CHRISTIAN
EDUCATION

CHRISTIAN EDUCATION

A Guide to the
FOUNDATIONS OF MINISTRY

Edited by

FREDDY CARDOZA

Baker Academic

a division of Baker Publishing Group
Grand Rapids, Michigan

© 2019 by Freddy Cardoza

Published by Baker Academic
a division of Baker Publishing Group
PO Box 6287, Grand Rapids, MI 49516-6287
www.bakeracademic.com

Printed in the United States of America

Library of Congress Cataloging-in-Publication Data
Names: Cardoza, Freddy, editor.
Title: Christian education : a guide to the foundations of ministry / edited by Freddy Cardoza.
Description: Grand Rapids, MI : Baker Academic, a division of Baker Publishing Group, [2019] | Includes bibliographical references and index.
Identifiers: LCCN 2019005913 | ISBN 9780801095597 (cloth)
Subjects: LCSH: Education (Christian theology) | Christian education.
Classification: LCC BT738.17 .C483 2019 | DDC 268—dc23
LC record available at https://lccn.loc.gov/2019005913

19 20 21 22 23 24 25   7 6 5 4 3 2 1

CONTENTS

ILLUSTRATIONS

CONTRIBUTORS

Editor

Freddy Cardoza (PhD, Southern Baptist Theological Seminary) is dean of Grace Theological Seminary and the School of Ministry Studies at Grace College and Seminary in Winona Lake, Indiana. He previously served as executive director of the Society of Professors in Christian Education and chair of the Christian Education Department of Talbot School of Theology.

Authors

Holly Catterton Allen (PhD, Talbot School of Theology) is professor of Christian ministries at Lipscomb University in Nashville, Tennessee. Her most recent book is *InterGenerate: Transforming Churches through Intergenerational Ministry* (ACU Press, 2018); she also coauthored *Intergenerational Christian Formation* (InterVarsity, 2012). Allen directs two international, cross-denominational conferences: InterGenerate and the Children's Spirituality Summit.

Leon M. Blanchette Jr. (EdD, Southern Baptist Theological Seminary) is chair of the Department of Christian Ministry at the School of Theology and Christian Ministry and professor of Christian education at Olivet Nazarene University. He is an elder in the Church of the Nazarene and has served as children's pastor for over thirty years.

Megan G. Brown (PhD, Talbot School of Theology) is associate professor of Christian ministries at University of Northwestern–St. Paul, where she has taught since 2014. She specializes in emerging adulthood and teaches courses on relationships, spiritual formation, developmental foundations, teaching methods, research methods, ministry practice, and Bible study methods.

Gregory C. Carlson (PhD, University of Nebraska, Lincoln) is chair and professor of Christian ministries and leadership at Trinity International University, where he has taught since 2007 in the areas of youth and family ministries, teaching the Bible, and leadership.

Jane Carr (PhD, Talbot School of Theology) is professor of Christian ministries at Talbot School of Theology, Biola University. She also serves as the book review editor for the *Christian Education Journal*, published by Sage Publishing. Prior to joining the full-time faculty at Biola University, she served on staff at Friends Church in Yorba Linda for twenty-six years. She currently is the founder and principal of Focus on Leaders, a private organization that provides executive coaching and leadership development training to corporate and nonprofit leaders.

Ken Coley (EdD, University of Maryland) is senior professor of Christian education at Southeastern Baptist Theological Seminary, where he has taught since 1996. He directs the doctor of education program and specializes in educational leadership and teaching.

Shelly Cunningham (PhD, Talbot School of Theology) is associate professor of Christian education at Talbot School of Theology, Biola University, where she has taught since 1989, specializing in the area of educational process and design. She currently serves as associate provost for faculty advancement at Biola University.

Jim Dekker (PhD, Trinity Evangelical Divinity School) is professor of ministry and division chair at Cornerstone University. He has taught sixteen years in Christian higher education and nine years as codirector for the Center for Youth Ministry Studies. He has served in youth ministry for over thirty years, and his specialization is adolescent resilience and spiritual direction.

Octavio Javier Esqueda (PhD, University of North Texas) is professor of Christian higher education at Talbot School of Theology, Biola University, where he teaches in the doctoral program in the areas of Christian higher education, theological education, and Christian education. He coauthored *Anointed Teaching:* *Partnership with the Holy Spirit* with Robert W. Pazmiño.

James Riley Estep Jr. (DMin, Southern Baptist Theological Seminary; PhD, Trinity Evangelical Divinity School) is the vice president of academics at Central Christian College of the Bible in Moberly, Missouri. He also serves as the resource director for e2 (effective elders ministries), a ministry committed to equipping church leaders.

Karen Lynn Estep (PhD, Michigan State University) currently serves as senior adjunct doctoral chair and faculty mentor for the Online College of Doctoral Studies at Grand Canyon University. She has served in Christian higher education for over fifteen years, working with educators at Lincoln Christian University and Greenville University.

Cheryl Fawcett (PhD, Trinity International University) is missionary specialist for the Association of Baptists for World Evangelism (ABWE). Since 2005, she has traveled the world ministering alongside other veteran missionaries, with an emphasis on serving youth and equipping youth workers in cultures around the globe.

James T. Flynn (DMin, Regent University) is an associate professor of ministry who directs the doctor of ministry program and serves as associate dean of instruction and operations at Regent University School of Divinity.

Paul G. Kelly (PhD, New Orleans Baptist Theological Seminary) is professor of educational leadership and chair of the Educational Leadership Department at Gateway Seminary, where he has taught since 2009. Kelly also serves as senior editor of the *Journal of Youth Ministry*, the peer-reviewed journal of the Association of Youth Ministry Educators.

Chris Kiesling (PhD, Texas Tech University) served in campus ministry and pastored churches in both rural and urban contexts before becoming professor of Christian discipleship and human development at Asbury Theological Seminary, where he has taught since 1998. He teaches various master's and doctoral courses and recently completed a four-year term serving as interim dean of the School of Practical Theology. He coauthored with David Setran the book *Spiritual Formation in Emerging Adulthood: A Practical Theology for College and Young Adult Ministry*.

Jonathan H. Kim (PhD, Trinity International University) is associate professor of Christian ministry and leadership at Talbot School of Theology, Biola University, where he has taught since 1999, specializing in the areas of Christian formation and discipleship.

Keith R. Krispin Jr. (EdD, Southern Baptist Theological Seminary) is professor of Christian ministries at Judson University, where he teaches undergraduate and graduate courses in ministry and leadership. He has over thirty years of experience in student ministries and other aspects of church leadership.

Jason M. Lanker (PhD, Talbot School of Theology) is associate professor of Christian ministry and formation at John Brown University, where he has taught for the last twelve years. He also serves as teaching elder at New Heights Church with oversight of discipleship.

Kevin E. Lawson (EdD, University of Maine, Orono) is professor of educational studies at Talbot School of Theology, Biola University, where he has taught since 1995. He has also served as editor for the *Christian Education Journal: Research on Educational Ministry* since 2003.

Mark A. Maddix (PhD, Trinity Evangelical Divinity School) serves as dean of the School of Theology and Christian Ministry and professor of practical theology at Point Loma Nazarene University in San Diego, California. He is a frequent contributor to the *Christian Education Journal* and the coauthor of *Practicing Christian Education* (Baker Academic, 2017) and *Discovering Discipleship* (Beacon Hill, 2010). He has coedited several books in the areas of spiritual formation, missional discipleship, ecclesiology, and neuroscience and Christian formation.

David Odom (PhD, Southwestern Baptist Theological Seminary) is associate professor of student ministry and director of the Youth Ministry Institute at New Orleans Baptist Theological Seminary. For over twenty-five years, he served as youth minister in churches in Texas and Alabama.

David P. Setran (PhD, Indiana University) is Price-LeBar Professor of Christian Formation and Ministry at Wheaton College, where he serves as graduate coordinator and teaches classes on the history and philosophy of Christian education, discipleship, and emerging adult spiritual formation.

Randall L. Stone (PhD, New Orleans Baptist Theological Seminary) served in local church ministry leadership for three decades and is now professor of Christian education at New Orleans Baptist Theological Seminary, where he has taught since 2011. He chairs the Discipleship and Ministry Leadership division and directs the EdD and DEdMin programs.

John David Trentham (PhD, Southern Baptist Theological Seminary) is associate professor of leadership and discipleship at Southern Seminary in Louisville, Kentucky, where he also serves as director of the doctor of education program and editor of the *Journal of Discipleship & Family Ministry*. In 2017, he was elected president of the Society of Professors in Christian Education (SPCE).

William R. Yount (PhD, Southwestern Baptist Theological Seminary; PhD, University of North Texas) served as professor of foundations of education at Southwestern Baptist Theological Seminary (1981–2012). He currently serves as ministry-based professor of Christian education at New Orleans Baptist Theological Seminary (since 2012) and adjunct professor of Christian education at Dallas Baptist University and B. H. Carroll Theological Institute.

ACKNOWLEDGMENTS

This book exists because of the collective efforts of innumerable people whose contributions may never be fully known. *But I know.* And I would like the reader to gain at least a glimpse into the backstory of this important work, which is designed as a foundation for study in Christian education.

This work follows the heritage and legacy of the 1992 and 2001 Baker Academic texts edited by my good friend and mentor, Michael Anthony. Those books, *Foundations for Ministry* and *Introducing Christian Education*, were landmark contributions to the field with a lasting impact. Upon Michael's recommendation and the unflagging and, indeed, stalwart support of executive acquisitions editor Robert Hosack and editor Julie Zahm, *Christian Education: A Guide to the Foundations of Ministry* came into being.

My sincere thanks go to the contributors of this edited work, each of whom is an accomplished scholar and choice person. Their skillful study, coupled with deep personal piety, has resulted in well-researched chapters addressing twenty-five themes relevant for ministry in this winnowing season of human history—the twenty-first century.

I offer my sincere gratitude to others whose direct and indirect support helped make this publication a reality: my editorial assistant, Jamie D. Smith; my mentor and former dean *par excellence*, Dennis E. Williams; and the other educators who inspired my Christian education career, Ed Buchanan, Bruce Powers, Wes Black, Mark Simpson, and Dennis Dirks.

I would also like to acknowledge colleagues who immediately supported this research and publication, including the fine faculties of Talbot School of Theology and Grace Theological Seminary. Additional thanks are extended to Clint Arnold, Scott Rae, Bill Katip, and John Lillis, who provided the needed time to complete this work through sabbaticals and sensitivity. Finally, I thank my students over the years and my beloved colleagues who are members of the Society of Professors in Christian Education. Your commitment to Christ continually inspires me and my work.

INTRODUCTION

FREDDY CARDOZA

Our world has changed. The twenty-first century brought a paradigmatic change as virtually nothing in society has been untouched by the digital age. It has presented humanity with tremendous possibilities and threatening peril.

Revolutionary innovation has occurred in every disciplinary field. Higher education has been shaken to its core. Much of what was assumed to be true in a variety of academic subjects has been deconstructed and laid bare. Current research and novel ways of thinking have challenged both the nature of truth and the very foundations of human knowledge. Biblical authority finds itself juxtaposed between these forces and the paradigmatic changes they have wrought as the world looks for clear convictions in a time of moral and existential uncertainty.

This new reality is radically reshaping our lives and redefining the essence of what it means to be human: how we think, feel, live, and relate. These divergent forces are creating a global crisis in which our world wobbles between unbounded optimism and uncertain pessimism. Together, these tensions are leading people to desperately search for hope, love, truth, and meaning.

It is within this challenging yet chaotic vortex that we Christian educators find ourselves. Like Issachar's sons of old, we must labor both to understand the times and to know what to do. A discerning look reveals that despite the global ambiguity of our time, divine truth remains. Even within cultural uncertainty, the imperatives issued by Christ continue unabated. And though societal supports shake, the church still stands as the pillar and foundation of truth (1 Tim. 3:15), resting firmly on Jesus, the chief cornerstone of the ages (Eph. 2:20).

On the sole and solid foundation of Christ (1 Cor. 3:11), God has provided his revelation to guide us. As Christian educators are fond of saying, "All truth is God's truth, wherever it may be found." This includes the unassailable truth of God's revealed Word (2 Tim. 3:16) and the corresponding truth divinely revealed

1

through general revelation in other areas of human endeavor (Rom. 1:19–20).

Despite the certainty of God's unchanging truth, no academic field of study has remained untouched in this season of human upheaval. This includes the area of Christian education. As times change, each generation of believers must take the truths it holds dear and pass them on to the next generation. This means doing the painstaking work of reconnecting the dots of our discipline so that they build bridges between Scripture and society, Christ and culture.

As was mentioned by Michael Anthony at the turn of the millennium in the literary predecessor of this text, *Introducing Christian Education* (2001), the very notion of Christian education is prone to misunderstanding and confusion. This remains true two decades later as the digital age advances fields of knowledge and creates human needs that Christian academies and ministries must, by necessity, boldly address.

Part of the reason for the misconception about Christian education has to do with the maturation of its many subdisciplines into fully-fledged fields of study. The popularity of Christian formation, childhood ministry, youth ministry, leadership administration, and other movements has led to related but sometimes independently organized disciplines within the broader professional progeny. Another source of misunderstanding about the nature of Christian education has to do with the wide expanse of academic programs and Christian ministries associated with the field. Practical theology degrees in colleges, universities, and seminaries continue to grow in diversity, and the proliferation of targeted church and parachurch programs continues at an epic clip.

What, then, is Christian education? In its essence, *Christian education includes all fields of study and related ministries whose purposes involve equipping in the biblical worldview, helping to make disciples, and facilitating transformation in the lives of believers through teaching-learning (education) and formation.*

Since Christian education is an area of practical theology, it involves both Christian educational ministry-type academic programs and related ministries in churches and parachurch organizations. More specifically, it involves those ministries and disciplines whose direct or indirect purposes relate to supporting or facilitating the lifelong process of disciple making and life transformation. To this end, every attempt is made to educate ministers with the knowledge, to instill them with the values, to train them with the competencies, and to provide them with the relational skills necessary to be and to make transformed disciples in obedience to the Great Commandment and the Great Commission.

As we move headlong into the third decade of the twenty-first century, these realities have created the demand for a new primary textbook in the area of Christian education. Building on the success of the aforementioned *Introducing Christian Education: Foundations for the Twenty-First Century*, edited by Michael Anthony, this work, *Christian Education: A Guide to the Foundations of Ministry*, represents the latest thinking and research from a combination of both newer thought leaders and trusted sages in our guild.

The current offering is divided into five parts. These parts represent a succinct overview of the field at this time. They cover Christian education from the ground up, including its educational foundations (part 1), educational theory (part 2), educational administration (part 3), educational ministries (part 4), and educational specializations (part 5). Each of these parts has five chapters, representing a total of twenty-five individual themes, each written by a different specialist.

This textbook provides an unapologetic evangelical perspective on the field of Christian education. The authors who have written the following essays are, first and foremost, persons of integrity and personal holiness. Each scholar is known to be an expert in many areas, including the one in which he or she has written. They are trusted colleagues who associate with the Society of Professors in Christian Education, an evangelical body of academic professors and professionals. They have a combination of grounded theological and theoretical training from the best programs in the discipline. They demonstrate expansive practical experience and ministerial expertise in their respective topics. These men and women represent a wide cross section of institutional types, geographical locations, and evangelical traditions.

Together, these scholars form a chorus of voices that blend into a beautiful harmony of perspectives with the advancement of God's kingdom as their aim and with Christian education as their method. It is our collective hope that ministry practitioners, professionals, professors, and pupils will greatly benefit from and be equipped by this work.

PART 1

EDUCATIONAL FOUNDATIONS

Christian education encompasses a large family of disciplines in the education and ministry fields that falls within one of the traditional areas of theology called practical theology. Sometimes called Christian ministries, practical theology includes pastoral ministries and Christian education—and sometimes other ministries. Because of the diversity of Christian education as a field, it provides ministerial training in a great number of areas. For this reason, though Christian education is the historical name of the discipline, this term is more often used today to describe what we do rather than to define it. Sometimes the historical name is replaced with other descriptive names such as educational ministries, church ministries, Christian ministries, discipleship ministries, educational leadership, and others. This great diversity simply points to the overall impact and growth of Christian education as a part of practical theology. It is an expansive field of study that continues to morph as Christian educators identify ministry needs and as the academic discipline forms around those ministry areas

to provide formal education, training, and support for those needing to be equipped.

Understanding Christian Education Foundations

Part 1 of this book covers educational foundations, which are the irreducible core of Christian education. Any person who seeks to understand Christian education as a field of study or wants to be trained in it needs to understand these things. To separate Christian education from its foundations would be akin to divorcing hermeneutics from biblical studies, language from the humanities, or math from the sciences. In each of these cases, one proceeds from the other. The foundations provide essential contextual understanding of the many supporting assumptions, axioms, and organizing principles that form the basis of the work of Christian education. Without the foundations, one cannot make sense of the collective agreement regarding the nature, terminology, boundaries, goals, and strategies of this field. The foundations also provide needed perspective and depth of understanding about the literature, subject areas, academic degree programs, and career fields of Christian education.

The Danger of Neglecting the Foundations

Without the foundations, people within Christian education, whether academic leaders, ministry practitioners, or current students, lack a unified understanding of what Christian education is, what it should do, and how it should be done. Absent these foundations, the result would be a weakening of the very fabric of the field into pragmatism.

One might argue that something akin to this has already happened to a degree. The fact that so many outside the field and, indeed, within the field do not have a clear understanding of Christian education at its most granular level may indicate a neglect of the foundations, and I suspect this is true. As one who has served in this field for over two decades, I have nurtured a lurking suspicion that one of the major strengths of Christian education may have become its greatest weakness.

As was stated earlier, Christian education is an area within practical theology. Practical theology is by definition *practical*. For this reason, those in the field place a high premium on applying ministry principles to real life and, specifically, doing what works. When doing what works is united with sound theory found in the foundations of the discipline, Christian education makes a tremendous impact. Being practical means that it is praxis-based—meaning a combination of theory and practice or, more technically, theory-informed practice.

The praxis-based impact of informed Christian education ministry is healthy and dynamic. It is what is needed and desired by churches, parachurch organizations, and institutions of higher education. Even so, a subtle danger exists. Because of the practical nature of Christian education and its many subdisciplines, it is possible for practitioners to begin to view the foundations and theories as known assumptions or, worse, as impractical and therefore unimportant.

A Call to Return to the Foundations

We may have subtly gravitated past praxis to pragmatism. When this happens, Christian educators and the ministry leaders they equip find themselves becoming increasingly gimmick-driven rather than doing the hard work of thinking about how to discern powerful and biblical strategies for potent kingdom impact. By immersing oneself in the mastery of the foundations, one can avoid the errors of pragmatism and discover the timeless truths of practical ministry.

The first part of this textbook issues a challenge for each reader, whether professor, professional, or pupil, to value and master the classical foundations of Christian education. These five chapters include a solid biblical-theological overview of Christian education and a review of its historical, philosophical, psychological, and practical foundations. Together, these form the irreducible elements of all Christian education–related fields.

1

Biblical-Theological Foundations of Christian Education

OCTAVIO JAVIER ESQUEDA

What comes into our minds when we think about God is the most important thing about us. . . . We tend by a secret law of the soul to move toward our mental image of God. . . . This is true not only of the individual Christian, but of the company of Christians that composes the Church. Always the most revealing thing about the Church is her idea of God.

—A. W. Tozer, *Knowledge of the Holy*

Our theology—our thoughts about and study of God—affects everything we believe and do and is foundational to Christian ministry. While knowledge of God is by nature primary for all Christian believers, disciplines, and ministries, we tend to compartmentalize theology and practical ministry, separating "theory" from "practice." Sadly, some perceive theology as mere dogmatic presuppositions that lack real implications for daily life and ministry.

When we do any of that, we act as if what we confess does not affect our behavior. However, as Dallas Willard has correctly pointed out, "We always live up to our beliefs—or down to them, as the case may be. Nothing else is possible. It is the nature of belief."[1] Therefore, our theology, or lack thereof, always guides and influences the process and the practice of Christian educators. We affirm that all truth is God's truth since "this world is not a neutral place. It's God's."[2]

This chapter explores key theological foundations from Scripture and explains how each person of the Trinity provides us with guiding principles for Christian education. Since

1. Willard, *Knowing Christ Today*, 309.
2. Naugle, *Worldview*, 26.

the Bible is essential for our understanding of the Triune God, overarching themes of the biblical narrative (creation, fall, redemption, and re-creation) are also discussed in this chapter.

God's Revelation and Christian Education

The everlasting Triune God is majestic and awesome beyond human understanding. God is the only "high and exalted One, Who lives forever, whose name is Holy" (Isa. 57:15 NASB). As finite creatures, we are able to know and understand God only through what he reveals to us. God makes himself known to us through the categories of general or natural revelation and special revelation.

General Revelation

Theologians refer to God's disclosure through his creation and the human conscience as general revelation. God's creation declares his glory and draws our attention to the supreme author of everything that exists (Ps. 19:1–6). This revelation is constant and invites all human beings to praise the Creator God of the universe. God's eternal power and divine nature are evident to all through his creation (Rom. 1:19–20). General revelation is vital for our understanding of God and stands as a permanent reminder of his love and power.

Unfortunately, we tend to forget about God's constant presence evidenced by creation. Everyday circumstances reveal routine but amazing phenomena we take for granted: the morning sunrise, our ability to breathe, the stimulating use of our five senses. Each of these is a constant reminder that the Lord designed us and desires for us to know him.

In short, general revelation spurs and enriches our understanding of God. We should pay attention to his voice through his creation and providence because our Lord is always present and speaking to us through his deeds.

Special Revelation

Our Triune God also speaks to us through the incarnate Word of God, Jesus Christ (John 1:1–3, 9–14; Heb. 11:1–2), and the written Word of God, the Bible (2 Tim. 3:16–17). This kind of revelation is known as special revelation. The focus of God's special revelation is Jesus; through him, we are able to know more about God and enjoy a personal relationship with him. The Bible is therefore the foundational curriculum in Christian education, and Christ is the standard for its interpretation and application.

Our Limited Understanding

There is, however, a theological tension we need to acknowledge. On the one hand, the Bible affirms that knowing God is possible and that this knowledge is worthy of praise. Even though humankind tends to base worth on human wisdom, power, or money, knowing and understanding God are of supreme worth and the only valid reasons for human boasting: "Thus says the LORD, 'Let not a wise man boast of his wisdom, and let not the mighty man boast of his might, let not a rich man boast of his riches; but let him who boasts boast of this, that he understands and knows Me, that I am the LORD who exercises lovingkindness, justice and righteousness on earth; for I delight in these things,' declares the LORD" (Jer. 9:23–24 NASB).

We are certainly able to know God and appreciate his attributes and deeds. On the other hand, because God is infinite, we can never *fully* comprehend his majesty. He transcends our finite understanding, as he has clearly stated in Isaiah 55:8–9:

> "For My thoughts are not your
> thoughts,
> Nor are your ways My ways," de-
> clares the LORD.
> "For *as* the heavens are higher than
> the earth,
> So are My ways higher than your
> ways
> And My thoughts than your
> thoughts." (NASB)

As Christian educators, we recognize that much will surpass our limited knowledge and understanding. If we were able to fully grasp God, then we would be his intellectual equals, and we are not. Our goal should be to learn and to apply what he has disclosed to us. The knowledge God has given is sufficient for effectively living our earthly lives in complete obedience to his commandments (Deut. 29:29; John 15:9–12). Hence, theology and Christian education are tasks involving receptivity, humility, and obedience to the Triune God.

The Triune God Is the Foundation for Christian Education

The Lord has eternally existed as three persons: Father, Son, and Holy Spirit. Each person, although distinct, is fully God and has the same divine attributes. The Father, Son, and Holy Spirit are equal in essence, but as separate persons, they relate differently to one another and to creation (Matt. 3:16–17; 1 Cor. 15:28). Robert Pazmiño argues that the mutual communion of the persons of the Trinity

(*perichoresis*), in which each divine person is a being for the others, provides the foundational model for Christian education aimed at "the formation and transformation of persons as beings for others."[3] Just as God exists in community (a three-in-one tri-unity), we human beings, created in God's image, mirror his attributes and exist to live in community characterized by love.

Defining the Trinity

The doctrine of the Trinity is a fundamental doctrine of the Christian faith and a good description of the God of the Bible: the Triune God perfectly represents unity (one God) and diversity (three persons). The Athanasian Creed establishes that whoever wishes to be saved must believe in the Trinity because it represents a core Christian belief. Though each divine person has a distinct role, the perfectly harmonious activities of Father, Son, and Holy Spirit always reflect a "deeper personal unity of conscious thinking, feeling, and willing" that reveals an "essential oneness of being."[4]

The Holy Trinity is the essential foundation for life and Christian education. The three persons of the Godhead always work together in perfect harmony and are the basis and model for Christian teaching. Christian education exists because the Father, the Son, and the Holy Spirit are teachers. At the same time, as distinct persons, they play different roles and provide various principles for believers and Christian educators. Pazmiño rightly argues that God the Father, as the Creator of the universe, is the *source* from whom all Christian education content originates; God

3. Pazmiño, *God Our Teacher*, 21.
4. G. Lewis and Demarest, *Integrative Theology*, 1:280.

the Son, as the Master Teacher, is *exemplar* or *model* for authentic Christian teaching; and God the Holy Spirit is the *tutor* and *counselor* who sustains the life of the Christian community and the wider society in order to fulfill God's purposes.[5]

God the Father

God the Father is transcendent, distinct, and separate from his creation and at the same time immanent, present, and constantly sustaining his creation. He is called the Creator, Ruler, Sustainer, and Judge of all. As such, he is majestic, glorious, and holy (Lev. 19:2). At the same time, God is intimately personal and full of intrinsic goodness (Ps. 25:8; 86:5; Jer. 33:11; Nah. 1:7). God's existence and deeds can truly be described as incomprehensibly awe-inspiring, for his greatness in all things far exceeds us all (Neh. 1:5; Ps. 66:5). God alone is the source and foundation for life and Christian education.

Character and Attributes of the Father

We can trust in God because we know his character, which he has disclosed to us. God's qualities or character patterns are generally described as divine attributes. Our God is unique, and there is no one like him (Isa. 43:10; 46:9). Therefore, some of his attributes are incommunicable because he does not share them with anyone or anything else (eternal, self-sufficient, immutable, impassible, omnipresent, omnipotent, omnibenevolent, and omniscient).

God also possesses communicable attributes, which he shares with human beings (personal, faithful, loving, holy, wise, and glorious).[6] Michael Lawson uses thirty-three words to describe the characteristics or attributes of God that can be used to help children understand what God is like: adorable, angry, beautiful, colorful, creative, everywhere, fair, faithful, famous, friend, generous, gentle, holy, huge, invisible, joy, kind, life, light, love, merciful, mysterious, patient, playful, righteous, scary, smart (omniscient), spirit, strong (omnipotent), tender, timeless, a trinity, and unique.[7] Ultimately, any human list of divine attributes falls short of completely representing the awesomeness of our God. Nevertheless, such a list is helpful in showing the breadth and depth of God's personality and being.

The Father as Source

Our God is also a loving Father who instructs and cares for his children. God revealed himself with the term *Father*, indicating that he is the source from whom everything else proceeds. Gordon Lewis and Bruce Demarest note that, in the Old Testament, *Father* denotes "God as the creator (Mal. 2:10), founder of the nation of Israel (Isa. 63:6; 64:8), and the One who entered into a saving, covenantal relationship with his people (Jer. 3:19; 31:9)."[8]

In the New Testament, the term *Father* is widely used, especially in the Gospel of John. In Christ, believers become God's children through regeneration and adoption. Consequently, Lewis and Demarest explain that the word *Father* "signifies the new relation of life and love that Christians enjoy with God (John 14:23; 20:17; 1 John 2:13; 3:1). The Aramaic term *abba*, 'dear Father' (Rom. 8:15; Gal.

---

5. Pazmiño, *God Our Teacher*, 33.

6. Bird, *Evangelical Theology*, 127–37.

7. M. Lawson, *Grandpa Mike Talks about God*.

8. G. Lewis and Demarest, *Integrative Theology*, 1:189.

4:6), is a title of special intimacy found on the lips of a young child."[9] As God's children, we should go with confidence to our heavenly Father to learn and to be instructed by him.

The Father as Teacher

Christian education exists because God is the ultimate teacher, as Job 36:22 clearly states: "Behold, God is exalted in His power; Who is a teacher like Him?" (NASB). Every time God reveals himself to us, he is teaching us about himself and about the way in which we should go (Ps. 32:8; Isa. 2:3). God anticipates that we will respond to his revelation with complete obedience. This is the simple but indispensable expectation when he teaches us.[10] Obviously, our obedience should come out of reverence and love for the merciful and gracious God of the universe, who is rich in unfailing love and righteousness (Exod. 34:6).

God teaches us in various ways. God teaches people according to their diverse circumstances and is not limited to a singular or a particular teaching method; rather, he uses different ways to communicate with us. For example, God's creative teaching methodology recorded in the Bible includes the following:

- He spoke directly and audibly from heaven.
- He wrote on tablets of stone.
- He became flesh.
- He revealed himself in supernatural beings.
- He gave vivid dreams and visions.
- He drew on walls of palaces.

- He made animals talk.
- He voiced truth through human prophets.
- He composed poetry.
- He provided visual reminders of promises.[11]

God is indeed the model and example of creativity in teaching. Since we have a creative God, Christian educators should imitate him as they help people grow in their relationship with the Lord.

God the Son

God the Son is the Lord of all (Phil. 2:11). He became flesh and dwelled among us in order that we may become children of God (John 1:12, 14). Therefore, as the sovereign God and head of the church (Col. 1:18), Jesus Christ is indeed King of Kings and Lord of Lords (Rev. 19:16). The Dutch theologian Abraham Kuyper (1837–1920) brilliantly summarized the centrality of Christ over creation, our lives, and Christian education: "There is not a square inch on the whole plain of human existence over which Christ, who is Lord over all, does not claim: 'This is Mine!'"[12]

Our Lord Jesus Christ is not simply a necessary cliché in Christian education; he is the fundamental person under whom everything finds its purpose and meaning. In addition, Jesus is the model for Christian teaching. The terms *teacher* and *rabbi* were frequently used to describe Jesus's earthly ministry. His followers were called disciples over two hundred times in the New Testament. Jesus was a teacher like many religious leaders, but he was

9. G. Lewis and Demarest, *Integrative Theology*, 1:193.

10. Esqueda, "God as Teacher," 35.

11. M. Lawson, "Biblical Foundations for a Philosophy of Teaching," 62.

12. Plantinga, *Engaging God's World*, xiii.

different because he taught with divine authority (Mark 1:21–22). Jesus was a consummate teacher and the only one with the right to be addressed with the title *Master Teacher*. Christian educators should imitate him and follow his example in order to become adequate representatives of Christ. In fact, they should try to live up to the challenge the late Christian educator Howard Hendricks gave to his students: If you want to be like the Master Teacher, you need to master the Master's life. Authentic Christian education flows from the words and the example of the Master Teacher. Specifically, Robert Pazmiño proposes viewing Jesus as the master of the context, content, and audience of teaching.[13]

Context of Jesus's Teaching

Jesus's teaching was always considerate of the social context. Even though he was a teacher sent from God (John 3:2), he was willing to teach wherever the occasion arose—a synagogue, the temple, the seashore, the countryside, and in people's homes. He taught in different regions, from metropolitan Jerusalem to little towns such as Bethany and Chorazin, regardless of their social importance. Christian educators can follow the example of Jesus by willingly adapting to the social and cultural environment in order to teach the good news of the kingdom.

In his teaching, Jesus used common language to reach his listeners. His illustrations connected his teaching with relatable ideas and activities from domains that everyone could understand: home, nature, work, business, social relations, government, and national traditions.[14]

13. Pazmiño, *God Our Teacher*, 60.
14. Dillon, *Jesus as a Teacher*, 94–95.

Content of Jesus's Teaching

The content of Jesus's teaching was grounded in the Scriptures (Matt. 22:29; Luke 4:21; 24:32; John 7:38; 10:35). Christian education honors Jesus's example of making God and his Word the core curriculum. The purpose of Christian teaching is not just imparting knowledge but also leading students into obedience to the Lord (John 14:15).

Audience of Jesus's Teaching

Jesus reached different kinds of people without discrimination. He was willing to teach elites such as the Pharisees, scribes, priests, and rich as well as marginalized outcasts such as the poor, the diseased, and tax collectors. Jesus clearly established that the transformation of lives was the goal of his teaching. He wanted those he taught to become like him: "A pupil is not above his teacher; but everyone, after he has been fully trained, will be like his teacher" (Luke 6:40 NASB).

The context, content, and audience of Jesus's teaching provide Christian educators with solid guidelines for their own lives and ministries. As Christian educators, we must aim to consistently become more like the Master Teacher (Matt. 10:24–25). All believers are followers of Christ and his disciples. Both teachers and students sit at the feet of the Master and by his grace learn how to become better imitators of him in words and deeds. Jesus Christ is the sovereign Lord and the model for and goal of Christian education.

God the Holy Spirit

The Holy Spirit is essential for the Christian life and for Christian education. As a member of the Godhead, the Third Person of the Trinity is God and shares all the divine attributes

(Matt. 28:19; Acts 5:3, 4, 9; 2 Cor. 3:17). The work of the Holy Spirit is fundamental for the transformation teachers need in their lives and the transformation they hope to see in the lives of their students. The Holy Spirit guides believers into God's truth (John 16:3), reveals God (1 Cor. 2:9–12), and motivates and counsels believers into following God's truths (John 14:26). This reality reminds us that the Holy Spirit is the only one who can change lives and that we should yield to his leading. We always need the Spirit in our lives and teaching because only the Holy Spirit can reach any person from any generation and life situation. Indeed, Christianity and Christian education are meaningless apart from the Holy Spirit.[15]

The Holy Spirit indwells, baptizes, and seals all born-again believers (1 Cor. 6:19; 12:13; Eph. 4:30). Through the Spirit, believers enjoy a personal and intimate relationship with the Father (Gal. 4:6). The Holy Spirit guides God's children to live lives that please the loving Father (Rom. 8:14). As the author of the Bible, God's written revelation, the Holy Spirit helps both teachers and students to understand God's message through illumination (Eph. 1:17–18). The purpose of illumination is to help believers comprehend God's biblical truths.[16] The Spirit also comforts, intercedes, and gives spiritual gifts to God's children (Acts 9:31; Rom. 8:14; 1 Cor. 12:7). Therefore, the ministry of the Holy Spirit is fundamental for all spiritual activities. His presence in our lives is vital, and as believers and Christian educators, we should walk by the Spirit in order to please the Lord (Gal. 5:16). Christian teaching involves working in partnership with the Holy Spirit.[17]

15. Esqueda, "Holy Spirit as Teacher," 75.
16. Esqueda, "Holy Spirit as Teacher," 76.
17. Pazmiño and Esqueda, *Anointed Teaching*, 9.

Theological Foundations from the Biblical Narrative

God's written revelation, the Bible, starts with creation, in which the Triune God formed the universe out of nothing. God, therefore, is the source of everything, who declared what he had made was "very good" (Gen. 1:31). The Triune God also created human beings in his own image, giving them special dignity and honor beyond the rest of creation. The biblical narrative then moves to the fall and its consequences. However, the Bible's main focus is redemption, which results in reconciliation, wherein the Lord actively seeks to redeem humanity from slavery to sin in order to restore a right relationship with him. Jesus Christ, the Messiah promised in the Old Testament, becomes not only the Savior in the New Testament but also the basis, center, and end of all things. The Bible ends with re-creation, a new heaven and a new earth where sin is finally and completely destroyed and God restores everything back to himself. The fourfold metanarrative of creation, fall, redemption, and re-creation in Scripture provides several important principles for Christian ministry and education.

Creation

The Lord created the heavens and formed the earth (Isa. 45:18). He created human beings according to his image and with specific purposes, according to Genesis 1:26–28:

> Then God said, "Let Us make man in Our image, according to Our likeness; and let them rule over the fish of the sea and over the birds of the sky and over the cattle and over all the earth, and over every creeping thing that creeps on the earth." God created man in His own image, in the image of God

He created him; male and female He created them. God blessed them; and God said to them, "Be fruitful and multiply, and fill the earth, and subdue it; and rule over the fish of the sea and over the birds of the sky and over every living thing that moves on the earth." (NASB)

The threefold commission, or creation decree, of human beings is (1) to have fellowship with and to worship the sovereign Lord in whose image and likeness we are created, (2) to have relationships with other human beings, and (3) to care for and exert dominion over creation as God's stewards. We exist to have a relationship with God, with others, and with creation.

Created by God (*Imago Dei*)

All human beings are essentially and ontologically the same, regardless of their culture, background, and generation. We all are created in the image of God. As bearers of God's image (*imago Dei*), we all, both males and females, share the same importance and self-worth. We are indeed "fearfully and wonderfully made" (Ps. 139:14 NASB). The image of God determines the nature, value, and dignity of humankind and defines our essence (Ps. 8:3–5). Our cultural, personal, and experiential variables are secondary and not essential. They are important but not fundamental. Therefore, Christian education reaches out to all people and considers everyone important and teachable.

Called to Relationship

We are created in the image of God as relational beings. We are individuals, but we are created for community. We are divinely designed for authentic community and exist to experience deep relationships with God

and with one another (John 17:20–21). For this reason, regardless of our generation and cultural background, we all long for sincere and profound interpersonal relationships. The New Testament is full of admonitions to live in community, as we can see in the many passages with the commonly repeated words, "one another" and "each other." In fact, Hebrews 10:24–25 reminds us that one of the primary purposes of getting together as the body of Christ is to support one another: "Let us consider how to stimulate one another to love and good deeds, not forsaking our own assembling together, as is the habit of some, but encouraging one another; and all the more as you see the day drawing near" (NASB). This is the communal goal of the teaching ministry in the church. Authentic Christian education and spiritual growth can flourish only in the context of the community of believers.[18]

However, individualism is a core value of American culture that subtly interferes with God's design for us. Soong-Chan Rah argues that "me, myself, and I" has become the unholy trinity of Western philosophy and shaped many Western societies. Sadly, the American church has a tendency to reduce the Christian faith to a personal, private, and individual faith.[19] In the same way, researchers Edward Stewart and Milton Bennett, in their excellent book *American Cultural Patterns: A Cross-Cultural Perspective*, point out that "personal relations among Americans are adapted to gaining emotional benefits from social interaction while preserving independence and avoiding obligations."[20] They continue, "It is probably accurate to say that in all of the

18. Esqueda, "Sin and Christian Teaching," 174.
19. Rah, *Next Evangelicalism*, 30.
20. Stewart and Bennett, *American Cultural Patterns*, 89.

world outside the United States, a relationship without obligation is simply not significant."[21] Relationships without commitment cannot produce authentic Christian community.

Commissioned as Stewards

Lastly, human beings created in God's image serve as divine priests of nature and society. The mandate to subdue creation as God's representatives stresses the importance of the world and of culture. Since God is the unifying element for all creation and everything was created for him and through him, there should not be a distinction between the sacred and the secular. Everything is sacred because it comes from the Lord. Christian education provides a holistic perspective of God's creation and our role as his representatives in this world.

Fall

God's creation is good and declares God's glory, but it unfortunately also declares the tragedy of fallenness, of chaos, of painful destruction.[22] Sin is not normal but contradicts God's ideal plan of human flourishing and shalom for his creation. Sin opposes God's holy character, and its fruits are the vandalism of shalom.[23] Sadly, sin "permeates our entire being and alienates us from ourselves, other people, our world, and most importantly, our creator."[24] The story of the fall and its consequences reminds us that apart from Christ, we are dead in sin (Eph. 2:1–10).

God's grace, which saved us and sustains us, can be fully appreciated only in the context of

the fall and its consequences. We are all sinners in desperate need of divine grace to support us and to empower us to serve the Lord as we teach and minister to others.[25] Sin and grace are crucial for a complete understanding not only of the gospel but also of our daily lives and ministries. As Christian educators, we are indeed messengers of grace and shalom.

The realities of Satan and spiritual warfare need to be acknowledged as central elements of the Christian life and ministry. Satan is "the prince of this world" (John 12:31) and the "god of this age" (2 Cor. 4:4). Therefore, we have a real struggle against Satan and his angels, who oppose God and his plan (Eph. 6:12). However, Christ came to destroy the devil's work (1 John 3:8) and to triumph over Satan and evil (Col. 2:15).

Redemption

The biblical story focuses primarily on the divine restoration of humanity. In the Old Testament, the sovereign and gracious Lord initiates the story of redemption through his covenants with his chosen people. These covenants are the backbone of the biblical narrative and find their fulfillment in the New Testament with the promised Messiah. Christ, by his grace, provides eternal life and the redemption of sin and its consequences (John 3:16; Eph. 4:2–10). Sin affects all areas of life, but Jesus Christ redeems everything sin has distorted. The Triune God of creation is the Triune God of salvation, restoration, and unity (Rom. 11:36).

Christ's death and resurrection are indeed the best news for humanity. As Christ followers, we are commanded to proclaim the good news of the gospel and to make completely

21. Stewart and Bennett, *American Cultural Patterns*, 95.

22. Plantinga, *Engaging God's World*, 47.

23. Plantinga, *Not the Way It's Supposed to Be*, 16.

24. Esqueda, "Sin and Christian Teaching," 164.

25. Esqueda, "Sin and Christian Teaching," 175.

committed disciples of our Lord. The Great Commission in Matthew 28:18–20 mirrors the Edenic commission of Genesis 1:26–28. Jesus Christ calls us to make disciples among all people because every person created in God's image is important.

Jesus Christ is the perfect image of God, to which his followers will also be fully conformed (Rom. 8:28–30; Col. 1:15). Christ is the head and prototype of the new humanity God is bringing into existence through the work of the Holy Spirit.[26] God regenerates sinners, gives them new life, and progressively transforms them into the image of Christ. People grow and mature differently, but one day God will perfect the work he started in every believer (Phil. 1:6). This transformation to become more like Christ is not merely personal; it also has a communal orientation. God's purpose and plan of Christlikeness is for all believers in the context of the body of Christ, the church (Eph. 4:11–16). Christian education, then, is the process of helping all believers grow together with the goal of being transformed into the fullness of Christ (Eph. 4:13).

Re-creation

The biblical narrative ends with the final redemption and restoration of the world as the new heaven and the new earth appear after the second coming of Christ.[27] The final consummation of God's redemptive work of humanity is still to come, and believers live with hope in the Lord, who is always trustworthy to fulfill his promises and will one day completely destroy sin and its consequences. The second coming of Christ is our blessed hope. Eschatology, the study of last things (Gk. *eschatoi*), is of fundamental importance for Christian theology and ministry. Brian Daley accurately defines eschatology as "the hope of believing people that the incompleteness of their present experience of God will be resolved, their present thirst for God fulfilled, their present need for release and salvation realized."[28] We expectantly remember Jesus's last words in the biblical narrative, "Yes, I am coming quickly," and echo John's response, "Amen. Come, Lord Jesus" (Rev. 22:20 NASB).

Conclusion

Our Triune God is the foundation of our lives and the source of Christian education. Only in God can we discern our identity as human beings created in God's image and our calling as God's children and messengers of grace and reconciliation in Christ. Since knowledge of God is fundamental for a complete understanding of all things, theology always directs our ministry and practice. Christian educational practices emerge from the centrality of God, who provides them with their meaning and purpose. In other words, to know God is the content and to make him known is the purpose of Christian education. Howard Hendricks accurately summarizes the importance of Christian education: "Christian education is not an option, it is an order. It is not a luxury, it is a life. It is not something nice to have, it is something necessary to have. It is not a part of the work of the church, it is the work of the church. It is not extraneous, it is essential. It is our obligation, not merely an option."[29]

26. G. Lewis and Demarest, *Integrative Theology*, 2:139.

27. Esqueda, "Biblical Worldview," 97.

28. Daley, *Hope of the Early Church*, 1.

29. Howard Hendricks, as quoted in R. Clark, Johnson, and Sloat, *Christian Education: Foundations for the Future*, 11.

Christian education exists because the Triune God is a teacher who desires to guide us into his path so we can follow him. The Christian educational goal goes beyond the transmission of content and focuses on the complete transformation of believers' thinking, attitudes, and behavior according to God's character and standards. Knowing, loving, and obeying God represent authentic and complete Christian education, for "the fear of the LORD is the beginning of wisdom, and the knowledge of the Holy One is understanding" (Prov. 9:10 NASB). A humble and teachable spirit is an indispensable condition for a flourishing experience of Christian education that pleases the Lord. Consequently, our attitude as Christian educators should mimic the one David expressed in Psalm 86:11: "Teach me Your way, O LORD; I will walk in Your truth; unite my heart to fear Your name" (NASB).

The Triune God is the Creator and sovereign Lord of all. Our knowledge of God (theology) affects everything we believe and do and is by nature foundational to Christian education. God graciously reveals himself and expects us to respond in faith and obedience to his revelation. The Trinity—Father, Son, and Holy Spirit—is the basis for life and Christian education. The loving Father adopted us as his children by the sacrifice of the Son and the power of the Holy Spirit. Jesus Christ is the goal and the focus of Christian teaching. The Holy Spirit is the one who produces spiritual transformation that pleases the Father. The biblical narrative, expressed through the categories of creation, fall, and redemption, provides important principles for Christian ministry and education.

2

Historical Foundations of Christian Education

KEVIN E. LAWSON

After his resurrection, as Jesus Christ prepared for his ascension and departure from his disciples, he placed on them a commission, a responsibility to fulfill as they awaited his return. As Christians living many centuries later, we have a responsibility to fulfill this commission as well: "And Jesus came and said to them, 'All authority in heaven and on earth has been given to me. Go therefore and make disciples of all nations, baptizing them in the name of the Father and of the Son and of the Holy Spirit, teaching them to observe all that I have commanded you. And behold, I am with you always, to the end of the age'" (Matt. 28:18–20 ESV).

This chapter explores the story of how God's people, for almost two thousand years, have attempted to fulfill this commission, particularly by "teaching them to observe all that I have commanded you" (Matt. 28:20 ESV). It focuses on the nonformal educational efforts of the church of the Western, post-Reformation Protestant church movement as it sought to ground congregational members in the faith and stimulate spiritual growth. The questions that shape this chapter include (1) What was the church facing during these different time periods? (What were the needs and challenges of the church?) and (2) How did the church develop ways to help people learn and grow in their Christian faith? Let's begin by looking at the church in its earliest years, with the teaching ministry of Jesus's disciples.

Educational Ministry in the Early Church

Paul and Teaching in the Apostolic Era

After Jesus's ascension, and with the coming of the Holy Spirit, the disciples took up the task of both proclaiming the good news of the gospel of Jesus Christ and instructing new believers in the faith. Acts provides examples of sermons preached by Peter and Paul and indicates that believers "devoted themselves to the apostles' teaching and the fellowship, to the breaking of break and the prayers" (Acts 2:42 ESV). The early church was a preaching and a teaching church. Leaders instructed believers in how Jesus fulfilled the messianic promises of the Hebrew Scriptures, how they were to live their lives as followers of Christ, and how they were to share this message of reconciliation with the world. They faced many challenges, including tensions between gentile and Jewish believers living together in the body of Christ, tendencies toward legalism or license, false teachers, and persecution of those who followed this new faith.

The apostle Paul extensively preached and taught. His letters to churches and church leaders are filled with instruction handed down from the Old Testament and early Christian teaching (catechesis), encouragement of moral formation and education (exhortation), and instruction for living in light of Christ's coming return (discernment).[1] Paul, other apostles, and those who worked closely with them taught new believers to place their faith in Christ and to help them learn how to live as his followers.

Hippolytus and Catechetical Instruction in the First and Second Centuries AD

Following the apostolic era, the bishops of the early church were viewed as successors of the apostles, who had carried on an authoritative preaching and teaching ministry. The *Monarchial Episcopate* refers to the practice

1. Osmer, *Teaching Ministry of Congregations*, 26–44.

of a bishop taking on the leadership responsibility for a region, usually working out of a major city. These bishops were responsible to preach and to teach within their region, to oversee those teaching others, and to ensure orthodoxy in the beliefs and practices of their people. During a time when many theological issues had not yet been fully clarified, they had the important role of identifying doctrinal issues that needed to be resolved, heretical teaching that needed to be countered, and instruction that would help train new believers in the faith.

In addition to this formal teaching authority of the bishops, leaders in house churches were involved in teaching the basics of the faith to those seeking to become Christians. These seekers, or *postulants*, would come to the church leaders with mature Christians who served as their sponsors, testifying to the genuineness of the seekers' faith, moral lives, and desire to be baptized. Following an extended time of instruction as *catechumens*, these new believers would then receive final instruction for a short period of time as *competentes*, preparing them for the sacraments of the church, including baptism and the Lord's Supper.

Following baptism, they were considered *the faithful* or *neophytes*. As new members, they were expected to participate fully in the life of the church and to continue growing in knowledge and faithfulness. Hippolytus, a presbyter of the church in Rome who is traditionally identified as the author of *On the Apostolic Tradition* (ca. AD 215), describes an example of the instruction of new believers. This included both adults and children, for a period of three years, and their ritual preparation for baptism. He also describes the ongoing teaching efforts of the deacons and presbyters of the church, who gathered the people for morning prayers and instruction.[2]

The earliest example of a catechism—or a curriculum of instruction for new believers—found to date is the *Didache*, which means "teaching," commonly called *The Teaching of the Twelve Apostles*. Written in the late first or early second century AD to instruct gentile believers in a new way of life as Christians, the *Didache* addresses moral behavior and practices of baptism, fasting, prayer, the Lord's Supper, hospitality, reconciliation, and giving.[3] This curriculum provides insight into the moral issues Christians were facing, including abortion and infanticide, and how the church responded to those issues and instructed new believers in faithful living.

Also during this time period, catechetical schools were established in some metropolitan centers. Though providing basic instruction in the faith, they also developed more advanced curriculum involving theological and philosophical issues, literature, science, logic, and the arts to address how the Christian faith could be presented and argued within the philosophical debates of the time. Alexandria was the first of these schools, led by teachers such as Pantaenus, Clement, and Origen. The second-most-influential catechetical school was in Syrian Antioch, featuring leaders such as Nestorius, Diodore, and Chrysostom.[4]

Augustine and the Catechumenate in the Third through Sixth Centuries AD

Following a time in which periodic persecution tested the faith of believers, Christianity became accepted within the Roman Empire and eventually the identified religion of the state under the influence of Emperor Constantine. This acceptance brought new opportunities to build places of worship, basilicas, which utilized the visual arts in their construction to portray important stories of the Bible in ways that both literate and illiterate could understand.[5]

This was also a time when many people sought to become Christians, resulting in the need for more extensive teaching by bishops and other church leaders. This was the era of the catechetical lecture, with bishops such as Ambrose, Cyril, and Chrysostom developing curriculum to present to large groups of believers prior to their baptism. During Lent, those who sought to become baptized would enroll in an intensive time of instruction in the faith and faithful living, leading to exorcisms, baptisms, and anointings with chrism. Following baptism at Easter, converts received another week of instruction, called *mystagogy*, regarding the sacraments of baptism and the Lord's Supper, which had just been experienced, and the Lord's Prayer.[6]

Ambrose, bishop of Milan (late fourth century), was one of the first church leaders to intentionally use music as a means to reinforce the teaching of the church.[7] He taught Augustine, who went on to be one of the most influential theologians in the history of the church. As bishop at Hippo, North Africa, Augustine taught new believers in the faith and instructed and encouraged other catechists.

One of Augustine's most insightful writings about teaching new believers is *First Catechetical Instruction* (ca. AD 405), a letter

2. Hippolytus, *On the Apostolic Tradition*, 103–6.
3. Milavec, *Didache*, 12–45.
4. Cross, "Adoptianism" and "Nestorius."

5. Jensen, *Understanding Early Christian Art*, 15–25.
6. Harmless, *Augustine and the Catechumenate*, 300–345.
7. Brown, "Ambrose."

written to Deogratias, a deacon in Carthage struggling in his teaching efforts. Augustine's letter shows a sympathetic understanding of what helps people learn and how teaching can be done more effectively. It also provides two examples of an initial lesson for those seeking to begin attending the church; the lesson begins with creation, presents the gospel story, and ends with eternal life with God in heaven.[8]

Children of believers were instructed in the faith by their parents at home. They participated in the life of the church but were not viewed as fully Christian until they had been baptized. One of the tensions that arose during this time period was due to concern over the consequences of children's guilt for original sin if they died before baptism. The prevailing theology held that baptism addressed the forgiveness of sins prior to baptism, not sins committed after baptism. The early church did not believe that baptism addressed both past and future sins, and it did not yet have a theology of repeatable penance for sins committed after baptism. This caused many believers to delay baptism until late in life, often just before death.

The development of a theology of repeatable penance and the acceptance of a doctrine of original sin impacting children led to a major change in baptismal and instructional practices. Now, children of believers were baptized immediately after birth, and the catechumenate that had been practiced for three hundred years eventually died out. In its place arose the practice of parents and godparents taking on the responsibility of teaching baptized children the basics of the faith and raising them to live moral lives, avoiding sin and

partaking of the sacraments of the church to seek divine forgiveness when they did sin.[9]

Educational Ministry and Renewal in the Medieval Church

Educational Efforts in the Early Medieval Period

The disintegration of the Western Roman Empire (AD 476) is often used as a marker for the beginning of the Middle Ages. As the political empire fell apart, the church grew in importance in uniting people across Western Europe. In the early years of this era, the main ways that people learned about and grew in the faith were through the instruction of godparents, occasional preaching, the use of the arts within church buildings, and the cycle of the liturgical calendar. Godparents were tasked with ensuring that children learned the basics of the faith, including the Apostles' Creed, the Lord's Prayer, and at times the *Ave Maria* and/or the Ten Commandments.

Preaching, which was mainly the responsibility of the bishops, was sporadic. When it did occur, it provided instruction in the Scriptures and faithful living. The wide use of a variety of visual arts reinforced the teaching of the church, focusing congregants' attention on critical aspects of God's saving work in and through Jesus Christ. Wall paintings, mosaics, frescoes, and sculptures all portrayed critical incidents in the salvation story. The cycle of the liturgical year, a series of festivals with particular emphasis on the life and ministry of Jesus (beginning with Advent and going through his death, resurrection, and ascension), provided annual experiential

8. Augustine, "On the Catechising of the Uninstructed."

9. Dujarier, *History of the Catechumenate*, 81; also K. Lawson, "Baptismal Theology and Practices," 135–39.

reinforcement of key elements of God's saving work.

In the early 800s, Charlemagne, the first emperor in Western Europe after the fall of the Roman Empire, took up the task of reforming the church, devoting much effort to a variety of educational initiatives. Along with the development of schools in every cathedral for formal education purposes, under his leadership the church also established schools in monasteries where boys could learn the Scriptures, grammar, and music. Priests were also required to explain the Lord's Prayer to the people and to preach basic elements of the faith to their parishioners.[10] This Carolingian Renaissance is a good example of the importance and use of education to further church reform efforts.

The Fourth Lateran Council and the Renewal of Catechetical Instruction

In 1215, Pope Innocent III held the Fourth Lateran Council. In addition to addressing issues regarding the church's continuing involvement in the Holy Land, the council focused on how to better form and reform the moral life of the laity, counter false teaching, and strengthen the faith of the people. The main responses from the council included expanding preaching ministry in the church and requiring more instruction of the laity to prepare them for confession and receiving the Eucharist at least once a year.[11]

Across Europe, the impact of the council was felt in the expansion of preaching in the church and the development of preaching and confessional manuals for pastoral use. In England, one example of the renewal of teaching in the church was seen in the work of Archbishop of York John Peckham. In 1281, at the Council of Lambeth, he laid out an ambitious curriculum for the church's teaching ministry that was to be taught by all parish priests to the laity four times a year in their own language. The curriculum included the Apostles' Creed, Ten Commandments, Seven Works of Mercy, Seven Vices, Seven Virtues, and Seven Sacraments. His model was adopted by other bishops and used throughout the country. It influenced the writing of others, including the "Lay Folks Catechism," developed by Archbishop of York John Thoresby in 1357.[12] This was the first officially published catechism in English. Later, in the early 1400s, Archbishop Arundel issued decrees limiting the preaching and teaching by parish clergy to the content of Peckham's syllabus as a way to counter Lollard preaching.[13]

The expansion of preaching in the church and the development of a catechism for use with the laity also led to the further development and use of various arts to instruct and reinforce the teaching of the church. Religious poetry and music were used to instruct the laity and to encourage contrition for sin to prepare them for confession. Religious drama grew, providing reenactments of biblical stories and the lives of saints, who served as models for moral behavior and faithful living. Wall paintings, stained-glass windows, and sculptures were all used as "books for the unlearned," a form of silent preaching to teach the illiterate the basics of the faith. Important Bible stories,

10. Logan, *History of the Church in the Middle Ages*, 76–77.

11. K. Lawson, "Learning the Faith in England," 144–54.

12. Simmons and Nolloth, *Lay Folks' Catechism*, ix–xiv.

13. C. Fraser, "Religious Instruction of the Laity," 30–31.

stories of various saints, and aspects of the Apostles' Creed, deadly sins, virtues, and acts of mercy were illustrated on the walls and in the windows of church buildings, reminding people of what God had done for them and how they were to respond in faith and faithful living.[14]

Educational Ministry during the Reformation

Martin Luther, Bible Study, and the Modern Catechism

In the later Middle Ages, groups such as the Brethren of the Common Life in the Netherlands and Lollards in England promoted the study of the Bible by the laity in their own language. Reform movements gained momentum and in the early sixteenth century led to the division within the Western church known today as the Protestant Reformation.

Martin Luther, one of the major figures of the Reformation and a proponent of the priesthood of all believers, brought about a number of influential educational initiatives that impacted the religious life and spiritual formation of the people in Germany. He translated the Bible into German so it could be studied and understood by the people. Using a question-and-answer format, Luther developed catechisms for use by the laity and the clergy. His *small* catechism was designed for use with children, and his *large* catechism was for use with adults, including clergy. His catechisms covered instruction in the Ten Commandments, the Apostles' Creed, the Lord's Prayer, and the sacraments (baptism and the Lord's Supper). The law was taught

so people would understand the demands of the law and their inability to meet them, the Apostles' Creed made known the grace of God in Christ and the need for a response of faith for salvation, and the Lord's Prayer showed how to relate to God as his child.[15]

This form of catechism was emulated by many other reformers, such as Ulrich Zwingli and John Calvin (Switzerland) and Thomas Cranmer (England), and also by Catholic leaders in their efforts to counter the Reformation movement. Understanding the impact of music in helping people remember and express what they had learned, Luther also wrote many hymns to teach Scripture. In terms of formal education, he promoted universal education for all children, not just the affluent, and the development of libraries in schools. He also emphasized the responsibility of parents to teach their children the Christian faith rather than leaving this responsibility to leaders in the church.

Another major educational ministry development of this time period was the renewal of practices of confirmation. Though confirmation had been directly tied to baptism in the early church, it became separated as a church sacrament. By the late Middle Ages, it was delayed to around ages twelve (girls) to fourteen (boys).[16] Ultimately, confirmation served as a time of instruction in the basics of the faith and thus became a prerequisite for first communion within many Protestant groups.

While confirmation was an important milestone for young people, catechisms were the dominant curricular model. Instruction of children was done in three settings: church, home, and school. A general pattern developed

14. K. Lawson, "More than Silent Preaching," 327–30.

15. Wengert, *Martin Luther's Catechisms*, 16–20.
16. Orme, *Medieval Children*, 218–19.

in which parents and schoolteachers taught children the catechism during the week, and then on Sunday afternoons clergy examined children's knowledge of the catechism and offered additional instruction as needed.[17] Preparing for confirmation in early adolescence became a driving force for instructing children in the faith, and catechesis remained the dominant instructional model from the early sixteenth century through the eighteenth century. Both the Protestant tradition and the Roman Catholic tradition, with differing theological commitments, relied on a question-answer format and focused on the same four pillars of the catechetical curriculum: (1) the faith and the Apostles' Creed, (2) the sacraments of the church, (3) the Ten Commandments and the divine law, and (4) the Lord's Prayer as a pattern for prayer.[18]

Puritan Conference: Small Groups for Spiritual Growth

One of the major movements within the Protestant Reformation was Pietism, which emphasized personal religious experience, Bible study, and spiritual practices to promote growth in holiness. Starting within the German reform movement, this emphasis also spread to other Reformed groups, including the English Puritans.

After the initial English Reformation provoked by Henry VIII in the 1530s, when Elizabeth I came to the throne in 1558, many Protestant clergymen fled the country and lived predominantly in the Netherlands, Switzerland, and Germany. There they connected with the Reformation movements of those countries. Later returning to England, they brought some influence of the Radical Reformation and the German Pietistic tradition. They tried to further reform the Anglican Church but were not able to bring it fully in line with the more Reformed beliefs and practices they embraced.

Puritans saw certain practices as means of grace, tools to assist believers in conversion and growth in godliness. One of these was conference, a practice of discussing biblical texts and sermons and sharing God's work in believers' souls. These regular, confidential, intimate small gatherings used questions to prompt reflection on the truths of Scripture and how God would use these truths to teach and guide their growth.

Conference was practiced within home settings with children and servants, among friends, and in ministerial groups.[19] These small group gatherings to reflect on Scripture and pursue personal spiritual growth were forerunners to the Methodist small groups of the eighteenth century and to many small-group ministry models today.

Educational Ministry in the Early Modern Era

In the first few centuries following the Reformation, Europe experienced both industrialization and urbanization. These societal changes brought disruption to traditional family and community life and required the development of new ministry approaches in light of changing needs. Several new ministry approaches emerged that supplemented the traditional catechetical instruction of the church.

17. Green, *Christian's ABC*, 93–98.
18. Marthaler, *Catechism Yesterday and Today*, 36–38.

19. Jung, *Godly Conversation*, 124–44.

John and Charles Wesley and Small-Group Discipleship

John Wesley and his brother Charles had grown up in a family in which conference practices were carried out by their parents, particularly their mother, Susanna. While in college at Oxford, both brothers were also involved in a small accountability group called the Holy Club. Following some time in mission work among Native Americans in the American colonies, they returned to England, where they ministered with the Anglican Church. With some influence from the Moravian bands' approach to small groups for spiritual growth, the Wesleys were instrumental in forming a strategy for ministry with seekers and new believers that utilized a set of group experiences. This new movement became known as Methodism.

Methodism was known for its orderly approach to discipleship. Methodist *societies* were large group settings for people who desired to experience conversion and grow in godliness. A *class* was a smaller group than a society, composed of about twelve to twenty people who met for fellowship, mutual accountability, confession of sin, and support in their efforts to grow in holiness. Membership in a class and regular attendance were required for participation in a society.[20] The *bands* were even smaller. These voluntary groups were for those with clear faith commitments who responded to accountability questions about the state of their souls and their fight against temptation and sin. A band was a place of mutual sharing and support and also the training ground for many leaders within the growing Methodist movement. Finally, *select societies*

were small gatherings of lay preachers and group leaders who met to attend to their own spiritual needs and growth.[21]

These small group settings were instrumental in helping seekers and believers consider their lives in light of God's requirements, providing the necessary support to change the orientation of their lives and old patterns of behavior. These ministry models have continued to have a strong influence on small-group ministries in the twenty-first century.

Robert Raikes and the Sunday School

Industrialization in the eighteenth century led to the use of child labor in many mills, making it difficult for children to receive an education. Several Christian leaders experimented with offering some education to working children on Sunday, their one day off from work each week. In 1780, Robert Raikes, a publisher and social activist, began a Sunday school in Gloucester, England. He paid a scholar to teach children ages six to fourteen to read (using the Bible as a text, supplemented by the catechism) and to take them to worship in the church. While some church and community leaders were not supportive, the Sunday school grew in popularity and spread quickly.

A Sunday School Society was formed in 1785, and this approach to ministry with children soon spread throughout England and the United States. Other organizations, such as the Sunday School Union, founded in 1803, promoted the spread of Sunday schools and the development of curriculum and training materials for teachers.[22]

---

20. D. Watson, *Early Methodist Class Meeting*, 93–98.

21. K. Watson, *Pursuing Social Holiness*, 72–81, 157.
22. Boylan, *Sunday School*, 6–8; see also Eavey, *History of Christian Education*, 222–29.

In the United States, the Sabbath School Society was formed in 1790, and the American Sunday School Union was established in 1824, promoting the planting of Sunday schools in new communities throughout the western territories. They enlisted missionaries to plant schools and provide inexpensive curriculum materials and small libraries to promote character and spiritual growth through reading.

In the southern states, where there was little motivation to provide a traditional education to black slaves, the Sunday school became a means by which many of them learned to read and write. Following the Civil War, northern missionaries went to the South to establish Sunday schools and churches, offering emancipated slaves an opportunity to develop literacy skills and to be instructed in the Scriptures for moral growth.[23] Adults also participated in Sunday schools in some places, but this became more common in the later nineteenth century. This nondenominational enterprise was very successful—by 1875, there were almost seventy thousand Sunday schools in the United States—but in time, hermeneutical differences and the formation of denominational publishing houses and Sunday school societies led to the fracturing of the movement.

While Raikes's Sunday school model focused on providing basic education and spiritual instruction to working children, as the Sunday school spread, social developments gave it new direction. Under leaders such as Horace Mann, the growth of universal public education in the United States in the mid-nineteenth century made basic education available to all children. As churches focused their educational efforts more on religious instruction and spiritual growth, a revivalist perspective provided new challenges to ministry practices with children.

The Second Great Awakening had been a dominant force in the church in the early part of the nineteenth century. With its focus on human depravity and consequent separation from God came an emphasis on teaching for radical conversion experiences.

Horace Bushnell, a Connecticut pastor within the Reformed tradition, offered a different perspective rooted in his understanding of covenant theology. In 1847, he published *Christian Nurture*, proposing that "the child is to grow up a Christian and never know himself as being otherwise."[24] That is, he believed that with God's work through the family unit, children of Christians could be nurtured in the faith of the parents and the congregation and be encouraged to exercise faith from their earliest years. He believed that God would grow children's responses in faith over time, eliminating the need for a radical conversion experience later in life.

While Bushnell's views were not well received at the time, his emphasis on instruction for spiritual nurture in a growing faith had a significant impact on the efforts of the Sunday school from the later nineteenth century onward. The Sunday school model of this era became the major educational ministry effort of congregations throughout the twentieth century and is still a strong model in churches today.

George Williams and the YMCA, Emma Roberts and the YWCA

Another result of industrialization and urbanization was the movement of young adults from rural to urban settings as they searched

23. McMillan, *To Raise Up the South*, 10–12.

24. Bushnell, *Christian Nurture*, 10.

for work. Urban living brought new challenges and temptations. Following a Puritan model of conference, apprentices met together weekly for prayer and religious conversation from as early as the 1630s. In the latter 1600s, religious societies for young men met weekly for spiritual discussions and moral improvement. By the early 1800s, many Young Men's Societies in the United Kingdom, France, and America were meeting for mutual improvement and Bible study.[25]

In 1844, George Williams was a young man working in a draper's shop in London. With a desire to help other young men pursue spiritual growth and avoid the temptations of city life, he formed a small group that met after work for prayer and discussion of Scripture and religious writings. This group led to the formation of similar groups in other businesses, becoming the Young Men's Christian Association (YMCA).[26] The ministry of this group grew, spreading to the United States and Canada in 1851. The focus of the work of the YMCA was to share the gospel with young men and promote spiritual growth through Bible study, worship, and service. Wherever men gathered, the YMCA sought to have a ministry; opportunities included colleges, the military, railways, and mission settings.

In 1855, a similar type of ministry began with young women. It started as a prayer meeting led by Emma Roberts, one of five sisters involved in leading a school for girls in Barnet, England. With a concern for the personal, social, and spiritual well-being of young women, the group grew and developed ministries with working young women in urban settings. Bible study, prayer, education for self-improvement, and practical assistance for young women as they negotiated the challenges of urban life characterized the group's efforts. The YWCA spread to the United States in 1858 and began work with college and university students in 1872. The first world gathering for this ministry took place in 1892, with representatives from seventeen countries attending, and led to the formation of the international organization.[27]

Both the YMCA and the YWCA were nondenominational lay ministry efforts that sought to reach out to men and women at a critical time of their lives, encouraging spiritual growth, moral formation, and practical support in work, college, and other demanding settings. They both grew rapidly and received broad support from churches and society as a whole. Over the years, the evangelistic and pietistic emphases of these groups waned, and other social agendas took their place.

Francis E. Clark and the Birth of Modern Youth Ministry

In 1881, Francis E. Clark was a young pastor of a church in Portland, Maine, with a significant outreach to young people in the community. As many responded with a desire to grow in their faith and relationship with God, he decided there was a need for a ministry approach that would get these youth actively involved in the life of the church, including meeting together for prayer and finding areas of service. He saw the Sunday school as a ministry that poured instruction into youth but lacked a means to draw acts of Christian service out of youth. Incorporating elements of an earlier youth ministry model

25. Ninde, Bowne, and Erskine, *Hand-Book of the History*, 31–33.

26. Ninde, Bowne, and Erskine, *Hand-Book of the History*, 30–31.

27. E. Wilson, *Fifty Years of Association Work*, 8–12.

used by Theodore Cuyler, a Baptist pastor in Brooklyn, Francis and his wife, Harriett, created the Williston Young People's Society of Christian Endeavor. Youth members signed a commitment to pursue daily Scripture reading and prayer, support the work of their church, actively participate in weekly prayer meetings, and attend monthly consecration and testimony meetings.[28]

Clark promoted this new ministry model through publications, annual conventions (regional and national), and travel to help congregations form similar societies. Growth was dramatic. Over twenty societies formed within one year, around three hundred societies formed within two years, and over sixteen thousand societies formed within ten years. In 1895, at the time of the fourteenth convention for these societies, there were over forty-one thousand societies in existence, with membership over two and a half million. By this time, there were also many societies in other countries, generally growing wherever there was mission work.[29]

Like the Sunday school and the YMCA and YWCA, Christian Endeavor was a nondenominational ministry effort, encouraging the formation of Christian Endeavor societies within every congregation. As time went on, various denominations grew discontented with the nondenominational approach and desired to use the ministry model to promote stronger denominational ties and a cohesive understanding of the faith for their young people. Methodists renamed their groups the Epworth League of the Methodist Episcopal Church. Baptists formed their own Baptist Young People's Union, and other denominations followed suit. In spite of this denominational fracturing, national and regional conventions continued and promoted interdenominational participation and cooperation.

Clark's simple ministry model became the dominant approach to ministry with youth in the late nineteenth and early twentieth centuries. Youth taking leadership roles, strong local church participation, personal devotional practices, and holding regional and national conferences were all utilized by different denominations in their ministry efforts. Many of Clark's ministry strategies would continue to exert influence in both nondenominational and denominational youth ministry efforts of the mid- and late twentieth century.

Educational Ministry in the Twentieth Century

The twentieth century saw churches experimenting with a wide range of new ministry models and the rapid growth of parachurch ministry organizations to teach and to train children, youth, and college students. The evolution of nineteenth-century paradigms continued, supplemented with new efforts to address the changing needs of society.

Vacation Bible School

The modern Vacation Bible School (VBS), which began in 1901 in New York City, was an effort to provide healthy recreation and Bible instruction for children during the summer. At those times, schools were out, and little was available for them to do in more urban settings. The early VBSs were taught by college students and ran all day, weekdays, for four to six weeks. In many ways, they were like a modern-day camp experience in the church. This ministry model caught on, and by 1949, there were

28. Lanker, "Francis E. Clark," 385.
29. F. Clark, *World-Wide Endeavor*, 56–60.

over sixty-two thousand VBS programs in the United States. As time passed and other summer options for children grew, VBSs shrank in duration. By the end of the century, most were staffed by church volunteers and operated for one week and for only part of the day.[30]

Camping Ministries

Christian camping also grew rapidly in the early and mid-twentieth century. Rooted in the revival movements of the nineteenth century and a reawakened appreciation of the value of time spent in God's creation, camp programs were developed by denominations, parachurch organizations, and churches. Some were more wilderness-based with many outdoor activities. Others were more of a conference experience with assemblies, speakers, and group instruction. Today, some parachurch organizations, such as Young Life, use camp programs as a major evangelistic outreach, while other camp facilities put on conferences for Bible instruction or spiritual growth for those who are already Christians. Camp ministries began with an emphasis on summer programs but have expanded to offer winter camps and facility rentals.

Released Time Education

Beginning in 1914, in Gary, Indiana, the school system allowed children to be released from their normal class instruction one day a week to attend religious instruction programs in local churches. As time progressed, some churches cooperated with one another to offer this kind of program. Others copied this model, and by 1948, weekday church school programs were operating in most states throughout America. While this ministry model continues today, legal challenges since the mid-nineteenth century and changes in laws in some states have led to its decline. Today, rather than releasing children from school for religious instruction, many communities have adopted an after-school approach, avoiding legal complications.[31]

Parachurch Ministries for Children, Youth, and Young Adults

While the church continued its traditional Sunday school programs and adopted VBS as a special summer ministry outreach, it needed additional help in designing and carrying out ministry to children and youth, particularly ministry that would reach beyond the membership of the congregation. In the early twentieth century, organizations such as Boy Scouts and Girl Scouts began, focusing on the physical, social, mental, and spiritual growth of youth. Most Scout troops were sponsored by churches and viewed as a means to shape the moral character of the younger generation. By midcentury, other groups developed that had a more evangelistic and evangelical theological faith commitment. Royal Ambassadors (1908), Christian Service Brigade (1937), Pioneer Girls (1939, now called Pioneer Clubs), and Royal Rangers (1962) had many similarities to the Scout programs but with more Bible instruction. AWANA Youth Association (1950) provided churches with a club structure of games and activities along with Scripture memorization.

Other parachurch ministries operated in the community, providing an evangelistic outreach to those outside the reach of the local church. Child Evangelism Fellowship (1923), Young Life (1941), Youth for Christ (1944), and

---

30. Eavey, *History of Christian Education*, 348–51.

31. Eavey, *History of Christian Education*, 352–58.

Fellowship of Christian Athletes (1954) acted as mission agencies in the local community. At colleges and universities, groups such as the Navigators (1939), InterVarsity Christian Fellowship (1941 in the United States), and Campus Crusade for Christ (1951) provided evangelistic outreach, discipleship opportunities, and leadership training for students. Like the YMCA and the YWCA of the nineteenth century, these organizations sought to shape the faith and the faithfulness of the generation emerging into adulthood.

Renewal of Small Group Ministries

In the latter part of the century, there was a resurgence in the growth of small groups as a ministry model, both within the church and in many parachurch ministry organizations. Bible study groups were common, as were groups for discipleship/accountability, self-help, adult Bible fellowship, sermon discussion, prayer, and outreach. Many of the principles and practices of the Puritans, Moravians, and Methodists were reexamined and effectively modified for contemporary use.

Vocational Church Staff to Lead Educational Ministries

Beginning with its national convention in 1903, the Religious Education Association promoted the growth of educational work within the church and religious instruction in public schools. The first church staff members to oversee a church's educational efforts were hired in the first decade of the century. These directors of religious education were likened to principals of schools, organizing and overseeing all of a church's educational efforts. It was not until midcentury that youth pastors began to be widely hired, and in the latter part

of the century, as many churches grew in size, associate staff members with various ministry specialties were also hired: children's pastors, family-ministry pastors, college-ministry pastors, and others.

Moving into the Twenty-First Century

Many of the ministry models developed during the last century still serve the church well today. However, as society changes, we must evaluate, refine, and create new approaches that both teach people about the faith and help them grow in faithfulness in light of God's work in and for us. In our era, technological advances provide opportunities to make content accessible to people anywhere in the world. But when information is easy to come by, discernment becomes even more critical. The extent and the nature of human relationships are changing as a result of the increasing use of social media, creating both opportunities and challenges as we seek to encourage others' spiritual growth. The culture around us is also changing in its assessment of the Christian faith, challenging old assumptions regarding morality and the role of religion in shaping culture and communities. In many areas, believers live in a post-Christian era, with some of the same challenges faced by those in a pre-Christian era. The church must continue to respond to the changing context in which it finds itself, equipping believers both to proclaim the gospel to the world and to live faithfully in a world increasingly hostile to the message of Christ. Christians have always faced such challenges, and looking back at what the church has faced and the ministries it carried out in truth, wisdom, and innovation can give us insights for faithful and impactful response in our present context.

3

Philosophy of Christian Education

DAVID P. SETRAN

Every Christian minister has a philosophy of Christian education that is marked by sets of presuppositions about the ways people learn, proper roles of teachers and students, and effective educational aims and methods. Yet for many, this philosophy is often shaped by forces other than careful reflection on biblical, theological, and philosophical realities. A philosophy may be shaped by personal factors, such as previous experience, personality, and gifting. It may also be shaped by larger cultural dynamics, such as societal values, contemporary fads, or entrenched social, institutional, or denominational traditions. And, of course, it may be shaped by simple pragmatism. If a method "works"—often defined in terms of generating larger numbers or more excitement—then it is perceived as an appropriate and God-honoring approach.

Such influences are not harmful in and of themselves. The problem emerges when these variables drive educational processes out of conscious awareness and when there is an absence of critical reflection. When they serve as implicit causes of action rather than carefully considered foundations, these elements can guide educators to positions that reflect mere personal and cultural bias. Christian educators must move beyond the shaping power of these hidden values and find ways to articulate and live into a consciously chosen philosophy.

This is not easy to do. The ways in which educators view teaching and ministry are shaped by the personal and cultural "glasses" they wear, glasses that distort and obscure certain aspects of reality. Since most people are comfortable with and often oblivious to their own ways of seeing, they often have a hard time analyzing their own beliefs and motivations. Christian educators must find a way, therefore, to hold their viewpoints up for examination, making the familiar strange so that they can properly scrutinize them in light of biblical values while also considering alternative options. By looking at various philosophies and filtering them through a biblical and theological grid, Christian educators can begin to critically evaluate their own philosophical ideals while also developing new perspectives to enhance ministry and teaching.

Constructing a Philosophical Framework

In order to evaluate competing philosophies of Christian education and to develop a philosophy of one's own, it is helpful to have a conceptual framework that can demonstrate the relationship between areas of conviction and their resulting practices. Useful along these lines is a model developed by educational philosopher William Frankena (see fig. 3.1 for an adapted version of this framework).[1] Drawing on the logical frameworks of Aristotle and John Stuart Mill, Frankena's model details the connections between important components of educational thought.

For Frankena, the key to educational philosophy is to determine desired outcomes for students—a profile of what an educator wants to see happen in students' lives (box C). Boxes A (mission) and B (worldview) provide rationales for why those outcomes are the most important, while boxes D (methodological principles) and E (curriculum) deal more with how the outcomes can be attained. The model therefore combines a theoretical line of thought (A, B, C) with a more practical line of thought (C, D, E).[2] This model provides a helpful structure to outline the components of a robust philosophy of Christian education.

1. Frankena, *Philosophy of Education*, 7–9.
2. M. Peterson, *Philosophy of Education*, 75.

Figure 3.1
The Frankena Model

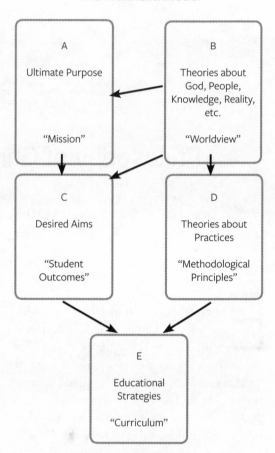

Worldview: The Foundation for Educational and Ministry Philosophy

From a Christian standpoint, it seems appropriate to begin one's philosophy of education with worldview (box B), since the ideals of which a worldview is composed largely determine the rationale for the mission (box A) and desired student outcomes (box C). Worldview encompasses one's belief structure, and in this sense it raises critical philosophical questions about metaphysics, epistemology, and axiology.

Metaphysics Deals with Ultimate Concerns

Metaphysics is the branch of philosophy that deals with questions of existence and the nature of reality. Of first importance, a metaphysically informed philosophy of education must address convictions related to theology: the nature and role of God, Scripture, the church, spiritual beings, eschatology, creation (cosmology), sanctification, and a host of other critical issues. Viewpoints on each of these subjects inevitably shape a teacher's goals for students, the scope and sequence of content, and teaching methodology. For example, one might assume that disparate views on spiritual warfare will greatly impact desired outcomes and methods for lessons on prayer. Likewise, different views on the role of the Holy Spirit will influence why and how one teaches about spiritual gifts or the role of spiritual disciplines in the Christian life.

Also important within the sphere of metaphysics is anthropology, the nature of persons. James K. A. Smith posits that "behind every constellation of educational practices is a set of assumptions about the nature of human persons."[3] Therefore, an accurate perspective on human beings is essential in forging a proper philosophy of Christian education. In this category, a teacher grapples with a series of key questions, such as the following: Are humans born essentially good or evil or as neutral blank slates? Are human thoughts and actions most fundamentally caused by genetics, the environment, or free self-determination? What does it mean that people are created in God's image? How do we define the different components of human beings (i.e., mind, body, emotion, will, soul, etc.) and describe

how they interact in the processes of transformation? What are the inherent differences between males and females? Different answers to these questions often lead to radically different educational and ministry approaches.

A last category of metaphysical concern is that of ontology, the study of "being." One primary ontological issue in education relates to whether ultimate reality can be found in matter, in spirit, or in both. For Christian educators, perspectives on this issue go a long way toward determining essential content and the aspects of students' lives and the world that are considered most important: mind or body, the soul or the created order.

Epistemology Deals with Knowledge

In addition to these metaphysical concerns, Frankena's box B also addresses epistemology, the branch of philosophy that looks at the nature, validity, and sources of knowledge. In other words, what constitutes knowledge? As George Knight suggests, questions about the nature of knowledge relate to whether truth can be known, whether it is relative or absolute, and whether it can be considered objective and independent of human experience.[4]

Perspectives on the sources of knowledge deeply influence Christian educators. While most would agree that people come to know about God and his world through multiple sources, it is nonetheless true that teachers favor certain sources over others. Some (empiricists) believe that knowledge is attained primarily through the five senses. Others (rationalists) hold that human reason and logic represent the chief vehicles of knowledge. Still others highlight authority, rooted in expertise and encoded traditions, or intuition, a "direct

---

3. James K. A. Smith, *Desiring the Kingdom*, 27.

4. Knight, *Philosophy and Education*, 20–21.

apprehension of knowledge accompanied by an intense feeling of conviction that one has discovered what he or she is looking for."[5] For Christians, divine revelation, or received knowledge from a location independent of the natural world, is obviously a critical source intersecting and ultimately transcending common epistemological approaches.

The relative weight given by educators to these sources has a significant impact on chosen ministry methods. For example, Christian educators leaning toward empiricism will be more likely to select teaching and worship styles that foreground sensory involvement. They will be more likely to utilize visual aids, encourage bodily movement, foster tactile engagement, include auditory prompts, and develop sensory-rich worship and teaching spaces. A teacher more attracted to rationalism will be more likely to highlight deep thinking about texts, apologetic and comparative doctrinal surveys, and reflection on theologically rich songs and documents. Rarely will a teacher be exclusively committed to only one epistemological source, but almost everyone favors one or the other.

Axiology Deals with the Good, Desirable, and Valuable

A final category in Frankena's box B relates to axiology. Axiological issues revolve around the larger question, What is of greatest value? Dealing with themes of ethics, aesthetics, and desires, axiological topics push teachers to identify those elements they consider to be most important, most lovely, and most valuable. It is critical to recognize, as Knight has pointed out, that axiological preferences are shaped by both metaphysical and epistemological beliefs.[6] Basic stances related to God, human nature, reality, and knowledge inevitably accentuate certain values over others. These chosen values, in turn, highlight particular desired student outcomes in the educational process.

Mission Clarifies an Educator's Ultimate Purpose

In light of the worldview described in box B in the philosophical model provided, educators should determine an ultimate purpose or mission (box A). This represents a teacher's sense of the basic ends of the educational process, the purpose for which everything else is done. For example, Aristotle viewed ultimate purpose in terms of human happiness. Others view ultimate purpose in terms of a utopian social order or self-actualization. Diverse Christians have expressed mission in many different ways, including glorifying God, loving God and neighbor, Christianizing the culture, and growing in Christlikeness, among others. The nature of box A (mission) directly reflects the metaphysical, epistemological, and axiological commitments described in box B (worldview).

Student Outcomes Clarify an Educator's Desired Aims for Learners

Student outcomes (box C) represent a description of what an educator wants to see happen in the lives of students in light of the commitments and values defined in boxes A and B. Such a description should account for the breadth of human experience. In other words, outcomes account for desired knowledge, attitudes, abilities, inclinations, virtues,

---

5. Knight, *Philosophy and Education*, 24.

6. Knight, *Philosophy and Education*, 28–30.

commitments, practices, behaviors, and other factors that constitute a student's life with Christ in the world. Outcomes, therefore, may be as diverse as a deeper knowledge of doctrine, a heightened compassion for the elderly, a growing capacity to relate to others, improved skills in Bible study, or a developing inclination to serve family members. These outcomes, as they are advanced, help students fulfill the ultimate mission (box A).

While the beliefs derived from worldview and mission set the parameters for desired outcomes, these aims are also shaped by the sociocultural and developmental context in which one is teaching. For example, educators may determine, by analyzing metaphysical and epistemological principles, that they value the development of students who serve the disadvantaged. As such, an axiological value is translated into student outcomes, and educators will express this objective differently if working in a fifth-grade, inner-city, after-school program as opposed to a suburban adult Sunday school class. They will express it differently in an African church than in an American Christian school. Differences in age, country, race, ethnicity, gender, and class highlight the need to nuance axiological values in ways that are sensitive to the particular context. In addition, cultural and developmental forces may work for or against their desired values, requiring that a teacher assess the opportunities and the barriers of their unique setting as they formulate outcomes and methods.

Method and Curriculum Reflect an Educator's Teaching Approach

Finally, boxes D (methodological principles) and E (curriculum) help an educator make decisions about the methods they believe will accomplish the aims set forth in box C (student outcomes). In box D, educators state theories of methodology, their beliefs about the practices most appropriate for achieving desired outcomes. These should relate to the accomplishment of student outcomes (box C), but they must also be consistent with one's worldview (box B). For example, while electric shock (box D) might pragmatically work as a means of enhancing scripture memory (box C), it would not be consistent with one's view of God and human nature (box B). Finally, box E makes these methodological theories concrete, providing space for the educator to think in very specific terms about the programs, resources, schedules, locations, and other practical guidelines for implementation. In this sense, it represents the "on the ground" ministry curriculum.

The Benefits of a Model for Christian Education Philosophy

A model like this provides a number of benefits. It helps leaders anchor ministry efforts in *conviction* rather than mere experience, popularity, tradition, or pragmatism. While many ministries begin with a set of outcomes, this model requires that teachers take a step back and look first at the biblical, theological, and philosophical convictions framing teaching aims. In addition, a model like this can provide *coherence* in a ministry, helping educators locate areas of contradiction and pushing them to seek consistency between ministry beliefs, aims, and methods. Using a model like this also helps with *centrality*. In many settings, educators take good outcomes (box C) and elevate them inappropriately to the level of ultimate purpose (box A). For example, the development of strong

Christian community might be an excellent outcome; however, when it assumes the status of ultimate purpose, community can adversely skew a whole ministry by directing it inward, diminishing outreach or evangelistic zeal. Models like this can reveal such inappropriate "idolatry." This kind of model also provides *criteria* for ministry evaluation. Utilizing this model, leaders can trace the effectiveness of practices not in terms of their completion but in terms of the fulfillment of appropriate outcomes. Finally, such a model serves as a tool for *comparison*. In order to properly compare competing philosophical models, a common rubric enables educators to identify areas of similarity and difference while also revealing the sources of variation.

In this light, the following section will introduce some typical philosophies of education, utilizing Frankena's categories to compare and contrast their presuppositions, desired outcomes, and recommended methods. After providing a brief historical context for the philosophy, these summaries will also attempt to examine what is helpful and unhelpful in each when considered from a Christian perspective.

Philosophies of Education: Issues and Options

Essentialism

Essentialism assumes that certain knowledge, an identifiable body of truth, is essential for every person in a group or population to possess. It posits that teachers and institutions are responsible to protect and preserve this knowledge by teaching it to current students, for now and posterity.

Essentialism has often been referred to as the back-to-the-basics approach to learning.

Emphasis is placed on the central ideas and physical realities of the universe and the need to pass along this rich storehouse of essential knowledge, skills, and values to the next generation. In this sense, essentialists tend to view education as a process of cultural transmission, one in which mature educators teach fundamentals to immature students so that they can steward this heritage.

While both rationalism and empiricism can accompany essentialist pedagogy, advocates of this approach tend to favor the use of reason and mental discipline in striving for knowledge mastery. Along these lines, they also hold that learning should be properly sequenced, moving from less to more complex concepts over time.[7]

Essentialist Outcomes

Essentialists hope to develop students with strong foundational knowledge derived from disciplined effort. They recognize that many important subjects will at first appear difficult, undesirable, and disconnected from life experience. Students, therefore, need to devote disciplined effort to acquire knowledge with the expectation that this will prepare them for the future.

Essentialist Methods

While various methods can be used to instill knowledge and skills, essentialists tend to advocate a traditional classroom setting in which the teacher is the expert authority and students are passive recipients of knowledge. The efficient transfer of knowledge through lecture is favored over discussion or other forms of active learning that may distract from

7. Knight, *Philosophy and Education*, 122–24.

mastery. Textbooks also tend to be favored because of their capacity to efficiently introduce students to a wide breadth of fundamental ideas. Since the teacher is set forth as the best source of knowledge and an intellectual role model, students are given little voice in selecting curricular components or connecting themes to their individual interests.[8]

Strengths of Essentialism

There is much of value in the emphases of essentialism. Christian educators can appreciate the concern for foundations, rooted as this is in a high view of content knowledge. Essentialism reminds Christian educators of the importance of biblical literacy and the disciplined acquisition of doctrines that frame orthodox belief and practice. Essentialists attribute great importance to the development of rational capacities, something Christians can affirm as they seek to foster the discipleship of the mind. In highlighting the orderly nature of learning, essentialism also encourages Christian educators to think about the logical progression of curricular units, teaching foundational truths before moving to more inclusive and complex topics. Finally, the essentialist emphasis on being guardians and propagators of truth mirrors the mandate of Jude, who said Christians should "contend earnestly for the faith which was once for all delivered to the saints" (Jude 3 NKJV).

Weaknesses of Essentialism

At the same time, Christian educators must also recognize that exposure to the Christian worldview does not always produce Christian commitments or ways of living. Knowing, in

8. Sadker and Sadker, *Teachers, Schools, and Society*, 417.

other words, does not always result in willing, feeling, and doing. Knowledge can easily be isolated, compartmentalized as an abstract belief system rather than woven into the very fabric of life. Ideas may be understood, even affirmed, without movement toward implementation of and responsibility for that knowledge.

In this sense, essentialist pedagogy often reflects an inadequate theological anthropology. Educators may teach in such a way because they envision students as purely cognitive beings, neglecting the complex interactions of mind, body, and spirit required for the transformation of the soul. Essentialism often neglects other ways of knowing, such as embodied practices and sensory experiences, by which humans are shaped to know, love, and worship. Christians may also lament the default passivity of students in the essentialist framework. As the parable of the sower (Matt. 13:1–23) points out, teachers must recognize both the seed (the Word) and the soil (students' souls) as critical factors in promoting student fruitfulness. It is incumbent on Christian educators, therefore, to consider the interaction between truth and students' inner lives in fostering a truly transformational education.

Perennialism

As its name implies, perennialism refers to an educational philosophy that highlights timeless ideas. These truths are a unified body of knowledge so valuable that it should command the full attention of teachers and learners alike. In perennialism, the content itself is the focus of education, even more so than the teacher or the learner.

Educators holding this philosophy believe these truths were, are, and will always be relevant and, for this reason, must be mastered. Perennialists believe in eternal truths that exist independent of human experience, and therefore they hope to inculcate these truths within students. Perennialists view students as rational creatures whose ability to think logically is what separates them from the animals. The use of reason to acquire and analyze lasting truths forms the basis of a perennialist epistemology and axiology.

Perennialist Outcomes

Educational outcomes, therefore, are linked to helping students discipline their minds for intellectual engagement. Looking to the past for rich insights into the human condition, perennialists appreciate the "great books" as resources to fuel the contemporary imagination. Textbooks are less desirable because of their tendency to provide students with watered-down, second-hand interpretations. Instead, perennialists aspire to invite students, through primary sources, into the long-standing great conversation on such grand topics as truth, freedom, authority, and love.[9]

Perennialist Methods

While lecture may be utilized for these purposes, perennialists also tend to support the use of seminar-style discussions to promote dialogue concerning great texts, music, and works of art. They are advocates of the liberal arts, though they tend to place more emphasis on the humanities than the hard sciences. Perennialists tend to endorse the so-called classical model of education, focusing on the grammar, logic, and rhetoric (*trivium*) of key academic disciplines. In this approach,

younger students learn and memorize great foundational concepts and ideas. As they get older, they begin to use this fund of knowledge in developing logical arguments. Finally, they learn the art of persuasion and expression, communicating their learning in written and oral forms.

In perennialism, teachers are viewed as subject experts but also as guides helping to connect students with the great teachers of the past. Students, therefore, are a bit more active in their learning, contributing thoughts and interpretations in dialogue with these historical authors. Perennialism obviously shares many ideals with essentialism, including the emphasis on mental discipline and a focus on foundational knowledge. At the same time, perennialists look more to the classical heritage than to modern knowledge, give more latitude for discussion and dialogue, and emphasize the intellect more than modern life skills.[10]

Strengths of Perennialism

The perennialist mind-set has much to offer Christian educators who desire to cultivate the Christian mind. This position tends to support the existence of eternal truths. Whether gleaned through revelation or reason, these truths provide solid ground from which to seek truth about the human condition. By placing great value on the voices from the past, perennialism also highlights educators' responsibility to connect students to the riches of historical voices, including the "great cloud of witnesses" (Heb. 12:1). This is critical because it frees students from the presentism that often obscures important and time-tested perspectives. In addition, by leaving room for

9. Knight, *Philosophy and Education*, 118–19.

10. Knight, *Philosophy and Education*, 124–25.

dialogical interaction, perennialism presses students to learn not only from texts and teachers but also from one another.

Weaknesses of Perennialism

Despite the noteworthy strengths of this educational philosophy, perennialism also has the potential to skew an educational philosophy toward rationalism, neglecting the importance of the material world (including the physical body) and the capacity to learn through the senses and/or intuition. In addition, this perspective may highlight theory over practice and academic life over concrete vocation. By denigrating the material world and mundane practices, in other words, perennialism may shortchange the importance of one's daily work, especially if this relates to physical forms of labor. Yet for Christians, all work that serves people's needs for the glory of God is dignified.[11] It is also worth noting that perennialism tends toward academic elitism. By elevating a certain canon of classical Western works, it may neglect other helpful sources, especially those coming from diverse racial, ethnic, or socioeconomic backgrounds.

Behaviorism

Behaviorism is an educational approach that seeks to shape learners' knowledge and actions, with an emphasis on producing observable and measurable behaviors. In this view, students are taught or trained using methods designed to create desirable outcomes. The behaviorist metaphysic is rooted in philosophical realism, the belief that reality is to be found only in physical and observable

matter (thus, it also draws from philosophical materialism). Favoring scientific methodology, a behaviorist epistemology primarily emphasizes empirical, sensory observation of the physical world, seeking natural laws that can explain human experience. Humans are viewed as existing within the same plane as the rest of the natural order and are therefore subject to the same laws.

Behaviorist B. F. Skinner, in fact, likened humans to complex animals. "'Animal' is a pejorative term, but only because 'man' has been made spuriously honorific," Skinner suggested. "Man is much more than a dog, but like a dog he is within range of a scientific analysis."[12] For this reason, behaviorist education often seeks to shape or manipulate learners to master knowledge or to exhibit behaviors through the skillful use of positive and negative reinforcements that guide learning toward educational objectives.

Behaviorism is driven by a unique vision of causality. Skinner noted that people, in order to maintain a sense of dignity and responsibility, assume they are driven by desires and intentions flowing from within. He argued, however, that this is a prescientific understanding of human nature. In reality, there are no internal causing agents—there is no "autonomous man" who originates actions.[13] In other words, Skinner and other behaviorists rejected the concept of humans having true inner states, or what might be called a soul.

Instead, as complex stimulus-response machines, people are shaped by the positive and negative consequences of their actions in the world. If they act honestly, it is because their environment has rewarded honest

11. Sherman, *Kingdom Calling*, 64–72.

12. Skinner, *Beyond Freedom and Dignity*, 201.
13. Skinner, *Beyond Freedom and Dignity*, 14.

behavior and thus reinforced such actions. While many critics argued that such a theory compromised human freedom and dignity, Skinner contended that it simply affirmed the need for experts to determine which environmental conditions would produce the behaviors best suited to human survival and flourishing.[14]

Behaviorist Outcomes

Because of the rejection of inner qualities, behaviorist outcomes consist strictly of behavioral objectives, observable and measurable actions consistent with a predefined "good." Sunday school or youth group leaders, for example, might identify concrete behaviors they hope to encourage in their ministries. This implies a rejection of affective goals common in other educational approaches, such as seeking to help students develop certain attitudes, values, or convictions. Therefore, instead of speaking vaguely about developing loving or patient students, they would be more apt to outline particular demonstrable behaviors: writing encouraging notes, holding the door for others, sitting quietly, and so on. The more precisely an action can be defined, the more readily it can be assessed.

Behaviorist Methods

Behaviorist methodology is expressed in terms of behavioral engineering or behavior modification. After specifying the desired behaviors and evaluation methods, an educator selects environmental reinforcements that have proved effective in eliciting these behaviors. Positive reinforcements apply something rewarding: material goods, verbal affirmation,

grades for achievement, and so on. Educators might also utilize negative reinforcement, the removal of something positive, or punishment, the application of a negative stimulus. Reinforcements, behaviorists note, should be provided immediately so that they are associated with the behavior in the student's mind. As the desired behaviors increase and become habitual, the reinforcements can be gradually slackened. For those who contended that this introduced too much control, Skinner countered by saying that educational environments have always shaped student behavior. His desire was simply to take this haphazard control and make it more intentional for the development of a better society.[15]

Strengths of Behaviorism

From a Christian perspective, behaviorism does make some positive contributions. It reminds educators of the shaping influence of environments and the powerful role reinforcements play in molding both desire and action. Behaviorism works in part because it reflects something that is true about how God created human beings. If people are created by God to seek pleasure and reward (Matt. 5:12; 6:1–6), it makes sense that desires and actions are shaped by positive reinforcement. At issue, however, is the type of reward that is highlighted. Behaviorism can train students to desire lesser rewards and therefore promote a craving for idolatrous "treasures on earth" (Matt. 6:19). Students may begin to develop a taste for trinkets, stars, and human approval, never realizing that the ultimate reward— Christ himself—is much greater.[16]

---

14. Ozmon and Craver, *Philosophical Foundations of Education*, 206–12.

15. Ozmon and Craver, *Philosophical Foundations of Education*, 212–20.
16. DeYoung, *Glittering Vices*, 15.

Weaknesses of Behaviorism

Christians will find much to critique in behaviorism's view of human nature, rooted in a purely materialist worldview that denies the existence of the soul. Because of this, behaviorism also emphasizes external behavior modification rather than the transforming work of the Holy Spirit. Jesus obviously condemned such a perspective, using graphic language to speak of the pharisaical "whitewashed tombs" (Matt. 23:27) that appeared clean on the outside but were corrupt internally. The Sermon on the Mount indicates that the human problem is not only external (i.e., murder and adultery) but also internal (i.e., anger and lust) (Matt. 5:21–30). What is needed is not just behavioral compliance—what Paul Tripp has called "fruit stapling"—but a heart that has been transformed by the Spirit so that right behaviors naturally flow from this renewed source.[17]

Existentialism

Whereas behaviorism sets forth a view that emphasizes behavior and denies inner realities, existentialism highlights internal realities as most critical. It describes humans as autonomous, free, self-determining agents. This school of thought suggests that existence precedes essence—that is, humans are said to be born without a purpose and must find purpose in order to live a life of meaning. Because of this freedom, existentialists also hold that students are responsible for their choices and actions. In terms of reality, existentialists note the primacy of human existence over essence, prioritizing individual personhood above all.

Existentialist Outcomes

Student outcomes flow naturally from this perspective. Existentialist educators desire to develop sincere and authentic students who can develop their own perspectives on truth and beauty and thereby can make choices about values rather than conforming to others' expectations. Students should be free and creative, self-actualized in their ability to carve out a chosen and fulfilling existence. Avoiding the personal alienation of standardization, an existentialist educator hopes that students can begin to answer the core question, Who am I?

Existentialist Methods

In light of these themes, methodology tends to focus on individual freedom and self-determination. An existentialist instructor assumes the role of facilitator, assisting students in their attempts to better understand themselves. A teacher's role is not to intentionally shape students' perspectives on issues but to create a safe space in which students can clarify their own beliefs and values. Freedom from fear, in fact, is a central methodological theme. Though existentialist pedagogy does not by nature reject traditional subjects, it does ordinarily specify that students help determine curricular content based on their own desires. Whatever content is chosen, teachers are urged to focus on the inner needs of students throughout the learning process.[18]

Strengths of Existentialism

Aspects of the existentialist emphasis on human individuality, uniqueness, and value can contribute to Christian education. Christians

17. Tripp, *Instruments in the Redeemer's Hands*, 63.

18. Ozmon and Craver, *Philosophical Foundations of Education*, 247–58.

can certainly affirm the rejection of passive conformity that anchors the existentialist critique of hierarchical and bureaucratized culture. As sociologist David Reisman has suggested, many in modern society fall prey to an other-directed consumer mentality, living out of others' expectations and changing personal convictions depending on environment.[19] In Christian education settings, students often conform to parents' and teachers' expectations, failing to internalize a deeply personal faith. The existentialist emphasis on authenticity highlights the necessity of developing convictions one personally owns rather than simply borrowing from authority figures. In addition, by emphasizing freedom from fear in the educational process, existentialism sets forth the worthy goal that children can learn in an environment of loving affirmation.

Weaknesses of Existentialism

Many aspects of existentialism clash with traditional Christian theological perspectives. Existentialism certainly leans toward a human-centered rather than a Christ-centered pedagogical framework, making the individual the basic unit of importance. In such a setting, truth quickly becomes relative, interpreted and evaluated in terms of individual desires rather than external standards. Individuals are not purely self-determining but are subject to God himself, the ultimate and authoritative arbiter of truth. Furthermore, while existentialists attempt to preserve student freedom and subjectivity at all costs, Christians affirm the authoritative roles of parents and other spiritual leaders in shaping young lives according to biblical standards. Christians may also take issue with the existentialist definition of

freedom as self-actualization. Scripture argues that self-determination actually fuels slavery to sin and to self. True freedom, by contrast, comes through enslavement to God and righteousness (Rom. 6:16–22). For Christians, freedom to be oneself can be viewed in positive terms only if that self is given to God and for others. As Galatians 5:13 reminds us, "You, my brothers and sisters, were called to be free. But do not use your freedom to indulge the sinful nature; rather, serve one another in love."

Progressivism

The term *progressivism* describes a philosophical movement emerging in the late nineteenth and early twentieth centuries that arose as an alternative to traditional pedagogy. It emphasizes student-led discovery and experiential learning. Progressivism elevates the learner and their intrapersonal development over the mastery of a body of knowledge or the acquisition of truth. The educational pursuit is facilitated by teachers who enable students to pursue their interests while working to develop life skills and solutions to personal and global issues.

Rooted in philosophical pragmatism, progressivism is heavily influenced by the Darwinian notion of continual adaptation to changing social conditions. Therefore, education is not about passing on static and unchanging knowledge; rather, it emphasizes the continual reconstruction of personal and social experience. Ideas learned in classes are considered instruments for solving problems with uncertain solutions. Therefore, the philosophy undergirding progressivism is sometimes called either instrumentalism or experimentalism.[20]

19. Reisman, *Lonely Crowd*, 17–24.

20. M. Peterson, *Philosophy of Education*, 52.

Progressivist Outcomes

For progressives, student outcomes are often phrased in terms of growth, but growth implies lifelong learning and continual development rather than a particular fixed end.[21] Educational growth means a person is able to connect learning to life in such a way that they are increasingly able to grow personally and communally in the future. What matters in learning, therefore, is not only the content but also the attitudes that are formed in the process, inner factors that will enhance students' ability to grow in subsequent experiences.

Progressivist Methods

John Dewey, one of progressivism's leading proponents, critiqued what he saw as the flawed methodology of both traditional education and the new education of the early twentieth century. While the former emphasized external and objective factors (content, materials, environment, and teacher), the latter emphasized internal factors (the needs, purposes, and desires of students). Dewey insisted that true progressive education emphasized instead the interaction between objective and internal factors.[22]

Most progressives view the child as the starting point in the educational process, hoping to connect students' needs and purposes with important content. Instead of motivating students externally, they utilize pupils' natural curiosity to motivate learning. They view students as active learners, using content to find solutions to their problems rather than passively receiving information handed down from teachers. Teachers are portrayed as fellow learners in the educational process, working together with students to problem solve while providing wisdom from their knowledge and life experience. In this sense, the classroom is depicted as a sphere of democratic learning, a space in which teachers and students work together through mutual dialogue and cooperation. For progressives, education is not a preparation for future living but actually life itself.[23]

Strengths of Progressivism

Christians can certainly embrace progressivism's high view of the learner, in keeping with the dignity of the *imago Dei*. Jesus himself deeply valued learners and often built his teaching on their needs and purposes, connecting life to divine truth. Christian educators can also appreciate the cooperative impulse of joint learning, especially when linked to the theological reality of the Holy Spirit's presence in teachers and students.

While Christian educators cannot endorse the lack of purposeful aim in the progressive notion of growth, they can support the idea of a continuous reconstruction of experience in communion with Christ through the Holy Spirit. Finally, they can value an education that is concerned with all of life, fostering an active interaction between content and student experience rather than maintaining an artificial separation between the two. As Lois LeBar suggested, Christian educators can appreciate the progressive emphasis on learning that is inner, active, continuous, and disciplined.[24]

Weaknesses of Progressivism

True progressivism, rooted in a pragmatist epistemology, also poses problems for professing Christians. Like existentialism, it tends

---

21. Dewey, *Experience and Education*, 36.
22. Dewey, *Experience and Education*, 36.
23. Dewey, "My Pedagogic Creed," 77–80.
24. LeBar, *Education That Is Christian*, 173–93.

toward a relativistic view of truth since ideas are validated only when they are found useful in solving human problems. Progressives also view truth in naturalistic terms, seeing it rooted in the material world and knowable only through the scientific method. Growth is certainly an admirable goal, but when it is detached from any kind of end rooted in biblical teleology, it lacks a sustainable, and indeed eschatological, purpose.

Reconstructionism

As an educational philosophy, reconstructionism is best described as a movement to utilize education for the purpose of social reform. In this view, the essential quest of education is to equip students to question assumptions about society and cultural structures and then to effect needed social change. Such reform is to take place through activism against systemic social, economic, and political realities that students perceive to be unjust, inequitable, ignorant, or corrupt. Over time, student activists should become beneficent leaders who usher in a society free from oppression of any form through the elevation of personal freedom, economic equality, world peace, and social justice in all its many forms.

Reconstructionists value individuals, but they emphasize that people must always be viewed within a social context that structures their thoughts, aspirations, and views of reality. Reconstructionists are chiefly concerned with physical reality, though they are also interested in the effects of social injustice on the human spirit. They seek to destroy the dualism that separates the material world and the spiritual world. While many Christians see the spiritual world as possessing a value not inherent in the physical creation, Christian reconstructionism suggests that physical realities possess significant spiritual importance.

Reconstructionist Outcomes

Reconstructionists aim for nothing less than a renewed social order built on principles of equity and human flourishing. For many of these theorists, traditional Christian education is too individualistic and too future-oriented. Established Christianity is perceived as commending an introspective spirituality concerned only with personal character formation and salvation. Likewise, it is perceived as disproportionately emphasizing heaven and eternal life, failing to consider the pressing current needs of this world. Reconstructionists argue that education must prepare students to become activists, agents of change, and reformers who use their knowledge and gifts to bring healing and justice to a broken society.[25]

Reconstructionist Methods

Reconstructionists tend to reject traditional teaching methods because these are thought to stifle creativity by reinforcing the status quo. Traditional methods, in other words, tend to indoctrinate students in present ways of living rather than empowering them to develop new solutions to world problems. Like progressives, reconstructionists favor more democratic approaches to learning that involve students and teachers working together in collective problem solving. They also tend to appreciate attempts to heighten student activism in real-world contexts, liberating them to experiment with social justice projects in concrete settings. Reconstructionism, in this sense, is closely allied with so-called

25. Ozmon and Craver, *Philosophical Foundations of Education*, 180–90.

critical pedagogy, an educational approach that highlights consciousness raising and the empowerment of oppressed groups.[26] In this way, reconstruction has roots in thought that view the world through the lenses of oppression, liberation, class, and power.

Strengths of Reconstructionism

Reconstructionism has much to commend it. As a critique of individualistic modes of Christian education, reconstructionism reminds educators that the role of teaching is one of both conservation—sustaining orthodox traditions—and reformation, echoing the calls of Scripture to let justice "roll on like a river" (Amos 5:24). Reconstructionism holds the capacity to open students' eyes to the broader world in which they live and to help them think carefully about their roles as agents of social change. It can help alert students to the fact that more traditional educational models—what Paulo Freire called banking models—can blindly perpetuate the status quo.[27] It indicates that teaching ministries must emphasize individual piety and social concern, both elements of true religion (James 1:27). It also reminds teachers and students of the responsibility to care for all of creation, including the physical environment and people's material realities. In a world in which injustice is historically perpetuated by social structures, it provides a rationale to ensure that students learn to love their neighbor in the broadest sense.

Weaknesses of Reconstructionism

Yet as with the other philosophies, we must be cautious. By placing the emphasis of educa-

26. Noddings, *Philosophy of Education*, 67–70.
27. Freire, *Pedagogy of the Oppressed*, 58.

tion strictly on social sin and injustice, reconstructionists can ignore or downplay the seriousness of personal sin, doctrine, and eternal life. As interest in broader social issues grows, in other words, it becomes easy to minimize the importance of holiness, salvation, and personal evangelism. Such a shift can be seen, for example, in many educational institutions that began with strong Christian roots but then allowed social action to displace doctrinal orthodoxy and personal spiritual vitality as essential aims.

Conclusion

As is evident from this brief survey, all the above philosophies have both positive and negative features when considered from a Christian perspective. Importantly, each one highlights certain domains of human personhood. Essentialism and perennialism emphasize the mind, accentuating the importance of knowledge and rational understanding. Behaviorism emphasizes human action, stressing the importance of students' behavior. Existentialism emphasizes students' desires, purposes, and emotions, highlighting internal authenticity. Both progressivism and reconstructionism emphasize students' relationship to the broader social order, employing education in the process of social change.

Effective Christian educators will note the importance of growth in mind, body, emotions, spirit, and the broader social world. Jesus "grew in wisdom and stature, and in favor with God and man" (Luke 2:52), and an educator's task is to help people grow to love God and neighbor (Luke 10:27). In fact, Dallas Willard suggested that all these dimensions of human life are critical for renovation of the heart.[28] A carefully articulated philosophy of Christian education, therefore, may be eclectic, drawing constructive elements from many different models while attempting to avoid their pitfalls.

In the end, the goal of developing a Christian education philosophy is not to construct the most complicated model possible; rather, the goal is to develop a simple but robust philosophy after having probed one's own perspectives and wrestled through competing alternatives. The process of creating such a philosophy should establish both a strong foundation for ministry decision making and serve as an antidote to the "mission drift" that is so common in ministry settings. Ultimately, a strong philosophy of Christian education provides a ministry compass, tethering ministry practices to one's central beliefs and convictions while providing clear and compelling navigation for all of one's efforts.

28. Willard, *Renovation of the Heart*.

4

Personal Foundations of Christian Education

JONATHAN H. KIM

Personal formation lies at the heart of Christian discipleship because our identity, morality, and spirituality are all bound inseparably with the development of a Christian self, grounded in being a new person in Christ (2 Cor. 5:17) and experiencing the transforming power of the Spirit (Phil. 2:13). This inextricable bond presents a challenge to understanding Christian discipleship and raises two questions: (1) What is Christian *personal* formation? and (2) What does Scripture tell us about the formation of a Christian self? To answer these questions, we will examine the core biblical concepts related to personal formation and discuss the biblical determinants that explain this developmental process. This chapter is divided into three sections: the first defines Christian personal formation based on the study of key concepts; the second introduces a stage model of personal

formation based on a biblical framework; and the last section briefly summarizes the model and concludes the chapter. It is my wish that the content of this chapter will assist readers to understand how central personal formation is to Christian life and offer relevant insights to those who are involved in Christian formation and disciple-making ministries.

Toward a Biblical Definition of Personal Formation

What is Christian personal formation? A growing number of people are using the term *personal formation* to explain an aspect of Christian sanctification. This trend is observed more significantly among those who study spiritual formation. Because the term is widely used in many ministry circles these

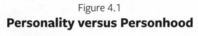

Figure 4.1
Personality versus Personhood

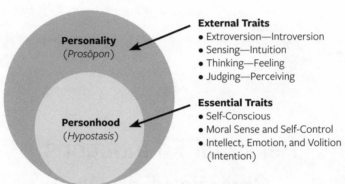

days, it is important to develop a biblical definition of personal formation. To do so, we need to examine a number of related concepts, such as person, personality, personhood, and formation. Since the Bible provides an immense amount of information about these concepts, we can easily rely on biblical categories in defining Christian personal formation. Let's start with the first key concept, person.

What Is a Person?

God is the Creator of human persons. We came into existence by the wonderful work of God, which began with Adam and Eve and extended to the rest of humankind (Gen. 1:27). No one came into being by chance or human effort alone. That is to say, our personhood stems from God's creative act. God made each one of us as a personal being according to his image, *imago Dei* (Gen. 1:26; James 3:9). While the *imago Dei* does not confer divinity, it indicates that God made us as beings who mirror his personal, rational, moral, and spiritual attributes. Thus, this chapter focuses on how the personal dimension of our selfhood grows in relation to God's sanctifying work.

From God's creative act, we understand that we are conscious, indivisible beings endowed with a distinct set of qualities and aptitudes that separate us from other creatures (Gen. 1:26; 5:1, 3; 9:6). The word *qualities* denotes our external traits, while the word *aptitudes* refers to our essential traits. They are also known as personality and personhood, respectively (see fig. 4.1).

Personality versus Personhood

When explaining what a person is like, we often use the terms *personality* and *personhood*. But what do they mean? Since these descriptors refer to the two different spheres of the human person, understanding their meanings offers important insights for the task of defining Christian personal formation.

Etymologically speaking, the concept of personality is connoted by the Greek word *prosōpon* (2 Cor. 5:12; 10:7). The term generally means "face, countenance, or presence" but more specifically the external traits of a person.[1] For instance, in the ancient Greek

---

1. Strong, *Enhanced Strong's Lexicon*, 4383.

theater tradition, a *prosōpon* was commonly known as a mask that gave stage actors a second face, another character. Shaped by this Greek meaning, the word *personality* came to signify the external traits of an individual that could be seen and distinguished by others, the personal characteristics that separate one person from another. Psychologists categorize these external traits into personality types using a variety of descriptions. A popular method is describing personality based on characteristics such as extroversion and introversion, sensing and intuition, thinking and feeling, judging and perceiving. These personality traits are believed to remain stable over time and distinguish one person from another.

Perhaps more significant for our study is the word *personhood*. This concept is traced back to the Greek word *hypostasis* (Heb. 1:3). This word is made up of the prefix *hypo* (meaning "under") and the verb *histēmi* (meaning "to stand or support"). Collectively, *hypostasis* means an upholding of the validity of some being from below[2]—meaning ontological traits that qualify a human individual as an intricate personal being.

In theology, the (English) term *hypostasis* refers to human beings having several capacities. First, we are self-and-other-conscious beings, each with a personal identity. Being capable of I-thou relationships, we have an innate ability to perceive our distinctiveness from and in relation to others. Second, we are born with an innate moral sense and an ability to control our own thoughts and actions (Rom. 2:14). Finally, we are living entities endowed with the faculty to reason, feel, and act freely. These intellectual, emotional, and volitional faculties allow us to exist as rational beings. The word *personhood*, therefore, refers to the essential capacities that we human beings possess inside.

What Is Formation?

Having articulated the human person as a conscious, indivisible being endowed with a distinct set of qualities (i.e., personality) and aptitudes (i.e., personhood), we will now examine the concept of formation. The word *formation* comes from the Greek word *morphē*, which means "the nature or character of something with emphasis upon both the internal and external forms."[3] The internal form is a nature of being, whereas the external form is a character of being. The word *formation* basically refers to the whole of a person going through changes. As an example, the apostle Paul used the word *morphoō* to command believers to be wholly transformed by Jesus Christ (Rom. 12:2; 2 Cor. 3:18). As we grow, both our nature and our character must be morphed into Christlikeness.

When we place our faith in Jesus Christ, God justifies and transforms (Gk. *metamorphoō*) us through the ministry of the Spirit. This process of renewal is what Scripture means by formation. With the righteousness of Christ imputed to us at conversion, God allows us to be fully morphed into Christlikeness so that we can regain the whole nature that was damaged by the fall (Gen. 3:1–24; Rom. 5:12–19). Despite the paradox of the "already and the not yet" in Christian life, believers are called to be transformed by the whole nature of Christ. This call remains effective until the full completion (Gk. *telos*) of sanctification is reached (Eph. 4:13; James 1:4). After all,

2. Louw and Nida, *Greek-English Lexicon of the New Testament*, 58.1.

3. Louw and Nida, *Greek-English Lexicon of the New Testament*, 58.2.

the Christian life is about how our relationship with God transforms us on the inside and the outside over time (Luke 10:27). While the physical body will progressively decline, the new nature will continually experience transformation until the Christlike nature is fully embodied within us.

Our analysis in the two previous sections suggests that the words *person, personality,* and *personhood* denote the ontological reality of a human person with individual qualities and aptitudes, whereas the word *formation* describes spiritual life having a goal-oriented focus, directing us to be changed into Christlikeness. Collectively speaking, Christian personal formation represents a development of a regenerated self toward Christlike maturity. It is a process of discipleship whereby a new self is matured through God's sanctifying work of grace until Christlike virtues are fully embodied in nature (Rom. 12:2; 2 Cor. 4:16; Eph. 4:23; Phil. 4:13). While some aspects of our formation may remain mysteriously hidden until the day of the Lord (Matt. 16:27; 1 Cor. 13:12; 1 Thess. 4:16–18; 2 Pet. 3:12; 1 John 3:2), much of our growth will become a visible reality in the earthly life.

Stages of Personal Formation

Having explored the biblical meaning of Christian personal formation, we are now ready to turn to the following question: How can we understand the formation of a Christian self within the boundaries of Scripture? The answer stems from careful hermeneutical study of biblical references to Christian selfhood and discipleship. To do this, first, I systematically identified all Scripture references that address the topics of the new self, the old self, the flesh, personality, personhood,

spirituality, growth, transformation, formation, and discipleship. Then I conducted a complete exegetical study of each reference before identifying relevant biblical categories. After I analyzed biblical categories and their related meanings, I organized the biblical data into a set of themes that outline the stages of Christian personal formation. My intention was to develop a Christ-centered model of personal formation using biblical principles. The following, then, is a process model of Christian personal formation in which there are four stages: the converted self, the conscientious self, the cohesive self, and the coherent self (see fig. 4.2).

Stage 1: The Converted Self

The first stage of Christian personal formation focuses on the converted self. Since this stage emerges as a result of having confessed one's faith in Jesus Christ as Lord and Savior, we need to understand what faith is and how it comes about. There are three components of biblical faith: knowing, believing, and trusting. They are also known as content, mental, and volitional dimensions of faith, respectively.

Knowing

The cognizance of spiritual truth regarding the narrative of God's redemptive love for humanity and plan for salvation is the first element of faith that leads to the formation of a converted self (John 3:16; 20:31; Rom. 10:14–17; 14:5; Heb. 11:6). Such an understanding is based on an intellectual recognition, acknowledgment, and acceptance of the biblical truth that affirms Jesus Christ as the Lord and Savior who gave his life to save humanity (John 1:14; 3:16; 8:32; 20:31). Knowledge about Christ is the crux of faith.

Figure 4.2
Stages of Personal Formation

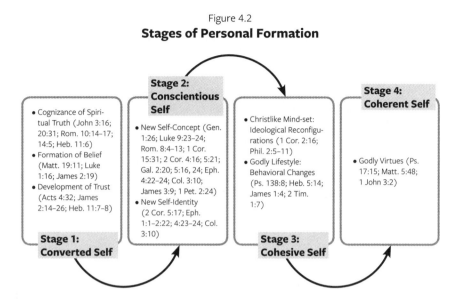

While the way we recognize the truth may vary, the Bible is clear that our knowledge needs to reflect some degree of intellectual recognition (Rom. 1:28) and acknowledgment (Gk. *hypolambanō*, Luke 7:43) of the facts of Scripture regarding God's message of salvation in Christ alone. This acknowledgment becomes personal knowledge if its values cohere with or correspond to our existing system of thoughts. Theoretically speaking, coherence and correspondence represent the ways our minds evaluate new ideas before they are integrated (Gk. *phroneō*, Gal. 5:10) into our existing pool of knowledge.

Although the process of knowing the truth seems to assume that a person must have highly developed intellectual ability to comprehend such abstract ideas, even a childlike understanding of the gospel message is sufficient for salvation. As a matter of fact, no matter how smart a person might be, no one can fully understand the complexity of God's truth. The fullness of God's reality lies beyond all human limitations of space and time.

Furthermore, without God's enablement, no one can understand his truth (John 6:44; Eph. 2:8–9). It is God's grace, granted through the Spirit, that enables us to comprehend his truth and be saved.

Believing

Belief is the second element of faith that leads to the emergence of a converted self. By definition, belief represents mental and emotional certainty of what we know to be true. It is a state of human consciousness that is predisposed to a certain set of propositions that have credible evidence in our minds. So to believe is to be aware of the reasons for our inner conviction and understanding.

In the Christian life, belief arises out of the truth value of the proposition we uphold. It first involves assuming certain ideas as trustworthy (Gk. *pisteuō*, James 2:19) and accepting them as a fact by reason of authority (Gk. *chōreō*, Matt. 19:11). Based on the reliability of an idea, either conceptual or experiential constructs emerge in our minds. Conceptual constructs are set by a related network of existing mental categories, whereas experiential constructs arise from emotional categories. As an example, when we encounter a new idea, we first evaluate its coherent or correspondent value based on either our cognitive or our affective goal. If an idea adheres to one of our goals, our minds begin to formulate a new conviction called *belief* by reframing our existing paradigm (Gk. *epistrephō*, Luke 1:16). Trivial or irrelevant ideas, on the other hand, are dismissed or mentally filed for later use.

When confronted with the content of the Christian faith as a body of knowledge, one is confronted with a new set of conceptual constructs. Assimilating those mental categories into one's value system—making them one's own—is what belief is all about. Thus, belief, resting on knowledge, is the second component of faith.

Trusting

Trusting Jesus as Lord and Savior is the third component of faith that leads to the converted self. The word *trust* means "confidence in" or "reliance on" something or someone. In the Christian life, to trust means to act on or to live according to what we believe (Gk. *pisteuō*, Acts 4:32). It connotes completely relying on God, being confident of his will, and living according to his plan.

Above, we demonstrated that belief requires knowledge. It is also important to understand the relationship between belief and trust. Belief, a mental act of faith, is rationally accepting something to be convincing, whereas trust, a volitional act of faith, is a concrete expression of the belief we hold. While belief is rooted in a rational assessment of knowledge, trust rests on the application of the belief we hold. For this reason, it is important that Christian leaders focus on helping people both to know and apply what they believe. In the absence of trust, belief becomes irrelevant and powerless. Trust is the only means of validating the legitimacy of the beliefs we hold.

Having discussed the three elements of faith, we can now define faith in the following way: faith is "the sum total of belief (Matt. 19:11; Luke 1:16; James 2:19) in the facts and truth of Scripture that produces the complete trust (Acts 4:32; Heb. 3:14) in and reliance on the person and work of Jesus Christ."[4] This faith necessitates "a firm and certain knowledge of God's benevolence toward us, founded upon the truth of the freely given promise in Christ, both revealed to our minds and sealed upon our hearts through the Spirit" (Luke 7:43; John 3:3–8; 16:8, 13; Rom. 1:28; 8:14; Eph. 2:8; Gal. 5:10; 2 Tim. 2:25).[5] While faith is a gift of God rooted in Christ's redemptive work, we need to mentally assent to receive his gift (John 6:44; Rom. 10:9–10; Eph. 2:8–9). We must learn the truth of the gospel, believe with conviction, and trust Jesus Christ as our Lord and Savior. God then provides a grace-filled path toward personal maturity (Rom. 6:23; 9:16; Titus 2:11; James 2:17). So as we close this discussion of the first stage of personal formation, we must remember that faith is the origin of the converted self. Without faith in Jesus Christ, there is no converted self. Also, while the first stage is a singular event that begins at the point of spiritual rebirth, the remaining stages become more concretely experienced throughout one's lifetime.

4. Estep and Kim, *Christian Formation*, 81.
5. Calvin, "Way in Which We Receive the Grace of Christ," 551.

Stage 2: The Conscientious Self

The second stage of Christian personal formation is marked by the development of the conscientious self. This stage focuses on how the relationship between the converted self and the Holy Spirit results in the development of a new self-concept and a new self-identity (John 14:26; Rom. 7:17; 8:26; 1 Cor. 3:16–17; Eph. 4:20, 24; Phil. 2:12–13; Col. 3:9–10). Self-concept and self-identity are associated with how we value and define our individualities.

New Self-Concept

The conscientious selfhood emerges when we understand our distinct individualities in Christ (Gen. 1:26; James 3:9). This stage begins with discovering our new self-worth through relationship with Jesus Christ. Prior to conversion, we exist as diffused selves (Jer. 17:9; Matt. 15:19; Rom. 3:10; Eph. 2:3), lost in sin (Eph. 4:24; Col. 3:9–10), experiencing futility (1 Pet. 1:18) and spiritual death (Eph. 2:1, 5; Col. 2:13). However, meeting Christ brings cognizance of our true ontology as children of God. As a result, we begin experiencing an intense peace that comes from understanding who we really are in God (Ps. 139:14). While the degree of this inner certainty may vary from person to person, as long as we are able to direct our thoughts according to God's truth, a meaningful self-concept will emerge. This new inner certainty is further materialized throughout the rest of the Christian life (Gen. 1:26–27; 5:1, 3; 9:6; 1 Cor. 11:7; 2 Cor. 5:17; Gal. 2:20; Phil. 1:21; 2:12; Col. 3:10; James 3:9; 1 John 3:2).

Rather than basing our self-value on internal sources such as our behavioral or emotional standards, we learn to focus on external sources such as God's eternal love and grace. God's estimation of an individual's worth provides a new framework to mend the behavioral-emotional biases of our old self-esteem. Then a more reliable, sustainable inner confidence emerges as a result. This process of normalizing the God-centered view of self causes us to find self-sufficiency through his standards of truth, removes a barrage of negative self-centered thoughts, and allows us to develop a new self-concept as children bearing the image of God the Father (Gen. 1:26; Ps. 139:14).

While growing in Jesus continually affirms our new, God-derived self-esteem (John 3:6, 15–16, 26), the inner struggle of the old self-concept may persist until the residue of the old self is totally obliterated through God's spiritual renewal (Rom. 7:15; 1 Cor. 15:52; 2 Cor. 3:18; 4:16; 1 John 3:2). The habits of sin that remain in our flesh will linger, seeking to pull us back to the old self (Rom. 6:12–14; 2 Cor. 5:4; 1 John 1:8). So whenever we are faced with discouragement and temptation, we must remember that our self-values are measured by God's standards of truth revealed in Scripture. For this reason, we must let the Spirit guide our conscience so that we might always view ourselves through the eyes of God.

New Self-Identity

Discovering a new self-identity in Christ is the second property of conscientious selfhood (2 Cor. 5:17; Eph. 1:1–2:22; 4:23–24; Col. 3:10; 1 Pet. 2:9). During this stage, a new self-definition arises as we realize the meaning of our existence in Christ. Comprehending this self-definition not only produces a new self-identity but also provides a new purpose in life.

Having a clear self-identity is an essential property of conscientious selfhood. Perhaps one way of understanding this significance is to remember the words of the apostle Paul to the Corinthian church. He told them that when they accepted Christ as Lord and Savior, they were given a new nature in Christ (2 Cor. 5:17). So Paul urged the Corinthian Christ followers to live not according to their old identity but according to their new identity in Christ (2 Cor. 5:15). This is true for all of us. Since our old nature was demolished at the cross, our former identity should no longer control us. We must enter into a new phase of selfhood as the people of God with an entirely new self-identity.

According to the Christ-centered view of selfhood, identity formation for Christians is based not on past experience but on the renewed life in Jesus Christ (Eph. 5:2). Conversion gets rid of the infirm identity of the past, and the new identity in Christ emerges as a result. Unlike the claims of developmental psychology, identity formation for Christians is not about having a sense of continuity between the past, the present, and the future. Rather, it is a result of breaking off the past and the present and embracing a new future in Christ (Eph. 4:17–24).

As explained, the major achievement during the conscientious-self stage is realizing our new self-worth and identity in Jesus Christ. During this stage, we receive a healthy dose of the Spirit's ministry based on God's grace and realize an entirely new self-value and existential meaning. Knowing our true selves leads to a purposeful life in Christ and helps us identify opportunities for further growth.

Stage 3: The Cohesive Self

The third stage of Christian personal formation focuses on the development of the cohesive self. At the core of this stage, transformation takes place at the ideological and behavioral levels. Ideological reconfigurations occur when we center our minds on the thought system of Christ (Rom. 12:1–2), and lifestyle changes occur when God's mission becomes our personalized life goal (Luke 9:23–24; Rom. 8:4–13; 1 Cor. 15:31; Gal. 2:20; 5:16, 24; 1 Pet. 2:24).

Christlike Mind-Set: Ideological Reconfigurations

The first characteristic of cohesive selfhood is having a Christlike mind-set. Since the attitude of the mind is the nucleus of life, the Bible calls each of us to reorient our minds to the thought system of Christ revealed in Scripture (Rom. 12:2; 1 Cor. 2:16; Heb. 11:3). While this exhortation encompasses personal transformation in all of its dimensions, the particular use of the word *mind* (Gk. *nous*) indicates that transformation begins with a renewed mind. This has important implications for our study in that the essence of personal formation is allowing godly thoughts to bring about ideological reconfigurations. One might ask, "In our flawed human state, is it possible for us to think godly thoughts?"

The epistemic issue here hinges on our participation in the life of grace offered by God. As we live under God's grace, the Spirit enlightens our minds to the reality of God's truth and removes the veil that sin placed over our minds. This restorative work reengages our epistemic capacity, illumines our thoughts, and brings order to our mental faculties so that we can think godly thoughts. The good news is that this grace-filled engagement of the Spirit is not just a one-time event that takes place at conversion; it is a continuous process that is contingent on our participation in the life of grace. The Spirit's empowerment is always available to those who respond to him with faith.

We need to replace our worldly system of thinking with faith and let Christ direct our thoughts, emotions, and wills (Phil. 2:5; 4:8; cf. Ps. 32:8; 1 Cor. 2:16; Col. 1:9; 3:2–5, 16; James 1:4). In this sense, ideological reconfiguration is not a matter of acquiring more human knowledge or having some type of mystical frenzy; it simply means that we trust Christ and place our minds in the environment of God's grace. If we do not, then we end up yielding to the lure of the flesh and infesting our minds with false beliefs, prejudices, and immoral thoughts. We need to cling to the Spirit to direct our minds according to the thought system of Christ revealed in Scripture. That is the only way that Christ's mindset can become ours and can reconfigure our ideology.

Godly Lifestyle: Behavioral Changes

The second property of cohesive selfhood is having a godly lifestyle. Believers ought to experience lifestyle changes not only as they attain godly thoughts but also as they live them out (James 1:22). This is where the Christlike mind-set becomes fully operative and produces a godly lifestyle.

As participation in the life of grace through faith is a necessary condition for ideological reconfiguration toward Christlikeness, it is also necessary for behavioral transformation. As we place ourselves in the environment of the Spirit, he binds our thoughts to the precepts of Christ and provides us with an objective view of life. So we are able to filter our subjective thoughts through the truth of the Bible and realize the results of our past life of sin. This process produces right thinking that

restores order to our lives and produces positive lifestyle changes that God desires (1 Pet. 1:14–16). While our circumstances may not immediately change, the Spirit will gradually change us over a lifetime.

During the cohesive-self stage, the Spirit confronts us with the cruciform life of Christ so that we can learn to embrace the whole sphere of Christian life that comes with the mission of God (Lat. *missio Dei*, Matt. 6:33; 28:18–20; cf. Matt. 23:11; Mark 10:45; John 4:34; 12:26; Rom. 12:1; Gal. 5:13). When we are able to apprehend a deep sense of purpose that comes with *missio Dei*, we can break out of self-centeredness, learn to embrace the mind of Jesus Christ (Phil. 2:5–8), and allow the Spirit to reshape our lifestyles (1 Cor. 2:11). However, the sinful tendencies and desires of the flesh may make many attempts to draw us back to old habits and life patterns. Fear, anxiety, regret, pain, and disappointment may linger, but if we obey the Spirit, we will be able to overcome them (1 Cor. 2:16; Phil. 2:5–11; 2 Tim. 1:7).

As indicated, the cohesive-self stage is marked by ideological and behavioral change. During this stage, we learn to reorient our minds to the thought system of Christ and experience lifestyle changes. Such a development takes place when we internalize Christ's truth (Rom. 12:2; 1 Cor. 2:16; Heb. 11:3) and personalize *missio Dei* as our life purpose (Matt. 28:18–20; Mark 16:15; John 20:21; 1 Pet. 2:9–10).

Stage 4: The Coherent Self

The final stage of Christian personal formation focuses on the development of the coherent self. This stage is characterized by embodying godly virtues based on a lifelong pursuit of spiritual formation (Phil. 4:8; 2 Pet. 1:5). The explanation below discusses the conceptual underpinnings of Christian virtues as they relate to personal formation, using the theology of sanctification as a touchstone. Obedient Christian living and growing in the virtues of Jesus are inseparable and lead to a coherent self.

At first glance, a discussion of personal formation in connection with virtues may conjure up negative feelings of dogmatic religious moralism. Rather than relegating the Christian life to religious moralism, we are referring to the responsibility that comes with being followers of Jesus Christ (Eph. 1:15–17; Phil. 2:12; 2 Pet. 3:18). Virtues are the properties of personal righteousness; they represent godly dispositions constitutive of mature Christian character (Gal. 5:16–18, 22–23; Phil. 2:2; 2 Pet. 1:5). This understanding is based on an evangelical view of virtues that asserts that God graciously allows his children to develop virtue in their lives. Furthermore, virtues are not something we possess in any absolute or mechanical fashion. Rather, they indicate a vibrant relationship with God. Only within the context of a transforming relationship with God through Christ can we embody godly virtues.

The Bible offers many examples of virtue: chastity, temperance, charity, diligence, patience, kindness, humility, hope, wisdom, justice, and so on. However, for this discussion, the term *virtues* is limited to the nine spiritual attributes listed in Galatians 5:22–23: love (John 13:34; 1 John 4:8), joy (John 15:11), peace (Prov. 16:7; John 16:33), patience (2 Thess. 3:5), kindness (Luke 6:37), goodness/righteousness (Rom. 1:17; 1 Cor. 1:30; 1 Pet. 1:15–16), faithfulness (Heb. 3:12; Rev. 19:11), gentleness (2 Cor. 10:1), and self-control

(2 Tim. 1:7). These nine virtues—fruit of the Spirit—are essential building blocks of coherent selfhood. While these virtues can be seen in both immature and mature Christians, only the mature can fully embody them as permanent dispositions of their character.

Developing godly virtues requires having first received Christ's atonement; conversion is the foundational basis for personal formation (Gen. 18:25; Deut. 32:4; Ps. 19:8; Isa. 45:19; Rom. 3:21–26). God then calls all believers to grow as disciples according to his standards of truth taught in the Bible so that they might mature to embody godly virtues as inner dispositions (Phil. 2:7; 1 John 3:2; 4:19, 21). While God grants his favor solely on the basis of Christ's atonement appropriated through faith, we are responsible for growing as "children of light" and producing spiritual fruit that glorifies God (John 15:16; Gal. 5:22–23; Eph. 4:17–24). In this sense, virtues are like good spiritual crops we produce in life.

Having explored godly virtues as constitutive elements of coherent selfhood, we will now examine two concepts that are often miscategorized as virtue in theological discussions. Some Christians use the terms *virtue*, *character*, and *righteousness* synonymously despite their straightforward meanings. This confusion is partly due to the lack of clear definitions that use semantic criteria. The following discussion examines the semantic distinctions between virtue, character, and righteousness so that we can understand exactly what virtue is and how it translates into coherent selfhood.

Virtue and Character

We all have a strong affinity for virtue and character, yet we may not understand what they mean and how they differ from each other.

A vast number of people, including pastors, use the terms synonymously. The confusion is partly due to the problem of not recognizing their inherent meanings. The word *virtue* is often used to translate the Greek word *aretē* (Phil. 4:8), which means "moral excellence or goodness." The word *character* comes from the cognate Greek word *charaktēr* (Heb. 1:3), which means the "representation, appearance, or enduring mark" of being. It is clear from these definitions that *virtue* represents a "principled quality" of a person, whereas *character* denotes an "exact representation" of a person's inner state. In other words, virtues are constitutive elements of Christian character. They represent our enduring character traits that are manifested in certain behavioral patterns. If we live a godly life, our character will be substantiated by virtuous qualities (Gal. 5:22–23). However, if we live an ungodly life, the content of our character will be marked by sinful or immoral qualities.

The capacity to possess godly virtues is possible only within the context of the imputed work of Christ and the enablement of the Spirit. This means we must be born again and need to live a Spirit-filled life as Christ's disciples (Gal. 2:20; 3:23–29; 2 Tim. 2:22; 1 Pet. 1:14–16; 1 John 2:3–6). As long as we are willing to obey God, the Holy Spirit will work in and with us to provide the capacity for growth until Christlike virtues are fully embodied in us (Rom. 8:13–14; Gal. 4:19; Phil. 2:13).

Virtue and Righteousness

One way of grasping how Christian virtues translate into cohesive selfhood is to study their relationship to the concept of righteousness. The Bible teaches two types of righteousness: positional (Rom. 3:22–28; 4:22–5:2; Eph. 2:8–9) and personal (Matt. 5:6, 10, 20; Phil. 2:12–13; 1 Tim. 6:11; 2 Tim. 2:22). The former is based solely on God's justifying grace, which attributes Christ's righteousness to us when we believe, and the latter is associated with day-to-day obedient living.

Positional righteousness is the righteousness that God grants us at conversion (2 Cor. 5:21). It means "being declared right" based solely on the justifying work of Christ. It is God's gift of grace made possible by the finished work of Christ on the cross and is not attainable by any merit. In order to possess positional righteousness, we, who are born of sin, must take hold of the righteous nature of Christ by faith in repentance (Phil. 3:9). We then become positionally right with God as his children (this is what justification means, whereby the righteousness of Christ is fully attributed to us). Following conversion, the Spirit begins the sanctification process and teaches us how to grow in personal holiness. As we respond in obedience, our faith grows and produces godly virtues. Theologically speaking, positional righteousness is the foundation on which Christian virtues are developed. Apart from having the righteous nature of Christ in us, we have no innate ability to pursue a virtuous life.

Personal righteousness, on the other hand, is the end result of our moment-by-moment obedience to God. It is a life characterized by godly living. Once we are declared positionally right with God, we can grow in personal holiness. Here we must anchor our faith in Christ and cooperate with the Spirit daily (1 Pet. 1:16; 2 Pet. 1:5). Inasmuch as the Spirit seeks to bring us into full submission to God's will, unless we obey, we will not be able to overcome the desires of the flesh and grow (1 Cor. 10:13; Gal. 5:24–25). When we pursue personal holiness, we mature and eventually embody Christlike virtues as the indicators of our personal righteousness (John 16:5–11; Acts 17:11; 1 Cor. 3:16; 2 Cor. 6:16; 1 John 1:9).

Virtue and righteousness are closely aligned. While virtue represents the quality outcome of godly living, righteousness indicates the state of being positionally or personally upright. As much as God's justifying grace brought positional righteousness to us, we are responsible to pursue a life of holiness until Christlike virtues emerge as properties of our personal righteousness. This is the aim of the coherent self.

Conclusion

With the premise that the development of a new self lies at the heart of Christian discipleship, this chapter explained the significance and the process of Christian personal formation. It began by discussing the core concepts that explain personal formation. Then it introduced a biblically derived conceptual model of personal formation containing four stages: the converted self, the conscientious self, the cohesive self, and the coherent self. The converted-self stage rests on God's redeeming love. The conscientious-self stage appears when we discover our new self-concept and new self-identity in Christ. The cohesive-self stage is marked by experiencing ideological and behavioral transformation. And the coherent-self stage emerges when we embody Christlike virtues in our nature.

My desire is that the content of this chapter will offer relevant insights to those who are involved in Christian formation and disciple-making ministries. As we close, let's remember that the reality of personal formation bears witness to God's redeeming grace. While human responsibility is required, the principal cause of our personal formation is the grace of God. By his grace, we are saved. By his grace, we are being transformed. So in humility, let us rely on God to complete his good work in us "until we all reach unity in the faith and in the knowledge of the Son of God" (Eph. 4:13).

5

Practical Foundations of Christian Education

PAUL G. KELLY

John's story did not begin well. His father abandoned his mother during her pregnancy with John, so he grew up fatherless. His mother emotionally abandoned him, too absorbed in her own life. She frequently left John to fend for himself, so he felt like a throwaway kid. Out of loneliness, he bullied peers at school and dabbled in the occult for power he could use to intimidate others. Not surprisingly, most of John's peers were afraid of him.

I met John when he was a high school freshman. I was leading a freshman Bible study, so I invited him to the class. He gave a noncommittal answer but told me where he lived and invited me to stop by anytime. I took him up on the offer the following Saturday. John's mother was out of town. He had been on his own for several days and seemed lonely. We sat on his porch and chatted. I asked John if anyone had ever told him about Jesus. I thought the question might end our conversation, but John seemed genuinely interested. We spent time looking at Scripture, and before I left, John embraced the gospel.

That Sunday John walked into the Bible study oblivious to the shock and fear on the other boys' faces. I handed John my Bible and asked him to read a passage aloud. He took the Bible and started to read about Jesus instantly healing a person. He stopped reading. I watched as he read the verse again silently. He looked up at me with wonder in his eyes and asked, "Is this true?" John fell in love with the Word of God at that moment.

This true story addresses an important question: Why should a church bother with Christian education? The way we answer this question impacts people like John, who need to know Christ and experience his love.

It impacts those who have grown up in the church but relegate Jesus to the background of their lives. It also impacts those who are hungry to dig deeper into their faith. In short, we do Christian education to make disciples—of everyone, everywhere.

The previous chapters laid a theoretical foundation for Christian education. That foundation is essential to effective Christian education, but the task remains unfulfilled until it is fleshed out in real lives. Christian education unites our ecclesiology (how we do church), anthropology (our understanding of people and human nature), sociology (our study of culture), and theology (how God and his truth relate to people), integrating them into a dynamic practice that communicates essential truth from one generation to the next. In this chapter, we will look at the *praxis* of Christian education through individual and corporate lenses, considering its impact on the lives of people in the church, universal and local.

The Goal of Christian Education

Jesus called fishermen to be his first disciples. Jesus used their vocation as a metaphor for what he wanted to do in and through their lives: "While walking by the Sea of Galilee, he saw two brothers, Simon (who is called Peter) and Andrew his brother, casting a net into the sea, for they were fishermen. And he said to them, 'Follow me, and I will make you fishers of men.' Immediately they left their nets and followed him" (Matt. 4:18–20 ESV). They, and most others, called Jesus teacher (Mark 4:38; 10:35; John 11:28). When Jesus called Simon and Andrew to follow him, they understood he was calling them to be like him. D. A. Carson explains, "Greek has several expressions for 'follow me,' but they all presuppose

a physical 'following' during Jesus' ministry. His 'followers' were not just 'hearers'; they actually followed their Master around . . . and became, as it were, trainees."[1] Jesus invited Simon and Andrew to watch him, listen to him, learn from him, and become like him.

But notice the end of Jesus's invitation to discipleship: "I will make you fishers of men" (Matt. 4:19 ESV). By following Jesus, Simon and Andrew would engage with other people. Howard Vos describes Jesus's meaning: "As they had caught fish and had brought them to shore for human use, so now by means of the gospel net they were to bring men to Christ for His use."[2] Jesus's teaching led his disciples to invest in other people, drawing them into restored relationship with God in Christ.

The purpose of Christian education today is the same. First, Jesus calls people to follow him as disciples. Then they become disciple makers as they invest themselves in drawing other people to the Savior. Disciples watch Jesus through the stories of Scripture, listen to his voice though the Holy Spirit, pay attention to his work in the world, and obey his teaching.

Christian education is about more than filling our heads. The goal of Christian education is to lead people who are following Christ to help others follow Christ. The result is abundant life now (John 10:10) and forever (John 3:16).

The Great Commandment and the Great Commission

Christian education focuses on transformation. This transformation involves both an

---

1. Carson, "Matthew," 119.
2. Vos, *Bible Study Commentary*, 43.

internal change of the heart and an external transformation of the habits. While the Bible talks at length about the Christ-centered life believers are called to live, two passages summarize the call especially clearly: the Great Commandment and the Great Commission.

The Great Commandment

A Pharisee once approached Jesus and asked, "Teacher, which is the great commandment in the Law?" (Matt. 22:36 ESV). Jesus responded with what has become known as the Great Commandment and the Royal Law (James 2:8): "You shall love the Lord your God with all your heart and with all your soul and with all your mind. This is the great and first commandment. And a second is like it: You shall love your neighbor as yourself. On these two commandments depend all the Law and the Prophets" (Matt. 22:37–40 ESV). Jesus began his reply by quoting the *Shema* (Deut. 6:4–5). He made it clear that true religion begins with loving God with all that we are—body, soul, and spirit (1 Thess. 5:23). Continuing his reply, Christ added a second command drawn from Leviticus 19:18. He made it clear that loving others is to be understood as a natural overflow of our love for God. Jesus explained that all of the law is fulfilled through these two commands.

The Great Commission

After his resurrection, Jesus met his disciples on a mountain in Galilee. There he gave them instructions to carry on the work he had begun. His words are known as the Great Commission: "And Jesus came and said to them, 'All authority in heaven and on earth has been given to me. Go therefore and make disciples of all nations, baptizing them in the name of the Father and of the Son and of the Holy Spirit, teaching them to observe all that I have commanded you. And behold, I am with you always, to the end of the age'" (Matt. 28:18–20 ESV).

Jesus had promised to make his disciples fishers of men. Before he ascended into heaven, he commissioned them to do this "fishing" by making disciples. How would they know how to make disciples? Jesus had spent two to three years making disciples of them. They were to teach others all that Jesus had taught them.

Jesus included two specific actions as part of the disciple-making process. First, those who had become disciples were to be baptized. Baptism symbolized death of the old self and resurrection of the new self (Rom. 6:3–4). Through baptism, disciples affirmed the work of the Holy Spirit in cleansing them from sin; identified with Jesus Christ, who was also baptized; and aligned with the church. Baptism was the initial step of discipleship.

Jesus also instructed the disciples "to observe all that I have commanded you" (Matt. 28:20 ESV). Teaching is at the core of Christian education and disciple making. Jesus did not tell the disciples merely to tell believers all that he had commanded. Jesus commanded the disciples to teach them "to observe," that is, *to obey*. Teaching is more than telling. The disciples were to guide people both to understand and to practice the commands of Jesus through both their words (teaching) and their actions (modeling). That is, after all, how Jesus taught the Twelve. Jesus did more than tell his disciples how to fish—he made them fishers. As a result, they turned the world upside down (Acts 17:6).

Jesus claimed "all authority in heaven and on earth." The disciples were to go and make disciples under the authority of Christ. They also experienced the presence of Jesus: "I am with you always." Discipleship was not to be a purely human endeavor. To make disciples, we partner with the Spirit of Christ. He works through us to draw the new disciple to himself.

The Essential Tasks of the Church

As discussed in chapter 2, from their beginning, the practices of the church were intended to make disciples. The early church was engaged in preaching, teaching, worship, fellowship, service, and evangelism. These are still essential practices for the church, each of which serves to shape people into disciples and has significance for the work of Christian education.

Kērygma: *Preaching*

Kērygma, preaching, was central to the ministry of the early church. Preaching was modeled by John the Baptist before the coming of Christ (Matt. 3:1). Jesus preached faith and repentance and the coming of the kingdom of God (Matt. 4:17; Mark 1:15). Jesus sent the disciples out to preach (Mark 3:14). Preaching is still central to the ministry of the church, and the venues of preaching have expanded over time. Preachers today preach to congregations gathered in church buildings on Sunday mornings, but they also preach through television and radio, post sermons on the internet, and stream messages live to multiple congregations at the same time. Still, the call to *kērygma* is the same. "How then will they call on him in whom they have not believed? And how are they to believe in him of whom they have never heard? And how are they to hear without someone preaching? And

how are they to preach unless they are sent? As it is written, 'How beautiful are the feet of those who preach the good news!'" (Rom. 10:14–15 ESV).

The late Haddon Robinson correctly said, "Through the preaching of the Scriptures, God encounters men and women to bring them to salvation and to richness and ripeness of Christian character. Something fills us with awe when God confronts individuals through preaching and seizes them by the soul."[3] Preaching is not the only way the church teaches, but it is a powerful way. For many, the first introduction to the life of a disciple comes through Christ preached in a church worship service, on television, or online.

Didachē: *Teaching*

From the moment Jesus called the first disciples, teaching (*didachē*) became a significant aspect of the ministry of the church. Teaching in the early church was varied in nature and location. Sometimes the teaching was more formal and sometimes less. The apostles taught in the temple and to groups that met in homes. They also taught in the marketplace, along the riverside, and even in an Ethiopian chariot. Christian teaching occurred almost anywhere.

Formal Teaching

Teaching is still of utmost importance in church ministry. As with preaching, the church today approaches teaching in a variety of ways. Some Christian teaching occurs in academic settings. Seminaries offer classes in New Testament, Old Testament, theology, church history, hermeneutics, practical ministry,

3. Robinson, *Biblical Preaching*, 4.

children's and youth ministry, and pastoral counseling. While many seminaries are primarily designed to train people for pastoral leadership in the local church, some Christian schools focus on integration, training working professionals to integrate their faith into their nonpastoral vocations.

Nonformal and Informal Teaching and Discipleship

Most churches offer nonformal teaching as part of their weekly ministry programming. This typically includes regular discipleship classes targeting people of all ages across the human life span—children, adolescents, and adults. Classes focus on diverse areas including general Bible teaching and training members in related areas such as spiritual disciplines, apologetics, and leadership development.

Some of the most significant teaching in the local church setting occurs informally. In some ways, the best classroom for Christian education is real life. Jesus taught his disciples everywhere they went, even as they walked along the road (Luke 24:13–35). Thus, Christian homes are an especially effective place for informal Christian education to occur. Parents who intentionally pass on faith and values to their children teach them lessons that may last a lifetime, ensuring the faith will be "once for all delivered to the saints" (Jude 3 ESV).

Leitourgia: *Worship*

The Bible uses the word *leitourgia* to describe service given to God in worship. The apostle Paul used *leitourgia* when he spoke of being "poured out" as a "sacrificial offering" for the sake of the Philippians (Phil. 2:17). According to Ralph Martin, there were three primary elements to worship in the synagogue:

praise, prayer, and instruction.[4] The early church drew heavily from its Jewish heritage, and each of these elements figured prominently in early church worship. There were also other acts of *leitourgia*. For example, the first-century believers shared the Lord's Supper as part of their worship. And financial gifts were sometimes part of worship.

Services of worship in American churches today include many of the elements used by the early church: prayer, songs of praise, words of instruction, and sacraments or ordinances of the Lord's Supper and baptism. We normally include ways for people to give offerings to God. And, like the early Christians, we understand that our service of worship is not to be practiced merely in formal settings. Our lives are to be lived as offerings of worship, punctuated with times when we gather with other disciples for mutual edification (Heb. 10:24).

Worship makes important contributions to Christian education. Certainly, sermons include important biblical teaching and application, but other elements of worship are instructive as well. Songs of praise are rich sources of theological truth. Singing them lodges truth into the memory and religious affections into the heart. We learn to pray by listening to others pray, and we learn about God when we see his answers to prayer. Baptism teaches us about Jesus's work in us and our collective membership in the body of Christ. The Lord's Supper allows us to periodically rehearse the power of Christ's atoning death and apply it to our lives. The truth of Jesus is reinforced by visuals in worship, whether stained glass, banners, paintings, projected images, or other media. Worship is a learning

---

4. Martin, *Worship in the Early Church*, 24.

environment, and each element has instructional value.

Koinōnia: *Fellowship*

The early church placed great emphasis on fellowship (*koinōnia*). *Koinōnia* was more than fond feelings or mere friendship. Christ followers were deeply invested in one another's lives. They shared material possessions (Acts 4:32) and meals (Acts 2:42) and carefully guarded their unity in the Holy Spirit and the community of faith (Eph. 4:1–6).

The apostles used several significant metaphors for the fellowship of believers. They called this fellowship the *body* of Christ, emphasizing the interdependence of Christian believers (1 Cor. 10:17). They called believers the *bride* of Christ, underscoring God's passionate pursuit of his people (Rev. 21:9). They described this fellowship as a *building*, the dwelling place or house of God (Heb. 3:6), and as a *family*, sharing brotherly love and offering familial support (Eph. 2:19). These and other metaphors serve to deepen our understanding of what it means to be in fellowship with God and others. Such biblical fellowship is the ideal environment for Christian education. According to Rick and Shera Melick, "Agape [God's unconditional love] is the natural greenhouse where spiritual learning can flourish."[5]

Diakonia: *Service*

Soon after Christ ascended, church controversy threatened to rip apart the new fellowship of believers. A group of Greek-speaking Christian widows were being treated inequitably in the distribution of food, so the apostles appointed seven godly men to oversee this ministry, a task with spiritual investment. *Diakonia* (service) took on a new dimension for the early church. For believers, service was a spiritual task done unto God. It was an act of worship but something that practically benefited brothers and sisters in Christ.

Diakonia "is the foundation of New Testament fellowship as believers serve others in the body who are in need."[6] The body of Christ is built up as individuals use their gifts to serve others in the church (Eph. 4:12). But Christian service also requires believers to care for the needs of those in the broader community. After all, James called believers to invest in the care of widows and orphans (James 1:27) and to care for the poor (James 2:1–6, 15–17). Though needy believers received this type of ministry, Christians were widely known for ministering to those outside the family of faith as well.

Like the early church, today's congregations carry out *diakonia* in many ways. They pray for and support those who are sick. They operate food pantries and clothing closets for the needy within and outside the church. They do prison ministry. They befriend those who are friendless. They repair homes and church buildings. These forms of service give insight into an important function of Christian education. Leaders in the church are called to equip church members for works of service (Eph. 4:12).

Equipping ministry is a central function of Christian education. Believers who volunteer for disaster relief need to know how to engage with people who have lost everything, how to prepare meals, how to distribute bedding.

---

5. Melick and Melick, *Teaching That Transforms*, 191.

6. Mounce, *Mounce's Complete Expository Dictionary*, 635.

Volunteers in youth ministry need to know how to connect with teenagers and how to guide them to spiritual growth. People who volunteer for a mission trip need to know what ministry they will be doing and learn how to do it. Bible study and small group leaders need many skills to effectively shepherd people toward Christian maturity. Overall, members need to be equipped for service. The equipping may happen in a classroom or on the job, but training is essential for *diakonia*.

Martyria: *Evangelism*

Central to the heart of God and the ministry of the church is evangelism, which consists of bearing witness (*martyria*) to the gospel. Jesus's final words to his followers exhorted them to bear witness to him (Acts 1:8). The disciples were to be witnesses, to give testimony to what they knew of Jesus. Within the first generation of the church, they bore witness across the Roman world (Col. 1:5–6). No church can be understood as fulfilling its biblical mandate when reaching people with the gospel is ignored or marginalized.

As we consider how to do evangelism in our own time, we can benefit from the example of Stephen. "But [Stephen], full of the Holy Spirit, gazed into heaven and saw the glory of God, and Jesus standing at the right hand of God. And he said, 'Behold, I see the heavens opened, and the Son of Man standing at the right hand of God.' But they cried out with a loud voice and stopped their ears and rushed together at him. Then they cast him out of the city and stoned him" (Acts 7:55–58 ESV). Even as they picked up stones to put Stephen to death, he was sharing the truth of Jesus.

Stephen was the original Christian martyr. He witnessed the most important event in human history—the crucifixion. He spoke from firsthand knowledge of the Son of God. His unwillingness to renounce his belief in Jesus led to his unjust death. This resolve demonstrates the degree of conviction that he (and countless others since) had for evangelism. This conviction should be understood as more important than life itself, but, practically speaking, it must be taught and lived.

The eyewitnesses to the earthly life of Christ are now gone, but the call to the church today is the same: we are commanded to be witnesses of Jesus. We are to tell the world what we know about the Son of God. The ministry of every Christian church should involve giving personal testimony as evidence to the claims of Christ. As we do, the Great Commission may be fulfilled in our time. Seeking this outcome, individual believers, congregations, denominations, and parachurch organizations need to develop intentional strategies for witnessing to the peoples of the world. A church is seldom effective at *martyria* if it does not focus on teaching and training individuals to give testimony of their faith. Without both a powerful visual and a verbal witness, the unbelieving world may misunderstand Christianity as nothing more than an altruistic nonprofit organization, a global relief agency, or a social justice movement. Placing the right emphasis on evangelism will ensure that biblical priorities are maintained in the proper order—the gospel, followed by the implications of the gospel. From the ministry of Jesus to the commissioning of the disciples to the first Christian martyr to today, sharing the message of Christ has been a central task for believers throughout the first two millennia of the church.

The Work of Christian Education

Christian education is more than a program of the church. Christian education facilitates discipleship. Discipleship, the epicenter of Christ's command, should naturally and intentionally occur through all the essential functions of the church. People grow as disciples through the preaching, teaching, worship, fellowship, service, and evangelism of the body of Christ.

Now that we have examined the nature of Christian education in the context of the church, we will shift our focus to the practical outworking of Christian education. We will examine both the functions of Christian education and the jobs needed inside and outside the local church to accomplish the work of Christian education.

It should be noted that this section is neither exhaustive nor timeless. The work of Christian education is dynamic. As our world and its needs change, the church must respond. For this reason, Christian education changes from time to time, from culture to culture, and even from church to church. No listing of functions and jobs can include every possible role of Christian education. And Christian education will continue to change as the surrounding culture changes. The church should continually explore better ways to make disciples. These new innovations in Christian education will require creative people to envision, lead, and staff them.

Functions of Christian Education

Churches approach the work of Christian education in a number of ways. The success of the field of Christian education has spawned specialty areas that have grown into movements in their own right. We celebrate these successes and recognize them as being within the legacy and heritage of this enormous task to which we are committed. Below are several categories that represent the work of Christian education.

Proclamation

Proclamation may normally be thought of as pastoral ministry rather than Christian education. However, the spoken word is the most common approach to teaching. In proclamation, a speaker attempts to instruct hearers in evangelism, theology, prayer, biblical interpretation, and Christian living. A preacher or pastor-teacher seeks to explain, illustrate, provide examples, apply truths to life, and inspire action. Proclamation normally takes place in a worship service, but it can also take place at a camp or retreat, over a meal, at conferences, on the street corner, or online. Whether in real time in flesh and blood or through digital delivery, proclamation is a key part of Christian education.

Normally, proclamation occurs in an open setting with learners of a variety of ages represented. At other times, the audience may be more targeted. Learners in these situations may include those with no commitment to Christ, new believers, maturing believers, and church leaders—all learning together. Some communicators use educational teaching tools such as printed outlines, projected images, or other visual media to aid with comprehension and retention. Measuring the learning that has taken place in these settings is often a challenge. For this reason, due to the purpose of proclamation, some preachers encourage people to make an explicit or public commitment to live out the truths they have been taught.

Bible Study

One of the key responsibilities of Christian education is faithful Bible teaching. While later chapters will cover the specifics of teaching, it is worth mentioning here that Bible study should have focal points. First, we teach the story of the Bible. While the Bible contains sixty-six books written over fifteen hundred years by dozens of authors, all the books together tell a remarkable and larger story about the God who pursues and redeems his people. Those who would follow Christ and teach the Bible need to understand the story of Scripture and be able to communicate that story to others. Second, we teach the Bible systematically. The Bible addresses key doctrinal questions: Who is God? What is the nature of Jesus? What is the church? What is salvation? What is sin? What is the nature of humanity? In systematic Bible study, a teacher gathers the various passages that address specific truths so people can examine all the teaching about a doctrinal issue. Third, we teach the Bible for life application. The Bible includes eternal principles that address various issues of life. Christians struggle with real-life problems—failing marriages, joblessness, substance addictions, relational strife, emotional problems, and financial pressures, to name a few. Believers need to know how to integrate the teachings of the Bible into their lives in practical ways.

Small-Group Fellowship

Small groups are used for all types of purposes in churches, including evangelism, assimilation, training, ministry, and leadership development. We often think of small groups being used for discipleship. Discipleship-based small groups should be Bible-centered. That is, small-group leaders should use a significant portion of the meeting time to teach the Bible. In addition, small groups should foster genuine Christian fellowship among members.

Members of a group should minister to one another's needs.

Small groups generally are an intentional mixture of seekers (those who have not yet made a commitment to Christ), new Christians, and mature Christians. Bill Donahue, an expert on small groups, suggests that groups should practice the discipline of an "open chair"—that is, a group should always be ready to welcome a new member into its membership.[7] While small groups are more likely to be based in homes, many adult Bible fellowship and other Sunday-school-type classes also fit the description of small groups and should perform many of the same functions.

Equipping

Beyond basic Bible instruction, Christian education is also concerned with equipping disciples. The church needs to equip people for leadership and service in the kingdom, both within and outside the church. Believers need help in discovering and utilizing their spiritual gifts for ministry. Teachers need to learn best practices for teaching from other well-equipped teachers. Ministry directors need to learn how to budget, organize, enlist, and train other leaders. Those who work with children and youth need to be trained in the appropriate care and shepherding of minors. Parents need instruction for raising their children in the faith. Believers need to be trained to manage their finances in a godly way. Equipping involves the development of life and ministry skills and requires an understanding of both principles and practice. Those who are properly equipped will be able to do what they have been called, gifted, and trained to do.

7. Donahue, *Leading Life-Changing Small Groups*, 161–62.

Discipleship

Churches often develop groups that are specifically designed to help disciples grow in their relationship with Christ. Often conducted as closed groups with restricted membership, these groups frequently involve covenant learning. In such an arrangement, members agree to prepare through personal study prior to group meetings. Closed groups allow for members to share deeply about their experiences and concerns. They require members to be accountable to one another for their growth. Members commit to be present each time the group meets unless providentially hindered. Commonly, new members are not permitted once the closed group has formed, except in the case of some long-term groups that admit new members periodically.

The instructional content of a discipleship group may focus on the study of a book, a workbook, or a specific portion of Scripture. Regardless of which is used, the learning process promotes authentic faith by including significant amounts of personal sharing, testimony, confession, and encouragement. Leaders for discipleship groups need a great deal of spiritual maturity. They also need an ability to facilitate deeper discussion among group members.

Personal Evangelism

Personal evangelism is a special issue in Christian education. As has already been noted, each person who shares the message of salvation becomes a teacher. A personal evangelist normally teaches in an informal setting as they guide another person to understand and apply the truth of Christ. Christian education also equips people for personal evangelism. A number of strategies for personal evangelism have been developed. Training for personal evangelism is normally most effective when a person is able to watch someone else share his or her faith and then practices sharing with a coach watching. Personal evangelism can take place over time or in the moment, anywhere and at any time.

Some approaches to evangelism involve memorized presentations. Others are more apologetic in nature and focus on answering a seeker's questions. God frequently uses established relationships in personal evangelism, but he also uses mass evangelism events such as crusades or revivals and direct evangelism in which no relationship has previously been established. It is important that ministers and ministry equippers understand the full breadth of biblical evangelism techniques so that the message can get out. There is a growing assumption that evangelism *requires* a relationship, but the only true requirements are an obedient believer, a lost person, and the Christian gospel. Best practices in evangelism normally focus on two things: the personal story of the evangelist and the gospel presented from Scripture.

Mentoring

Much of the teaching that happens in the church involves a more mature believer passing on information and insights to a less mature believer. Mentoring is a structured way for this to happen. Mentoring relationships may be formal or informal. Mentoring may focus on a number of different aspects of spiritual and personal development. Mentors may work with protégés to develop specific disciplines or character traits. Often mentors simply invest in the spiritual lives of their protégés. This may be the kind of relationship Paul had in mind when he instructed Titus:

"Older women likewise are to be reverent in behavior, not slanderers or slaves to much wine. They are to teach what is good, and so train the young women to love their husbands and children, to be self-controlled, pure, working at home, kind, and submissive to their own husbands, that the word of God may not be reviled" (Titus 2:3–5 ESV). Churches may set up mentoring programs that connect people to mentors. Churches might also encourage those who are reaching maturity to invest in individuals who are young in the faith.

Assimilation

One of the challenges in a church is the assimilation of new church members, particularly new believers, into the life of the church. Assimilation includes several components. Assimilation is relational, as new members need to find friends in the church who will love and support them. Assimilation teaches new members foundational truths of the faith. New Christians need to understand how the church operates and what is expected of a church member. Assimilation helps new members find a place of service within the church. An assimilation plan for new believers may include a new member class. It normally includes encouragement to participate in a small group. It might include a spiritual gifts survey and an introduction to the various ministries in the church.

Coaching

While similar to mentoring, coaching is more focused on providing targeted training that results in specific professional and often work-related expertise. Mentoring is more oriented to teaching, whereas coaching is more about facilitating growth through guiding discussions, asking questions, providing resources, and helping a person grow in skills and overall competency. Coaching relationships are more often than not short-term experiences. A coach often possesses a broad and/or deep understanding of certain desired abilities or traits and systematically and efficiently helps the other person cultivate those needed qualities. When targeted skills in any area of professional or pastoral leadership are needed, coaching is a practical tool church leaders should know about and use.

Administration

Finally, Christian education includes the work of administration. Effective ministry requires attention to the details that make it possible. Administration has to do with guiding a ministry toward organizational goals and developing organizational structures needed to support and advance the work of ministry. It includes the allocation of money, facilities, staff, and other resources for the accomplishment of ministry. It also includes the development of organizational systems and communication tools for completing the work of the church. Proper administration is sometimes neglected in ministries, resulting in inefficient or ineffective organizational operation. Good administration is needed at both the macro (church-wide) and the micro (ministry) level for proper functioning to take place.

Jobs in Christian Education

We have examined several functions of Christian education. Now let's turn our attention to the roles that support effective Christian education. While all church ministry positions are intended to support the ministry of the church, several positions call for the type of

Table 5.1. Church Ministry Positions

Church Staff Role	Ministry Focus	Responsibilities	Emphases and Competencies
Education or Discipleship Pastor	All life-stage ministries (children, youth, and adult), with a special emphasis on adult education	• Give leadership to Christian education and discipleship or spiritual formation • Responsible for the teaching ministries of the church, including small group ministry and Sunday school • Enlist and train teachers • Develop programs and curriculum	• Leadership • Educational administration • Life span development • Curriculum development • Biblical/theological knowledge
Executive or Administrative Pastor	Church staff and leaders, especially those who make use of facilities and work with vulnerable populations or who manage staff	Responsible for the administrative work of the church: finances, organizational structure, facility use and maintenance, policy development and implementation, legal issues, and basic human resources	• Administration • Communication • Bookkeeping • Legal and liability issues for churches • Biblical/theological knowledge
Senior Adult Pastor	Senior adults (usually sixty-five years and older)	• Provide ministry and pastoral care to senior adults • Coordinate service opportunities and community gatherings for seniors	• Effective Bible teaching • Senior life stage and end-of-life issues • Pastoral counseling
Family Pastor	Families, especially parents with children or grandchildren in the childhood or teenage years	• Provide Bible teaching, training, and support to families • Provide opportunities for marriage enrichment, parenting skills training, and multigenerational worship • May oversee life-stage ministries for children and youth	• Effective instruction of children and youth (pedagogy) and of adults (andragogy) • Administration • Family and parenting issues • Pastoral care and counseling • Biblical/theological knowledge
Single or Emerging Adult Pastor	Single adults of all ages, college students and postcollege young adults	• Develop opportunities for study, fellowship, and ministry that address the unique needs of single adults • Understand unique issues of single adults (singleness, divorce/separation, single parenting)	• Effective instruction of adults (andragogy) • Administration • Pastoral care and counseling related to single adults' issues • Biblical/theological knowledge
Youth or Student Ministries Pastor	Adolescents (usually middle school and high school students)	• Provide opportunities for teenagers to grow and develop in their faith • Train and supervise leaders • Navigate adolescent development, youth culture, ministry to parents, and pastoral care for students	• Best practices for teaching adolescents • Curriculum development • Administration • Legal and liability issues when working with minors • Biblical/theological knowledge
Children's Pastor	Newborn through elementary-school-age children and their parents	• Provide a healthy environment in which children can grow • Develop studies, events, and projects for children • Support parents in their role as spiritual shepherds of their children • Train and supervise leaders	• Child development • Best practices in education of children at various developmental stages • Curriculum development • Ministry to parents • Legal and liability issues when working with minors • Biblical/theological knowledge

specialized training that Christian education programs provide. Table 5.1 includes a survey of church ministry positions that would be well served by a candidate with Christian education expertise and formal training.

In addition to these positions, there are other Christian education jobs outside the local church: nongovernmental organization (NGO) or Christian nonprofit leader; camp director; recreation leader; Bible curriculum writer; college campus ministry director; parachurch ministry leader; Christian school-teacher; Christian education professor; and Christian school, college, or university administrator. Since another chapter is devoted to parachurch ministry, these positions are not explored in detail here. Even so, Christian education students should understand the types of positions for which they are being professionally equipped in their academic programs and institutions. These and many other positions provide ample professional ministry opportunities for the well-equipped Christian education graduate.

Conclusion

This chapter has provided a broad look at the practical work of Christian education. Simply put, the focus of Christian education is disciple making. Christian education serves people at all life stages. It involves formal and informal learning environments and permeates the ministry of the church, from worship services to the mission field.

PART 2

EDUCATIONAL THEORY

At its core, Christian education centers on the teaching-learning process. There are many things Christian educators are equipped to do, and these include an ever-expanding array of competencies and specializations. Yet nothing is as essential to the work as providing transformational teaching that results in the making of disciples. Christ himself said as much in the Great Commission, when he charged us to make disciples, teaching them to observe all he had commanded (Matt. 28:20).

Educational Ministry

Christian teaching is the essence of educational ministry. The ministry of teaching fosters disciple making—both directly and indirectly. Directly, effective teaching results in the making of disciples by imparting truth to believers (2 Tim. 2:2). Indirectly, effective teaching contributes to the making of disciples by equipping saints for ministry (Eph. 4:11–13). These two aspects of Christian teaching, biblical instruction and ministry

equipping, are central to the work of educational ministry. Both are explored in detail throughout this book. In part 1, the foundations of Christian education were identified. Part 2 is a deep dive into key areas of teaching theory. Parts 3, 4, and 5 will then focus on equipping. Together, these provide the basic knowledge needed for effective ministry in Christian education.

It can be said that teaching is both the heart and the heartbeat of Christian education. Teaching is, however, not an end unto itself. The real value of teaching is its *effect*—what it produces. In this way, teaching is a means to an end. The end, meaning the goal, is learning. Teaching is the catalyst that produces the desired result of Christian education.

Understanding Educational Theory

Education focuses on all aspects of teaching and learning. This understanding recognizes the importance of the teacher and the learner in the educational process. What makes education *Christian*, however, is both the content

73

of the teaching and its aim. The teaching content is fundamentally truth, and God's Holy Word, the Bible, in particular (2 Pet. 1:19–21). The teaching aim is learning—specifically, learning that fosters renewed minds resulting in the formation of Christian character (Gal. 4:19) that produces permanent life change (Rom. 12:2).

Effective Christian education produces ministry-ready disciples who have experienced genuine personal transformation from the inside out, whose lives embody the power and presence of the living Christ. They know, love, and live for Christ and love others in his name (Matt. 22:37–39). They have adopted God-honoring knowledge, beliefs, worldviews, attitudes, motivations, convictions, values, actions, behaviors, lifestyles, and relationships.

Those qualities are the telltale signs of a Jesus follower. Yet how are these types of believers produced? Through biblically informed Christian education rooted in solid educational theory. For the Christian minister or teacher, educational theory has to do with the why, what, and how of teaching and learning. It involves being aware of the educational process and the assumptions and presuppositions that should guide an educator's understanding about what learning really is. It informs one's acceptance or rejection of theories and theorists in the field of education. It equips one with the needed didactic tools to produce the desired type and degree of knowledge students need. It provides tips and techniques for helping students of different ages and developmental levels reach specific learning goals.

A Call of Commitment to Educational Theory

The aspects of educational theory mentioned make up a comprehensive system of ideas that serve as a framework for Christian education. Developing such a framework is not optional. Every teacher approaches the task of teaching from a particular perspective, whether or not they recognize that. Accidental educators without an understanding of theory teach from a relatively random, uninformed, and aimless reference point. Indeed, this lack of attention to theory may explain some of the ineffective teaching and disciple making in many of today's churches.

Intentional educators, on the other hand, are those who discipline themselves to acquire the perspectives needed by learners and expected of teachers. It is incumbent on ministry professionals to consistently invest the time, attention, and energy needed to master these nonnegotiable perspectives held by all true Christian education professionals. When Christian teachers take educational theory seriously, they become increasingly skilled in helping produce spiritually formed, biblically informed, and personally transformed Christian disciples. Let's commit ourselves to becoming conversant in, and ultimately mastering, the essentials of theory presented in the following chapters.

6

Learning Theory

WILLIAM R. YOUNT

A Triad of Theoretical Explanations

Scripture presents Jesus of Nazareth as prophet, priest, and king. These three roles reflect distinctions in human life and learning, designed by God and codified over the past 140 years as behavioral, cognitive, and humanistic systems by educational psychologists.

Jesus was a prophet (Matt. 13:57; 21:11; Luke 24:19; John 6:14) as he proclaimed the objective yet nonmaterial kingdom of God. He used stories and illustrations to explain the nature of this kingdom. As a prophet, Jesus focused on the objective elements of faith. He expounded the Old Testament through contemporary illustrations and stories. He transformed the thinking of listeners through parables, using familiar objects (concrete) to explain the spiritual (abstract). Jesus asked objective questions to deepen understanding and expose misperceptions. He explained kingdom concepts by giving examples of comparison and contrast. In all these things, he showed himself a "Master of intellect,"[1] teaching from the mind (head), the cognitive sphere of learning.

Jesus was a priest (Heb. 3:1; 4:14) as he identified with his people, loving them and giving his life, figuratively and literally, daily and ultimately for others. As a priest, Jesus focused on the subjective elements of faith. He accepted people as they were (the adulterous woman, the leper, Nicodemus the Pharisee, Matthew the tax collector, the Roman centurion, Judas the traitor), offering them new life by his love. He cared for people: the crowds, women, children, the sick, and the afflicted. He befriended the disciples, providing for their needs. In all these things, Jesus showed himself humane and humanitarian, teaching from the heart, the humanistic sphere of learning.

1. Willard, *Divine Conspiracy*, 146.

Jesus was king (Mark 15:2; Luke 23:3; John 18:37; Acts 17:7) as he demonstrated kingdom life, providing the kingdom model to emulate. He commissioned his followers as teaching ambassadors to make disciples of all nations (Matt. 28:19–20). As king, Jesus was Lord and leader, rewarding those who followed and obeyed him. He called men and women to action (Matt. 5–7; John 17:20), declaring that they would be known by their fruit (Matt. 7:16–17). He defined spiritual wisdom as hearing and practicing his commands (Matt. 7:24–27). In all these things, Jesus showed himself proficient and skillful, teaching as demonstrator (hand), the behavioral sphere of learning.

Behavioral Theories of Learning

Traditional Behavioral Theories

We begin with traditional behavioral theories of learning, the oldest theories. Ivan Pavlov's classical conditioning and B. F. Skinner's operant conditioning reflect the essential nature of teaching for behavioral change. Albert Bandura's social learning theory emphasizes behavioral learning but includes cognitive elements.

Classical Conditioning Theory

Ivan Pavlov (1849–1936) discovered a simple connection between food (stimulus) and salivation (response) in dogs, called the stimulus-response (S-R) bond. Food causes salivation naturally, without training. Pavlov called food an unconditioned (natural) stimulus and salivation the unconditioned (natural) response. But Pavlov's dogs salivated at the mere sight of the lab assistants who fed them, even without food. The assistants were conditioned stimuli, associated by the dogs with food. Salivation caused by seeing the assistants was a conditioned response. Classical conditioning explains the (unconscious) creation of associative links between stimuli and behavioral reactions to those stimuli.

Learners who avoid participation in class activities do not necessarily choose to behave this way. Their hesitancy is associated with bad experiences in the past. A classroom's climate is full of possibilities for positive or negative associations, depending on the teacher's personality and teaching style. Do learners know we want them to succeed? Is our feedback corrective and uplifting or punitive and humiliating? Are we kind or gruff toward learners? Regardless of method, manner matters in climate control. Classical conditioning emphasizes behaviors that are involuntary and unconsciously elicited by specific stimuli but does not explain how new behaviors are intentionally established and shaped.

Operant Conditioning Theory

B. F. Skinner (1904–90) emphasized the acquisition of new behaviors in his theory of operant conditioning. Learners "operate" on their environment (response) and receive a reward (reinforcing stimulus), creating R-S bonds. Responses are voluntary and emitted by people or animals. Rewarding emitted behavior increases the likelihood that the behavior will be repeated.

By providing reinforcing stimuli (food pellets) for increasingly complex (emitted) behaviors, Skinner was able to teach pigeons to play the piano and table tennis. The R-S principles discovered by Skinner are effective and powerful. They are used by teachers to program behavior in schoolchildren, by medical doctors to program behavior in mental patients, and by dictators to program behavior in entire nations.

Given this power and its potential for abuse, is human programming ethical? Programming behavior is ethical when principles are used for justified purposes[2] and when changes occur for reasons that learners accept.[3] If the behavioral outcomes are honest, and students knowingly cooperate with the process, then programming human behavior is neither manipulation nor bribery.

Social Learning Theory

Albert Bandura (b. 1925) observed that many persistent behaviors are learned without direct reinforcement. They result from learners observing the actions of respected models (parents, older learners, or teachers). Bandura wrote *Social Learning Theory* (1977), which emphasized vicarious, rather than direct, reinforcement. Vicarious reinforcement refers to behavior changes in observers caused by reinforcement of models. Bandura incorporated mental encoding of behavior, a cognitive construct, which Skinner opposed his entire life.[4]

Behavioral Theories of the Twenty-First Century

Textbooks continue to cite sources on traditional behavioral theories from the 1960s and 1970s. Research continues, however, with emphasis on analyzing and correcting dysfunctional behaviors in the classroom.

Applied behavioral analysis (ABA) provides a framework to study past and present environmental circumstances thought to explain persistent behavior problems. From this analysis, educational specialists determine how to shape classroom behaviors that are less disruptive and more productive.[5]

Functional analysis identifies personal, social, and environmental factors associated with specific behaviors. Specialists generate intervention plans, called functional behavioral assessments, which are more comprehensive than ABA since they are derived from a broader understanding of student misbehavior.[6]

Positive behavioral support (PBS) creates and monitors plans, based on functional behavioral assessments, which include suggestions for changing classroom environments, creating predictable daily routines, providing opportunities to make choices, and adapting curriculum.[7] Though time-consuming, PBS procedures are effective in improving learning environments when other approaches fail.[8]

Bandura's inclusion of mental encoding in his behavioral social learning theory took a significant leap in 1986 with the publication of his *Social Foundations of Thought and Action: A Social Cognitive Theory*. Social cognitive theory went beyond imitated behavior and vicarious reinforcement to propose a more complex view of learning.

The increased complexity resulted from the interaction of three elements—namely, personal characteristics, behavioral patterns, and the social environment. Personal characteristics reflect both cognitive (thought processes, self-perceptions) and affective (emotional states) components. Behavioral patterns and the social

---

2. Justified purposes would include helping learners improve skills.

3. An example of such a reason would be losing weight.

4. Sprinthall, Sprinthall, and Oja, *Educational Psychology*, 230. Older references such as this one refer to facts not subject to change or ideas that have not changed.

5. Ormrod, *Educational Psychology*, 321; Woolfolk, *Educational Psychology* (2004), 310.

6. Ormrod, *Educational Psychology*, 322.

7. Ormrod, *Educational Psychology*, 322.

8. Ormrod, *Educational Psychology*, 324.

environment (interactions with others) reflect social learning theory's behavioral foundation.

In 2018, Bandura turned ninety-three. Even at that age, he continued to research and write, pushing his theory further into a cognitive perspective. Contemporary issues include self-control, self-regulation, and self-efficacy. Self-control is the control of one's own behaviors in the absence of reinforcement or punishment. Self-regulation is the consistent use of self-control skills in new situations. Self-efficacy is the strength of one's belief in their ability to handle particular tasks.[9]

Cognitive Theories of Learning

Cognitive theories differ from behavioral theories in their focus on the mind rather than the nervous system, insight rather than S-R/R-S bonds, and understanding meaning rather than programming behavior. Cognitive theories focus on the mental processes people use to make sense of the world. Cognitivists view learning as the reorganization of perceptions, extracting meaning from facts, in order to develop a clear and coherent understanding of the subject.

Traditional Cognitive Theories

Jerome Bruner's discovery learning and information processing theory reflect the essential nature of cognitive learning.

Discovery Learning Theory

Jerome Bruner (1915–2016) saw little value in studying rats, cats, or pigeons (favorites of behaviorists) to understand how children learn in a classroom setting and instead gathered his data from actual children. Bruner viewed the goal of teaching as promoting a general understanding of a subject. He believed that the facts and the concepts children discover through their own explorations are more usable and better retained than material they merely commit to memory. Bruner found that discovery learning helped children develop better problem-solving skills and greater confidence in their ability to learn. In other words, Bruner emphasized the importance of "learning how to learn."

Structure reflects his view that any content can be organized into an interrelated system of essential and supporting concepts. This conceptual system can be reduced to diagrams, sets of principles, or formulas, increasing the power of learning. Economy emphasizes the need to provide learners with small doses of information, followed by problem-solving activities that use the information. When content is conceptually organized (structure), conceptually concentrated (power), and conceptually distributed (economy), learners understand that content more deeply than when they are overwhelmed by long recitations of facts.

Bruner believed that all children have an innate will to learn. Intrinsic motivation (coming from within) springs from personal curiosity as well as the desire for competence and cooperative work with others. These are rewarding in themselves and thus self-sustaining. External rewards, such as stars or candies, are artificial and therefore ineffective as motivators. Bruner held teachers responsible for ensuring that innate motivators not be impaired by boring presentations, abusive discipline, and unwholesome competition among students.[10]

9. Ormrod, *Educational Psychology*, 331.

10. Yount, *Created to Learn*, 244.

Information Processing Theory

Information processing theory (IPT) was born of E. C. Tolman's (1886–1959) work in the 1920s and 1950s in cognitive mapping and the personal computer (1960s). IPT echoes the behavioral perspective of man as machine (mind as computer) but is considered a cognitive theory because of its emphasis on internal mental processes.

Learning is controlled by the interaction between cognitive structures and cognitive processes. The cognitive structures, or memory stores, are information storage units in the brain that operate much like those in a computer, which processes incoming data from inputs (keyboard, mouse) in its volatile random-access memory (RAM) and saves results to a permanent storage device (hard disk). The traditional IPT model consists of sensory registers (SR), inputs; short-term memory (STM), RAM; and long-term memory (LTM), hard disk. The three-component model, SR-STM-LTM, remains the most common depiction of IPT.

Cognitive processes are mental actions that transfer information from one structure to another while transforming information into various kinds of memories. These processes include attention, recognition, maintenance rehearsal (repetition), elaborative rehearsal (connecting new material to old), encoding (organized storing), and retrieving (remembering). Metacognitive processes are executive controls that govern the operation of the other cognitive processes.[11]

IPT proposes a series of steps in the processing of incoming sense data. These steps are (1) attending to a sound (sight, touch, smell), (2) recognizing the sound, (3) transforming the sound into a mental representation, (4) comparing the sound to sounds already stored in memory, (5) assigning meaning to the sound, and (6) acting on the sound.[12] IPT explains how we learn (i.e., how cognitive structures are created), why we forget (disuse, distortion, repression, interference), and how we can improve our ability to remember (active recall and use, elaboration and mnemonics, safe and pleasant environment, and clear organization).[13]

Cognitive Theories of the Twenty-First Century: Constructivism

Contemporary cognitive theories use the inclusive term *constructivism*. Learners construct their own knowledge and understanding through perceptions of the world. Constructivism has three major branches: cognitive, social, and radical.

Cognitive Constructivism

Cognitive constructivism is closely tied to Piaget's work in cognitive development and Bruner's discovery learning. Cognitive constructivism emphasizes individual, internal constructions of knowledge.[14] It stresses the personal search for understanding as learners interact with information and modify existing concepts. Disequilibrium[15] motivates accommodation[16] and assimilation,[17] which

11. Eggen and Kauchak, *Educational Psychology* (1994), 307.

12. Snowman, McCown, and Biehler, *Psychology Applied to Teaching*, 245.

13. Yount, *Created to Learn*, chap. 9.

14. Woolfolk, *Educational Psychology* (2004), 323.

15. The uncomfortable conflict between "what is already known" and "what is experienced."

16. Changing "what is already known" to fit "what is experienced" (exegesis).

17. Changing "what is experienced" to fit "what is already known" (eisegesis).

produces learning (adaptation).[18] Cognitive constructivists see interaction with others as important but primarily as a means of generating disequilibrium in individuals.

Cognitive constructivism emphasizes experience-based activities (Piaget and Bruner) but has been influenced by postmodern thought. Proponents distrust direct instruction by teachers.[19] Since perceptions are individually constructed from personal experience, the "essence of one person's knowledge can never be totally transferred to another person." Since constructed perceptions are heavily influenced by age, gender, race, ethnicity, and prior learning, "one cannot duplicate what they've learned in another."[20] Further, proponents insist that teachers "guard against imposing their thoughts and values on developing learners."[21]

What, then, is the role of the teacher in such a student-dependent, self-constructing system? "This question hasn't been satisfactorily answered."[22]

Cognitive constructivism is anchored in Piaget, who promoted the "construction of knowledge" in the form of mental schemes (concepts). Such knowledge has objective correspondence with the world. Disequilibrium between scheme and world is least when the correspondence between them is best, so held Piaget.[23]

Today's proponents, however, reinterpret Piaget's views in increasingly subjective ways. Contemporary constructivism, even in its most objective form, reflects postmodernism by de-emphasizing objective correspondence in favor of subjective coherence—the self-derived, personal, internal constructions of reality and truth by learners. Disconnecting "what we think" from "the world as it is" undermines the meaning of learning in particular and the academic goals of education in general.[24]

Social Constructivism

The second branch, social constructivism, integrated Bruner's discovery learning with Lev Vygotsky's (1896–1934) Communistic[25] emphasis on communal learning. Social constructivists emphasize environments in which learners exchange ideas and collaborate in solving problems. Learners construct understanding together in ways not possible for individuals. Knowledge reflects the world "as it is filtered through and influenced by culture, language, beliefs, and interactions with others."[26] Cognitive development is the internalization of socially derived meanings.

Piaget emphasized individual cognitive development as primary and social interaction as a secondary and natural outcome. Vygotsky emphasized social interaction as primary and individual cognitive development as a secondary and natural outcome. This distinction between Piaget and Vygotsky captures the essential

18. Yount, *Created to Learn*, chap. 4.
19. Eggen and Kauchak, *Educational Psychology* (2007), 235.
20. Snowman, McCown, and Biehler, *Psychology Applied to Teaching*, 326.
21. Eggen and Kauchak, *Educational Psychology* (2007), 235.
22. Eggen and Kauchak, *Educational Psychology* (2007), 236.
23. Cherry, "Understanding Accommodation in Psychology," reflects this desired correspondence between cognitive structure and external reality.

24. Is the study of biology to produce "biology as I see it" (subjective coherence) or "biology as it is" (objective correspondence)? Increasingly, American educators are opting for subjective coherence, continuing the decline of American education.
25. Vygotsky was a Soviet psychologist and a prolific writer in the 1920s. Despite his passionate defense of Communism, his writings were suppressed by Stalin.
26. Woolfolk, *Educational Psychology* (2004), 326.

difference between cognitive and social constructivism. Social constructivism has become the "view that is most influential in guiding the thinking of educational leaders and teachers."[27]

Radical Constructivism

Radical constructivism, the third branch, emphasizes the subjective creation of knowledge by individuals and is the most subjective view of the three. It is discussed in the section on humanistic theories of learning. Constructionism, not to be confused with constructivism, considers all knowledge socially constructed. Constructionism projects the strongest degree of relativism, in which all knowledge and all beliefs are equal. Since it is more concerned with public policy than learning, it is not discussed here.

Taking cognitive and social constructivism together, we can list five general characteristics of teaching and learning. First, learners are active builders, not passive recipients. Learners are actively engaged in constructing knowledge and understanding that makes sense to them.

Second, new learning depends on prior learning. The ideas constructed by learners are strongly influenced by their prior knowledge. An analysis of 183 studies (1999) concluded that learners' prior knowledge and their present performance are strongly related.[28]

Third, engaging others in learning-based tasks facilitates personal learning. Cognitive (individual) constructivism emphasizes interaction as a source of disequilibrium (motivation for learning) for individual learners.

Social (group) constructivism emphasizes shared or negotiated meaning,[29] which is then internalized by individual learners. In both, learning is enhanced when learners engage one another.

Fourth, meaningful learning occurs through real-world tasks. Rather than confront learners with abstract principles that are "often irrelevant to real-world conditions," constructivists use authentic activities. For example, students use math skills to balance a checkbook or writing skills to complete a job application.[30] Apparently, these proponents are not concerned with critical thinking or abstract analysis.

The final characteristic is a *softening* of *objective truth*. Educational texts reflect a continuing shift from objective to subjective truth. Postmodern influences have moved constructivism as a whole toward the position of radical constructivists, for whom the personal constructions of learners are more important than the correctness of those constructions. This is a critical issue for Christian teachers (for whom truth is both knowable and eternal), and one we will discuss more in the section on humanistic learning theories.[31]

Cognitive Theories of the Twenty-First Century: Information Processing Theory

As constructivist views became more prominent, interest in information processing theory

27. Eggen and Kauchak, *Educational Psychology* (2007), 237.

28. Snowman, McCown, and Biehler, *Psychology Applied to Teaching*, 325.

29. Snowman, McCown, and Biehler, *Psychology Applied to Teaching*, 327.

30. Eggen and Kauchak, *Educational Psychology* (2007), 241.

31. *Constructivism* is sometimes used to describe these various camps without distinction, adding to the confusion. Woolfolk characterizes constructivism as a "vast and woolly area in contemporary psychology, epistemology, and education." *Educational Psychology* (2004), 323.

(IPT) waned. However, IPT has rebounded with the advances in neuroscience in the last twenty years. IPT offers a conceptual bridge between the mental aspects of cognitive theory and the neurological aspects of brain-based learning.

The three-component IPT model (SR-STM-LTM) has been criticized as either simplistic or too compartmentalized. It is seen as simplistic by those who point to the many subsystems and interactive subprocesses that make up these components. The three-component model is seen as overly compartmentalized by those who consider the various memory functions—SR, STM, and LTM—nothing more than various levels of processing of a single memory.[32] Three contemporary models attempt to address these concerns.

The Parallel Distributed Processing Model

The parallel distributed processing model (PDP), or connectionist model, emphasizes connections between elements in memory more than the elements themselves. The concept "dog," for example, is stored as a network of various elements—"animal," "barks," "furry," "four-legged." The concept "dog" exists not as a single entity but as elements linked in a network of connections.[33] Activation of one element (or node) in a network may prompt activation of others (elaboration). Activation of nodes occurs along many parallel connections in various networks, giving rise to the PDP label.

Without the connections between nodes, concepts would not exist. The connectionist model is appealing because it "seems to have

a direct tie to the biology of the brain."[34] IPT (cognitive functioning) and neuroscience (biochemical functioning) have been converging in the literature for years, and the connectionist (PDP) model supports this convergence.

The Working Memory Model

The traditional three-component model uses the term *working memory* as a synonym for short-term memory (STM). The working memory model (WM) uses working memory to identify an active part of LTM that also includes STM. WM holds the most recently activated portion of LTM and moves activated elements in and out of temporary memory stores. Whereas STM (three-component model) is a passive receptacle of data, WM is active in integrating acoustic and visual data, organizing information into meaningful chunks, encoding concepts, and linking new information to existing forms of knowledge in LTM.[35] WM is the "workbench of memory" where active mental effort is applied to new and old information.[36]

One subcomponent of WM, called the central executive, "focuses attention, oversees the flow of information throughout the memory system, selects and controls complex voluntary behaviors, and inhibits inappropriate thoughts and actions." Other subcomponents handle visual data, auditory information, and meanings.[37] WM manages many of the cognitive controls formerly discussed under metacognitive processes.

34. Sternberg and Williams, *Educational Psychology*, 283.

35. Sternberg and Williams, *Educational Psychology*, 283–84.

36. Woolfolk, *Educational Psychology* (2004), 243.

37. Ormrod, *Educational Psychology*, 193. Ormrod quotes five studies from 2000 to 2004.

32. Elliot et al., *Educational Psychology*, 281.

33. Sternberg and Williams, *Educational Psychology*, 282.

The Levels-of-Processing Model

Responding to the criticism of compartmentalization, the levels-of-processing model (LOP) replaces the three distinct memory stores (SR, STM, LTM) with as many memory stores as are needed to encode items.[38] The LOP model rejects the idea of distinct boundaries between memory stores, suggesting instead that memory storage is allocated along a continuous dimension of depth of encoding.[39]

The goal in learning is to process meanings as deeply as possible. Simple repetition of words and definitions results in shallow processing. Providing synonyms for words (elaboration) requires deeper processing. Determining whether words describe learners (the self-reference effect) requires still deeper processing.[40]

The increased complexity of newer IPT models reflects recent discoveries of how the human mind processes information. Unfortunately, this increased complexity does little for the classroom.

The PDP model suggests that neural networks are strengthened when teachers provide learners with background information related to new topics, review information and concepts already studied, and provide intentional opportunities for repetition and practice.[41] The WM model suggests the use of active recall[42] and the integration of new information with existing knowledge.[43] The LOP model emphasizes elaboration and meaningfulness. These suggestions add nothing to what is presented in the traditional three-component IPT model.[44]

Current educational psychology texts present IPT in its three-component form.[45] Discussions of alternative models vary from text to text. The fact remains that, however components are classified or subdivided, IPT helps explain how the human mind processes information.

Humanistic Theories of Learning

Humanistic theories of learning embrace the affective domain of learning, emphasizing learner openness, responses, valuing, prioritizing, and lifestyle. Humanists emphasize the uniqueness of each learner in terms of attitudes, emotions, and values.

Traditional Humanistic Theories

Abraham Maslow, Carl Rogers, and Arthur Combs, leading psychologists in the 1960s and 1970s, developed traditional humanistic methods of education.

Abraham Maslow (1908–70) believed that children make wise choices for their own learning when given the opportunity. Teachers should arrange attractive and meaningful

---

38. LOP was first proposed in 1972, but Sternberg and Williams, *Educational Psychology*, and Woolfolk, *Educational Psychology* (2004), continue to cover it.

39. Sternberg and Williams, *Educational Psychology*, 285.

40. Sternberg and Williams, *Educational Psychology*, 285.

41. Sternberg and Williams, *Educational Psychology*, 281–83.

42. Active recall is learner recall, as opposed to passive recall, which is teacher review.

43. Sternberg and Williams, *Educational Psychology*, 284.

44. Sternberg and Williams, *Educational Psychology*, 284.

45. Alexander, *Psychology in Learning and Instruction*, 67; Eggen and Kauchak, *Educational Psychology* (2007), 203; Ormrod, *Educational Psychology*, 191; Snowman, McCown, and Biehler, *Psychology Applied to Teaching*, 248; Woolfolk, *Educational Psychology* (2004), 239.

learning situations and allow students to select those they find personally valuable. He
rejected teacher-directed classroom management for the motivating power of self-chosen
activities.

Carl Rogers (1902–87), a psychotherapist
by profession, developed learner-centered
teaching methods from his work as a counselor. Rogers believed that teaching should revolve around learners' feelings and preferences
rather than the agendas of teachers. Thus, his
views emphasized perception of reality over
reality itself.

In Rogers's view, good teachers provide
opportunities for learning and trust students
to do their work to the best of their ability.
Teachers strive to be sincere and transparent
facilitators, viewing learning experiences from
students' perspectives. The result of these efforts, according to Rogers, is that students
take responsibility for their own learning and
learn more effectively.

Arthur Combs (1912–99) stressed that
teachers should be facilitators of learning. His
views paralleled Bruner's views on discovery,
but Combs placed more emphasis on sharing
personal views and less on objective (cognitive) problem solving. For Combs, meaning
is not inherent in the subject matter. Rather,
the individual instills subject matter with its
meaning. Combs's dilemma was not how to
present subject matter but how to help students derive personal meaning.

Humanistic learning theories enjoyed
great popularity in the 1960s and 1970s. By
the 1980s, declining achievement and falling
standardized test scores soured administrators and teachers on humanistic approaches.
Students did not routinely choose to study. By
the 1990s, humanistic learning (Maslow, Rogers, Combs) had been dropped or moved to

units on motivation. One is hard-pressed to
find any contemporary reference to the system
in educational psychology textbooks.[46] By all
accounts, humanistic learning theory is dead.
Affective education, however, is not.

Humanistic Theories in the Twenty-First Century

Though the humanistic learning theory
label has faded, the tenets of humanistic learning have not. Learner-directed activities, personal choice, teacher as friend, the exploration
of feelings and emotions, subjective evaluations, and other humanistic values have been
absorbed into radical constructivism or into
broader-based, hybrid learning approaches,
such as cooperative learning.[47]

Radical constructivism is to educational psychology what existentialism is to philosophy,
where self and choice, championed by secular
humanism, continues to flourish. Now those
ideas have merged with relativism, language de-
construction, and postmodernism's rejection of
metanarratives. The result has been a new way
of thinking about knowledge, teaching, and
learning. Radical constructivism views learning as creating one's own knowledge. Radical
constructivists believe that "objective reality or
truth is an educational illusion. The only reality
is what the individual mind can conjure."[48]

Radical constructivists are less concerned
about the correctness of student answers
than about the exploration of students' self-

46. I continue to include humanistic learning in the
teacher's triad because personal commitment is essential
to Christian education and spiritual formation. Christian
educators reject secularism but embrace humanitarian-
ism and humaneness.

47. Yount, *Created to Learn*, chap. 10.

48. Alexander, *Psychology in Learning and Instruction*, 69.

generated ideas. Teachers "appreciate and build on whatever interpretations or constructions the students have made—constructions as unique as fingerprints."[49] Truth under this system has no meaning beyond self. Facts mean just what individuals choose them to mean, neither more nor less. As American education is moving in this direction, it is producing social chaos in the process (Judg. 17:6).

Suggestions for System-Specific Teaching Principles

The different types of learning (see Table 6.1) call for different approaches to teaching.

Behavioral principles work best with unmotivated learners who have difficulty behaving appropriately in class or where skill mastery is highly prized. Here are some suggestions:

- Use cues (actions) and prompts (explanations) to establish new behaviors. For example, "It is fine to talk with one another when you arrive, but when I stand with my Bible open [cue], I need your attention so we can begin."
- Praise behaviors specifically and judiciously. Generally praising the class is ineffective. Motivated learners resent such praise; unmotivated learners ignore it, knowing it is undeserved. Praise learners for specific, well-defined successes.
- Provide informative feedback on student work.[50] The best feedback involves appropriate praise for correct answers and specific correction for wrong answers. Practice, without corrective feedback, does not improve performance.[51]
- Use removal punishment (penalty) rather than presentation punishment.[52] Take away what learners want (recess, extra credit) rather than giving what learners do not want (public humiliation, criticism).
- Focus on behaviors rather than persons.[53] Praise the best answers, not the best students.

Cognitive principles work best with curious learners in academic learning groups where understanding is highly prized. Some suggestions include the following:

- Use verbal and visual explanations. Explain concepts by comparison and contrast. Use diagrams and illustrations to give visual support to verbal explanations.
- Arouse curiosity. Ask thought-provoking questions that are relevant to students' need to know.[54] Encourage informed guessing and help students analyze wrong answers to correct misunderstandings. Use a variety of learning materials to increase curiosity. Mechanical teaching and rote memorization hinder curiosity and the desire to understand.

49. Alexander, *Psychology in Learning and Instruction*, 69.
50. Eggen and Kauchak, *Educational Psychology* (1994), 281.
51. Sprinthall, Sprinthall, and Oja, *Educational Psychology*, 235.
52. Eggen and Kauchak, *Educational Psychology* (1994), 280.
53. Woolfolk, *Educational Psychology* (1993), 217.
54. "What are the differences between the research hypothesis and the statistical hypothesis?" Students will be writing both in future research proposals.

Table 6.1. Summary of Seven Key Characteristics of Learning by System

Theory	Who is the learner?	What is learning?	What is the goal of learning?	How is learning strengthened?	What guides learning?	What motivates learning?	How should feedback be given?
Behavioral	An organic machine to be programmed	Mechanical, stamping bonds into the nervous system	Behavior (habits, skills)	Repetition (recitation, drill, and practice)	Direct or vicarious reinforcement	Primary and secondary drives	Direct, focused on performance, and immediate
Cognitive	A mind to be engaged	Rational (objective) and interactive (social)	Understanding of content (concepts, principles)	Insight (problem solving)	Objective application to life	Curiosity, meaningfulness, and achievement of delayed goals (a degree, status)	Clarifying, focused on understanding, and delayed, providing time for reflection.
Humanistic	A person to be befriended and nurtured	Personal (subjective) and interactive (social)	Appreciation for content (attitudes, values, priorities)	Personal sharing (testimonies, stories, experiences)	Personal satisfaction	Personal desires and values	Warm, focused on effort, and personal

- Encourage students to ask questions in class. Discuss tangential questions raised by students. Such flexibility reinforces learning by connecting spontaneous questions with prepared material. It also enhances motivation by showing students that their questions are important.

Affective principles work best with self-motivated learners in voluntary (nonacademic, self-help, or adult education) learning groups where personal engagement is highly prized and appreciation of subjects is the primary goal. Here are some possible applications:

- Focus on learner experiences to improve attitudes toward subject, self, cooperation, and school. [55]

- Use small-group processes in a relaxed, safe class environment to maximize personal interaction.

- Model openness by sharing personal experiences and using role-playing activities to help learners intensify their sharing. [56]

- Allow students to direct their own learning. Let learners select topics and resources, set goals, and evaluate outcomes with minimal guidance. [57]

- Emphasize affective outcomes. Focus class time on helping learners achieve personal goals, clarify personal values, and improve interpersonal skills. Affective learning emphasizes personal growth over content mastery.

55. However, academic achievement suffers as objective meaning is deemphasized.

56. LeFrancois, *Psychology for Teaching*, 250.
57. Slavin, *Educational Psychology*, 298.

Neuroscience and Learning in the Twenty-First Century

At the base of all *psychological* learning theory lies the *physiological* function of the brain. This electrochemical machinery has been the focus of educators for more than a decade. Neuroscience analyzes the functions of the brain that support human personality, language, and learning.

One hundred years of "settled brain science" was overturned by revolutionary discoveries in the 1990s.[58] Educators were quick to claim and adopt these discoveries, creating the field of brain-based learning, the newest fad in classroom education. The 2000s reverberated with books, articles, and conferences dedicated to teaching the brain.

Unfortunately, cell-level brain functions resisted translation into classroom practice. In some cases, theorists made grand leaps of logic from esoteric brain functions to classroom applications. In others, what was known from classroom observation and experience was simply repeated, using brain-based jargon.[59]

Practitioners realized they did not need to understand how potassium ions leap synapses to help learners any more than they needed to understand Ohm's law[60] to use electric lights and equipment. Despite the fascination of axons, dendrites, and electrochemical pulses, the teaching-brains frenzy began to subside by 2009,[61] joining educational fads of the past.[62] Little in brain-based learning enhances what is already known about intentional educational processes, with one great exception: the revolutionary discovery that mind (what we give attention to) controls the physiological structure and wiring of the brain.[63]

The most revolutionary development in neuroscience in the 1990s was the relationship between the brain and the mind. In 1990, most neuroscientists believed that the brain was fixed (wired) by age six and that the immaterial mind was a brain-based illusion. By 2005, the majority of neuroscientists were convinced, based on intentional experimentation and verifiable fMRI and PET scans, that the brain changes throughout life and that these physical changes (rewiring) are created and controlled by means of mental attention.

What does this mean in terms of educational practice? Here is my evaluation: *Whenever we focus learner attention (instruction) on the facts, concepts, values, and skills in our disciplines, learner **brains** respond immediately by **creating new brain cells** ("neurogenesis") that form **new physical networks** ("neuroplasticity") to support **new concepts** (cognitive), **new values and priorities** (affective), **and new skills** (behavioral). This continues for **as long as we live**.*[64]

58. In January 1990, President George H. W. Bush declared the 1990s the "Decade of the Brain," and millions of dollars were spent on neuroscience research.

59. Examples are neurons (brain cells); synapses, the empty space between axons (the transmitting branch of one neuron) and dendrites (the receiving branches of others); and specific regions of the physical brain: the frontal lobes, amygdala, hippocampus, and others. Yount, *Created to Learn*, chap. 16.

60. George Ohm stated the fixed relationship among voltage (volts, E), current (amperes, I), and resistance (ohms, R) in electric circuits: $E = IR$.

61. A website for McGraw-Hill's popular *Annual Editions: Educational Psychology* listed forty-three articles for review for inclusion in the 2009–10 edition. None of them addressed brain-based learning.

62. Instructional television (1950s), programmed (computerized) education (1960s), open classrooms (1970s), authentic assessment (1980s), and learning styles (1990s).

63. See Yount, *Created to Learn*, 528–29, for specific examples.

64. Yount, *Created to Learn*, 559.

A Christian Meta-analysis of Learning Theory: The Teacher's Triad

I developed the teacher's triad (fig. 6.1) in order to synthesize the three learning theory systems into a single meta-approach to teaching and learning.[65] The numbers in the following discussion refer to the circled numbers in the figure.

The Reality of Imbalance in Teaching

Teachers have a dominant teaching-learning preference that unconsciously[66] controls their choice of methods, classroom atmosphere, and grading philosophy. We have briefly addressed these theoretical distinctions as learning characteristics and principles of teaching. We now turn to the real-world preferences (imbalance) of thinkers, feelers, and doers and the extremes these preferences generate when they are emphasized to the exclusion of others.

Thinker-teachers (4) focus on facts, concepts, principles, and meaningful content mastery. Their concept-based approach emphasizes explanations, discussions, and problem-solving activities. Content-rich PowerPoints, illustrations, examples, questions, and problems are common in thinker-teachers' classrooms. Their goal is to help learners master content. Their unconscious assumption is that proper understanding eventually results in skilled behavior and positive attitudes.

Feeler-teachers (5) focus on the personal relevance of subjects to learners. Their learner-based approach emphasizes learner experiences, values, and relationships. The freedom *from* PowerPoint lectures, programmed structure, and "arbitrary" testing and the freedom *to* personally share and react to content, choose from a variety of learning options, and do one's best without correction are common in feeler-teachers' classrooms. Their goal is to help learners discover themselves. Their unconscious assumption is that heartfelt experiences eventually result in skilled (enough) behavior and clear (enough) understanding.[67]

Doer-teachers (6) focus on student skills, competencies, and real-world applications. Their skill-based approach emphasizes systematic programming, drill and practice, recitation, and feedback. Demonstrations, activities, and projects are common in doer-teachers' classrooms. Their goal is to help learners master skills derived from the content. Their unconscious assumption is that proper programming results in clear thinking and positive affect.

The social dimension of teaching creates a dynamic that is more complex than the three systems alone. Teachers (thinkers, feelers, or doers) stand before classes that consist (in rough thirds)[68] of student-thinkers, student-feelers, and student-doers. Teaching—no matter how effective when measured against its preferred system—consistently misses two-thirds of the students unless intentional steps

---

65. Yount, *Created to Learn*. See especially chap. 11, "The Christian Teachers' Triad."

66. The preferences are certainly knowable (and are described here), but teachers are unaware of what controls their choices until they intentionally study alternative views.

67. Falling standardized test scores proved this assumption false in the 1980s and spelled the doom of formal humanistic learning theory.

68. For twenty years, in scores of classes at home and abroad, I have asked students to divide themselves into thinker, feeler, and doer groups based on characteristics given here. The result *in every case* is three roughly equal groups. Each of these groups approaches teaching and learning in distinctly different ways.

Figure 6.1
The Teacher's Triad

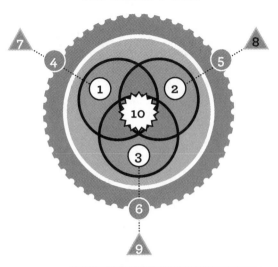

The Learner (white solid circle surrounding 1, 2, 3, and 10)	1. **Rational thinker**: cognitive learning theories 2. **Personal chooser**: humanistic learning theories 3. **Skillful doer**: behavioral learning theories
The Teacher (outer circle intersecting 4, 5, and 6)	4. **Explainer**: cognitive techniques 5. **Friend**: humanistic techniques 6. **Coach**: behavioral techniques
The Toxic Extremes (triangles 7, 8, and 9) that hinder learning	7. Cold intellectualism 8. Warm superficiality 9. Dry ritual, burnout
The Perfect Center (10)	10. **Christ** as Internal Teacher (Col. 1:27) helping us . . . think clearly (Col. 1:9–10), value and empathize warmly (Rom. 12:15), and minister skillfully (Matt. 11:29–30). Spiritual maturity is found in the synergism of all three spheres (Eph. 4:11–16).

are taken to match teaching methods with learner needs.

The Triadic Solution to Imbalance

Effective teachers engage all their students by pushing themselves out of their comfort zones (thinker, feeler, or doer) and into the other less-well-traveled two. Familiarity with learning theories facilitates changes that move teachers into all three spheres where students live.

We see the fluidity of Jesus's approach through many teaching encounters in the Gospels. When learners were confused, he explained. When they were hurt or sick, he embraced and nurtured. When they lacked skills, he demonstrated and corrected. Let us commit ourselves to teach with this same focus, using whatever principles—behavioral, cognitive, or affective—a particular learning problem calls for.

As we move among conflicting methods, solving learner problems as they arise (head, heart, or hand), we grow more holistic, more triadic, as Christ's equippers of disciples (Eph. 4:12). In Christ, we learn to help every learner grow, maturing in Christ (head, heart, and hand). Along the way to this golden goal, we become more useful to the Master, who teaches through us (prophet, priest, and king) to transform life itself, as we give him freedom. Learning theory helps. Selah.

7

Educational Taxonomies, Part 1

Analysis and Design in Teaching and Learning

MEGAN G. BROWN AND SHELLY CUNNINGHAM

Shopping lists, planners, mobile applications, budgets, travel itineraries, blueprints, maps, cost estimates, proposals—all of these are tools we use to help organize our time and our projects. They are primarily intended to be used as preparatory, or management, strategies to ensure that consideration is given to what is important and strategic to accomplish a goal or project. A similar tool is needed to design an effective learning situation.

God created human beings with the capacity to learn and to grow; however, like plants that require watering and pruning, the educational process requires attention and shaping to maximize the capacity for growth and development.

Scripture challenges us to "count the cost" of being a disciple of Jesus. "Suppose one of you wants to build a tower. Won't you first sit down and estimate the cost to see if you have enough money to complete it?" (Luke 14:28). God has given us the ability to be intentional and decisive about our spiritual call to discipleship. That intentionality needs to expand wide and deep enough to encompass our learning contexts, in which there is the potential for transformative learning and growth to happen.

Unfortunately, when it comes to teaching and learning, sometimes we focus more on the event itself than on the time and effort needed to prepare and manage the teaching-learning process. Although drawing her observations from the higher education context, Dee Fink's challenge to educators to "raise the bar" in the arena of course design can be applied to almost any teaching-learning situation.

When we teach, we engage in two closely related, but distinct, activities.

Figure 7.1
ADDIE Model

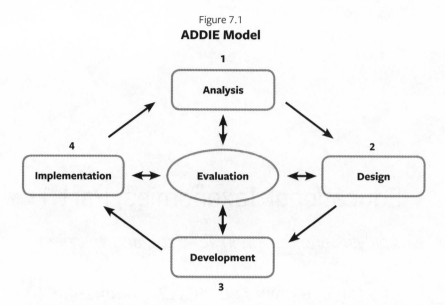

Diagram adapted from http://edweb.sdsu.edu/Courses/EDTEC700/ETP/addie.htm. Process written by Peyri Hamada, based on Helen Barrett's "Framework for the Multimedia Development Process."

First, we design the course by gathering information and making a number of decisions about the way the course will be taught. Second, we engage in teacher-student interactions as we implement the course we have designed. . . .

Of these two activities, our ability to design courses well is usually the most limiting factor. Most of us have had little or no training in how to design courses. In addition, during the last two decades research on college teaching and learning have led to some new ideas about course design that have, in essence, "raised the bar" in terms of what is possible. These include ideas such as active learning, significant learning, and educative assessment.[1]

The challenge can be transferring concepts of organization and design to instructional contexts in ways that are connected and integrated. There are many possible models to follow, although there is frequently some overlap in core components. One model that has proven effective in laying out a systematic framework applicable to a variety of instructional design settings is the ADDIE model of instructional design. Instructors who follow the stages in the ADDIE model will be led to institute a learner-centered approach as opposed to a teacher-centered approach.[2]

The ADDIE model consists of five stages: analysis, design, development, implementation, and evaluation (see fig. 7.1). Analysis is the critical first stage, in which one gathers information about components such as the target audience, learning context parameters, and available resources. Design is the brainstorming stage. Here one drafts or creates a teaching-learning program, course, or curriculum that meets the criteria identified in the analysis stage. During the development

1. Fink, "Self-Directed Guide."

2. Petersen, "Bringing ADDIE to Life," 227–41.

stage, one constructs an effective educational program that builds on the analysis and design results. Everything goes live during the implementation phase, but it may also include preprogram components such as training and so on. Finally, one conducts an evaluation comparing the original learning outcomes to the results.[3] This chapter and the chapter that follows focus on these five stages and discuss how to approach the teaching-learning process.

Analysis

The first stage in the ADDIE model of instructional design is analysis. This stage consists of gathering information that will be used to assess needs, set learning objectives, and appraise a variety of components within the learning context that will impact the design, development, and implementation of the teaching-learning situation.

This section outlines a planning approach to analysis that begins with the big questions and general considerations and then moves to the specifics. For each of the categories included in the analysis section, you will find a list of questions to aid you in gathering the type of information you need to make good decisions about course design, development, and implementation. Depending on the general context of your teaching-learning situation, some questions may be more relevant than others.

General Context of the Teaching-Learning Situation

Although there are many similarities in the basic building blocks used to design effective

3. "ADDIE Model."

teaching-learning experiences, the general context in which the learning experience occurs shapes the components involved. Some of the questions to answer related to the context include the following:

- Will the learning take place in a church, as part of a parachurch ministry (such as a camp or campus ministry), or in a more formal and structured academic or school setting?
- What physical/structural resources (building, location, etc.) and monetary resources are available?
- Given the context, what is the role of the teacher? (Paid or volunteer? Are there credentialing and educational degree requirements? etc.)
- What is the expected or anticipated role of the learner? (Must the learner enroll, register, apply, have parent/guardian permission, pay fees, meet age or residency requirements, fulfill prerequisites, demonstrate competency before advancing, etc.?)

These components will be discussed in more detail below and in chapter 8.

General Parameters of the Teaching-Learning Situation

No matter how much apparent flexibility is given to the person, team, or committee responsible for making decisions about the shape of a learning experience, it is wise to begin by researching questions related to institutional and/or denominational expectations. Analysis in this category will include researching answers to questions such as the following:

- Who is primarily responsible for the design and development of the course? Will the same person or team implement the design? Who will oversee the process?
- What kind of course is being designed? For example, will this be a multiple-session class? Weekend workshop or retreat? Repeated seminar? How many lessons, sessions, and/or units will be developed? What is the estimated length of the course (number of days, weeks, etc.) and the time frame?
- Has this course or material been taught in the past? By whom? For whom? Were any recommendations made for changes?
- What expectations or overarching goals does the department, sponsoring institution, or organization have about this course or any of its components?
- Is there a curriculum map outlining the scope and sequence of the content? Where does this fit with other courses or programs?
- Is there a preapproved curriculum to be implemented?
- What internal approval processes need to be followed while this learning module is being developed (for teacher recruitment, curriculum design and selection, expenditures, advertising and promotion, etc.)?
- What external approval processes need to be followed while this learning module is being developed (for alignment with guidelines disseminated by academic or professional regional accrediting bodies, etc.)?

Learner Characteristics/Needs and Relevant Subject-Matter Content

Working within the general parameters, one still has great freedom to design a learning experience that will lead to lasting behavioral change and growth in the lives of the participants. However, only information that is meaningful to the learners will be transferred into long-term memory to influence this behavior change. As a result, identifying connections between the subject or content and the needs and characteristics of the learners is necessary. Analysis in this category will include researching answers to questions such as the following:

- What is the primary purpose and/or overall goal of the teaching-learning situation?
  - Cognitive? Affective? Behavioral? Theoretical? Practical? A combination?
  - Is it to challenge? Inform? Develop skills? Encourage? Build community and connections?
- At what level is the information targeted?
  - Beginning, developing, or mastery/advanced?
- What are the characteristics of the learners who will be participating in this teaching-learning experience?[4]
  - Approximate size of the group?
  - Characteristics of the group (gender, age, life stage, socioeconomic status, cultural and ethnic identities, educational background, employment, religious affiliation, etc.)?
  - Learning style(s) of the group?

4. Fink, "Self-Directed Guide."

- What are the needs of the learners who will be participating in this teaching-learning experience?[5]
  - What do you know about the generational characteristics associated with the learners?
  - What is reflective of their cohort group?
  - What cultural influences have they shared in common since birth?
  - What tends to motivate or drive this group?
  - What unique or challenging life situational factors might influence learner responses?
  - What prior knowledge of, or experience in, this subject area do the target learners have?
  - What predisposition for, or possible feelings about, this topic do the target learners have?
  - What interests and desires do the learners possess?
  - What expectations and learning goals exist for this experience?
- Given your analysis of the characteristics and needs of the learners, what approaches will be most effective to target and recruit learners for this instructional event?

Teacher Characteristics/Needs

The role of the teacher, leader, counselor, or director is central to the design and delivery of the learning experience. Even if the curriculum is a prescribed curriculum, the shape of the delivery will be directly influenced by the values and style of the teacher(s). Analysis in this category will include researching answers to questions such as the following:

- What values and beliefs does the teacher or leader have about teaching and learning?
- What is their attitude toward the content? The learners?
- What level of knowledge and experience do they have with the topic area?
- What are their strengths in teaching? What teaching style do they have?[6]

In summation, the analysis process involves considering the general context of the teaching-learning situation, the general parameters of the teaching-learning situation, and both the learners' and the teacher's characteristics and needs. Although this is only the first stage in the ADDIE model of instructional design, it is critical that careful consideration be given to the various questions listed in this section. A well-laid foundation will provide a strong base on which to build a teaching-learning situation that can target needs for transformative change and support a dynamic learning context that is able to adapt as necessary throughout the design, development, and implementation phases. The next stage is design.

Design

"Teachers are designers."[7] The second stage in the teaching-learning process is design.

---

5. Fink, "Self-Directed Guide."

6. Fink, "Self-Directed Guide."
7. Wiggins and McTighe, *Understanding by Design*, 13.

At this stage, you are free to dream, create, and imagine what the curriculum plan for the course, class, workshop, or seminar can become. This stage is where your creative freedom as teacher-planner can flourish as you build a framework, or a foundation, and preplan for the task at hand.

If you have spent intentional and focused energy working through the analysis phase of understanding the teaching-learning process, you will have a strong foundation on which to build the design elements. The analysis phase is invisible in terms of identifiable curriculum pieces; however, its influence will heavily impact the shape of the design that becomes the framework for the entirety of the learning experience. A number of key areas to consider include selecting objectives/outcomes, selecting content, and selecting the instructional format.

Selecting Objectives/Outcomes

The first step in the design stage is selecting objectives, or outcomes, to accompany the overarching goals identified during the analysis stage. The objectives you select will serve as the intended outcomes of the educational experience—whether that is a course, class, workshop, seminar, or other educational experience.[8] Learning objectives are statements that specify what learners will know or be able to do as a result of the learning activity (i.e., the outcomes that students must meet on the way to reaching a goal). The difference between outcomes and goals is that, generally, "outcomes are more precise, specific, and measurable than goals. There can be more than one outcome related to each goal and a particular learning outcome can support more than one goal."[9]

It is important to revisit the overall goals you have for the course, class, workshop, or seminar and create objectives that meet those goals. In so doing, consider cognitive, behavioral, and affective areas you hope the teaching-learning process will address. Also, be sure to consider scope and sequence. Scope addresses what the learners need to know, while sequence addresses the order or chronology of the material.[10]

In some settings, creating goals and objectives is downplayed and seen as unimportant. However, when considered as a part of the entire teaching-learning process, this step is instrumental in determining the direction of the course, class, workshop, or seminar. The importance of this step cannot be overstated—in any setting. If you face opposition in the goal- and objective-writing process, explain the importance of these benchmarks as a guide for gauging understanding (cognition), action (behavior), and transformation (affect) during the teaching-learning process. The goals and objectives you select will set the direction for the educational experience and aid in keeping both the teacher and the learners on track. On a broader scale, objectives can help to integrate courses with other courses and with program goals. In the end, objectives will form the basis for evaluating the effectiveness of the instruction, the mastery level of the learners, and the strength of the curriculum.[11]

As you work to select objectives to complement the learning goals, a few taxonomies are worthy of consideration. In his *Taxon-*

---

8. Posner, *Analyzing the Curriculum*, 77.

9. "How to Write Program Objectives/Outcomes."
10. Phenix, *Realms of Meaning*, 267, 290–91.
11. "Effective Use of Learning Objectives."

Figure 7.2

Bloom's Taxonomy of Measurable Verbs

Benjamin Bloom created a taxonomy of measurable verbs to help us describe and classify observable knowledge, skills, attitudes, behaviors, and abilities. The theory is based on the idea that there are levels of observable actions that indicate something is happening in the brain (cognitive activity). By creating learning objectives using measurable verbs, you indicate explicitly what learners must do in order to demonstrate learning.

			Verbs That Demonstrate *Critical Thinking*		
					Evaluation
					Appraise
				Synthesis	Argue
				Arrange	Assess
			Analysis	Assemble	Choose
			Analyze	Collect	Compare
		Application	Appraise	Combine	Conclude
		Apply	Categorize	Comply	Estimate
	Comprehension	Complete	Compare	Compose	Evaluate
	Compare	Construct	Contrast	Construct	Interpret
Knowledge	Describe	Demonstrate	Debate	Create	Judge
List	Discuss	Dramatize	Diagram	Design	Justify
Name	Explain	Employ	Differentiate	Devise	Measure
Recall	Express	Illustrate	Distinguish	Formulate	Rate
Record	Identify	Interpret	Examine	Manage	Revise
Relate	Recognize	Operate	Experiment	Organize	Score
Repeat	Restate	Practice	Inspect	Plan	Select
State	Tell	Schedule	Inventory	Prepare	Support
Tell	Translate	Sketch	Question	Propose	Value
Underline		Use	Test	Setup	

Adapted from http://www.taasa.org/wp-content/uploads/2012/04/Working-on-the-Wow-Side-Handout-31.pdf.

omy of Educational Objectives, psychologist Benjamin Bloom, well known for Bloom's taxonomy, provides a helpful starting point for thinking through goals and objectives.[12] Bloom outlines three areas, or domains (cognitive, affective, and psychomotor), of learning objectives and provides details concerning the cognitive domain. Cognitive objectives focus on knowledge—what is it you want the learners to know? Affective objectives focus on attitudes, values, and dispositions—what is it you want the learners to feel or care about or be motivated to change? Psychomotor (behavioral) objectives focus on skills and practices—what is it you want the learners to be able to do or implement as a result of the learning experience? As you work on the goals and objectives for your course, class, workshop, or seminar, you may find it helpful to keep Bloom's taxonomy (fig. 7.2) available for reference.

Bloom's taxonomy addresses six levels of cognition: knowledge, comprehension, application, analysis, synthesis, and evaluation. As demonstrated in the figure, each level requires a higher order of thinking (cognition) moving from left to right. As you select goals and

12. Bloom, *Taxonomy of Educational Objectives*.

objectives, keep in mind the age group you anticipate working with and what those within that age group are cognitively capable of demonstrating. For example, if you are working with adults who have a foundational understanding of the material or topic, you may choose to utilize higher-order thinking and include some objectives that require analysis, synthesis, or evaluation. Specifically, if you are leading an adult Sunday school class, you may ask adult learners to do one or more of the following (key words from Bloom's list are italicized):

- Students will *interpret* one of Jesus's parables.
- Students will *debate* or *argue* for their side of a controversial topic.
- Students will *design* or *create* a resource to teach the Beatitudes to their children.
- Students will *compare* and *contrast* parallel passages of Scripture.

However, if you are working with a group of students, adult or otherwise, who are unfamiliar with the topic, you may want to rely more heavily on lower-order thinking areas: knowledge, comprehension, and application. Here are some examples of objectives for these areas:

- Students will *recall* or *repeat* the key details of the biblical story presented.
- Students will *recognize* important characters from the biblical story presented.
- Students will *demonstrate* an ability to *apply* the principles of the biblical story to their lives.

Overall, as noted by Ralph Tyler, the objectives you select should be attainable and should express both what the student should develop and how that should function within the area being studied or life in general.[13] The goals and objectives you select should have the learners in mind and should be developed so that the learners, not the teacher, are the central focus. The goals and objectives will be the central and driving focus of the learning experience, which "takes place through the active behavior of the student; it is what he does that he learns, not what the teacher does."[14]

Building on the foundation Bloom provided, Lorin Anderson and David Krathwohl revised Bloom's original taxonomy to include the following areas of cognition: remember, understand, apply, analyze, evaluate, and create (see fig. 7.3).[15] Like Bloom's, Anderson and Krathwohl's taxonomy addresses cognition from lower-order thinking to higher-order thinking.

Krathwohl also edited a volume of the original text by Bloom to address the affective domain of learning. Krathwohl suggested five levels of affective learning: (1) listening to an idea, (2) responding to the idea, (3) developing values or commitment to the idea, (4) developing a value system based on the idea, and (5) being characterized by the idea or value.[16]

B. J. Simpson developed a learning taxonomy for the psychomotor (or behavioral) domain (see table 7.1). He identified several levels moving from perception and set at the

13. Tyler, *Basic Principles*, 46–47, 65.
14. Tyler, *Basic Principles*, 63.
15. L. Anderson and Krathwohl, *Taxonomy for Learning*, 67–68.
16. Krathwohl, *Taxonomy of Educational Objectives*.

Figure 7.3

The Cognitive Process Dimension: Categories and Cognitive Processes and Alternative Names

Lower order of thinking skills ——————————————→ Higher order of thinking skills

Remember	Understand	Apply	Analyze	Evaluate	Create
Recognizing	**Interpreting**	**Executing**	**Differentiating**	**Checking**	**Generating**
• Identifying	• Clarifying	• Carrying out	• Discriminating	• Coordinating	• Hypothesizing
Recalling	• Paraphrasing	**Implementing**	• Distinguishing	• Detecting	**Planning**
• Retreiving	• Representing	• Using	• Focusing	• Monitoring	• Designing
	• Translating		• Selecting	• Testing	**Producing**
	Exemplifying		**Organizing**	**Critiquing**	• Constructing
	• Illustrating		• Finding coherence	• Judging	
	• Instantiating		• Integrating		
	Classifying		• Outlining		
	• Categorizing		• Parsing		
	• Subsuming		• Structuring		
	Summarizing		**Attributing**		
	• Abstracting		• Deconstructing		
	• Generalizing				
	Inferring				
	• Concluding				
	• Extrapolating				
	• Interpolating				
	• Predicting				
	Comparing				
	• Contrasting				
	• Mapping				
	• Matching				
	Explaining				
	• Constructing models				

Adapted from Anderson and Krathwohl, *Taxonomy for Learning*, 67–68.

lower levels, through guided response and mechanism in the middle, to complex or overt response, adaptation, and origination at the higher levels. As in Bloom's taxonomy, related action verbs are included to help in developing specific and measurable learning-objective statements.[17]

It is often helpful to consult these taxonomies in order to assess whether consideration has been given to bringing the learners through a full spectrum of learning activities that will result in outcomes being achieved at both lower and higher levels in the various domains. A holistic learning experience will generally include at least one outcome targeted for the cognitive, the affective, and the behavioral domain, but determining how many for each category will depend on the decisions documented in the analysis stage.

Dee Fink has given consideration to this holistic perspective in "A Taxonomy of Significant Learning." Although sharing several

17. Simpson, "Learning Taxonomy."

Table 7.1. Learning Taxonomy: Simpson's Psychomotor Domain[a]

Level and Definition	Illustrative Verbs	Example
Perception: the ability to use sensory cues to guide motor activity. This ranges from sensory stimulation, through cue selection, to translation.	chooses, describes, detects, differentiates, distinguishes, identifies, isolates, relates, selects, separates	• Listening to the sounds made by guitar strings before tuning them • Recognizing sounds that indicate malfunctioning equipment • Estimating where a ball will land after it is thrown and then moving to the correct location • Adjusting the heat of a stove to the correct temperature by the smell and taste of food
Set: readiness to act. This includes mental, physical, and emotional sets. These three sets are dispositions that predetermine a person's response to different situations (sometimes called mind-sets).	begins, displays, explains, moves, proceeds, reacts, responds, shows, starts, volunteers	• Knowing how to use a computer mouse • Having an instrument ready to play and watching the conductor at the start of a musical performance • Showing an eagerness to assemble electronic components to complete a task • Knowing and acting on a sequence of steps in a manufacturing process • Recognizing one's abilities and limitations
Guided response: the early stages in learning a complex skill that include imitation and trial and error. Adequacy of performance is achieved by practicing.	assembles, builds, calibrates, constructs, dismantles, displays, dissects, fastens, fixes, grinds, heats, manipulates, measures, mends, mixes, organizes, sketches	• Using a torque wrench just after observing an expert demonstrate its use • Experimenting with various ways to measure a given volume of a volatile chemical • Performing a mathematical equation as demonstrated • Following instructions to build a model
Mechanism: the intermediate stage in learning a skill. Learned responses have become habitual, and the movements can be performed with some confidence and proficiency.	assembles, builds, calibrates, constructs, dismantles, displays, dissects, fastens, fixes, grinds, heats, manipulates, measures, mends, mixes, organizes, sketches	• Demonstrating the ability to correctly execute a 60-degree banked turn in an aircraft 70 percent of the time • Using a personal computer • Repairing a leaky faucet
Complex or overt response: the skillful performance of motor acts that involve complex movement patterns. Proficiency is indicated by a quick, accurate, and highly coordinated performance, requiring a minimum of energy. This category includes performing without hesitation and automatic performance. For example, players often utter sounds of satisfaction or expletives as soon as they hit a tennis ball or throw a football because they can tell by the feel of the act what the result will produce.	assembles, builds, calibrates, constructs, dismantles, displays, dissects, fastens, fixes, grinds, heats, manipulates, measures, mends, mixes, organizes, sketches	• Dismantling and reassembling various components of an automobile quickly and with no errors • Maneuvering a car into a tight parallel parking spot • Operating a computer quickly and accurately • Displaying competence while playing the piano

Level and Definition	Illustrative Verbs	Example
Adaptation: skills are well developed, and the individual can modify movement patterns to fit special requirements.	adapts, alters, changes, rearranges, reorganizes, revises, varies	• Using skills developed while learning how to operate an electric typewriter to operate a word processor • Responding effectively to unexpected experiences • Modifying instruction to meet the needs of the learners • Performing a task with a machine that was not originally intended to do that task
Origination: creating new movement patterns to fit a particular situation or specific problem. Learning outcomes emphasize creativity based on highly developed skills.	arranges, combines, composes, constructs, creates, designs, originates	• Designing a more efficient way to perform an assembly line task • Constructing a new theory • Developing a new and comprehensive training program • Creating a new gymnastic routine

a. Psychomotor learning is demonstrated by physical skills such as coordination, dexterity, manipulation, grace, strength, speed; actions that demonstrate fine motor skills such as the use of precision instruments or tools; or actions that evidence gross motor skills such as the use of the body in dance or athletic performance.

components with Bloom's taxonomy, Fink's taxonomy includes six major types of significant learning and several subcategories (see fig. 7.4).

Each of the six types can be matched with a question that can be used to craft relevant learning objectives.

- Foundational knowledge: What key information, ideas, and perspectives are important for the learners to know?
- Application: What kinds of thinking, complex projects, and skills are important for the learners to be able to do or manage?
- Integration: What connections should the learners be able to recognize and make within and beyond the particular learning experience?
- Human dimension: What should the learners learn about themselves and about interacting with others?

- Caring: What changes in the learners' feelings, interests, and values are important?
- Learning how to learn: What should the learners learn about learning, engaging in inquiry, and becoming self-directed?[18]

Similar to Bloom's taxonomy of verbs, the document "Effective Use of Learning Objectives" also provides a verb list for each of these dimensions of learning that can be used to write clear and measurable learning objectives for the various categories.[19]

Characteristics of Learning Objectives

One acronym that is helpful to use in crafting effective learning objectives is SMART. A SMART learning objective is

18. "Effective Use of Learning Objectives."
19. "Effective Use of Learning Objectives."

Figure 7.4
Taxonomy of Significant Learning

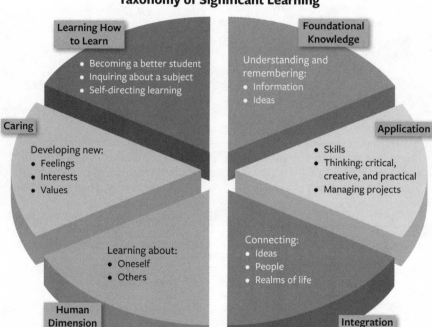

One important feature of this particular taxonomy is that each kind of learning is *interactive*. This means that each kind of learning can stimulate other kinds of learning. This has major implications for the selection of learning goals for your course. It may seem intimidating to include all six kinds of significant learning, but the more you can realistically include, the more the goals will support one another—and the more valuable will be your students' learning.

Adapted from Fink, "Self-Directed Guide."

- specific
- measurable and observable
- attainable and reasonable for the learners working under the given conditions (as clarified in the analysis stage)
- relevant and results-oriented
- targeted to the learners and the desired level of learning[20]

Selecting verbs from the taxonomy charts referenced earlier to create your learning

20. "Effective Use of Learning Objectives."

objective statements will help to ensure that the outcomes are specific and measurable.

How to Write Learning Objectives

Objectives need to be written from the perspective of the learners—what it is that the learners should achieve by the end of the teaching-learning experience. They are often stated with a sentence stem such as the following: "By the end of this course/class/workshop/seminar, the learners will be able to . . ." Objectives do not specify what it is the teacher is doing, although the teaching behaviors will be directly connected to the objectives in ways that will help facilitate the learners' accomplishment of the objectives.

Here is an example of stating a learning objective that demonstrates fine-tuning from poor to best.

Poor: Students should know the historically important systems of psychology.

This is poor because it says neither what systems nor what information about each system students should know. Are they supposed to know everything about them or just names? Should students be able to recognize the names, recite the central ideas, or criticize the assumptions?

Better: Students should know the psychoanalytic, Gestalt, behaviorist, humanistic, and cognitive approaches to psychology.

This is better because it says what theories students should know, but it still does not detail exactly what they should "know" about each theory or how deeply they should understand whatever it is they should understand.

Best: Students should be able to recognize and articulate the foundational assumptions, central ideas, and dominant criticisms of the psychoanalytic, Gestalt, behaviorist, humanistic, and cognitive approaches to psychology.

This is the clearest and most specific statement of the three examples. It clarifies how one is to demonstrate that he/she "knows." It provides even beginning students an understandable and very specific target to aim for. It provides faculty with a reasonable standard against which they can compare actual student performance.[21]

Selecting Content

After selecting objectives, the next step in the design stage is selecting the content for the course, class, workshop, or seminar. Overall, content involves the subject matter that will be covered over the course of the teaching-learning experience and includes "facts, concepts, generalizations, principles, and theories."[22] The selection of content also accounts for learning styles and means of processing information (which will be addressed later in this chapter). As you begin to think through the content step, consider what will best meet your goals and objectives and carefully "determine what knowledge students need in order to succeed."[23]

As you work to select content, the first consideration is the *scope* of the content. In other words, how much do you want to cover (depth and breadth) in the amount of time allotted for the course, class, workshop, or seminar? Second, consider the *sequence* of the curriculum plan. In other words, how will you ensure continuity of learning and build on previous lessons as the teaching-learning process progresses? Depending on the material covered and your goals and objectives, it may also be important to consider how you will integrate the material into real-life situations and provide practical applications for the learners.[24]

In regard to the content selection process, curriculum experts have created a number of technical models that may prove helpful.[25] The needs-assessment model considers the current state of the learners and what acceptable learner-based end goal should be achieved. The needs-assessment approach includes

21. This example is from "How to Write Program Objectives/Outcomes."

22. Ornstein and Hunkins, *Curriculum*, 234.
23. Ornstein and Hunkins, *Curriculum*, 233.
24. Ornstein and Hunkins, *Curriculum*, 186–90.
25. McNeil, *Contemporary Curriculum*, 113–23.

"four steps: (a) formulating a set of tentative goal statements, (b) assessing priority to goal areas, (c) determining the acceptability of learner performance in each of the preferred goal areas, and (d) translating high-priority goals into plans."[26]

The futuristic model takes into account that learners are a part of both the present and the future and anticipates new and different educational challenges and needs.[27] Therefore, the futuristic model considers goals, objectives, and content that will prepare learners for their future. This approach often requires strategic planning and an integrative or multidisciplinary approach to content selection and curricular design.[28]

The rational model is often referred to as an ends-means approach to design.[29] This model constantly considers how the learners will meet the goals and objectives laid out in the initial analysis phase and what educational tools (content and learning activities) will be best suited to help them attain the desired results.[30]

Finally, the vocational or training model focuses more on behavioral or skill-based outcomes and the content needed to reach those competencies.[31] While this model has a narrower focus than some of the others, it can be particularly helpful in select settings in which skills or basic behaviors are the educational focus. For example, this model may be helpful when creating a training seminar for nursery workers.

When integrating a biblical approach to content selection, a biblical worldview should also be considered during this stage of the design process. As Harro Van Brummelen suggests, while Scripture does not provide a road map for curricular design and development, "a biblical approach keeps us humble."[32] Keeping a biblical worldview in mind will be helpful as you select the content you hope to cover and what facts, skills, concepts, generalizations, principles, and theories you hope to address.[33]

In summary, as you work through this stage of the teaching-learning process, these questions may be helpful to consider.

- Will you need a textbook, a workbook, or ready-made curriculum, or will you need to create your own curriculum?
- What material do you hope/plan to cover and in what detail?
- How does what you plan to cover fit with other classes (within your church or academic setting)?
- How does the content selected meet the educational needs of the learners?
- How can you best address the cognitive, affective, and behavioral dimensions of learning?
- How can you best organize the subject matter?

Selecting the Instructional Format

Finally, after considering objectives and content, you need to give thought to the instructional format that is most conducive to the setting in which you will be teaching. Here are a few questions to consider:

26. McNeil, *Contemporary Curriculum*, 114.
27. McNeil, *Contemporary Curriculum*, 116.
28. McNeil, *Contemporary Curriculum*, 116–17.
29. McNeil, *Contemporary Curriculum*, 123.
30. McNeil, *Contemporary Curriculum*, 118.
31. McNeil, *Contemporary Curriculum*, 122.
32. Van Brummelen, *Steppingstones to Curriculum*, 79, 81.
33. Ornstein and Hunkins, *Curriculum*, 76.

- Will the setting be formal, nonformal, informal, self-directed, digital (see chapter 14 for more details), or a combination of several formats?
- How will you determine the format?

In addition, an important consideration as you think about the instructional format is the process you will utilize to recruit and identify the learners. Here are some questions that could be asked:

- How many learners do you anticipate having?
- Will the number change your format? If so, in what way or ways?

In addressing these initial questions concerning format, keep the learners in mind and what you hope they will gain from the teaching-learning situation. There are four instructional formats to consider.

Formal

A formal instructional format is most commonly associated with degree and certificate programs within educational institutions.[34] Wesley Black defines formal education as an "approach to learning focused on acquiring skills, knowledge, attitudes, and values growing out of planned, intentional learning experiences."[35] This process of learning often takes place in a classroom setting with a planned, focused curriculum.[36] In addition, Arlen Etling, borrowing from Philip Coombs, defines formal education as "the hierarchically structured, chronologically graded educa-

tional system running from primary school through the university and including, in addition to general academic studies, a variety of specialized programs and institutions for full-time technical and professional training."[37]

This instructional format places more emphasis on the teacher and their choices than on the learners' choices. In a ministry setting, formal education can be particularly helpful for Sunday school programs, organized Bible studies, and other organized church-based learning opportunities. This instructional format can also be particularly useful in settings in which material is new to the learners and the teacher needs to take the lead within the teaching-learning context. Direct instruction lends itself well to structured settings. Overall, a major strength of this instructional format is the value placed on planning.

Nonformal

The term *nonformal education* was first discussed by Philip Coombs in the 1960s and made popular in evangelical circles by Ted Ward in the 1970s.[38] A nonformal instructional format relies on "deliberate educational strategies based on meeting people's needs outside of the formal educational setting."[39] This approach is often more learner-centered than formal education and provides the learners with greater decision-making opportunities.[40] Nonformal education can also be change-oriented, making it an interesting educational approach.[41]

Within ministry, nonformal education can be a powerful and useful tool. For example,

---

34. Mocker and Spear, "Lifelong Learning."
35. Black, "Formal Education," 298.
36. Black, "Formal Education," 298.

37. Etling, "What Is Nonformal Education?" 73.
38. Newton, "Nonformal Education," 505–6.
39. Newton, "Nonformal Education," 506.
40. Mocker and Spear, "Lifelong Learning," 6; and Newton, "Nonformal Education," 506.
41. Newton, "Nonformal Education," 506.

internship experiences and some forms of discipleship are nonformal in nature. Overall, within a Christian context, nonformal education can be quite useful because it is flexible but still purposeful and focused on meeting the needs of the learners. A major strength of this instructional format is the flexibility it offers within the learning context.

Informal

An informal instructional format is even less structured than nonformal education and involves everyday learning opportunities that are not planned, scheduled, or organized. Wesley Black defines informal education as "an approach to learning focused on acquiring skills, knowledge, attitudes, and values growing out of student interactions with experiences or environments."[42] When something happens that is explained or interpreted by a peer, parent, coach, counselor, or other individual, informal education takes place. In ministry, many informal educational opportunities exist. Mission projects, trips, and unstructured mentoring are often avenues for informal education. A major strength of this instructional format is that it takes advantage of the everyday opportunities that present themselves for both new learning and reinforcing learning.

Self-Directed

Self-directed learning is the most student-centered of all the instructional formats discussed here. Donald Mocker and George Spear suggest that "self-directed learning represents the ultimate state of learner autonomy."[43] In this format, the learners decide what they would like to discover and then set the course for themselves without formal direction and can choose to discontinue the learning venture at any time. Within a ministry-based setting, if discipleship and formal educational opportunities have been successful, then self-directed learning should begin to take place in the individual lives of believers. For example, church members who study Scripture on their own, practice various spiritual disciplines, and participate in prayer are all exercising a self-directed learning format. A major strength of this instructional format is that the learners have the ability to continue learning without the direct aid of a teacher, leader, minister, or counselor.

A Combination of Instructional Formats

With each instructional format in mind, you may find that your teaching-learning process would be executed most effectively by incorporating several of the formats discussed. Intentionally planning to incorporate several instructional formats can strengthen the learning process for the learners involved. For example, when formal and nonformal options are combined, the learning can move beyond the classroom time and provide the learners with hands-on experiences to complement the classroom learning. In most teaching-learning situations, implementing a combination of instructional formats allows the most effective learning to take place.

In summation, the design process involves selecting objectives/outcomes, content, and the instructional format. However, this is only the second phase of the teaching-learning process. The remaining steps will be addressed in the next chapter.

42. Black, "Informal Education," 362.
43. Mocker and Spear, "Lifelong Learning," 11.

8

Educational Taxonomies, Part 2

Development, Implementation, and Evaluation in Teaching and Learning

MEGAN G. BROWN AND SHELLY CUNNINGHAM

The previous chapter detailed the foundational steps needed for an effective teaching-learning process. Once the groundwork has been laid, the details can then begin to take shape.

Development

The third step, the development stage, is the next piece of the puzzle in the teaching-learning process. This stage of the process involves planning and detailing the specifics of the lesson or program plan. Before jumping into the actual planning process, it is helpful to understand a number of potential instructional development frameworks. This chapter gives an overview of several common frameworks. After reviewing the available options, considering which may work best for your teaching-learning environment, and developing an initial plan, you can begin the exciting process of lesson planning.

Understanding by Design (UbD)

Understanding by Design (UbD) is a well-known option for curriculum development made popular by Grant Wiggins and Jay Mc-Tighe.[1] UbD operates as a backward model of curriculum design and development in that it focuses on end goals, desired results, and assessment options and works backward to develop the curriculum itself. UbD pays particular attention to the learning audience and

1. Ornstein and Hunkins, *Curriculum*, 216.

considers the learners' instructional needs.[2] Ultimately, the desired result at the end of the instructional time is at the forefront of this model of curriculum development.[3]

Understanding by Design includes three stages of development: "(a) Identify desired results, (b) Determine acceptable evidence, and (c) Plan learning experiences and instruction."[4] The first stage considers cognitive competencies, content, and what the teacher hopes the learners will carry with them after the course, class, workshop, or seminar.[5] Generally speaking, the first stage is all about priorities, deciding what is most important and what can be reasonably covered in the time allotted.

The second stage considers how the desired results identified in the first stage will be assessed. During this stage, it is important for the teacher to consider how they will determine whether or not a learner has achieved the desired results identified. This step, as suggested by Wiggins and McTighe, allows the curriculum planner to "think like an assessor."[6] Determining how to assess students up front allows the teacher to more intentionally plan lessons and learning activities in the next stage.

The third stage addresses the actual curriculum plan. Here the teacher selects appropriate instructional activities to meet the goals and assessment needs identified in the first two stages of the UbD model. At this stage of the development process, "purposeful task analysis"[7] must be employed to be sure goals

are reached and assessment means are considered. This is the final, and perhaps most laborious, of the three stages.

To help put this method of curriculum design into practice, Wiggins and McTighe developed several helpful templates.[8] The templates are useful in a number of educational settings, including ministry-based settings. Should you find the UbD model most helpful for the teaching-learning process you are preparing for, select and use your choice of template as you design and develop your course plan.

Hook, Book, Look, Took (HBLT)

Hook, Book, Look, Took (HBLT), introduced by Lawrence Richards, is another method of instructional development. This method follows a four-step process of lesson planning. The four steps follow the title of this method. First, hook involves enticing the learners to enter the learning experience. Richards and Gary Bredfeldt suggest that an effective hook involves (1) gaining the attention of the learners, (2) bringing a need or a longing to the surface, (3) setting the direction for the class or session, and (4) leading naturally into the content of the class or session.[9]

The second step, book, involves addressing the content of the lesson and clarifying the meaning, theories, or principles being studied. Richards and Bredfeldt suggest a number of instructional methods that can be effective for this step of the teaching-learning process.[10] For example, student-focused methods (i.e.,

2. Wiggins and McTighe, *Understanding by Design*, 13.
3. Wiggins and McTighe, *Understanding by Design*, 14.
4. Wiggins and McTighe, *Understanding by Design*, 18.
5. Wiggins and McTighe, *Understanding by Design*, 17–18.
6. Wiggins and McTighe, *Understanding by Design*, 18.
7. Wiggins and McTighe, *Understanding by Design*, 19.

8. Wiggins and McTighe, *Understanding by Design*, 327–32.
9. Richards and Bredfeldt, *Creative Bible Teaching*, 155–56.
10. Richards and Bredfeldt, *Creative Bible Teaching*, 156.

discussion groups) or more teacher-focused methods (i.e., lecturing) can be helpful for this step. The ultimate goal of this step is to help the learners gain a greater understanding of the material.

The third step, look, deals with implications of the material being studied. Here the teacher assists the learners in making connections between the material studied and daily life. This step moves the learners from mere cognitive learning to higher-order thinking, practical application, and transformation.

The fourth and final step, took, encourages the learners to respond to the lesson. As Richards and Bredfeldt suggest, this often takes place outside the classroom or direct learning environment.[11] However, during the classroom experience, the teacher can urge the learners to consider how they can respond to the material outside the learning environment. Simply challenging the learners to utilize what they have learned can be an effective way to help them take the material beyond the classroom setting.

In Christian teaching, the HBLT method can be quite impactful. Consider the flow of the method alongside the process of discipleship and sanctification. The HBLT method allows space for creativity and intentionality in the instructional process as well as transformation, the goal of Christian education. Utilizing this method may prove helpful for Bible studies in a large group or small group, specific programs, and mentoring within the church. If you think this developmental model is ideal for your teaching-learning experience, consult the lesson planning worksheet developed by Richards and Bredfeldt to aid you in the HBLT process.[12]

Instructional Theory into Practice (ITIP)

A third framework that may be helpful in developing your course, class, workshop, or seminar is Madeline Hunter's Instructional Theory into Practice (ITIP) model. Hunter's model addresses content, student behavior, and instructor behavior with seven helpful lesson planning and preparation elements. The seven steps include (1) goals and objectives, (2) anticipatory set, (3) input or modeling, (4) understanding check, (5) guided practice, (6) independent practice, and (7) closing or wrap-up.[13]

The first step deals with goals and objectives, which were addressed in detail in chapter 7. However, Hunter's model emphasizes selecting goals and objectives that contain an appropriate level of difficulty and correlate with the appropriate levels of Bloom's taxonomy. The goals and objectives should be selected with attention to the learners' current needs and perceived abilities and where the teacher hopes they will be at the end of the course, class, workshop, or seminar.

The second step deals with motivation and the learning task. At this stage of the teaching-learning process, it is important to consider the learners' previous knowledge of and experience with the topic being addressed. Learning activities should be selected with care and intentionality. This stage of the development process is similar to Richards and Bredfeldt's hook stage.[14]

The third step involves the actual teaching process. Here the teacher decides what information needs to be covered and how best to achieve the objectives outlined. During this

---

11. Richards and Bredfeldt, *Creative Bible Teaching*, 158.

12. Richards and Bredfeldt, *Creative Bible Teaching*, 160–65.

13. M. Hunter, *Enhancing Teaching*, 87–95.

14. Richards and Bredfeldt, *Creative Bible Teaching*, 154–56.

step, the instructor provides clear instruction on the concepts under study. As with many of the other models discussed, a number of instructional methods can be utilized to appropriately and effectively input or model the topic of the lesson.

The fourth step in Hunter's ITIP model is an understanding check. This step involves observing, interpreting, and evaluating the learners' learning. This can be done formally with immediate feedback and further instruction or as a more formative and ongoing assessment that allows the teacher to adjust the instructional format to meet the learning needs of the students. Overall, this step of the process assists the teacher in evaluating how well, or not, the teaching-learning process is going.

The fifth step in Hunter's model is guided practice. This step allows the learners time and space to demonstrate, practice, and express their learning. This can be done via group discussion, answering reflection questions, demonstrating a skill or behavior, or solving a problem. Hunter suggests the teacher give immediate feedback as students complete guided practice and then reteach or review areas that are still unclear or in which students appear to lack mastery. Overall, this step is guided and overseen by the teacher.

The sixth step involves the learners practicing the material learned on their own. This may involve in-class practice or, in traditional settings, may be accomplished via homework assignments, projects, or outside-of-class experiences. While this step is not always visible to the teacher, it is an important part of the learning process. This step should not be completed until the teacher is certain the learners have a substantial grasp of the material being covered and are able to work independently.

Finally, Hunter suggests the instructor close or wrap up the course, class, workshop, or seminar. This final step may involve recapping the material and a final understanding check. However, not all topics can be wrapped up nicely and may require ongoing learning and practice (lab experiments, mission or service opportunities, etc.).

Overall, Hunter's model is a useful and workable model for curriculum design. While the steps have been explained here as a step-by-step process, it is important to note that some steps may be omitted or repeated for specific learning situations. Hunter simply provides a model to aid in the development process. As you consider your teaching-learning situation, this is yet another model that may prove helpful within both ministry-based and more academic settings.

Experiential Learning Model (ELM)

The Experiential Learning Model (ELM), developed by David Kolb, grew out of the work done by John Dewey, Kurt Lewin, and Jean Piaget and focuses on a series of steps. The basic premise of this model is the underlying understanding that human beings can, and do, learn through experience.[15] The initial steps of Kolb's model include (1) concrete experience, (2) reflective observation, (3) abstract conceptualization, and (4) active experimentation. Kolb later expanded his theory to account for learning styles and developmental stages. Kolb's expanded model includes four areas of learning: feeling, watching, thinking, and doing. Within each quadrant, Kolb defined the type of learning experienced. For example, learning that involves feeling and

15. Kolb, Rubin, and McIntyre, *Organizational Psychology*, 3.

Figure 8.1
Kolb's Learning Styles

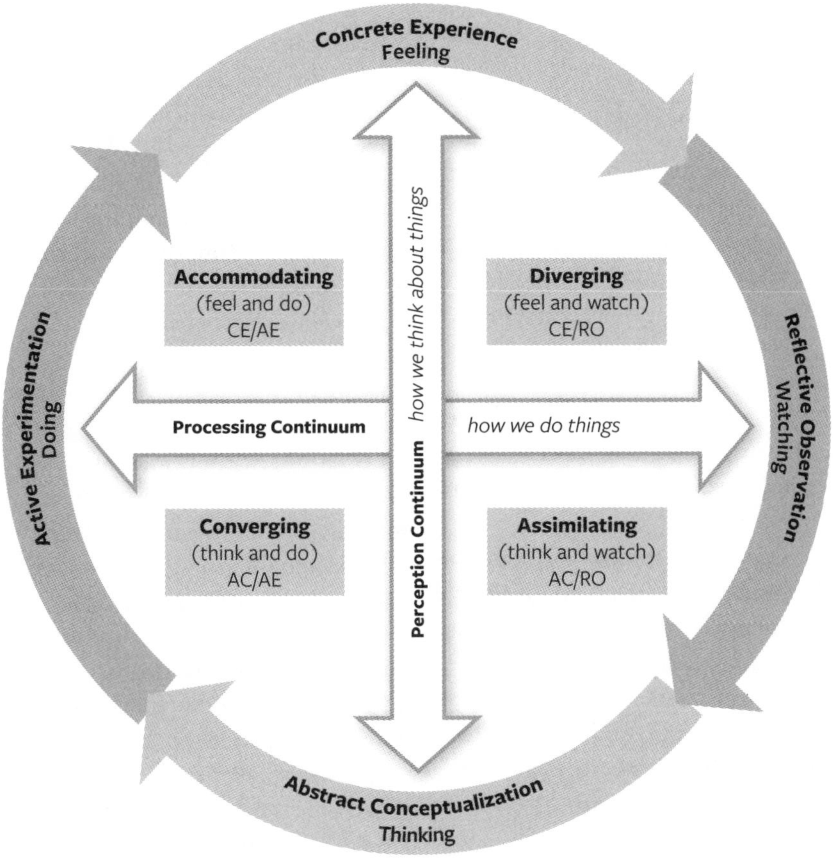

doing is called accommodating, learning that involves feeling and watching is called diverging, learning that involves watching and thinking is called assimilating, and learning that involves thinking and doing is called converging (see fig. 8.1).

Overall, Kolb's model proposes that learning is more about a holistic process, involving transformation and experience, than the rote learning promoted by some other learning models. Kolb believed that learning involves a process of thoughts being "formed and reformed through experience."[16] However, Kolb also recognized that concerns of developmental and learning style play a role in the learning process and how learning takes place.

This method of curriculum design and development has been resurrected and restructured for use in e-learning formats. The experience-based learning this method promotes works well with online educational

16. Kolb, Rubin, and McIntyre, *Organizational Psychology*, 26.

formats. In addition, models of internship and apprenticeship, laboratory, studio art, co-operative learning, and mission-service learning fit well with Kolb's ELM model.[17]

Teaching Methods and Learning Activities

With the aforementioned models of development and lesson planning in mind, you should consider which teaching methods and learning activities will be most effective for the learners with whom you anticipate working. It is important that you select teaching methods and learning activities that meet the distinct learning needs and preferences of the learners. These learning needs and preferences are often described as "modes of knowing"[18] or "multiple intelligences."[19]

Howard Gardner's careful work on intelligences and how people learn is an invaluable asset to the teaching-learning process in both ministry-based and academic settings. In 1993 Gardner first identified seven intelligences: (1) musical intelligence, (2) bodily-kinesthetic intelligence, (3) logical-mathematical intelligence, (4) linguistic intelligence, (5) spatial intelligence, (6) interpersonal intelligence, and (7) intrapersonal intelligence.[20] However, the latest edition of Gardner's work discusses two additional intelligences: (1) naturalist intelligence and (2) existential intelligence.[21] Gardner suggests that naturalist intelligence is the eighth intelligence but that he is not yet ready to add existential intelligence as a ninth intelligence.[22] Overall, Gardner states that he is comfortable suggesting there are eight and a half intelligences.[23]

Using Gardner's work can be helpful in the teaching-learning process. As you plan for your situation, consider the learners you will be working with and what learning needs they may have. When possible, include a variety of learning activities that meet a number of learning styles, or multiple intelligences. Additional information concerning teaching methodology and learning activities will be discussed in later chapters.

In summation, the development process involves careful planning and considering a variety of curriculum models or frameworks. While a number of options are available, you should consider which model will work best for the teaching-learning situation you are planning and preparing. As you select a framework, plan lessons, and prepare for the next stage in the ADDIE model of instructional design (implementation), allow the Holy Spirit to enter into the development process. In reflecting on planning and preparing, Benedictine nun Joan Chittister writes, "Thinking a thing through and planning how to do each part of it are not the same. One enables us to imagine what we will need to complete the journey, whatever changes we may need to make on the way. The other sets us on a road no one has ever been on before with an old map for a guide and not a clue about where else this road might take us on the way."[24] As you enter into the development process, invite the Spirit to join you. Think the teaching-learning process through, but, as Chittister suggests, leave room for "whatever changes [you] may need to make on the way."[25]

17. Kolb, Rubin, and McIntyre, *Organizational Psychology*, 5.

18. Van Brummelen, *Steppingstones to Curriculum*, 97.

19. Gardner, *Multiple Intelligences*, 8–18.

20. Gardner, *Multiple Intelligences*, 8–18.

21. Gardner, *Multiple Intelligences*, 18–21.

22. Gardner, *Multiple Intelligences*, 21.

23. Gardner, *Multiple Intelligences*, 21.

24. Chittister, *Sacred In-Between*, 15–16.

25. Chittister, *Sacred In-Between*, 15–16.

Implementation

The fourth stage in the ADDIE model of instructional design involves carrying out the plan. This stage is where you begin to see all your hard work from previous steps come alive. The implementation phase may include a number of steps, depending on the type of teaching-learning process you are planning. At this stage, you need to consider administrative support, going live, and formative assessment.

Administrative Support

You will need to do some assessments before "going live" with the teaching-learning process. The first area to consider during implementation is administrative support. This involves reviewing the budget, considering marketing and promotion, recruiting and training staff, identifying resource personnel, getting needed permission, and collecting supplies and needed material.

Reviewing the Budget

Before going live with the teaching-learning process, you should review your budget. Consider how you will spend the funds allocated for the teaching-learning process using these questions:

- Given the number of learners anticipated, what amount of supplies will be needed?
- What rental fees need to be considered?
- What, if any, stipends or salary will be offered to support staff?

Taking a final look at the course plan and what you hope to accomplish may help with the budget overview. If you do not have an allotted budget, consider how you can raise the needed funds or gain support through donations or fund-raising.

Considering Marketing and Promotion

Before going live, it is also important to consider how you will promote your teaching-learning situation. A few questions to help you include the following:

- Do posters, flyers, postcards, or other promotional materials need to be created and sent out?
- Will a simple announcement or social media message suffice?
- Do you need to inform a board or a department head about the course?
- Who is your audience, and how will you let them know about this learning opportunity?

Recruiting

Recruiting and training needed staff is essential in both academic and ministry-based settings. Whether you will be working with paid or volunteer staff, this is an important part of the process.

The first item for consideration is how many staff members you anticipate needing. Second, consider how you will fill the needed positions. Ask yourself the following questions:

- Are there current staff members who could take on responsibilities for this teaching-learning task?
- Will additional staff need to be recruited or hired?
- What is the most efficient way to advertise for, interview, and hire new staff?

There are a number of ways to identify and recruit needed staff members, including listing openings on a church or other relevant website, announcing the opportunity in your church during worship, or intentionally seeking out qualified personnel and providing them with a thoughtful, personal invitation to take part in the teaching-learning situation.

During the implementation process, be sure to periodically thank your staff for the good work they are doing to ensure the teaching-learning process goes smoothly. Simple notes, small treats, or gift cards can make a significant statement and let your staff members know you appreciate their hard work.

Identifying Resource Personnel

Identifying resource personnel is a key part of the implementation process. This step may involve making a list of individuals or departments that can assist you throughout the teaching-learning process. Consider these questions:

- Who is responsible for ordering supplies and materials?
- Who should be contacted for specific materials for the course, class, workshop, or seminar?
- Are there any experts you would like to have as guest speakers or resource personnel available to your learners? If so, how can you contact them and schedule a class session or time slot for them to join the teaching-learning process?

While this step may involve a number of areas, it can be instrumental in the success of the teaching-learning process and providing students with the most effective learning opportunity possible.

Getting Needed Permission

Another area to consider during the implementation process is permission needs. Before utilizing any print materials, images, handouts, video clips, or other class aids that are not your own original work, be sure to obtain permission from the author or appropriate source. Many churches own licensure to utilize various media and other educational resources. Check with your church office concerning what is covered and not covered. For academic settings, an instructional aid department may be able to assist you in obtaining permission to use specific materials.

Also, do not forget to obtain permission forms, medical forms, and needed waivers for field trips and service projects if needed. Such trips can provide meaningful learning opportunities but may be attended only if the required permission is obtained. Therefore, before planning and building such opportunities into the teaching-learning process, discuss any permission requirements with your institution and put those into your course plan.

Collecting Supplies and Needed Materials

Also part of the implementation stage is making sure you have all the needed supplies for the teaching-learning process. Consider the following questions:

- What media-based supplies will be needed (projector and screen, laptop, tablet, DVD player, etc.)?
- Will the space you plan to utilize be fully equipped to meet your needs?
- What tangible supplies will be needed (textbooks, workbooks, handouts, learning activity aids, markers, whiteboards, etc.)?

- What steps will need to be taken to acquire the needed supplies and prepare
the teaching-learning environment?

Going Live

After you've addressed all the details of administrative support, the teaching-learning situation you have diligently planned for will soon
begin. As you and your teaching staff prepare
for each course, class, workshop, or seminar,
take a few moments to pray for the teaching-
learning process, collect your thoughts, and
review your curriculum plan. As students arrive, greet them and welcome them into the
teaching-learning process. Utilize your plan to
the fullest while leaving space for the working
of the Spirit and flexibility for adjustments as
needed. During the teaching-learning situation,
be attentive to things that work well and things
that could be improved. Keep a list of notes to
reflect on later during the evaluation phase (see
the next section in this chapter). Finally, enjoy
the moment and the opportunity to both lead
and participate in learning.

Formative Assessment

The final aspect of the implementation
stage is formative assessment. This is a means
of regularly assessing the teaching-learning
process and monitoring how well the learners are performing or mastering the goals and
objectives. Assessment can be done a number
of ways during the implementation stage. Two
of the most common means of assessment are
individual assessment and group assessment.
Maria Weurlander, Magnus Söderberg, Max
Scheja, Håkan Hult, and Annika Wernerson
found that conducting formative assessment
impacts student motivation, can aid students
in an awareness of their own learning, and can

impact both the learning process and the final
outcome.[26] While the researchers noted that
the teaching-learning environment impacts
the formative assessment process and function, it is still a valuable tool for a variety of
teaching-learning environments.[27]

As you consider conducting formative assessment, ask yourself the following questions:

- Are the originally outlined goals and
objectives being fulfilled?
- Are the learners progressing as anticipated?
- What areas may need to be revised
moving forward?
- What areas are going well?
- What areas may need to be revised if
this curriculum is utilized in the future?

In summation, the implementation stage
involves administrative support, including
reviewing the budget, considering marketing and promotion, recruiting and training
staff, identifying resource personnel, getting
needed permission, and collecting supplies
and needed materials; going live; and formative assessment. However, this is only the
fourth phase of the teaching-learning process.
The final step is evaluation.

Evaluation

You are almost at the end of the ADDIE
model of instructional design for the teaching-
learning experience. It is often tempting, upon
reaching the end of a course, class, workshop,

26. Weurlander et al., "Exploring Formative Assessment," 747–60.
27. Weurlander et al., "Exploring Formative Assessment," 756.

or seminar, simply to close the door and file away the notes. However, even if the event appeared to be successful, important questions need to be answered: Did the learners learn? In what way(s)? To what extent? How do you know? What are the next steps for further growth? How might the instructional design need to be remodeled to build on what you have discovered and to take the learning to the next level? Evaluation, the final step in the ADDIE model of instructional design, focuses on these questions.

Let's return to an overview of the instructional design process; however, instead of seeing it as a linear arrangement, we will now look at the model as a loop. This loop is commonly referred to as the assessment cycle (see fig. 8.2). The term *evaluation* is more commonly used in nonacademic and nonformal instructional contexts, while the term *assessment* is the preferred term in academic contexts. Both terms refer to similar processes and encompass the same general components.

The assessment cycle begins with the formulation of the outcomes for student learning (see "Design" in chapter 7). At the time of evaluation, these outcomes will be reviewed and used as the assessment criteria. Assessment or evaluation will be effective and informative only if the learning outcomes were well constructed in the design phase and written in such a way as to be specific, measurable, observable, and attainable.

Next, teaching-learning activities are designed to facilitate the achievement of these outcomes. In order for the evaluation to result in substantive data or information with which to answer the assessment questions, consideration needs to be given at the design and development stages to the types of activities that will give evidence of or demonstrate

Figure 8.2
The Assessment Cycle

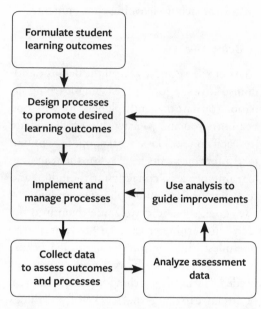

Adapted from the San Dieto State University Curriculum Guide, 2006.

student progress made toward achievement of the learning outcomes.

One of the core tenets of the Understanding by Design (UbD) model referenced earlier is that effective curriculum should be planned backward, beginning with stating the long-term desired results and then identifying what type of product or practice will give evidence that the result was achieved. The rest of the model focuses on developing the overall learning plan that will lead the students to demonstrate or produce this evidence.[28]

Grant Wiggins and Jay McTighe categorize assessment into performance tasks and other evidence.[29] Other evidence includes

28. Wiggins and McTighe, *Understanding by Design*, 14–16.
29. Wiggins and McTighe, *Understanding by Design*, 153.

the more traditional assortment of quizzes, tests, samples of work completed, and observations. A performance task, on the other hand, is designed for students to apply what they are learning to new situations that are "authentic" and "real-life." Such tasks assess their understanding of the concepts and their ability to transfer their learning. They might involve solving real-world problems or creating a context for an activity that engages a particular audience.[30]

Dee Fink calls this kind of assessment "forward-looking assessment" and defines it as follows:

> Forward-Looking Assessment incorporates exercises, questions, and/or problems that create a real-life context for a given issue, problem, or decision to be addressed. To construct this kind of question or problem, the teacher has to "look forward," beyond the time when the course is over, and ask: "In what kind of situation do I expect students to need, or to be able to use this knowledge?" Then, create a question or problem that replicates this real-life context as closely as possible.[31]

Bringing this kind of perspective to the design and development stages of the instructional design process promotes a learning-centered course and avoids a narrow evaluation process that seeks to determine only if the students got it or not.[32] Incorporating a forward-looking or real-world paradigm for learning activities is especially well suited to ministry contexts in which the primary goal is life application and evidence of transformative learning.

30. McTighe and Wiggins, *Understanding by Design,* 154.
31. Fink, "Self-Directed Guide."
32. Fink, "Self-Directed Guide."

After the design framework is in place, the third step in the assessment cycle is the actual implementation—going live with the learning event and all its curricular components, both inside and outside the classroom. At this point, you are midway through the evaluation process.

The fourth step in the cycle involves collecting data to assess the achievement of the student learning outcomes. This data is the evidence that you identified in the design and development stages to indicate student achievement of the learning outcomes. It includes such data as quizzes, tests, papers, reports, projects, problem-solving scenarios, case studies, journals, presentations, performances, demonstrations, proposals, observation reports, and various web-based products (websites, blogs, etc.). The data can be collected throughout the duration of the learning experience, at the end, or at a point in time beyond the conclusion of the course, class, workshop, or seminar.

Interestingly, it is not unusual in ministry contexts to neglect or ignore the need to collect evidence that students are making progress toward the learning outcomes. However, this might better be understood as a stewardship issue for those in ministry. It is not unlike the request made for an accounting of progress in the parable of the talents (Matt. 25:14–30). If we desire to create instructional experiences that demonstrate fruit and growth toward Christlikeness in the lives of the learners and that are intentional, focused, and worth the time and resources of student, instructor, and organization or church, we need to consider how we know, at the end, if the learners truly learned and to what extent.

Data can be presented in a quantitative or a qualitative form. Quantitative data is

generally defined as data that can be measured and deals with numbers. Quantitative
forms may include counts, charts, number
scores, letter grades, or checklists. In contrast,
qualitative data deals with descriptions and
can be observed but not measured. Qualitative
forms may include content analyses (lists of
key phrases, themes, etc.), narrative reports,
descriptions, performances, demonstrations,
audiovisual products, oral presentations, and
so on. Sometimes these can all be combined
into a portfolio that contains representative
samples of a learner's work during the course
or program.

The fifth step in the cycle is to analyze the
assessment or evaluation data that was collected to determine to what degree the learning outcomes were achieved. Depending on
the nature of the learning outcomes, assessment data may be analyzed by plotting scores
on graphs, listing percentage summaries, or
forming representative focus groups of learners to assess learning-outcome achievement.
Analysis may also be obtained by distributing
some kind of self-report survey to participants
or by surveying stakeholder groups (employ-
ers, family members, etc.) for their assessment
of evidence of learning-outcome achievement
observed in the lives and practices of the learners in real-life contexts.

Finally, the last step in the assessment
cycle is to use the data analysis conclusions
to make decisions about improvements to
bring to the course or learning context in the
future. In reality, this is not a final step; it is
a bridge step to propel continued and better learning for students. Improvements may
need to be made at the design stage or at the
implementation stage or at both. Whatever

improvements are made, the next review process should compare student progress in the
areas in which improvements were made and
before-and-after achievement results. This is
considered closing the loop and is a robust
way to approach the process of evaluation
and assessment.

In summary, evaluation is best understood
as a cycle or a loop that begins with a review
of the original learning objectives/outcomes.
Next, it involves monitoring (formative evaluation) and reviewing (summative evaluation)
how effectively the learning outcomes were
woven into the design, development, and
implementation stages of the instructional
process. Finally, it involves studying quantitative and/or qualitative data produced by the
learners as evidence of their learning achievements. This assessment is then used to revise,
as necessary, the design, development, and implementation stages of the instructional process to better achieve the learning outcomes
the next time the course, class, workshop, or
seminar is taught.

Conclusion

This chapter and chapter 7 gave an overview of
the ADDIE model of instructional design. The
ADDIE model lays out a systematic framework
for designing an effective teaching-learning situation. The five stages of the ADDIE model
are analysis, design, development, implementation, and evaluation. Following these steps,
or a similar process, will help to ensure that
consideration is given to what is important
and strategic in order to accomplish the goals
of a teaching-learning situation.

9

Educational Methodology

KEN COLEY

Jesus was called Rabbi throughout the New Testament Gospels. Ever since our Lord stunned the multitudes with his dynamic communication of truth, Jesus has been known as the Master Teacher. He thrilled audiences of thousands with his riveting storytelling and tales of divine power and majesty. Yet beyond his exquisite mastery of public speaking skills, something more profound was at work: Jesus's intimate understanding of human nature and how to shape it through Christian teaching. Jesus's educational methodology is the central theme of this chapter.

Long before modern teaching-learning theory, Jesus understood and demonstrated unique educational prowess, utilizing techniques that now fill academic textbooks. Millennia before the concepts of multiple intelligences and learning styles were formally conceptualized, Jesus mastered an ability to challenge people to embrace new thoughts,

beliefs, understandings, convictions, attitudes, values, choices, behaviors, and lifestyles. The teaching-learning approach practiced by Jesus remains peerless.

Throughout the Gospels, we encounter Jesus engaging his disciples in the teaching-learning process. He engaged their imaginations ("Consider the lilies of the fields"), provoked discussion ("Who do men say that I am?"), provided object lessons ("I am the bread of life"), and encouraged active learning ("You give them something to eat"). With the example of Jesus in mind, we pause to ask, "Why do teachers teach the way they do?" Many longtime teachers have never pondered this question. The most frequent response relates to how teaching was modeled: "I teach the way I do because my favorite teacher taught that way."[1] Or they select instructional techniques based on the ways, or modalities, that they

1. Felder, "Teaching Teachers to Teach," 176.

learn best. But is there another choice related to the craft of teaching that acknowledges the current research on the complexities of the teaching-learning process?

In order to address these important questions, this chapter argues two points. First, effective teaching is not merely the transmission of new ideas or course content but, as Jesus's teaching illustrates, includes the holistic engagement of the learner. Gary Newton explains, "Learning happens most effectively through active engagement of every aspect of the person. The more engaged and active a person is in the learning process, the greater the potential for learning to take place."[2] Second, effective engagement of learners demands differentiation. That is, effective teachers deliver the same material in different ways in order to meet the needs of different learners. An instructor dedicated to differentiation "provides different avenues to acquiring content, to processing or making sense of ideas, and to developing products so that each student can learn effectively."[3] Effective teaching requires that instructors do more than present content in a fashion that they find appealing. It requires planning, creativity, and training so that every learner can grasp and live out the key concepts of the instructional encounter.

We will begin by considering the teaching-learning process, with special attention given to current research on effective teaching, including awareness of the learner's schema and metacognitive processes. Then a robust discussion of active learning theory and techniques will be taken up, aimed at equipping the reader to cultivate engaged learning through differentiated teaching.

Defining the Teaching-Learning Process

For the purpose of clarity, let us establish what is intended when discussing the teaching-learning process. In short, this can be defined by one word: *change*. This change can be in a learner's beliefs, understanding, perception, or attitude, but most importantly, it is hoped that change is also ultimately reflected in the learner's behavior. Where no change has occurred, no effective teaching and no learning have taken place. But the teaching and learning experience will not succeed if the learner is not engaged in the process. The greater the engagement, the more significant the potential change in the learner and the deeper the personal meaning will become.[4]

Rick and Shera Melick agree with these two concepts of change and engagement and reflect their approach in a unique term: *transformactional*. They explain:

> Learning is more than mental. It is emotional. It is volitional. It is active. Transformation is indeed mental, but transformation also produces better living through informed action. In using the word "*transformactional*," we hope to stress two important aspects of learning. First, real learning includes action. Second, the process of learning is active. It actively seeks, embraces, and applies knowledge. In the case of Christian education, the learner actively seeks, embraces, and applies the truths of Scripture so that the learner develops Christlike character and lifestyle.[5]

In the Christian view, learners discover truth rather than construct it. Truth is understood as being genuinely eternal and issuing forth

---

2. Newton, *Heart-Deep Teaching*, 107.
3. Tomlinson, *How to Differentiate Instruction*, 1.

4. Coley, *Teaching for Change*, 6.
5. Melick and Melick, *Teaching That Transforms*, 4.

from God himself as a form of either general or special revelation, not as a brand-new creation of student learners. In other words, truth is something God gives that learners come to perceive because God deliberately intended for them to do so. This understanding of truth, revelation, and illumination gives insight into the nature of Christian teaching. As John Milton Gregory puts it, "Teaching is arousing and using the pupil's mind to grasp the desired thought or to master the desired art. Learning is thinking into one's own understanding a new idea or truth or working into habit a new art or skill."[6]

Martha Elizabeth MacCullough refers to this educational dynamic as interactive learning—the process whereby learners take in new information from their surroundings and use prior categories, vocabulary, and understandings to begin to process, make sense of, and store the information for retrieval and use. MacCullough's educational method presents four basic elements in an interactive teaching model:

1. Engaging the mind: activating the student's mind toward the topic of study.
2. Providing new information: giving new information or creating a student activity that requires the student to get it from an outside source.
3. Creating student processing activities: assisting students with opportunities to make connections with prior learning, draw conclusions, or practice a new skill.
4. Assessing learning: using student work products that represent the

construction of their understanding as feedback on student achievement.[7]

Meaningful engagement that leads to transformational learning seldom occurs by accident, but it can be a significant part of each instructional episode through systematic planning. The discussion that follows includes five terms that are prominent in the contemporary literature on effective teaching, and the routine practice of these concepts leads to deeper learning according to current research. These five themes are schema of the learner, metacognitive analysis, formative assessment, reflective practice, and active learning techniques.

Schema of the Learner

The first responsibility of the teacher in facilitating learner engagement involves the schema (i.e., schemata) of the learner. Schema has to do with how students process and organize new content in order to establish a basic meaning of that information, and then how they develop a more sophisticated understanding of that knowledge as a whole. The success of learners in building a schema or framework of understanding directly relates to the quality of their educational experience. When teachers or learners fail in this task, students are often unable to develop a comprehensive, systematic, and accurate awareness of information. The result is student confusion, academic underperformance, and incomplete understanding of knowledge.

John Milton Gregory explains, "The lesson to be mastered must be explicable in the terms of truth already known by the learner—the unknown must be explained by means of the

---

6. Gregory, *Seven Laws of Teaching*, 5.

7. MacCullough, *By Design*, 100–101.

known."[8] So teachers must be able to successfully bridge new content to learners' existing knowledge for it to be assimilated into their preexisting frameworks.

Research on the concept of schema supports the instructional techniques used by Jesus thousands of years ago. A modern educator need only consider Jesus's "I am" sayings found in John's Gospel to recognize how Jesus connected with the general schema of disciples of all generations and cultures. All of humankind can grasp the temporal meanings of bread of life, the vine and the branches, and the door. From this basis of the concrete, Jesus connected to the eternal truth of his identity and his mission.

Two concerns arise related to students' use of new information and the construction of new concepts. Lorin Anderson and David Krathwohl point out that research reveals that many students do not integrate what they learn in classrooms with their lives outside of school. "Students often seem to acquire a great deal of factual knowledge, but they do not understand it at a deeper level or integrate or systematically organize it in disciplinary or useful ways."[9] This may be an issue of perceived irrelevance. It is not uncommon for most learners at one time or another to wonder whether the content they are learning is actually relevant to their lives. The perception that the content being communicated by the teacher has no personal value or practical application may undermine students' motivation to learn. For this reason, it is important that teachers work to counter this common educational problem by working to connect learning with life. This involves teachers thinking

deeply about how to help students make vital connections between theory and practice so that knowledge does not become detached from practice.

A second concern about the integration and application of knowledge is that students construct conceptions that "do not coincide with authentic aspects of reality or with well-accepted, normative conceptions of the information."[10] Stated another way, students can misunderstand the correct meaning of a concept and reach conclusions that are incorrect. Students unfamiliar with the new information can and often do misunderstand content. If and when this happens, learning has not taken place and the educational process has failed. Effective teachers must make sure that truth, as understood in the mind of the learner, corresponds to reality. When what is in the mind of the student matches what is real, actual, and true, learning has legitimately taken place, and meaningful use of that powerful knowledge can also take place.

Metacognitive Analysis

The second responsibility of the teacher in facilitating learner engagement involves what is called metacognitive analysis. Though it is a complex term, the concept is simple: it involves helping learners think about how they think. Consider this question: As a teacher, have you paused in your lesson preparation to consider how you personally learned the concepts you are preparing to teach? Taking the time to consider your own mental processing is known as metacognitive analysis. "*Metacognition* . . . refers to the processes learners use to plan, monitor, and evaluate

---

8. Gregory, *Seven Laws of Teaching*, 2.

9. L. Anderson and Krathwohl, *Taxonomy for Learning*, 42.

10. L. Anderson and Krathwohl, *Taxonomy for Learning*, 38.

their understanding and performance. Metacognition includes a critical awareness of both *one's action* of thinking and learning, and also of *oneself* as a thinker and learner."[11]

Ruth Schoenbach, Cynthia Greenleaf, Christine Cziko, and Lori Hurwitz give an excellent description of metacognitive conversation.

> The metacognitive conversation is carried on both internally, as teacher and students individually read and consider their own mental processes, and externally, as they talk about their reading processes, strategies, knowledge resources, and motivations and their interactions with and affective responses to tests. . . . Participants become consciously aware of their mental activity and are able to describe it and discuss it with others. Such conversation enables teachers to make their invisible cognitive activity visible and enables teachers and students to reflectively analyze and assess the impact of their thinking processes. A great deal of research in the past two decades has identified metacognition as key to deep learning and flexible use of knowledge and skills.[12]

Ken Bain agrees, noting that highly regarded professors possess the ability to think about their own thinking in a way that provides them with an understanding about how other people might learn. "They know what has to come first, and they can distinguish between foundational concepts and elaborations or illustrations of those ideas. They realize where people are likely to face difficulties developing their own comprehension, and they can use that understanding to simplify and clarify complex topics for others."[13] Thus, effec-

tive instruction requires more than planning opportunities for these types of reflections; master teachers must be able to anticipate how students should best approach new information and help them overcome potential hurdles.

Formative Assessment

The third responsibility of the teacher in facilitating learner engagement involves formative assessment. James Popham defines formative assessment as a "planned process in which assessment-elicited evidence of students' status is used by teachers to adjust their ongoing instructional procedures or by students to adjust their current learning tactics."[14] In other words, teachers are responsible to develop a plan to monitor the learning process and to make teaching adjustments as needed in order to ensure student learning.

Active learning often has the potential to reinforce formative assessment, if the teacher and the students take note of the achievement level of the class or individual students. Teachers ought to ask, "What is the quantity or quality of the responses I am getting from the learners?" Students should ask, "How do I need to adjust my personal study to perform at the level of expectation established by the teacher?" When both teacher and student take personal responsibility in the learning environment, authentic learning happens.

Popham emphasizes that the formative assessment activities are planned, not spontaneous or spur-of the-moment reactions to an unresponsive class. Robyn Jackson agrees with the importance of this approach: "Formative assessments are one of the most powerful ways

11. Chick, "Metacognition."
12. Schoenbach et al., *Reading for Understanding*, 25.
13. Bain, *What the Best College Teachers Do*, 25.

14. Popham, "Formative Assessment," 17.

to improve student achievement because they provide real-time feedback to you and your students on their progress toward the learning goals, and they help students see a direct relationship between how hard they work and what they learn."[15] Jackson suggests some activities called "dipsticking" that give quick feedback during instruction, including one-question quizzes, thumbs-up/thumbs-down, and unison responses.[16]

In their book *Classroom Assessment Techniques: A Handbook for College Teachers*, Thomas Angelo and Patricia Cross effectively summarize how such discussion of learning takes place.[17] They have found that as teachers use formative assessment techniques, they promote metacognition by teaching students to self-assess. This self-assessment takes place as the teacher provides guided practice in using these techniques and gives feedback on student responses. Angelo and Cross conclude, "Once again, as with active involvement and faculty-student interaction, there is strong evidence from education research that explicit instruction in metacognitive skills and strategies leads to more and better learning—especially when students learn a variety of discipline-specific skills and strategies."[18] In summary, when Christian teachers provide constant educational feedback to learners, students think more about how and what they are learning *while they are learning*, resulting in more effective educational experiences.

15. R. Jackson, *Never Work Harder than Your Students*, 131.

16. R. Jackson, *Never Work Harder than Your Students*, 132.

17. Angelo and Cross, *Classroom Assessment Techniques*, 373.

18. Angelo and Cross, *Classroom Assessment Techniques*, 373.

Reflective Practice

The fourth responsibility of the teacher in facilitating learner engagement involves reflective practice. Reflective practice has to do with the requirement that Christian teachers not only teach but also evaluate their teaching. James Stronge describes this practice as follows: "Effective teachers continually practice self-evaluation and self-critique as learning tools. Reflective teachers portray themselves as 'students of learning.' They are curious about the art and science of teaching and about themselves as effective teachers. They constantly improve lessons, think about how to reach particular children, and seek and try out new approaches in the classroom to better meet the needs of their learners."[19]

Reflective practice does not automatically occur in all Christian teaching settings. Sometimes teachers resist self-evaluation or the evaluation of their teaching by others. In many educational settings, reflective practice is a formal process ensured by regular teaching evaluations. As evaluations are given, teachers are often asked to reflect on their own teaching and to make adjustments, in addition to being held accountable for teaching improvement. In Christian ministry settings, self-evaluation is often informal and irregular, but such reflective practice should be a priority.

Reflective practice supports effective Christian education by preventing the teacher from repeating the same teaching errors year after year. Some experienced teachers have perfected the educational errors of a first-year teacher over a career of decades! Figure 9.1 depicts the process employed by educators who are committed to engaging their students in ways that lead to the construction of under-

19. Stronge, *Qualities of Effective Teachers*, 30.

Figure 9.1
Teaching and Learning Process That Leads to Engagement

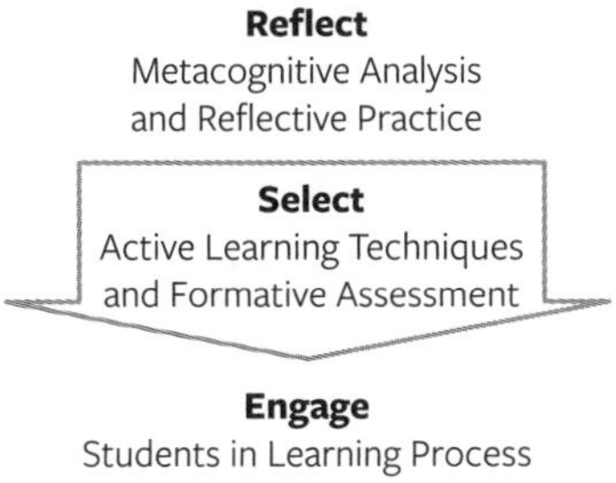

Reflect
Metacognitive Analysis
and Reflective Practice

Select
Active Learning Techniques
and Formative Assessment

Engage
Students in Learning Process

Coley, "Active Learning Techniques," 362.

standing, deep learning, and the continued and confident use of new knowledge.

These are concepts of extreme importance. It would be a grave mistake for students entering educational ministry leadership to ignore these essential educational issues. Would-be Christian teachers of all kinds must reflect on their own learning processes. It is also helpful for students in Christian education settings to interact with other students about their personal learning and teaching experiences.

Active Learning Techniques

The final responsibility of the teacher in facilitating learner engagement involves active learning techniques (sometimes abbreviated ALTs). Richard Felder and Rebecca Brent have done extraordinary research in the field of active learning at the undergraduate and graduate school levels. Active learning is "anything course-related that all students in a class session are called upon to do other than simply watching, listening and taking notes."[20] For various reasons and in certain situations, lecture-based teaching can be effective and

20. Felder, "Teaching Teachers to Teach," 177.

may be necessary. Even so, active learning should be integrated into the educational process even when lectures are employed.

Utilizing Active Learning

Adult learners are more learning-focused when they are actively involved in a lesson as opposed to simply being passive listeners. A teacher who merely asks, "Does anyone have any questions?" is not providing meaningful discussion or participation. Teachers must intentionally plan to include participation opportunities in their lesson plans. This is not to say that a lecture is an altogether inferior method to active learning. There needs to be a balance between teachers presenting information that they have researched prior to class and episodes in which the class members interact with the teacher, Scripture, and one another.

The teacher who is new to this approach might consider setting a goal of including two active learning techniques (ALTs) in each teaching setting, placing new ones at different places in the lesson each week. As both the teacher and the class become used to the new expectations, the number of ALTs could increase to three or four during each class time. There is a misconception that active learning requires a great deal of time, but these techniques can often be integrated quickly using minute changes. The teacher can transform a regular lecture into active learning simply by asking class members to show their responses to a question by giving a thumbs-up or a thumbs-down response. Active participation in learning can involve simple techniques such as this one, which involves as little as a few seconds, or more complex exercises that drive student reflection even deeper. Active learning simply requires Christian educators to have a commitment to utilizing these important educational principles consistently in their teaching.

Examples of Intrapersonal Active Learning Techniques

The following active learning techniques involve individual learners and represent an ever-increasing level of engagement, from thinking (and no movement) to highly involved engagement that includes physical movement around the classroom. Keep in mind that as the suggested activities increase the level of student engagement, the amount of instructional time needed to employ the techniques also increases.

Thinking

In this form of active learning, the teacher invites the students to imagine a specific situation or call to their mind's eye a picture or memory. The teacher does so in an effort to connect with a prior experience that may include an emotional connection. While no movement or conversation is required, the learners have the opportunity to become more engaged than simply listening passively. For example, the Bible study teacher can invite students to think back to a recent confrontation with someone that required them to exercise love. No verbal responses are offered, and the activity requires only a brief amount of time.

Reading

Interacting with printed text is crucial in almost every discipline but particularly in Bible study. Every class session or group meeting should include reading God's Word aloud,

silently, or both. Even so, sometimes students do not remain focused while reading a given passage. The technique of reading with a purpose is an approach that engages students, holds their attention, and assists them in constructing new insights. Here is how it works.

1. The teacher leads a brief discussion that is related to both the students' schema and a major point in the text they are about to read.
2. The teacher poses a question related to the text and asks the students to look for one or more specific ideas while the text is read aloud or silently.
3. The teacher asks students to present their responses to the question given in step 2. As the teacher gauges the students' level of understanding, the teacher can probe for deeper insights.
4. Depending on the readiness of the group, the teacher then assigns additional reading, usually longer than the first portion in step 2. Once again, the teacher poses one or more questions and asks students to think about them as they read.

Writing

Writing is an excellent place for metacognitive reflection and formative assessment. The one-minute paper method is a popular approach that is most often used at the conclusion of an instructional episode. The teacher requests that all students, using a note card or half sheet of paper, record what they believe to be the most important point(s) in the lesson. Another approach is called the muddiest point essay. In this technique, students are asked to describe a point in the lesson that was confusing to them and, if possible, to explain how the material or presentation was perplexing. Another approach is to encourage students to write random ideas or reactions on easel paper posted around the room. The comments need not be tightly organized or formatted a certain way. Thus, the technique is called graffiti board.[21]

Responding to a Poll

One of the quickest ALTs, polling, includes formative assessment. Using as little as ten seconds, the instructor can gauge audience awareness, opinion, or level of understanding. The teacher poses a brief question and asks the class members to respond in one of many ways, including the following:

- Raise your hand if you are familiar with . . .
- Show me thumbs-up or thumbs-down if you agree or disagree . . .
- Show a frequency by the number of fingers you hold up, with your fist being zero.
- Indicate your level of agreement with five being strongly agree, and so on . . .
- Select the correct multiple-choice answer: one finger is A, two fingers represent B.

Examples of Interpersonal Active Learning Techniques

Having reviewed some intrapersonal active learning techniques, let us move to methods that involve students engaging other learners through interpersonal activities. Like before,

21. Guillaume, Yopp, and Yopp, *50 Strategies for Active Teaching*, 81.

keep in mind that as the suggested activities increase students' levels of engagement, the amount of instructional time required to use these methods also increases. Each of the following techniques involves interactions among students in proximity to one another.

Think-Pair-Share

In this interpersonal active learning technique, the teacher begins by posing a problem and having the students work on it individually for a short time. Then the learners form pairs to reconcile and improve their solutions. Finally, the teacher calls on several individuals or pairs to share their responses. This takes a bit more time than a simple group activity, but it includes individual thinking in group settings and therefore leads to greater learning and collaboration.

Thinking-Aloud Pair Problem Solving

Thinking-aloud pair problem solving (TAPPS) is a powerful technique for helping students work together to understand a problem solution, case analysis, or text interpretation or translation. The students get into pairs and designate one member of each pair as the *explainer* and the other one as the *questioner*. The explainers explain the problem statement (or explore the first part of a case study history or interpret or translate the first paragraph of the text—whatever the problem-solving element happens to be) to their partners. The questioners ask questions when explanations are unclear or incomplete. After the allotted time, the teacher calls on several individuals to explain things. After the teacher gets a satisfactory explanation, the pairs reverse roles and continue with the next part of the problem solution, case analysis, or text interpretation or translation. In the end, students will understand the material to an extent that no current instructional technique can match.[22]

Movement-around-the-Room Methods

Numerous versions of ALTs have been created that involve learners moving throughout the educational space in order to facilitate learning. In tea party, the teacher thinks of several questions connected to that day's lesson to which students can respond without preparation. As students enter, the teacher hands each one a card that contains a question. After students think about a response, they find someone with a different color card (containing a different question). Each person reads their question and shares a response. Repeat as time permits.

Another movement-related method is the gallery walk. This technique follows a cooperative group activity during which students recorded their thoughts on easel paper. (This work product is usually significant and contains too many ideas to be presented orally in class.) All groups post their papers on the walls of the classroom, and students are given time to browse around the room and look at the postings, much the same as one does in an art gallery. If necessary, each group leaves behind one member to serve as a docent, or guide, to answer questions.

A similarly interpersonal active learning approach is the Post-it note technique. Each student responds to a question or a challenge by writing a response on a Post-it note and then puts their response in the appropriate category on the board.

22. Felder and Brent, "Active Learning," 3.

Active Learning Methodologies for Christian Teaching

The final section of this chapter on educational methodologies introduces eight additional active learning techniques for use in Christian teaching. Along with these methods are suggestions for how to use these techniques in nearly any Bible study setting. Keep in mind that one should not utilize all of these techniques in a single lesson plan but should integrate them throughout one's teaching repertoire.

The following examples are meant to demonstrate how the activities can occur at different times in a lesson. The reader is encouraged to explore *Creative Bible Teaching*, by Lawrence Richards and Gary Bredfeldt, which provides a helpful discussion on the placement of active learning techniques throughout one's lesson plan. Their pedagogical approach is known as Hook-Book-Look-Took.[23] Similarly, in *Teaching That Transforms*, Rich and Shera Melick describe the placement of forty-three ALTs at various points in a lesson plan.[24] Dan Lambert also presents an extensive list of ALTs in his text *Teaching That Makes a Difference* under the heading, "The World's Longest List of Teaching Methods."[25]

Warm-up activity (used as an advance organizer to motivate student learning). Prior to the lesson, the teacher prepares five statements that connect with the theme or topic of the session. As each member enters, they are given one of the statements and asked to consider a brief response. As others arrive, class members

23. Richards and Bredfeldt, *Creative Bible Teaching*, 188.
24. Melick and Melick, *Teaching That Transforms*, 294–327.
25. Lambert, *Teaching That Makes a Difference*, 149–65.

are encouraged to interact with other students who have a different statement. (The approach here is the tea party technique.)

Review (used to clarify and concretize learning). During any part of the lesson, the teacher simply asks a question such as, "How many of you encountered a situation this week that reminded you of the lesson theme from our last lesson? Raise your hand." (The approach here is the polling technique.)

Connect (used to connect new information with a student's existing knowledge). To activate this method, the teacher finds ways of connecting to the learner's schema or current framework of knowledge. For example, assume this week's lesson involves the concept of forgiveness. The teacher asks students to think for a few moments about a time they chose to forgive someone who had offended them. The teacher pauses for approximately thirty seconds as students process the issue. Then the teacher asks students to turn to the person next to them and briefly describe the decision they made. Allowing for student feedback takes approximately a minute. Finally, the teacher thanks students for participating and asks for volunteers to share with the entire class what they and their partner discussed. (The approach here is think-pair-share.)

Context (used to provide cultural or biblical information needed to understand the lesson). Context is necessary for learners to make sense of principles, facts, and truths across vast periods of time and across diverse cultures. Good teachers work to bridge the contextual gap between what happened in the biblical text and how that relates to today. The teacher mentions that the events discussed in the lesson influenced the culture and the political environment of the time. The teacher breaks the students into teams and asks them

to place the events discussed in the lesson in chronological order. For added fun and competition, the teacher could provide the team that finishes first a special treat or an opportunity that can later be shared by all. (The approach here is get it straight.)

Content (used to establish the focal point of the Bible study). It is crucial that learners comprehend and remember the content being taught. This is especially true with reading comprehension of the Scriptures. One way to solidify learning content is through the following example. If a Scripture passage from the Gospels is being used, the teacher asks the students to review the verses and to look for the identity and description of the group Jesus was addressing. Give them ample time to begin reading. The teacher asks the students to look up when they have made the proper identification so it is evident they are ready to answer. The students identify the biblical characters and discuss their findings. Then, knowing who the players are, the students continue to read, looking for information about how the people in the passage responded to Jesus's teachings. Again, they look up when they have an answer. As teachers use this method or similar approaches, students are guided through active learning to a more comprehensive understanding of the content being taught. (The approach here is reading with a purpose.)

Check for comprehension (used for formative assessment, to establish the degree to which students are learning). Active learning techniques can help teachers ascertain the degree to which learners comprehend what is being taught. An example of this method is the following. The teacher gives each student three cards and then asks some important questions about the lesson. For each question, the students hold up one of the three cards to indicate their level of understanding. Holding up the red card means, "Stop. I am not ready to move on." Raising the yellow card means, "I'm not sure. I need to examine this some more." Lifting the green card means, "I got the concept and I'm ready to move on." This feedback allows learner and teacher alike to assess the degree of comprehension that has taken place thus far in the lesson. (The approaches here are the stoplight technique and checking for levels of understanding.)

Confirm conviction (used to establish personal commitment to a biblical principle). One of the most important aspects of Christian teaching is affective learning. Affective learning involves ensuring that students develop the attitudes, values, and convictions scriptural truth requires. An example of this method is a continuation of the previous method, the comprehension check. The teacher asks students to reflect on the day's lesson and to identify the most important issue confronting their lives related to the study. Then using one of the three cards from the previous exercise, students write a statement about what they think the Holy Spirit is asking them to change and how they plan to respond. The teacher lets them know this issue is between them and the Lord and that they will not be asked to read their cards. They should seal their commitment to the Lord in private as the teacher leads a prayer of devotion. (The approach here is writing for understanding.)

Challenge for application (used to challenge learners to make a decision that will impact their behavior or choices). Christianity is nothing if it is not lived. Truth is meant to be applied, and a great part of Christian teaching is aimed toward life application. To utilize this active learning technique, the teacher reminds students that the Lord wants to impact people around them each and every day. Then the teacher asks the students to write down on Post-it notes what they can do this week as a response to the day's lesson. After they have written on one or more notes, the students can place their notes under one of the four categories the teacher has written on the board: home, church, work, or other. (The approach here is the Post-it note response.)

These active learning techniques are expressions of taking our responsibility as teachers seriously. We have been given a divine responsibility to teach, and with this duty comes a higher level of accountability to God (James 3:1). For this reason, it is incumbent on Christian teachers to develop a greater understanding of the teaching-learning process and to fan their teaching gift into flame, as the apostle Paul challenged the younger Timothy (2 Tim. 1:6). As this is done, the prospect and the goal of transformation in the lives of learners become a greater possibility.

Conclusion

This chapter began by presenting Jesus the Master Teacher as the archetype for effective Christian teaching. We bridged those timeless teaching principles of Jesus with educational theory and the significant role the teacher plays in the process of Christian education. We examined various personal, interpersonal, and intrapersonal methods designed to help learners become actively engaged in the educational process through techniques that help facilitate learner engagement. In all of this, we must recognize the supernatural effect of the Word of God and the indwelling of the Holy

Spirit, both of which serve as primary influences in the teaching-learning process.

As Christian educators, we carry out a mandate to engage disciples in the teaching-learning process. We do this by being aware of and using the most current and most effective instructional techniques available. In return, we have confidence that it is the Lord's work and will to help bring about total life transformation in his people through our teaching ministry. May we commit ourselves to the skillful development and exercise of our teaching gifts for the building of his kingdom and the magnification of his glory.

10

Transformational Teaching

GREGORY C. CARLSON

Why is there so little Christlikeness amid so much Christian teaching? Many factors may address this nagging, disconcerting question: the nature of people, ignorance of the substance of biblical thinking, no essential experience with Christ, novice or immature faith, misconceptions about the nature and work of God, sin impeding progress in holiness, or one of a number of other factors. It is little wonder the apostle Paul grieved, "My dear children, for whom I am again in the pains of childbirth until Christ is formed in you" (Gal. 4:19). To which we respond by wondering, how do those involved in educational ministry understand and participate in the process and goals of *Christian* education? Is there any difference in the way that followers of Christ perceive and perform in the educational endeavor? Can it be that all we are doing in church education is identical to the secular enterprise, only with Bible verses attached? Or is there a distinctiveness,

a persistent quality that produces not only an obvious work of God in a person but also life change toward Christlikeness?

Let's clarify some assumptions. By now, you have studied your way through the journey of theology (chap. 1), history (chap. 2), philosophy (chap. 3), psychology (chap. 4), practice (chap. 5), theories (chap. 6), taxonomies (chaps. 7 and 8), and methodologies and styles (chap. 9) of learning. The foundational tools and skills these chapters afford help us stake our claim to effective ministry. However, the real test is when we actually seek to *do* the activity of teaching. That ministry will most certainly require clarity about the means (process) and the ends (goals) of education.

This chapter focuses on teaching for transformation. First, the goals that should be pursued in "education that is Christian"[1] will be discussed. Then, the definition of what

1. LeBar, *Education That Is Christian*.

132

is meant by transformational teaching, especially within a Christian educational context, will be addressed. The teacher used of God for supernatural change needs to be rock solid about the gospel and to know that God is a partner in this endeavor. Finally, this chapter demonstrates goals within specific core elements of the teaching-learning process.

Goals of Transformational Teaching

Let us begin with the end in view. What is God's purpose in the life of an individual believer? The apostle Paul asserts that those who are "called according to his purpose" are "to be conformed to the image of his Son" (Rom. 8:28–29). God's intent is for a believer to bring glory to Christ by being like him. Likeness training, or the process of becoming like someone, assumes time, intimate relationship, imitation, appreciation, and repetition of action. When we see couples that have been together for many years, we often see similar actions, attitudes, and thought patterns. The parents of a college graduate were being complimented by a casual friend of their daughter: "You must be very proud of your daughter! She is just like you!" What the friend did not know was that the daughter was adopted. In the same way, our "adoption" (Eph. 1:5) results in us being like our Lord Jesus Christ.

All aspects of a person's life are in focus as Christian education engages the teaching-learning process. Walking into a learning situation, a pupil is not just a head to be filled or a heart to be touched. They are more than just a "Christian soldier" or a conduit for presenting the gospel. Each student is a person who is being formed into the nature of Christ: "He is the one we proclaim, admonishing and

teaching everyone with all wisdom, so that we may present everyone fully mature in Christ" (Col. 1:28).

In the preceding chapters of this text, authors shared helpful guidance about how an educator should think about the teaching-learning relationship. A focus on the goals of the educational methodologies described in chapter 9 follows.

Domain-Specific Goals

Goal setting has sometimes been criticized. Some teachers say that the Holy Spirit's work cannot be measured, so we should not set goals. Ronald Habermas and Klaus Issler assert, "Every teaching situation involves explicit and implicit aims. An aim represents a value statement—it prescribes what ought to be. In teaching that is Christian, the broader aim of every teacher is that students grow to full maturity in Christ."[2] The development of goals can shape, guide, clarify, and strengthen the teaching-learning process. Not only does it allow the teacher to express intentions, but it also invites the student to join in the mutual purposes of learning to live the life of Christ.

The Cognitive Domain

The realm of cognition, involving what are sometimes referred to as knowledge aims, should not be diminished in Christian teaching. Christian college or seminary professors consistently report a decline in knowledge of Scripture among incoming students. Some have the opinion that this erosion is due to professors deemphasizing cognitive learning

2. Habermas and Issler, *Teaching for Reconciliation*, 137.

and placing greater emphasis on the affective and behavioral domains. Despite this possible imbalance and neglect of content-based learning, it should be underscored that the fullness of a person's life cannot be just "knowing." The teaching of the Bible should be paramount, but "the goal of Christian teaching, while it certainly includes the communication of Bible facts, must extend beyond that. . . . Teaching is not merely giving out information; it involves guiding others into finding the truth for themselves."[3] A former Christian college president was fond of saying, "We're not educating a head on a stick!"[4] What he meant is that we should see our students as multidimensional, needing care for all aspects of life—not just knowing, but moving toward obedience.

Others tell us that we need to worry only about getting people to know the Bible. Often in children's ministry settings, a leader will recite, "My word . . . will not return to me empty" (Isa. 55:11). Turning the discussion to their pupils, the teacher asks, "Does knowledge guarantee spiritual growth?" Just as a seed needs optimal soil to flourish, so a person needs a full cultivation of aspects of life to grow in faith. If knowledge is all that is necessary for godly living, then university towns would be the most holy and spiritual places on earth! We smile, because we know that "knowledge puffs up while love builds up" (1 Cor. 8:1).

On the other hand, it cannot be emphasized enough how important knowing the Bible is. Through the Scriptures, one comes to know the truth of Christ (John 5:39), sanctification in truth (John 17:17), cleansing

holiness (Eph. 5:26), salvation's wisdom (2 Tim. 3:15), the "teaching, rebuking, correcting and training in righteousness" that equip the believer for "every good work" (2 Tim. 3:16–17), and growth in salvation (1 Pet. 2:2). In other words, the Scriptures are essential to our start and growth in faith. "Faith comes from hearing the message, and the message is heard through the word about Christ" (Rom. 10:17).

What is the key aim for this dimension of a person's life? To believe in Christ as Lord and Savior, growing in faith, being obedient to what is learned, showing love for him. "And this is love: that we walk in obedience to his commands" (2 John 6). A Christian teacher could tease the class, "You people are educated *way beyond* your obedience! And you want to know more!" Goals in this domain should promote knowledge that leads to faith and obedience.

The Affective Domain

Should our educational goals be geared toward change in the domain of emotions, attitudes, and passions? Yes. Unfortunately, "while research is increasingly demonstrating that emotion is not the enemy of reason . . . relatively few scholars and practitioners . . . regard emotion as integral to the meaning-making process."[5] Oxford moral educator John Wilson suggested that a large part of religious education should be "education of the emotions." He proposed that religious education has three options: teaching *about* religion, which avoids indoctrination but does not necessarily address the heart; teaching *into* religion, which is persuading and too indoctrinating; and educating *in* re-

---

3. Zuck, *Teaching with Spiritual Power*, 150.

4. Gregory Waybright, personal conversation, May 2007.

5. Dirkx, "Engaging Emotions in Adult Learning," 16.

ligion, which in his view includes attitudes and emotions as central to faith.[6] The transformational teacher builds a relationship with the student. A repeated refrain at a Christian college is "Ministry is best done in the context of relationship!" These relationships mirror Paul's close ties with the church in Thessalonica: "You are witnesses, and so is God, of how holy, righteous and blameless we were among you who believed. For you know that we dealt with each of you as a father deals with his own children, encouraging, comforting and urging you to live lives worthy of God, who calls you into his kingdom and glory" (1 Thess. 2:10–12).

The Behavioral Domain

In one sense, all observable goal accomplishments may be said to be behavioral. How does one know about spiritual progress except through confirming conversation? How do we know if someone is obeying the Lord unless we see it lived out? Good intentions too often result in nothing more than a salve for delayed obedience. The apostle John reminds us that our claims do not hold up to truth if our lives disobey the commands of Scripture (1 John 1:6–10). Demonstrating our relationship with God in observable actions so that people will "see [our] good deeds and glorify [our] Father in heaven" (Matt. 5:16) is the thrust of Jesus's teaching.

But behavioral goals must not be the only objectives in view in our teaching. Gary Newton cautions, "Behavioral objectives must never be isolated from the other dimensions of the person that also influence the heart to change. Rather, they need to be integrated

with objectives from these other dimensions to produce a change in heart."[7]

The Spiritual Domain

The spiritual aspect of a person's life should also be included when setting goals; however, this presents a common tension for the Christian teacher. Gary Parrett and S. Steve Kang have evaluated the approaches prominent among secular educators: "Perhaps these theories may help us understand certain dimensions of how Christians learn, grow and experience certain aspects of a faith. Yet they are all fundamentally limited in that these theories cannot begin to describe the spiritual dimension of learners."[8]

Scholars such as Dallas Willard, Robert Mulholland, and Kenneth Boa have opened evangelical educators to a new understanding of teaching for spiritual impact. Often the terms *spiritual formation* and *transformational teaching* are interchanged. The domains discussed above are not in conflict with the growth of a Christian. Viewing a person from a holistic viewpoint, we want to avoid what David Dockery calls "a false dichotomy between the life of the mind and the life of faith."[9]

The Transformational Goal of Teaching

What is the transformational goal of teaching? The life of Christ should permeate and energize all the thinking, attitudes, decisions, and actions of a believer. This Christ-life is imputed to a believer when regeneration occurs and prompts the basis of growth: dead to sin, alive in Christ (Rom. 6:2, 8). Theologian

---

6. John Wilson, *Education in Religion and the Emotions*, 161.

7. Newton, *Heart-Deep Teaching*, 12.
8. Parrett and Kang, *Teaching the Faith*, 237.
9. Dockery, *Renewing Minds*, 15.

Millard Erickson expressed it this way: "It is as if, with respect to one's spiritual status, a new entity has come into being. It is as if Christ and I have been married, or have merged to form a new corporation. Thus, the imputation of his righteousness is not so much a matter of transferring something from one person to another, as it is a matter of bringing the two together."[10] This is not just an example to follow; it is a life to live! "Christ in you, the hope of glory" is how the apostle Paul expressed it (Col. 1:27). This Christ-life, a transformed life, involves knowing the Lord through his Word. It impacts and changes patterns of thinking, feeling, and action. There is a response to what is known.

Some cautions may be in order. We can know sound doctrine (as do demons [James 2:19]) and still not have the life of Christ. We can have much character and virtue (Matt. 19:20) or zeal for God (Rom. 10:2) and still not have the life of Christ. We can do great service in Christ's name (Matt. 7:22–23) and still not have the life of Christ. How is this life grasped? By faith! The life of Christ is received by faith (John 1:12). By faith, we grow in Christ (Col. 2:6–7). Faith in Christ causes us to overcome (1 John 5:4).

Defining Transformational Teaching

Transformational *teaching* must be based on transformational *learning*. To say that one has taught well, with no one having learned, is presumptuous and ridiculous. The story is told of a professor who stepped out of his classroom while showing a video of the lesson and upon returning early found just a few

students and several recorders in the room. Information was being transferred (albeit in a tenuous manner), but learning was not happening. The interaction was not there.

Can we be so bold as to say that teaching doesn't happen until learning occurs? The pioneering Christian educator and publisher Henrietta Mears stated, "A teacher has not taught a lesson until his pupil has learned it."[11] Howard Hendricks, longtime seminary professor and leadership/teaching expert, said, "Teaching is causing. Causing what? Causing people to learn."[12] A young pastor was driving home with his spouse after a Sunday morning service. Looking for some encouragement and affirmation, he asked, "What did you think of the sermon?" His wife responded, "We'll see if our people obey!" The emphasis of transformational teaching is not the performance of the teacher; it is the response of the learner. Teaching requires cognizance of the change happening in the life of the student. So what is learning?

Teaching as Change

Learning is essentially a means for *change*. "Change, then, is imbedded in the very nature of the created universe. It will always be a part of the human experience."[13] In defining Christian education, Dennis Williams, longtime Christian education professor and dean, stated, "Change is the goal and the change is defined as conformity to the image of Christ."[14] To remain the same after teaching, with no strengthening, adaptation, revision, or creation of a new thought, attitude, or

10. Erickson, *Christian Theology*, 818.

11. Mears, *431 Quotes*, 41.
12. Hendricks, *Teaching to Change Lives*, 122.
13. Richards, *Expository Dictionary of Bible Words*, 155.
14. Dennis Williams, "Christian Education," 132.

behavior, seems to be an exercise in busywork. Learning can be incremental, and associations that create change may take more time than classroom or conversations allow, but if there is no ultimate difference, can it be said that *learning* has occurred? "Learning is the process through which experience causes permanent change in knowledge or behavior."[15] But learning for a Christ follower should be more than just a change of behavior or cognition. Christian educators Klaus Issler and Ronald Habermas developed a basic and yet inclusive definition: "Learning for Christians is change that is facilitated through deliberate or incidental experience, under the supervision of the Holy Spirit, in which they acquire and regularly integrate developmentally appropriate knowledge, attitudes, values, emotions, skills, habits, and dispositions into an increasingly Christ-like life."[16] Note the values expressed in this definition. Experiential learning under the guidance of the Holy Spirit with integrative development toward Christlikeness—that is transformative teaching!

The change that happens within an individual must involve more than just *knowing* and *showing*, as significant as these dimensions are. Two experienced professors of education defined transformative teaching in this way: "an act of teaching designed to change the learner academically, socially, and spiritually."[17] L. Ted Johnson, Christian education director for an evangelical denomination in years past, stated, "Change is modification. It is either adding or subtracting something that alters the present. Such alteration may affect structure and organization, methods or behavior. When change

affecting behavior is introduced, it is directed either at the knowledge level (changing what people know), or at the feeling level (changing attitudes), or at the action level (changing the way people respond or behave)."[18] This change must be comprehensive. The descriptions of a person's cognitive, affective, and behavioral dimensions are good and necessary. But we, as educators, can err by dissecting the person. And people must be seen as having a *spiritual* core or heart.

Discipleship professor Gary Newton described heart, spirit, and will as component aspects of the same entity.[19] Each term allows a specific window into the nature of the learner. We should be teaching in accordance with the perspective of our Lord Jesus, who commanded, "Love the Lord your God with all your heart and with all your soul and with all your mind and with all your strength" (Mark 12:30). Jesus added *mind* to the Old Testament verse. Leaving out the mind from Christian education is certainly a diminishing of the potential of teaching and learning.

Teaching for Meaning

Learning is also *meaningful* change. Jack Mezirow, one of the major proponents of transformative education, defined the learning process as "the extension of our ability to make explicit, schematize (make an association within a frame of reference), appropriate (accept an interpretation as our own), remember (call upon an earlier interpretation), validate (establish the truth, justification, appropriateness, or authenticity of what is asserted), and act upon (decide, change an attitude toward, modify a perspective on, or

15. Woolfolk, *Educational Psychology* (2001), 200.
16. Issler and Habermas, *How We Learn*, 23.
17. Rosebrough and Leverett, *Transformational Teaching*, Kindle location 235.

18. Johnson, *Teaching Church*, 78.
19. Newton, *Heart-Deep Teaching*, 25.

perform) some aspect of our engagement with the environment, other persons, or ourselves."[20] Note that meaning may be derived from the physical environment, from relationships with other people, or even from internal change of thought or attitude. Schemata then can be extended, strengthened, or diminished, but rarely are they created out of nothing. These structured patterns (schemata) of thinking, feeling, skill, and response are guides to organizing and using vast amounts of information[21] to make sense of the changes in our environment, others, and ourselves.

In a milieu characterized by social media, ease of travel, and communication, we would expect to have an increasing connection to meaning. However, "we are in danger of consuming huge amounts of information divorced from purpose and meaning. 'Why' and 'because' are often casualties in the quest for an education to match the perception and challenges of this time."[22] Christian educators must rely on the work of the Holy Spirit and creatively integrate process and purpose.

A closer look at the need for teaching for meaning and its connection to life change may be helpful. Using Mezirow's terms *engagement* and *interpretation*, we can outline a spectrum of change (or the lack thereof). To one extreme, there is no meaning and no change in the educational endeavor (i.e., no engagement or interpretation is possible). This phenomenon may be observed in an early morning college classroom the day after a paper or project is due. Interaction is nonexistent, and presentation is difficult. Both teacher and student seem to be confused by what is transpiring.

Additionally, teachers can observe that there is change without meaning; there is much activity but not significance. Students may be exhausted. Teachers may be fatigued. Resources are drained. It is difficult to maintain motivation, for the adjustments of life seem out of kilter with anything usable for the future, meaningful in the present, or memorable from the past. Dawson Trotman, founder of the Navigators ministry, warned that being busy would curtail the actual discipleship process.[23]

Neither of these polar plateaus is in the "learning zone," which corresponds to Lev Vygotsky's "zone of proximal development."[24] Maintenance of the status quo might seem to be a virtue for some, but it will eventually reveal resistance to change. Recent changes in developmental theory have "challenged Christian educators to exit the trap of transmissive education that lends itself to a reductionist rationalized faith and a false bifurcation between content and method."[25]

Where does maximum learning happen? Where we attribute "old meaning to a new experience."[26] An example of this is when a professor asks about a ministry internship, "How has what you have learned in class helped you in your ministry to youth?" Too many times new opportunities for learning do not have meaning because of little reflection or thinking. However, "the transformation of meaning perspective" almost always involves

20. Mezirow, *Transformative Dimensions of Adult Learning*, 11.

21. Woolfolk, *Educational Psychology* (2001), 253.

22. Rosebrough and Leverett, *Transformational Teaching*, Kindle location 30–31.

23. Trotman, *Born to Reproduce*, 12.

24. Woolfolk, *Educational Psychology* (2001), 50.

25. Espinoza and Johnson-Miller, "Catechesis, Developmental Theory, and a Fresh Vision," 11.

26. Mezirow, *Transformative Dimensions of Adult Learning*, 11.

critical reflection on the foundation of expectations[27] and adjustments in thinking, attitude, response, and behavior.

In other situations, old experiences can have new interpretations. This becomes obvious when we share the gospel with others. When the Holy Spirit makes a person a new creation (2 Cor. 5:17), they often come back saying, "*Now* I understand this verse. Before, it didn't make sense." This is an example of creating new expectations and perspectives from familiar events, activities, habits, and thinking of the past.

Defining Teaching as Transformation

With the rise of adult educational theories during the last half of the twentieth century came a renewed interest in learning designs that emphasized a more holistic approach.[28] However, the "self-directed" aspect did not seem to sufficiently answer the totality of learning.

Transformational teaching began to emphasize a different perspective than the behavioral or information-processing models of education. Jack Mezirow and associates framed the transformative learning theory during the last few decades of the twentieth century. He defined transformational learning as the challenging of assumptions that are found to be "distorting, inauthentic, or otherwise invalid" and then the development of new schemes to renovate those perspectives.[29] Is this not the meaning of "the renewing of your mind" of

Romans 12:2? New Testament scholar W. E. Vine defined renewing as "the adjustment of the moral and spiritual vision and thinking to the mind of God, which is designed to have a transforming effect upon the life."[30]

The transformative view of learning, then, in turn changes how one goes about teaching. It changes how one views the teacher's role and that of the learning group: "Informational teaching implies that the teacher holds all the knowledge and students are empty vessels to be filled. Transformational teaching implies that a fundamental change takes place among the members of a learning community."[31]

Perhaps the most contrasting turn for the transformational teacher is the view of the scope of the student. "Transformative learning is best facilitated through engaging multiple dimensions of being, including the rational, affective, spiritual, imaginative, somatic, and sociocultural domains through relevant content and experiences."[32]

Yet based on the underpinnings of most transformative theorists, Rick and Shera Melick highlight three cautions that Christians should consider.

(1) Transformative theorists generally believe that all truth and knowledge is relative. We, as Christians, understand that our lives are based on the absolute truth of Jesus Christ and Scripture. (2) Most transformative theorists put great value on inclusiveness and acceptance. The moral aspects of right and wrong are less significant. While Christians believe in loving and accepting others, we cannot accept the sin of others. That is,

27. Mezirow, *Transformative Dimensions of Adult Learning*, 167.
28. See, for example, Knowles, *Modern Practice of Adult Education*, 236–39.
29. Mezirow, *Transformative Dimensions of Adult Learning*, 6.

30. Vine, *Expository Dictionary of New Testament Words*, 3:279.
31. Rosebrough and Leverett, *Transformational Teaching*, Kindle location 440–41.
32. Tolliver and Tisdell, "Engaging Spirituality," 38.

we love the person but not always their ideas and actions. . . . (3) Transformative theorists generally believe that a major purpose of dialogue is to merge ideas into the greater truth. Students are to dialogue in order to morph their personal understanding of truth with that of others. The Christian engages in dialogue, hoping to influence others through a clear understanding of Scripture, positive Christian experience, and genuine compassion for all in need. Christians may learn significantly through dialogue, but in the end, commitment to the Lordship of Jesus Christ and the authority of the Bible shape our understanding of truth. We cannot negotiate on those points.[33]

The Gospel as Central in Transformation

The gospel, the good news of Jesus Christ, is central to the transformation of people. It is the power for transforming a believer. Believing in the gospel results in salvation (Rom. 1:16). Salvation can be understood from the New Testament in three ways: (1) justification, God's imputing of our sin to his Son and crediting Christ's righteousness to our account (Eph. 1:13–14); (2) sanctification, growth in the life of Christ that results in comprehending (grasping) sound doctrine and causes a believer to live out the life of Christ (2 Thess. 2:13–14); and (3) glorification, the bringing of ultimate glory to Christ when believers will experience the fullness of life in Christ (Heb. 9:28). Paul was careful to present the essence of the gospel to the Corinthians: "By this gospel you are saved. . . . For what I received I passed on to you as of first importance: that Christ died for our sins according to the Scriptures,

that he was buried, that he was raised on the third day according to the Scriptures" (1 Cor. 15:2–4). J. I. Packer summarized the gospel in three words: "God saves sinners!"[34] The gospel then renovates all the goals of every domain of education.

The Gospel as Holistically Transforming

The Cognitive Domain

The gospel informs and enlarges the cognitive area of a student's thinking. William Lane Craig challenges us, "It is part of the task of Christian academics to help create and sustain a cultural milieu in which the gospel can be heard as an intellectually viable option for thinking men and women."[35] Knowing the gospel shows that one has a *reasonable* faith.

The Affective Domain

The gospel impacts one's way of life. It is the basis of one's relationship with God (vertical) and the impetus of one's relationship with other believers (horizontal). "When we lean toward the vertical *or* horizontal, we disintegrate discipleship. When integration is lacking, disciples easily become disillusioned and their character distorted."[36] Understanding the gospel results in an *ardent* faith. Such a faith produces people with godly convictions, affections, attitudes, and values.

The Behavioral Domain

The gospel motivates and guides the actions of a believer. The apostle Paul stated that sinful lifestyles, and "whatever else is contrary

33. Melick and Melick, *Teaching That Transforms*, 145–46.

34. As quoted in Parrett and Kang, *Teaching the Faith*, 103.
35. Craig, "Concluding Thoughts," 178.
36. Dodson, *Gospel-Centered Discipleship*, 46.

to the sound doctrine," should not be a part of a believer's life; they do not "conform" to the gospel (1 Tim. 1:10–11). Robert Coleman, noted evangelist and educator, asked, "Why are so many professed Christians today stunted in their growth and ineffectual in their witness? . . . Is it not because among the clergy and laity alike there is a general indifference to the commands of God, or at least, a kind of contented complacency with mediocrity? . . . It would appear that the teachings of Christ upon self-denial and dedication have been replaced by a sort of respectable 'do-as-you-please' philosophy of expediency."[37] The gospel supposes an *obedient* faith.

The Gospel in Transformative Teaching

"All Christian education should evangelize, but conversely, evangelism can bear lasting fruit only when sustained by good Christian education."[38] The comments of Catholic educator Thomas Groome highlight how the gospel permeates and propels teaching that transforms. It is essential that Christian ministers include evangelism in the goals of their activity. A frustrated children's ministry leader approached her pastor. "We have a well-run club! Why aren't kids coming to know Christ as their Savior?" After evaluation, two ingredients were added to the patterns of the ministry: prayer for the Holy Spirit to reach youth and an intentional, regular presentation of the gospel in the teaching ministry. As a result, the same children's ministry participants responded significantly to the claims of Christ.

The case could be established that evangelism is one of the first priorities in bridging the span between the sound doctrine of Scripture and the effective practice of ministry. However, Timothy Keller developed a model that outlines a middle layer of experience that he calls "theological vision." Between the "doctrinal foundation—what to believe" and the "ministry expression—what to do" is "a faithful restatement of the gospel with rich implications for life, ministry, and mission in a type of culture at a moment in history."[39] The ministry vision (middle layer) so described is too often missing in the transformative education in our churches.

The Holy Spirit in Transformation

A chapter on education that transforms would be remiss if it did not discuss the dynamic ministry of the Holy Spirit. The Holy Spirit's ministry is not an added attachment, neither to his character nor to our mutual process of teaching. The Holy Spirit *is* a teacher. This teaching aspect of his ministry—perhaps the *entirety* of his ministry—is frequently neglected, diminished, or even unwanted.

The Holy Spirit is qualified to be the Master Teacher because he is God. As Teacher, the Holy Spirit has mastery over every aspect of the transformative teaching process. Regarding content, the Holy Spirit who inspired the Bible also interprets it.[40] Teacher and student are not set adrift in a sea of relativity but are drawn toward truth. This shapes the foundation and the practice of the educational experience. The Lord Jesus Christ is the focus and the image that the Spirit illuminates. Regarding learners, the Holy Spirit regenerates

37. Coleman, *Master Plan of Evangelism*, 59–60.
38. Groome, foreword to *Christian Education as Evangelism*, xii.

39. Keller, *Center Church*, 20.
40. Quoting Peter Stephens in Thiselton, *Holy Spirit*, 265.

believers (Titus 3:5) and also transforms them (2 Cor. 3:18) through sanctification. The Holy Spirit "will no longer let [a believer] continue in sin comfortably"[41] and moves each one to increasing conformity to Christ. Regarding teachers, any human teacher is a junior assistant to the Holy Spirit. The Spirit bestows the gift of teaching (1 Cor. 12:4, 28) and guides teaching (John 16:13). He is the one who empowers for love (Rom. 5:5), witness (Acts 4:31), prayer (Rom. 8:26), and service (1 Cor. 12:4–5). Roy Zuck asserted, "The work of God's Spirit in the lives of regenerate teachers is needed so that they may be effective instruments in the hands of God. God's servants must be properly adjusted to the Spirit of God. The powerless, ineffective, carnal living of many believers attests to the fact that being rightly related to Christ (salvation) does not necessarily mean being rightly related to the Holy Spirit (in spirituality)."[42]

Regarding the learning environment, the Holy Spirit does his work in the life of a believer. Therefore, wherever a believer lives is where the life of Christ may be lived. "I have been crucified with Christ and I no longer live, but Christ lives in me. The life I now live in the body, I live by faith in the Son of God, who loved me and gave himself for me" (Gal. 2:20). "Remember . . . that the Holy Spirit affects not only the teacher and the learner, but also the subject matter and the environment. His power permeates truth wherever it is found."[43] Regarding methodology, the educational experience may be poised and polished, but if the Holy Spirit is not present, it is not Christian education. The Holy Spirit is essential for education to transform people into the image of Christ. Regarding learning goals, the Holy Spirit is divinely able to move a believer toward Christlikeness, the ultimate goal of transformative education that is Christian. Subsidiary goals in each of the domains will most certainly be related to teaching from the Scriptures, and as Jesus told the Pharisees, "These are the very Scriptures that testify about me" (John 5:39).

Sample Goals for Transformative Teaching

This section provides examples of instructional goals that could be used in a teaching ministry. Below, the key elements of education (God, humans, and content) are reviewed. Longtime Southern Baptist educator Findley Edge described a well-crafted teaching aim: "(1) brief enough to be remembered, (2) clear enough to be written down, and (3) specific enough to be attainable."[44] The following brief, clear, and specific sample goals may be refined and adjusted for your own teaching. Outcomes are labeled by domain: cognitive (C), affective (A), and behavioral (B).

Teaching Outcomes in Reference to God

"What comes into our minds when we think about God is the most important thing about us."[45] To miss a deep, life-changing relationship *with* God when studying *about* him would be tragic. Sample outcomes: (C) Each person will develop a description of the changes that occur when one becomes a child of God. (A) Each person will explain how they

---

41. Donald Williams, *Person and Work of the Holy Spirit*, 73.

42. Zuck, *Teaching with Spiritual Power*, 16.

43. Gangel, "What Christian Education Is," 20.

44. Edge, *Teaching for Results*, 51–52.

45. Tozer, *Knowledge of the Holy*, 7.

are led to honor, appreciate, and praise the Lord God for one of his characteristics or actions, given a list of the attributes of God and time to examine the list using the Scriptures. (B) Each person will assess one aspect of their relationship with God that they could share with a friend or relative this next week and devise a plan to do so.

Teaching Outcomes in Reference to Humans

How should one view the actions and the nature of a student in an education that is transformative? "Transformative learning theory is the student-centered negotiation of new understanding and changing circumstances."[46] It is important to keep the students in view as we teach. An exegesis of the text should be complemented with an "exegesis of the student." Sample outcomes: (C) Each teacher (teacher in training) will define *imago Dei* and the impact of sin and the fall on our lives. (A) Each teacher will evaluate the joys and the struggles they are experiencing in their walk with Christ and how those joys and struggles are evidenced in the lives of their students. (B) Each teacher will record five prayer needs from group members so that they can use them in their personal time with God this next week.

Teaching Outcomes in Reference to Content

The subject matter of transformative education must focus on solid truth and therefore point toward the Bible. "The Bible is not just information about God communicated in revelation, but is God revealing Himself through information about Himself."[47] Sample outcomes: (C) Each student will compare and contrast the Bible's portrayal of truth with a current model of education. (A) Each student will outline a personally developed profile of how the Bible can guide one's own thinking about truth. (B) Each student will memorize one verse about the place of the Scriptures in life and ministry and share that application with at least one other person this next week.

Conclusion

Teaching, if it is about anything, is about transformation. Teaching is not an end in itself. It is a purposeful activity that must drive learners toward life change in either the cognitive, affective, or behavioral domain. In other words, they should know God's Word, love God's Word, and live God's Word. What's more, transformed learners know Christ, love Christ, live for Christ, and love others. This is the essence of the Great Commandment. When asked to summarize what God really expected of his people, Jesus replied, "'Love the Lord your God with all your heart and with all your soul and with all your mind.' This is the first and greatest commandment. And the second is like it: 'Love your neighbor as yourself.' All the Law and the Prophets hang on these two commandments" (Matt. 22:37–40).

---

46. Melick and Melick, *Teaching That Transforms*, 129.

47. Gannett, "Teaching for Learning," 107.

EDUCATIONAL ADMINISTRATION

A major focus of Christian education is the study of leadership and, more broadly, the field of administration. Indeed, administration and leadership are, at last, inseparable because they have mirror functions required of those given the authority and the responsibility to oversee organizations. Administration and leadership work synchronously and are intrinsically linked in their mutual goal of serving people by advancing the mission of any organization. Though both terms are used here in part 3, the word *administration* is used as an umbrella term that includes leadership and that applies to the many areas of competency needed to fulfill the function of ministry oversight. Each of the five chapters in this part discusses an essential component of the broad skill set needed to lead twenty-first-century ministry.

The Nature of Administration

The word *administer* comes from the Greek word *kubernēsis* (1 Cor. 12:28), which is a term used in the navigation of ships and means "steering."[1] Steering has to do with piloting or governing a large vehicle and those it carries to their destination. Similarly, Christian educators equip ministers with the skills to lead organizations to fulfill their God-given mission.

In addition to the historical use of the Greek word in Scripture, the term's more recent usage is telling. As the word *administer* developed from Latin, to French, to current English use, it consistently referred to the act of ministering.[2] This concept relates closely to the biblical model of leadership. Jesus described the essence of Christian leadership as nothing other than service when he said, "Anyone who wants to be first must be the very last, and the servant of all" (Mark 9:35). The hallmark of Christian ministry leadership is rooted in servanthood, as is administration. In these ways, administration and leadership are united.

1. "Kubernēsis."
2. "Administer."

The connection between education and administrative leadership is equally intimate. Both are multidisciplinary fields that share origins in theology, the social sciences, and the humanities. For a Christian, to study administration, leadership, or education is to be exposed to content from God's Word as well as philosophy and history (humanities), anthropology, psychology, and sociology (social sciences). Together, these merge to form today's applied disciplines of management and education.

The Importance of Administration

In the 1940s, leadership began to be explored as an educational field of study.[3] This endeavor began with Ohio State University, followed by the University of Michigan,[4] then MIT.[5] In time, Christian institutions introduced courses and then degrees in both administration and leadership. Today, essentially all Christian colleges, universities, and seminaries have administration courses, with many devoting entire academic programs to the study of leadership.

Far from being falsely categorized as *secular* enterprises, administration and leadership are intrinsically biblical in nature. God gave us both, and excellence in both is needed in the advancement of the kingdom of God and of local church congregations, which happen to be part and parcel of the largest and oldest organization in the history of the world—the church of the living God. It is no surprise, then, that God gave the church three spiritual gifts directly tied to this task: the gift of teaching, which is a primary function of Christian education (1 Cor. 12:28); the gift of administration (v. 28), which is a primary function of organizational management; and the gift of leadership (Rom. 12:8), which is a primary function of organizational oversight.

A Call of Commitment to Administration

As Christian educators, we are responsible for integrating the important and necessary principles of administration with a thoroughgoing biblical perspective in order to lead people and manage organizations in the most effective, God-honoring ways. This part seeks to do just that. Each chapter provides content essential to Christian educators regardless of the type of parachurch or local church role they hold: organizational administration, discipleship, mobilizing volunteers, digital learning, and executive leadership. You are invited to read and think deeply about these subjects and their related issues as leaders in the field mentor you toward more effective ministry.

3. Khurana, *From Higher Aims to Hired Hands*, 354.
4. Boje, "Isles Leadership."
5. McGregor, "Human Side of Enterprise."

11

Organizational Administration

JAMES RILEY ESTEP JR.

s administration a ministry? Isn't it just a necessary evil? Surely filing systems, bureaucracy, and tedious policy and procedure manuals must be destined to impede the ministry of the church. In reality, administration both is essential to ministry and *is* ministry. It is the appropriate combination of leadership and management required to fulfill an organization's vision for ministry. This chapter addresses two principal themes: (1) the nature and practice of Christian leadership in organizational administration and (2) the relationship between administrative functions and the effectiveness of Christian ministry. Ultimately, effective administration positions the church to fulfill its calling as God's people.

Christian Educators as Administrators

Christian educators must be both leaders and managers, not one or the other. Leaders per-petually ask, "What's next?" They are future-focused, change-oriented, and mission-driven. Effectiveness is their measure for success ("How well are we fulfilling our mission?"). We think of leaders in Scripture as those who were on the move, leading God's people toward new destinations or making positive, progressive changes. Leaders are those out in front of the crowd, forward-thinking, seeing what lies ahead before others do, and calling others to follow them. As Leighton Ford observed, "Leadership always involves change, moving people from one point to another, from the old way of doing things to the new, from the security in the past to the insecurity in the future."[1] The Old Testament speaks of the sons of Issachar as "men who understood the times and knew what Israel should do" (1 Chron. 12:32), giving an abbreviated portrait of leadership. Moses, Joshua, David,

1. Ford, *Transformational Leadership*, 251.

Solomon, Hezekiah, Ezra, Nehemiah, Peter, Paul, and certainly Jesus were leaders of God's people.

Managers are different from leaders. Focusing on both present and past, they care about structure, control, and organization. Managers gauge success by efficiency ("Are we using our resources responsibly?"). Managers attend to operational items, working within the institutional framework, accepting its limitations. In contrast, leaders think outside the box, renewing an organization's vision, structure, and strategy; removing existing institutional limitations; and challenging its assumptions. Warren Bennis captured the notion best when he wrote, "Leaders are people who do the right thing; managers are people who do things right."[2]

The qualities of both leaders and managers are essential for administration, since the qualities of one without the qualities of the other usually result in failure. Leaders are visionaries and dreamers, but those with their heads in the clouds can trip over the stone at their feet. Similarly, managers can be so attentive to the specific details of a project or a plan that they fail to lift up their heads and proceed to run into a wall, failing to see the big picture. Effective administration requires leadership *and* management. Without management, administrators are just idealists, espousing lofty but unrealized principles. Without leadership, managers are just bookkeepers and chroniclers drifting aimlessly into the future. Administration requires both in the appropriate measure to fulfill God's mission for the church.[3] Christian education needs both visionaries and bean counters.

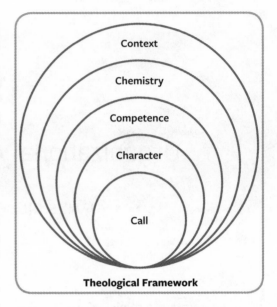

Figure 11.1
Five Key Elements of Leadership

Context

Chemistry

Competence

Character

Call

Theological Framework

Toward a Christian Model of Leadership

Leadership that is Christian is composed of five key elements (see fig. 11.1), each of which the Christian educator must have and continue to develop over the course of a lifetime.[4]

First, Christian leaders ought to have a sense of calling. "Where is God leading me?" or "With what has God burdened me?" Jeremiah said his call was like "a fire shut up in [his] bones" (Jer. 20:9). The apostle Paul expressed it as a kind of imperative: "Woe to me if I do not preach the gospel!" (1 Cor. 9:16). Without a deepening sense of God's call, confusion will ensue. His call is essential, the thing that influences all the other elements of leadership. Paul explained to Timothy that an elder in the church must desire the office

---

2. Bennis and Nannis, *Leaders*, 21.
3. Estep, "Leadership Strategies," 354–56.

4. See Estep, "Leadership Strategies," 350–54, for further discussion on the subject.

(1 Tim. 3:1), responding to the call of God on their life. A leader's personal calling translates into direction and vision for a ministry.

Second, Christian leaders should have Christian character. Examining character means asking, "Am I the right person?" It is a matter of being a leader, not just doing leadership. Even a cursory examination of leadership qualifications leads to the conclusion that a leader must be an exemplar, blameless (Titus 1:6–7), above reproach (1 Tim. 3:2), and an example to the flock (1 Pet. 5:3). This does not mean perfection but that those being led recognize the leader as a person of character. Being a "good person" does not automatically guarantee that a person is an effective leader, but without character the results can be disastrous. Christian leaders must have values, ethics, convictions, and spiritual maturity; a lack of character will only breed mistrust.

Third, Christian leaders should be competent. A leader must possess the abilities to fulfill the task to which God has called them. This is not just a matter of fulfilling a position description but of possessing the necessary skills and capacities to teach, motivate, equip, and encourage others to serve alongside them. This element involves asking, "Am I able?" It is a matter of the actual function of leadership in the church, what a leader does. Without a constructive level of confidence in one's abilities, only anxiety will persist. How can others learn to lead effectively from an incompetent leader? God does not call leaders to be passive or disengaged from action but rather engaged in the heart of a congregation's ministry, setting an example not only in character but also in service and performance.

Fourth, leadership requires chemistry, the ability to work productively with others and to lead through relationships. This is not

popularity, charisma, being liked, or being able to please people. Rather, leaders recognize their limitations and in response build teams, address conflict, facilitate change, pastor those in need . . . lead *people*. Through leaders' relational skills and networking, synergy is produced that enhances a ministry and enables their ministry to be fulfilled and multiplied.

Finally, Christian leaders serve from a context, a position. Ironically, while this is the last element in the list, it is often the first encountered when one is being introduced. The title and office, with the accompanying authority and power, within the context enable a Christian educator to have a voice, set a course, and lead a ministry. The context provides a position and a platform from which to exercise leadership. However, it can also be a restrictive feature when it hinders a leader's ability to fulfill their call, exercise their abilities, or engage the necessary teams for support. Paul addressed his letter to the Philippians, "To all God's holy people in Christ Jesus at Philippi, together with the overseers and deacons" (1:1), illustrating that congregations have discernible, identifiable leadership positions.

What makes leadership *Christian*? The approach to leadership must be theologically consistent with the life and ministry of the congregation. Scripture informs each of the five leadership components previously mentioned. Scripture gives insight into God's call, explains the expected character of believers as exemplified in Christ, and informs the responsibilities expected of all Christians, the nature of genuine Christian relationships, and the nature of leadership positions in the community of faith.

The five components of leadership must be theologically oriented to provide a distinctively

Christian model of leadership suitable for the Christian community. Applying a nontheologically informed approach to leadership within the church would be tantamount to introducing a virus into the body of Christ, an alien body into the congregation—one that would become pervasive and eventually redefine and redirect the church away from God's purpose and direction. In short, a theologically informed model of leadership, as illustrated in figure 11.1, is essential for the administration of Christian education.

Several caveats about this leadership model should be outlined. First, it is a dynamic model, since changes to any sphere will influence the others. The spheres do not operate separately from one another but are interconnected. For example, a change in one's skill set (competence) could lead to a new position (context). A comprehensive view of the model is necessary for it to be practical.

Second, no one is complete in all the elements. Completion of the model is the result of people working together as leaders, enabling themselves to fulfill God's purpose. Administration in Christian education is not just about being a leader but about developing others to their own fullness through the teaching ministry of the church.

Finally, congregations have to be concerned about an imbalance within the model. For example, what if the sense of call is replaced with the desire for position? A politician may end up leading the congregation. Similarly, if a congregation focuses on chemistry and none of the other qualities, only the most popular individuals will become leaders. We must focus on all five components in sequence, continually remembering that calling is the primary characteristic of a Christian leader.

Leading a Christian education ministry involves forming a vision, which leads to intentional ministry, which in turn calls us to minister and equip believers to serve, organize and resource them for effective ministry, and assess our effectiveness and efficiency for a continual cycle of improvement and advancement.

Maxims for Ministry Leadership

How do Christian educators exercise their administrative leadership and avoid slipping into a management posture, potentially impairing their ministry? Speaking broadly to this question, the following practices can minimize the risk of forsaking leadership for management.[5]

Maxim #1: A leader should consistently practice theological reflection on their mission and calling. Every aspect of ministry must be assessed in light of a leader's theological heritage and convictions. In order to remain a faithful leader, a Christian must frequently, and without exception, theologically reflect on their motives, performance, relationships, and place in ministry. In effect, Christian educators must be practical theologians.

Maxim #2: A leader should have a development plan. Consider batteries versus electrical outlets. Batteries drain quickly, having a limited power supply; if not recharged, they are soon empty. Wall outlets have alternating current wherein power flows two ways, providing virtually uninterrupted electricity. Leaders who do not have an intentional development plan are running their ministries on batteries and face burnout. However, with a development plan, a leader is plugged into the power

5. See Estep, "Leadership Strategies," 261–64. This is partially based on an interpretation of D. Anderson, "When 'Good' Isn't Enough," 39–41.

source and is able to access new resources, networks of people, fresh insights on ministry, and spiritual renewal. Such a plan reflects an attitude of humility and an acknowledgment of the need for continual growth rather than self-reliance. A leader's development plan is an investment in a ministry's future.

Maxim #3: A leader must lead from the front, manage from the back. No one leads from behind. Shepherds lead sheep, but ranchers drive cattle. God used the metaphor of sheep, not cattle, throughout the Scriptures to describe his people. A leader sets the example for those who follow by having a visible presence and assuming personal responsibility for the ministry. One common practice in this regard is MBWA, "ministry by walking around." An office is a suitable location for management, but a leader has to engage with people to move them forward in fulfillment of the church's mission.

Maxim #4: A leader should empower the development of other leaders. God's call extends to more than just one leader or ministry staff team; it encompasses numerous individuals across the gathered body. A leader seeks to empower others to fulfill their own calling, their full potential as leaders in the church. A leader values people not as mere resources but as important participants in ministry.[6]

Maxim #5: A leader should value accountability. By nature, leaders challenge their own comfort zones, pressing their own boundaries. However, when accountability is lacking, falling into a rut, embracing the certainty of the tried and true, becomes far too easy. These patterns signal the downfall of one's leadership potential and capabilities. The routine practice of accountability with Christian

6. Estep, "Theology of Administration," 44.

leaders or ministry colleagues provides an opportunity for answerability beyond oneself and the motivation to keep growing. In fact, a leader's personal lack of accountability will inevitably be transferred to the congregation, leading to mission drift and crisis.

Maxim #6: A leader should focus intently on the congregation's mission, vision, and core values. A sense of identity that informs, directs, and shapes its ministry is essential to every congregation. The mission, vision, and values are the cornerstone of the congregation's identity and ministry design. A leader ensures the integrity of the mission by integrating it into every aspect of the congregation's life. The mission-drivenness of a Christian leader guards against the onset of mere pragmatism, compromise for the sake of convenience, and institutionalism, wherein the congregation focuses on past successes rather than mission-driven future innovations to ministry. Articulating the congregation's mission, casting a vision for ministry, and clarifying values create a climate for perpetual, uninterrupted advancement of ministry.

Administrative Leadership and Ministry Effectiveness

Leadership and management are integral features of any purposeful ministry, especially Christian education. As previously indicated, administration is ministry. Successful pastors and congregations realize that administration provides the appropriate mix of mission-driven and mission-supportive endeavors needed to increase the influence and the impact of their ministry. They value administration. But how is administration really ministry? How does administration contribute to ministry effectiveness?

By Developing a Sense of Corporate Calling

Administration is ministry because it desires to see God's purpose for the church fulfilled in a congregation. The church is on a mission! Oftentimes we refer to the Great Commission as the indispensable mission of the church (Matt. 28:19–20). However, congregations must digest this passage and express it for themselves. God calls not only pastors but also congregations. A mission statement is a general description of God's ultimate purpose for a church. Because it is based directly on Scripture, it is virtually unchangeable, expressed in one sentence that captures the core calling of the congregation. It expresses what the congregation must *do* in order to actually *be* the church. Without it, it ceases to be a church. However, a mission statement alone is almost worthless unless it is further expressed, translated into a clear, shared, and compelling vision for the future.

The vision statement of a congregation is directly based on its mission. It is like an exegesis or a commentary on the mission. A vision statement expresses in broad terms what the congregation will do to fulfill the mission. Unlike the mission, which is virtually unchanging over the course of time, the vision has a shelf life. It may be valid for only a relatively short time, often as little as three to five years. Why? Because once plans are fulfilled, Christian educators must ask, "What's next?" Communities, congregations, social dynamics, and people all change, and those changes require a church to reenvision its ministry in order to be relevant to those both inside and outside the faith community. Hence, mission tells us what the ministry must do, its calling; vision expresses generally what next steps are required to fulfill the mission.

But how does a Christian educator, or a church, determine a vision? Figure 11.2 illustrates the formation of a vision for ministry in three sequential steps: (1) catalytic elements, (2) vision synergy, and (3) vision casting.

Figure 11.2
Formation of Vision for Ministry

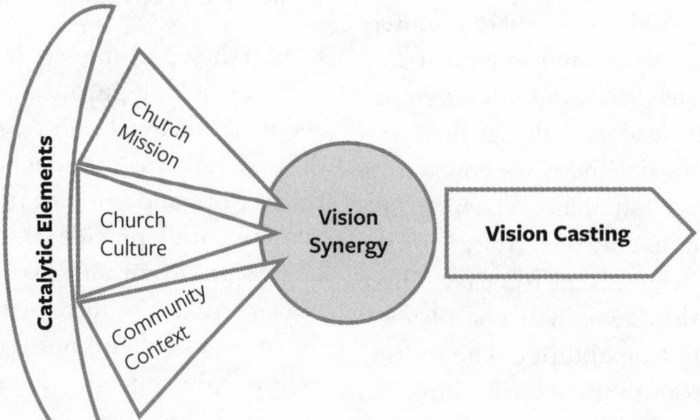

Catalytic Elements

Christian educators, along with other congregational leaders, should connect their thoughts first to the mission of the church, then the church's culture. That culture consists of the congregation's resources, attitudes, values, and relative health. The apparent needs and opportunities presented by the community as well as the context of the ministry are also important. A congregation should always keep a focus outside its walls.

Vision Synergy

Through prayer and dialogue, these items coalesce into an understanding of the reality in which the church ministers. The synergistic dialogue that ensues from the continued processing of these items becomes the source for determining the ministry's direction to fulfill the mission, accentuate the congregation's positives, and minister to both those in the congregation and those in the community. Ultimately, this is expressed by a vision statement, which is shared with those serving in the ministries of the congregation and with the congregation as a whole.

Vision Casting

Christian educators must never grow complacent or settle for simply managing the current ministries of the church. Rather, by routinely engaging in a vision casting process, they will ensure that their ministry is vibrant, pertinent, and a significant contributor to the faith formation and outreach of the congregation. This vision becomes the congregation's wayfinder as it moves into the future. Routine articulation, explanation, and incorporation of it is essential to a healthy congregation.

By Designing a Comprehensive Ministry

Administration is ministry because it endeavors to provide a comprehensive ministry design as a means of maturing the faithful. Engaging the process of revisioning as previously described will ensure the continued relevance of the Christian education ministry. But how can a congregation maximize its influence on people's lives on multiple levels of spiritual readiness and maturity? As a ministry, Christian education needs to encompass those who are nonbelievers, those who have spent a lifetime of faithfulness in the church, those who are novices in the faith, and those who are knowledgeable, spiritual leaders within the congregation. Hence, the notion of "one size fits all" does *not* readily apply when an organization is designing a comprehensive ministry of Christian education.[7] Table 11.1 provides a five-tiered template for ministry in the church, of which Christian education is a part.

The first two tiers of ministry are designed for those in the community outside the congregation rather than those already within the congregation (i.e., evangelism). The first tier, community engagement, involves building connections between the congregation and the outside community. These activities are not overtly Christian because they are intentionally designed for nonbelievers to become comfortable interacting with Christians. Hence, the Christian content at this tier is shallow and tangential. If these encounters and interactions spark an interest in the Christian faith through new realizations and relationships, then in the second

7. See Estep, "Biblical Principles for Christian Education," 50–51, 62–64, for the biblical basis of multitiered educational ministries.

Table 11.1. Template for Ministry in the Church

Evangelism (community)	**Community Engagement** sporting groups, support groups, holiday programs, popular seminars, opportunities outside the church, coffees and teas
	Expresses Interest in Christian Faith
	Outreach worship services, specialized classes, personal evangelism, some learning opportunities
	Accepts Christ as Savior
Spiritual Growth (congregation)	**Assimilation** small groups, Sunday school, basic classes, mentoring, special events for new believers
	Two Years of Discipleship
	Service and Study equipping, training, and resourcing for doing ministry outreach in the congregation and the community; opportunities for deeper, more advanced study of Scripture, theology, and spirituality
Leadership (congregation)	Recognized as a Leader
	Equipped to Lead preparation for new leaders, leadership events and retreats

tier, outreach, the gospel can be presented through a variety of means with the intent of leading the individual into a relationship with Jesus Christ. This is the first significant introduction of Christian content into the ministry, as it is the first occasion when Christ is introduced to the nonbeliever after they have expressed an interest in learning more about the Christian faith.

Christian education must not limit itself to those who have already expressed faith in Christ; it must also provide instructional opportunities and experiences for those who are not yet believers. These first two tiers are evangelistic, designed to introduce nonbelievers to the faith through interactions with

Christians and to acquaint them with the gospel message.

After someone accepts Christ, Christian education must intentionally shift toward a different ministry posture, one of spiritual growth. The new Christian must be assimilated more fully into the congregation through a ministry tier designed specifically for them: assimilation. Many recommend that new believers participate for two years in a small group, discipling relationship, or specialized ministry designed specifically for them.[8]

During those two years, the believer's interests, talents, relationships within the congregation, knowledge of Scripture, practice of spiritual disciplines, and sense of personal call are incubated until they are ready to serve in the ministry of the congregation and/or advance to a deeper level of study of and engagement with God's Word, theology, and spirituality. Christian education must provide meaningful contexts for the new believer to receive "pure spiritual milk, so that by it [they] may grow up in [their] salvation" (1 Pet. 2:2), but it must also eventually provide "solid food . . . for the mature" (Heb. 5:14). This means Christian education cannot simply be a single ministry initiative; instead, it must include intentionally tiered programs of small groups, Bible studies, retreats, and field trips, and even provision of self-study materials, such as are provided in church-based libraries, where available. It must also prepare and resource the new believer for meaningful service in the congregation and the outside community.

Finally, after a period of service and study, some individuals will demonstrate their call and ability to lead a ministry or eventually be on the congregation's leadership team. This

8. See Hawkins, *Move*, for the two-year duration rationale and importance of small groups.

will be recognized both by those with whom they serve and by existing congregational leaders. Christian education must provide for the equipping of new as well as existing leaders. This final tier, equipping members to lead, calls the Christian educator to multiply their ministry by facilitating leadership formation in the lives of those who evidence God's call. However, all five tiers of the comprehensive ministry design require people to teach, disciple, serve, facilitate, and lead.

By Preparing God's People to Serve

Administration is ministry because it prepares God's people to minister to one another and the world. Administration is not just about programs, policies, plans, or things; it's about people. Administration oversees and coordinates a congregation's ministries that provide spiritual nurture, prepare people for service, and form individuals into a distinctively Christian community. It is all about reasonably ensuring that ministry happens.

The previous section about ministry design reflects this commitment to providing for the spiritual lives of believers at various stages of their Christian walk, providing a progressive, comprehensive environment for spiritual formation. The administration of the Christian education context possesses a pastoral quality. Ultimately, it must contribute to the spiritual formation of believers. For this to occur consistently, learning objectives must be established for each ministry initiative. Here are some examples.

- Christians should consistently apply a Christian worldview to all of life.
- Christians should grow in piety and ethics as they grow in faith.

- Christians should commit their talents to the ministry of the church.

Each of these objectives would require further explanation or the itemizing of specific learning outcomes,[9] underscoring the necessity of providing for an individual's spiritual formation and preparing them to personally contribute to the corporate maturity of the church. Administration supports ministry effectiveness by providing training and teams as well as individual and corporate attention to the spiritually maturing believer, preparing them for real service in the church.

Every ministry of a church requires qualified, trained individuals to serve. Christian education is the ministry designed specifically to prepare people to serve in a congregation's ministries. Training is one of the essential tasks of administration. Small groups, Sunday school, youth groups, and children's worship all require trained and equipped people to lead them.

How can Christian education prepare believers to lead in these ministry contexts? No one format of preparation is sufficient. Rather, a combination of the following four formats—overlapping and creating a learning dynamic between them—can help fully prepare someone to serve as a teacher, sponsor, leader, or guide.

Group instruction is training done in clusters. Learning is best when it is done in groups, forming a community of learners. Jesus trained his disciples in groups (Matt. 16:13–20; Mark 4:10; actually his entire ministry to the Twelve), as did the apostle Paul on occasion (1 Cor. 11:2, 23; 15:3; 2 Thess. 2:15). Gathering people to study a book, share

9. Estep, "Toward a Theologically Informed Approach to Education," 265–69.

experiences, read through Scripture, and receive new information is perhaps the most basic form of training.

Spiritual mentoring, by contrast, is a process in which a more mature believer pours their life and faith into the life of another believer. An example is the early relationship shared by Barnabas and Paul (Acts 4:36; 9:27; 11:26, 30; 12:25; 13:2, 7) and other leaders (1 Cor. 4:17; 1 Tim. 1:18; 2 Tim. 2:1; Philem. 10). Through a one-on-one relationship or a triad of believers, people hold one another personally accountable, provide spiritual direction, and fulfill the admonition of Paul: "Follow my example, as I follow the example of Christ" (1 Cor. 11:1). Serving in the church requires more than precise skills. It also requires a spiritual disposition and a level of maturity, which a mentoring relationship can foster.

On-task supervision gives a trainee practical experience under the guidance of an experienced person (cf. Luke 9:1–6, 10–11). Essentially, this is learning by doing—on-the-job training. It involves a trainee developing ministry skills by seeing others exercise them, participating in ministry with those others, and doing tasks under the supervision of others until the trainee is able to perform them well independently.

Self-study, on the other hand, requires an individual to be internally motivated to learn and prepare for service (Ezra 7:10; 2 Tim. 2:15). Those best prepared to serve in the church's ministries not only have been taught, mentored, and supervised by others but also have adopted the practice of teaching themselves. They commit to reading books, magazines, and digital resources; attend conferences; and even visit healthy congregations to glean new insights and ideas for their congregation's ministry.

A comprehensive approach to equipping people to serve in a Christian education ministry involves all four of these components, each contributing an essential piece to the learning process. The culminating effect is a knowledgeable, capable, lifelong learner thoroughly prepared to serve as a teacher, sponsor, leader, or guide.

The task of creating ministry teams is not just a matter of training, which tends to focus on individual capabilities and achievements, but also a matter of placing the right person with the right people in the right context to fulfill a ministry purpose.[10] Teams have a synergistic dynamic that separates them from mere groups. Teams define their identity by the common objective that all the members assume responsibility for. They are like a successful football team. The individual talents of the players cannot win the game, but working together, the players align themselves toward the common goal, each contributing their best to the team's success.[11]

Several basic principles contribute to successful teams. First, team leaders should be spiritually mature believers who are personally committed to the purpose of the team. For such a commitment to grow, the purpose must be clearly articulated as a specific, measurable objective. Second, participants should be willing to serve, not just assigned or drafted into it, and they should possess expertise, faithfulness, wisdom, and commitment to spiritual growth. Third, teams require collaboration among participants. This does not negate conflict, nor does it assume that everyone on the team likes one another. Rather, relationships are based on a

10. Estep, "Transforming Groups into Teams."
11. Based on a figure in Estep, "Transforming Groups into Teams," 338.

shared, central ministry objective that invites open dialogue and trumps any individual agenda. Finally, successful teams require manageable team logistics. The three logistical matters that impact team success are size (too few or too many participants), deadline (the amount of time to accomplish the objective), and commitment duration (short-term task force versus yearlong commitment). Placing spiritually growing, trained individuals into a team dynamic advances ministry effectiveness through administrative oversight.

By Organizing and Planning for Ministry

Administration is ministry because it efficiently manages the resources of a congregation to help it fulfill its vision for ministry. Administrators are managers of a church's ministry. In this regard, Scripture presents the image of a household steward, one entrusted with the owner's valuables for their proper care, use, and handling (1 Cor. 4:1–2; Titus 1:7; 1 Pet. 4:10). Ensuring that a ministry is sufficiently organized and resourced to succeed is integral to making it effective.

Christian educators often need to be reminded that they lead in an organism, the body of Christ, not an organization, like a business (1 Cor. 12:27; Eph. 4:12). But even a single-cell organism has organization, structures that provide the resources necessary to sustain its life and help it reproduce itself.

The idea of organization is not contradictory to effective ministry but essential to it. Organization is more than flow charts depicting a hierarchical command structure and lines of communication. It is the congregation's nervous and circulatory systems, which must change and adapt as the congregation grows. The following are administrative principles of organizational structure in effective ministries.

- *Structures are temporary.* They are not an end in themselves but a means of achieving a desired ministry objective. Thus, they are changeable. When structures become permanent, institutionalism prevails and innovation is discouraged in favor of preserving the status quo. For this reason, an organization's structure should be purposeful, not permanent.

- *Structures support ministry initiatives.* Structure is the servant of change, not the impediment to it. Structures should support creativity and advancement of new ideas. To do so, structures must be adaptable and responsive to new ministry needs, favoring task forces and action units over large standing committees.

- *Structures should be no more complex than necessary.* They should be as lean and as simple as possible to ensure that communication flows readily, to avoid redundancy (unnecessary duplication) and the rise of bureaucracy (unnecessary complexity), and to encourage more significant participation. Clustering similar groups together fosters synergy and makes the use of resources more efficient and effective.

- *Organizational charts depicting structure require explanation.* We have all most likely seen an organizational chart outlining the divisions and hierarchical structure of a congregation. While the boxes are readily understood as ministry teams, two important items are often absent, and their lack can lead to confusion. These items are the lines between the boxes and the rationale for the grouping. First, the lines on the chart, which typically depict lines of communication or accountability, require clarification and explanation. Is communication to be written or spoken? Does accountability mean permission must be sought? Second, the rationale for the grouping of ministry teams, whether it is by age, location, spiritual readiness, or some other demographic, should be clarified.

Organizing a ministry means more than providing administrative structure. It also requires policies and procedures to guide the ministry's practices and decisions, to give direction to the ministry teams. When addressing the spiritual gift controversy in Corinth, Paul provided some principles and practices to guide the congregation, concluding that "everything should be done in a fitting and orderly way" (1 Cor. 14:40). Paul intimated that the Ephesian congregation maintained a list of those widows eligible to receive financial support (1 Tim. 5:11). Once again, when writing to the Corinthians about a substantial financial resource, Paul urged them to take "precaution that no one will discredit us in our administration of this generous gift; for we have regard for what is honorable, not only in the sight of the Lord, but also in the sight of men" (2 Cor. 8:20–21 NASB). Administrators provide policies and procedures to guide and direct ministries toward greater effectiveness by ensuring quality and control.

Similarly, policies and procedures often overlap with planning as part of a congregation's organizational structure. Time is a resource that must be used wisely, and planning helps us make the most of it. Some Christians resist planning for "spiritual reasons." Jesus was speaking of spiritual decisions but used matters of administrative planning and decision making to illustrate his point (Luke 14:28–32). Contrary to popular interpretation, James wasn't against planning for the future but rather planning in the absence of faith or focus on God (James 4:13–17). When we seek God's will while planning, we are acting in faith. Fulfilling his call for a congregation implies that he is already where he wants the congregation to be, and we must heed his call to join him. Therefore, we are developing the necessary structure, in terms of organizational arrangements, policies, and procedures, and planning for the future in which we will fulfill his call.

As previously mentioned, vision is often viable for only three to five years, and strategy is sometimes viable for only one to two years. Hence, a congregation should make a three-year plan and then each year update the existing plan by adding an additional year, creating a perpetual three-year plan. Several recommendations for effective planning are as follows:

- *Connect all planning to the congregation's vision and values.* Whatever is being planned must advance the stated mission of the congregation. Thus, the plan must state how ministry initiatives relate to the mission.
- *Involve engaged individuals in the planning process.* Ministry team leaders, heavily invested volunteers, and the church staff should be involved in the planning process. This creates a

ground-up dynamic that leads to support for the congregation's mission and acceptance of the plan.

- *Keep the planning process simple.* The more elaborate or cumbersome the process of developing and approving the plan, whatever it may be, the greater the likelihood of confusion, resistance, and failure.

- *Celebrate and communicate the plan's outcomes.* Once the plan is implemented or used by the congregation, positive results need to be shared to encourage support and further involvement in the ministry initiative.

Administration aids ministry effectiveness by organizing ministry. It simultaneously purposefully aligns the ministry teams of the church while eliminating bureaucratic entanglements. Similarly, it enables the organizational structure with relevant policies, procedures, and a perpetual process of planning to maintain effectiveness.

By Assessing Advancement

Administration is ministry because it values ever-increasing quality in a congregation's ministry.[12] Ministries base themselves on one of two things: assumption or assessment. When a congregation does ministry, members determine its success either by assuming that everything the church envisioned, planned, and resourced actually reached the expected level of achievement or by intentionally arranging to receive feedback and relevant data and deliberately reviewing the ministry's performance compared to the intended indicators

12. Estep, "Conducting Performance Reviews."

Figure 11.3
Cycle of Assessment

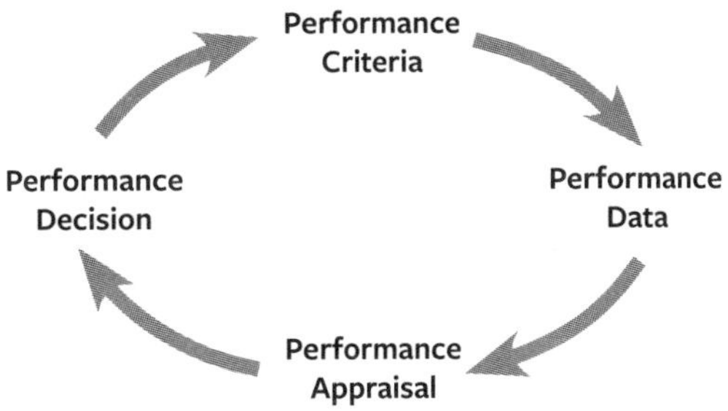

of success. A basic model of assessment is illustrated in figure 11.3.

Assessment begins with stated criteria for performance, which are typically expressed in a job description or expected program outcomes. These are the minimum, agreed-on standards of performance. A means of collecting relevant data is used to gather information about the actual performance of the individual, team, or program, typically in two forms: numbers, such as attendances or survey results, and words, describing what was gained through interviews or observation. The third step in assessment is appraisal, the honest comparison of the criteria to the information. Using this appraisal, a congregation can make decisions regarding improvements and adjustments to increase impact and effectiveness. By engaging in a regular cycle of assessment, a congregation can make it an expected part of a ministry's training and development process.

Conclusion

Paul told the Corinthians that the authority that the Lord had given him was "for building up and not for tearing down" (2 Cor. 13:10). Ultimately, the ministry of administration is to build up the people of God, the ministry of a congregation, and the church's influence in the world. Progressive leadership, competent management, attention paid to a congregation's mission, comprehensive ministry design, equipping and resourcing people to serve, responsive organizing and resourcing of ministry, and engaging in assessment all cumulatively result in effective ministry.

12

Discipleship

JASON M. LANKER

Educational ministry is essential, yet Jesus's timeless words in the Great Commission place the ultimate focus of ministry on disciple making (Matt. 28:19–20). Though most Christian educators would agree with this focus, disciple-making efforts appear to be lacking. In *unChristian*, David Kinnaman and Gabe Lyons reveal that nearly 70 percent of all Americans claim to have made a personal commitment to Jesus Christ at some point in their lives.[1] This should be exciting news, proof that the church excels evangelistically. However, this research also reports that only about one-third of the population, less than half of those self-identifying as born-again Christians, is committed to the church and its mission. Furthermore, only around 5 percent of Americans hold a biblical worldview—one of the factors that influence people's everyday actions the most.

From this research, it seems reasonable to conclude that today's church is doing an effective job of reaching out and getting people to agree to their need for God's gift of salvation. Unfortunately, that commitment may lack substance (James 2:14–26). Both formal research and casual observation indicate that most people are not experiencing the abundant life that Jesus offers (John 10:10).

Motivated to understand this phenomenon, Robert Coleman researched and wrote *The Master Plan of Evangelism*, first published in 1964. Coleman also observed "our spectacular emphasis upon numbers of converts, candidates for baptism, and more members for the church, with little or no genuine concern manifested toward the establishment of these souls in the love and power of God, let alone the preservation and continuation of the work."[2] Frustrated with the halfhearted

1. Kinnaman and Lyons, *unChristian*, 75.

2. Coleman, *Master Plan of Evangelism*, 33.

affirmations of the general public, Coleman focused on Jesus's teaching ministry to understand how he made such a long-lasting impact on this world. He concluded:

> Jesus was a realist. . . . The multitudes of discordant and bewildered souls were potentially ready to follow Him, but Jesus individually could not possibly give them the personal care they needed. His only hope was to get men imbued with His life who would do it for Him. Hence, He concentrated Himself upon those who were to be the beginning of this leadership. Though He did what He could to help the multitudes, He had to devote Himself primarily to a few men, rather than the masses, in order that the masses could at last be saved. This was the genius of His strategy.[3]

Coleman illustrated how Jesus powerfully shared the gospel by *first* focusing on discipleship. Since Jesus did it, this approach may seem unfailingly effective, but emphasizing both evangelism and discipleship has proven elusive for many congregations. Over time, churches tend to focus on evangelism at the cost of discipleship, or vice versa. So if Coleman is correct, we must ask ourselves the following questions: (1) If discipleship was so central to Jesus's message, what is discipleship all about? (2) How can discipleship occur in a way that more regularly produces Christlike development? (3) How can it be done to regularly introduce people to Christ?

Reimagining Discipleship

When Jesus called people to discipleship, what exactly was he offering? Discipleship scholar

Michael Wilkins explains that to answer this question we must first understand the position of disciple (Gk. *mathētēs*).[4] It was a very prized position of intimate connection with a recognized master. In its earliest forms, it primarily had to do with being a learner or a student, but Wilkins is quick to point out that by the time of Jesus, "the emphasis was not upon 'learning' or upon being a pupil, but upon adherence to a great master. Hence a 'disciple' . . . was one who adhered to his master, and the adherence was determined by the master himself."[5]

The Bible on Discipleship

In the New Testament, discipleship is less about *learning from* Jesus and more about being intimately *connected to* Jesus; the learning came through a focus on building that relationship. From Jesus's repeated statements for potential disciples to give up father and mother, houses and land, we see that being connected to Jesus was so valuable that giving up the treasures of this life was not only necessary but also beneficial (Matt. 8:18–22; 10:34–39).

How could this message have been a part of the good news Jesus was proclaiming? First, our commitment to Jesus is met with an even greater commitment from God back to us. Jesus comforts us as he comforted his disciples: "And remember, I am with you always, to the end of the age" (Matt. 28:20 CSB). This is great news because his promise is that those who are with him will ultimately become like him (Matt. 10:24–25; Rom. 8:28–30). The notion that Jesus, the Son of God, will be our constant companion is indeed good news!

---

3. Coleman, *Master Plan of Evangelism*, 33.

4. Wilkins, *Discipleship in the Ancient World*, 42.
5. Wilkins, *Discipleship in the Ancient World*, 42.

He will guide and instruct us through his indwelling Spirit on how to live perfectly in every situation of life (Eph. 4:17–24; Gal. 5:16–26). Through him, we receive all that we need for life and godliness (2 Pet. 1:1–3).

Unfortunately, many times when we share God's great gift of salvation, we emphasize forgiveness from past guilt and freedom from future corruption but leave out the offer of present healing.[6] This leads Wilkins to state, "Discipleship is virtually identical with the rest of the New Testament teaching on sanctification."[7] So in evangelism, we must share the promises of forgiveness of sin *and* the transformative spiritual process that will shape our lives to become more like his (Rom. 8:1–7; Phil. 2:12–13). By our simple and continued obedience to the Spirit's leading in our lives, we will be holistically and progressively transformed back into God's image (Gal. 5:16–24). As God is doing this work in us, he is also reconciling everything back to himself through us, accomplishing all that he has designed for us and our world (Matt. 6:9–13; Rom. 8:18–25; 2 Cor. 5:16–21; Col. 1:13–20). This *is* good news!

The Heart of Discipleship

The heart of discipleship may be best explained by the word *adherence*, related to *adhere*: "to give support or maintain loyalty"; "to hold fast or stick by"; "to bind oneself."[8] This, as Wilkins explains, is central to what it means to be a disciple. Yet how exactly do we help people adhere more completely to Christ and his body, the church? A simple analogy

may suffice. Consider how a piece of household tape adheres to something. If believers are to adhere to God, they must place themselves in direct, trusting contact with the one to whom they wish to be adhered.

While adherence seems a simple concept, it is not always a simple task. In our broken and fallen world, Christ's disciples are consistently connected to other things, while they attempt to adhere also to God. This is why one of the first priorities in discipleship must be the desire to "free the apprentices of domination, of 'enslavement' (John 8:34; Rom. 6:6), to their old habitual patterns of thought, feeling, and action."[9] Only as we are freed from entanglements will we be available to fully adhere to God.

Christian educators play a critical role in accomplishing the spiritual adherence of discipleship. Effectively connecting believers to the Triune God is an intensive and time-consuming process. It is also one that is difficult because, although we may provide all that a disciple needs to experience Christ's healing, significant change will not take place until the disciple desires to actually experience it (Matt. 11:28–30).[10] Unfortunately, this simple truth is often missed by those performing the ministry of teaching. Perhaps unwittingly, many organize their teaching around the belief that Christlike formation will simply follow in the lives of believers when their minds have been filled with God's truth. Honest reflection on our experiences says otherwise. The mind's exposure to truth, by itself, cannot produce holistic personal transformation. Thus, the disconnect between what the average churchgoer says and does is vast. Dallas Willard suggests that this is because we rarely provide

6. R. White, "Salvation," 1049.
7. Wilkins, *Discipleship in the Ancient World*, 135.
8. *Merriam-Webster's Collegiate Dictionary*, 11th ed. (2008), s.v. "adhere."

9. Willard, *The Divine Conspiracy*, 322.
10. Willard, *Renovation of the Heart*, 33.

vision, intention, and means (VIM) in our teaching.[11]

What he means is that we must do much more than provide great content. We must supply a "vision of life in God's kingdom and its goodness that provides an adequate basis for the steadfast intention to obey Christ."[12] Without a vision for the Christ life available to them, disciples can look at the Scriptures as an ancient piece of literature: old, important, and even essential historically but hardly relevant to life today. Christian educators must work to fill a disciple's mind with such an overwhelming sense of God's immanent power that they cannot escape "the vision of life now and forever in the range of God's effective will—that is, partaking of the divine nature."[13] Believers also need to understand their freedom from sin and the present availability of God's saving grace that is offered through Christ alone (Rom. 6; Eph. 4:17–24; Col. 3:1–14). Until they do, many believers will populate Sunday school classes and small groups, unclear about their current role in God's kingdom plans or unaware of how the Spirit could work through their simple obedience (Rom. 8:1–17; Gal. 5:16–25).

Discipleship as Transformation, Not Merely Behavior Modification

As Christian educators move people toward a grand vision of discipleship, they must invest their energies in shaping people's thinking and beliefs rather than merely encouraging them to modify their behavior. As Willard coaches, "We must never forget, in

moving toward the faith 'on the rock,' that our 'doing' comes—or fails to come—from what our beliefs actually are. Hence if we would train people to do 'all things,' we must change their beliefs."[14] Stated another way, renewal of the mind and the apprehension of truth shape beliefs, and those firmly held beliefs then lead to behavioral change and, ultimately, life transformation.

Beliefs Mature into Convictions over Time

The importance of belief formation is masterfully explained by James Moreland and Klaus Issler. First, beliefs come in degrees. The more we believe something or the stronger our conviction becomes, the more we will act on that belief.[15] Sometimes disciple makers expect people to act appropriately simply because they *know* God's truth. We must remember that, practically speaking, beliefs become life changing to the degree they are empowered by strong conviction, and the development of greater spiritual certainty takes time.

Because the formation of strong beliefs and deep convictions takes time, it may be too optimistic to expect disciples to regularly make enormous, instantaneous, and permanent life changes after each and every devotional lesson. A more effective disciple-making approach might be to encourage believers to make small, incremental changes in their lives as they grow in their faith. As a rule, people are more likely to receive, believe, and apply simple truths *incrementally*. This type of continual action, in which believers are taught God's truth and challenged to respond

---

11. Willard, *Renovation of the Heart*, 85.
12. Willard, *Renovation of the Heart*, 89.
13. Willard, *Renovation of the Heart*, 87. See also 2 Pet. 1:4; 1 John 3:1–2.

14. Willard, *Divine Conspiracy*, 331.
15. Moreland and Issler, *In Search of a Confident Faith*, 27.

with increasing devotion, is what progressively changes them in radical ways.[16]

To foster this kind of growth, we should regularly give disciples the opportunity to enact the thoughts or feelings that have arisen out of our teaching.[17] We must provide physical and psychological space for personal reflection so that learners can adapt their beliefs as needed. Finally, Christ's disciples must be challenged to life-test those new concepts in light of what is known or believed, and then we as teachers must reengage them with the cyclical learning process—to broaden their beliefs and deepen their conviction. This reflective process of faith formation is essential to effective Christian education. Unless disciples' foundational beliefs are clarified, tested, and confirmed as convictions, we should not expect to see significant permanent changes in the lives of those we disciple.

Knowing God Is More than Merely Knowing the Bible

A second important element in helping disciples change their beliefs into convictions involves helping them cultivate an intimate relationship with God. Biblical fidelity is essential, but depth of spiritual conviction does not come by merely having confidence in an abstract set of theological tenets. Conviction should be rooted in trust in Jesus Christ. According to Moreland and Issler, this involves realizing the distinction between having confidence *in* and having confidence *that*. Confidence *in* something is ultimately directed toward an object or a person, while

confidence *that* is simply directed toward a proposition.[18]

This may seem an unimportant distinction until we pay attention to the language and experiences of our teaching environments. It is important that we help people commit their lives to knowing Jesus rather than merely affirming Bible facts—as important as those are. Belief *in* Christ should then lead people to accept the veracity of his teachings rather than merely affirm propositional facts alone.

For example, when teaching, we regularly ask questions such as "Do you *believe that* Jesus is the Son of God? Do you *believe that* Jesus died on the cross for your sins? Do you *believe that* Jesus will come again to judge the living and the dead?" When "belief that" is the focus of our teaching ministries, we may unwittingly bypass the essential element of Christian faith—namely, a relationship with and belief in the character of the Triune God (Prov. 3:5–6; John 20:31).

This is why Jesus proclaimed that eternal life is found in knowing God (John 17:3) and Paul said that the loss of everything is incomparable to the overwhelming value of knowing Christ Jesus the Lord (Phil. 3:8). In both instances, the term for *know*, as is the case for most of the referents in the New Testament, is the Greek term *ginōskō*. In contrast to the Greek word *oida*, the other commonly used New Testament term for *know*, which "signifies having an opinion of some object or matter with no guarantee that it really is as supposed," *ginōskō* "takes place in man's dealings with his world, in experience. It denotes close acquaintance with something."[19] This means that if Christ's disciples are to eternally

16. Moreland and Craig, *Philosophical Foundations*, 130–53.

17. Kolb and Fry, "Towards an Applied Theory of Experiential Learning" 33–57.

18. Moreland and Issler, *In Search of a Confident Faith*, 17–18.

19. Bultmann, "Γινώσκω," 689.

experience God's kind of life, we as Christian educators are going to have to help them move beyond mere head knowledge about God to regular reliance on his holy character. God must progressively become so immanent and transcendent that the Triune God is not only tangibly present in all of life's circumstances but also infinitely reliable.[20]

Discipleship in the Body of Christ

As important as knowing and loving God is to the process of discipleship, it is not merely an individual pursuit. Knowing and loving others as the body of Christ is also an essential part of the Great Commandment (Matt. 22:37–40). This is because "New Testament community is an emergent interdependency of people in Christ who are in the process of loving each other genuinely, a process of becoming one."[21]

James Wilhoit articulates our need for others in the process of discipleship when he reminds us that "people change most readily when they are in environments that foster change as they learn to live out their unique communal calling. Such environments supply both support and challenge, and participants accept community responsibility as a way of life."[22] Unfortunately, spiritually intimate relationships don't just happen. In order to form these types of deep relationships, we must create an environment conducive to producing this type of needed intimacy.

Creating a Nurturing Environment for Discipleship

As Christian educators, we may invest most of our attention into curriculum development or programming. When this happens, we find out that "even the most compelling [disciple-making] vision is thwarted because, in spite of all the right structures being in place, little to no attention has been given to the climate."[23] To avoid the pitfalls of a primarily programmatic approach to discipleship, we should work to systematically establish a spiritually nurturing environment that "places the first focus on climate, not tasks. In the context of a healthy climate, a vision is developed."[24] When this type of shared vision for genuine Christian discipleship exists, the circumstances required for producing deep heart change within the larger community of faith become a possibility.

In order to foster the deep relationships needed for effective ministry-wide discipleship, we must put in place at least three environmental factors. The first is a climate of transparent trust. Greg Ogden suggests that to accomplish this we must first find tangible ways to affirm and encourage those whom we are discipling, quipping that "a hundred affirmations for every rebuke is just about the right ratio."[25] Unfortunately, in our desire to help foster connections with the Holy God, we often focus on the needed areas of improvement rather than the places where God's image is already being uniquely displayed. This needs to change because starting a discipleship relationship by emphasizing areas of brokenness tends to close people off to the experience, whereas environments of affirmation "give people the permission to drop their defenses and allow deep change to take place."[26]

Affirmation is essential to building this climate that nurtures deep and trusting relation-

---

20. Willard, *Divine Conspiracy*, 61–62.
21. Issler, *Wasting Time with God*, 59.
22. Wilhoit, *Spiritual Formation*, 184.

23. DeVries, *Sustainable Youth Ministry*, 79.
24. DeVries, *Sustainable Youth Ministry*, 80.
25. Ogden, *Transforming Discipleship*, 156.
26. Hull, *Complete Book of Discipleship*, 161.

ships. Affirmation fosters "an environment of grace [and] allows people to be broken before God and to deal with unconfessed sin, shame, and the other inner-life issues that destroy our good effort at discipleship."[27] A culture that affirms people in their struggles is important because there are times when we as Christ followers need to come to terms with the darker issues in our lives. This is necessary because, as Dietrich Bonhoeffer wrote, "In confession we break through to the true fellowship of the Cross of Jesus Christ."[28] Until believers feel the security of this type of nurturing community, they are unlikely to go below the surface of superficiality and to embrace deep, transformative relationships with God and others (1 John 1:5–10). This type of atmosphere is one in which we can safely speak the truth in loving ways and, together, grow up into the image of Christ with those on this journey with us (Eph. 4:15).

The other environmental element needed to produce a healthy discipleship climate is regularly speaking about God's truth. Ogden calls this "speaking truth in community."[29] This is what helps ensure that discipleship moves from being informative to being transformative. Cultivating this type of environment is a necessary part of producing healthy disciples. When these intentional, relational, and accountable communities are developed in our ministries, they become disciple-making vehicles that transform people, families, churches, and communities.

Four Types of Discipleship Teaching

As we work to create the types of ministries being described, it is essential that our disciple making be strongly biblical in a way that models the apostolic vision provided in Scripture. In 2 Timothy 3:16–17, Paul charges us to build our discipleship efforts around four types of teaching: teaching, reproof, correction, and instruction in righteousness. These four principles have to do with disciplers using God's Word to teach biblical content and to do it in such a way that people understand God's expectations for their lives as his followers.[30]

First, as the word *didaskalia* ("teaching" or "doctrine") implies, disciples should receive regular teaching, specifically in the basic doctrines and structure of Scripture. This is essential because our "society [is] moving more and more toward becoming post-Christian and religiously pluralistic." Disciples, whether new converts or cradle believers, need to know "the essentials of the Christian worldview. The basic story line of the Bible—creation, fall, redemption, and consummation—needs to be told honestly, creatively, passionately, relevantly, clearly, winsomely, and urgently to any and all who will listen."[31]

Our teaching must help believers not only delve into the actual text but also grasp the scope of previous thought about and interaction with the subject. As Gordon Lewis and Bruce Demarest sought to accomplish in their work *Integrative Theology*, we should strive to provide enough historical, biblical, systematic, apologetic, and practical background to our doctrinal teaching to enable theology to overcome the perception of irrelevance in the contemporary church. When that happens, teaching doctrine as Paul commanded will again be considered a powerful

27. Hull, *Complete Book of Discipleship*, 161.
28. Bonhoeffer, *Life Together*, 114.
29. Ogden, *Transforming Discipleship*, 162.

30. "Are the Four Profitable Areas in 2 Tim 3:16 Covering Doctrine and Practice?"
31. Estep, Anthony, and Allison, *Theology for Christian Education*, 221.

and convincing source of God's revelation and liberation—to the body of Christ and also to the world.[32] Without this foundational knowledge of the faith, disciples can easily fall into historical errors, progressively living the same type of lives that Paul was seeking to redirect in the Ephesian church (2 Tim. 3).

Second, proper discipleship teaching should include reproof. The reality is that, from time to time, we make spiritual missteps. God understands this and wants us to avoid prolonged exposure to the harmful effects of sin. His Word is a powerful cleansing agent capable of penetrating our souls and spirits in order to judge the thoughts and attitudes of our hearts (Heb. 4:12–13).

The concept of reproof points to situations in which people, through hearing God's Word, are challenged to live with integrity and authenticity. The apostle Paul points to the importance of biblical instruction that is convictional and that convincingly illustrates a biblical standard, resulting in a conviction of sin and, ideally, a confession of sin.[33] This is necessary because the Bible teaches not only truth itself but also the truth about us—and in doing so provides believers with a great many warnings and sharp statements about how to live their lives.[34] Even so, a careful balance must be maintained. Although we need to regularly see God's holiness and our brokenness, Ogden points out that reproof should not leave believers wallowing in unhealthy self-condemnation and guilt.[35]

Third, along with reproof must also come corrective instruction, not based in mere

moralism but in a call to holiness that consistently points to the grace of God (Eph. 2:8–9). Here the focus of good teaching to Christ followers is their restoration. Paul, under the inspiration of Scripture, challenges teachers to teach believers to live in a "right state" before God. He speaks to the ongoing need to challenge believers to seek personal restoration and to live uprightly, as they ought. This echoes the command of the apostle Peter, who chided believers, saying, "For you have spent enough time in the past doing what pagans choose to do" (1 Pet. 4:3).

In today's world of good intentions and soft discipleship, the words of Scripture about reproof and correction may sound foreign. The timeless words of truth, however, provide us with the exact and perfect balance needed for our lives so that we do not fall into the excesses of license or the restrictions of legalism. Proper teaching toward discipleship can help believers more easily walk the tightrope of Christian living as they seek to keep in step with the Spirit (Gal. 5:25). Through this bifurcation of reproof and correction, Christ's disciples can learn the balance between resting on God's empowering grace and passionately working out their salvation—no matter how many times they may fall (Phil. 2:12–13).

The fourth and final principle in Paul's exposition on the place of Scripture in discipleship is that of instruction in righteousness. Though we have sought to be incredibly careful in this textbook and, indeed, in this chapter to guard against any hint of self-righteousness or legalism, the apostolic teaching makes it clear that God's Word should bring about comprehensive Christian education and holistic training of disciples, leading to the

---

32. G. Lewis and Demarest, *Integrative Theology*, 9.
33. "Are the Four Profitable Areas in 2 Tim 3:16 Covering Doctrine and Practice?"
34. P. Williams, *Opening Up 2 Timothy*, 85.
35. Ogden, *Transforming Discipleship*, 165.

cultivation of a Christian mind and a life of Christian virtue.[36]

Being holy, after all, is at the very heart of the discipleship process (1 Pet. 1:14–16; 2 Pet. 1:2–4). Since God alone is righteous, and Jesus is the image of the invisible God (Heb. 1:3), the focus of this type of teaching is on helping disciples display more Christlikeness. Fortunately for believers, this is not a task they must do on their own, as God has given us his Spirit—the same one that led Jesus in the path of righteousness during his time on earth (Matt. 4:1; Acts 1:2; Heb. 12:2).[37] So teaching that fosters a trust in the guidance of the Spirit and an obedience of the heart is the essence of what biblical discipleship is and does (Gal. 5:16–26).

Discipleship is an intensive and never-ending process. This explains why Jesus commanded his disciples to continue teaching people to obey everything he had commanded. This is because he knew that "the student is not above the teacher, but everyone who is fully trained will be like their teacher" (Luke 6:40). After surveying Jesus's teaching methods, Roy Zuck concluded, "Unquestionably this small band of men was profoundly affected by the Lord Jesus. Because of the Master, their lives were changed, their hearts transformed. And, as we see in the book of Acts, they became powerful witnesses for Jesus Christ. Having been touched by the Savior they in turn became his agents in touching the lives of many hundreds of others by leading them to faith in Christ."[38] The result of this type of discipleship is that believers will know Christ, love Christ, live for Christ, and love others (Matt.

22:37–39). And those Great Commandment Christians will become Great Commission Christians who heed Christ's command to "go and make disciples of all nations, baptizing them in the name of the Father and of the Son and of the Holy Spirit" (Matt. 28:19).

Reimagining Evangelism

Having discussed the nature of discipleship, we must enter the fray regarding, arguably, one of the most neglected areas of many local church ministries, at least in the United States: evangelism. If believers are becoming disciples in the way the New Testament teaches, then dynamic evangelism will naturally result. After all, "making disciples" cannot happen without the good news of Jesus, the gospel, being shared in one form or another.

The Necessity of Gospel Proclamation

In Romans 10:14, Paul asks the questions—and these are not just rhetorical: "How, then, can they call on him they have not believed in? And how can they believe without hearing about him? And how can they hear without a preacher?" (CSB). He goes on to answer his own question, saying, "So faith comes from what is heard, and what is heard comes through the message about Christ" (Rom. 10:17 CSB).

Evangelism should be viewed as an absolute essential of Christian education ministry if for no other reason than the incalculable importance of each human soul. Jesus spoke of his own ministry, saying, "For the Son of Man came to seek and to save the lost" (Luke 19:10). Besides affecting the individual eternal destiny of each person in the world, the presence or absence of effective evangelism has

---

36. "Are the Four Profitable Areas in 2 Tim 3:16 Covering Doctrine and Practice?"

37. Issler, *Wasting Time with God*, 76–78.

38. Zuck, *Teaching as Jesus Taught*, 127.

a profound effect on the spiritual condition of families, communities, and local church congregations.

A disturbing current trend in the United States is a growing number of "nones," those with no religious affiliation. The percentage of American nones in 2015 was 21 percent and rising, according to a Pew study.[39] Meanwhile, it's a truism that both the number of US congregations and the number of their congregants is declining. A 2017 study revealed that even in the most evangelistic of evangelical denominations only 35 percent of churches were growing—with 9 percent plateaued and a full 56 percent in decline.[40] The statistics of many American churches are precipitously worse. Simply stated, there is a direct correlation between evangelism, discipleship, and local church growth.[41] For these reasons, biblically, ecclesiastically, and sociologically, Christian educators must place a high priority on the proclamation of the gospel, including personal and church-based evangelism.

Evangelism in the Context of Disciple Making

As important as evangelism is, sharing the gospel is not the end; it is a means to helping people become fully devoted followers of Christ. After all, Christ commanded us to make *disciples*, not simply *converts*. The work of evangelism in the context of discipleship occurs through the communication of God's truth. Through proclamation, people come to know Christ; through teaching, people come to grow in Christ.

If Christian educators earnestly sought to provide the same type of transformative teaching as has been described above, it seems that we could also see a witness as powerful as what was seen in the early church (Acts 17:6). As Christ's disciples, we have been made witnesses to what God has done.[42] Unfortunately, some evangelistic efforts start with a formula or a creedal statement that does not seem to necessitate a personal experience of God's salvation. It is not uncommon in many churches for large percentages of members to report not having had any type of new-birth experience, nor is one necessarily expected.[43] No wonder some evangelistic efforts lack the passion of one rushing to share from personal experience the news of our great King's victory over sin and death!

The Evangelistic Power of Changed Lives

When we begin our discussion with a focus on discipleship, we are acknowledging the simple truth that effective witness comes about only from what has first been seen or heard. Jesus's teaching ministry was centered on this truth. From beginning to end, the central offer of Christ's teaching ministry was discipleship unto him (Matt. 4:12–22; 19:16–30).[44] It was from this intimate relationship that Jesus released his disciples to make of the world the same thing he had made of their lives (Matt. 28:19–20).

If we are to more effectively share the good news, then the offer of transformative discipleship must take a more prominent place in Christians' lives. This is because, as we commonly say, "actions always speak louder

39. Zylstra, "Pew: Evangelicals Stay Strong."
40. Rainer, "Dispelling the 80 Percent Myth."
41. Rainer, *Unchurched Next Door*, 36.

42. B. Stone, *Evangelism after Christendom*, 279–312.
43. Zylstra, "Pew: Evangelicals Stay Strong."
44. Wilkins, *Following the Master*, 174–93.

than words." If we offer life transformation without providing visible examples of what God can actually do in people's lives through their submission to this process of discipleship, evangelism will always be a hard sell.

In trying to make the gospel something that is truly understandable and attractive, we might be helped by following Mark Mittelberg's formula for fostering a Christianity that is truly contagious.[45] What he suggests, as do Robert Coleman and others, is that the church's first priority is to create high-potency Christians.[46]

The second step is to take a cue from Jesus's teaching ministry and make close proximity with the world essential to the life of discipleship (Matt. 5:1–2; Mark 1:29–2:13). Unfortunately, in the current cultural climate, this will not be a simple task. As research consistently shows, how people both inside and outside the church view Christians is not pretty.[47] This means we are going to have to work extremely hard to demonstrate how Jesus has changed us into loving and lovable people.[48] So how did the Son of God do this? He focused his ministry on people—radically identifying with the world and radically serving their needs.[49]

The Power of Personal Evangelism

If we are going to foster deep relationships, we in the teaching ministries must provide teaching environments that help people truly

be themselves. This is because evangelism is centered on the simple sharing of ourselves; we become the *message* because we have become a *witness*.

As Rebecca Pippert explains, "Our problem in evangelism is not that we don't have enough information—it is that we don't know how to be ourselves."[50] When we can't help Christ's disciples realize this, we are up against an even bigger issue because "evangelism isn't something we *do* 'out there' before returning to our 'normal' lives. Evangelism involves taking people seriously, getting engaged with their needs and concerns, and then sharing Christ as Lord in the context of our natural living situations."[51]

As Christian educators responsible to equip the saints to do this work of ministry (Eph. 4:11), we must prepare people to become effective evangelists. An effective way to awaken disciples to the simplicity of evangelism is to help them understand how their gifts and callings have led them into certain occupations or interests. One's profession or expertise could be one of the most natural and effective means of sharing the gospel. This is because many adults not only work outside the home but also spend a majority of their waking hours in the marketplace. As educators, we should use our times of teaching to help disciples grow in their ability to point others to God's love, grace, and mercy in the person of Christ, resulting in more effective evangelism.[52]

An effective means of developing evangelistic disciples is equipping them to ask the kind of questions that can help others dig deeper into what they themselves really believe. In doing so, Christians will gain opportunities

45. Hybels and Mittelberg, *Becoming a Contagious Christian*, 39–52.

46. Hybels and Mittelberg, *Becoming a Contagious Christian*, 39–52.

47. Kinnaman with Hawkins, *You Lost Me*; Kinnaman and Lyons, *unChristian*.

48. Kinnaman and Lyons, *unChristian*, 206.

49. Pippert, *Out of the Salt Shaker*, 55–82.

50. Pippert, *Out of the Salt Shaker*, 22.

51. Pippert, *Out of the Salt Shaker*, 28.

52. Pippert, *Out of the Salt-Shaker*, 129–37.

to humbly share God's truth in ways that can influence those deep inclinations of the heart.[53] When our ministry models help to create these kinds of people, we should begin to see more effective evangelism in the workplace and the marketplace.[54]

In instances like these, as real friendships begin to develop, the gospel will soon surface as a topic of legitimate conversation. Evangelism can be effective without an already-formed relationship, but it is often very powerful in the context of friendship. Personal testimonies, though rough and unpolished, carry weight when people know and respect the Christian people who speak them. Authentic faith in the context of genuine relationship never fails to deeply impact hearts, sometimes leading to evangelistic fruit.

The Importance of Church-Based Evangelism

Along with equipping disciples to live a lifestyle of sharing their faith, we must also bring evangelism into the regular teaching of the local church. To accomplish this, we are going to have to more purposefully integrate evangelism into our teaching. One of the greatest hurdles to this is our fundamental assumption that evangelism is only aimed at nonbelievers. Ernest Best's exegesis of Ephesians takes that belief to task when looking at the role of the evangelist in the building up of the body (Eph. 4:11–13). Best states, "The gospel in fact speaks as much to believers as to unbelievers; they continually need to be brought back to what in the first place led them to become Christians. There is no point in their lives at which they can move beyond the fundamentals of the gospel."[55]

Conclusion

In all this, the local church is central in gospel proclamation. Not only is the gospel preached, leading to evangelism, but as it is preached and the principles of discipleship taught, Christians also better understand their responsibilities as members of the body of Christ. As local churches produce better-informed and transformed disciples, they will increasingly experience the power of God in their lives. As they do, the vision and the commission of Jesus in Acts 1:8 will come to pass: "But you will receive power when the Holy Spirit comes on you; and you will be my witnesses in Jerusalem, and in all Judea and Samaria, and to the ends of the earth."

---

53. Willard, *Divine Conspiracy*, 317–18.
54. R. Fraser, *Marketplace Christianity*, 135–46.   55. Best, "Ephesians," 391.

13

Mobilizing Volunteers

KEITH R. KRISPIN JR.

Over the years, anyone fortunate enough to have been part of a nurturing church environment has undoubtedly been blessed, shaped, and impacted by countless people serving faithfully in the local church. Pause to consider those who have deeply impacted you. What do many of these and countless others have in common? They are ministry volunteers, ordinary people with various gifts, talents, and passions who love Jesus, love people, and serve God and his church faithfully each week (without compensation and in their "spare" time).

Church leaders are called to mobilize God's people for God's purpose in this world. Unlike many companies that rely on paid employees to fulfill their mission, churches are primarily volunteer-run organizations. The amazing efforts of local congregations are led and orchestrated by church leaders, diligent employees, and devoted volunteers who together serve God and others. The purpose of this chapter is to (1) provide a biblical foundation for volunteer mobilization, (2) define and describe the nature of volunteerism, and (3) outline a practical model for volunteer mobilization.

A Biblical Foundation for Volunteer Mobilization

A Christian approach to volunteer mobilization must be first and foremost rooted in a biblical understanding of volunteers. In examining the Scriptures, one can see a number of principles that inform volunteer mobilization. Based on foundational constructs in the Old Testament and specific precepts in the New Testament, what follows is a theological framework for faithful, volunteer-driven ministry.

173

Biblical Examples of Equipping and Developing Volunteers

There are many places in Scripture where people are commanded by God to serve and to use their spiritual gifts. Only two such passages, however, are archetypal. Fittingly, one appears in each of the Bible's testaments. In the Old Testament, the book of Exodus gives the best biblical argument for a leader's responsibility to equip others for service. In the New Testament, Ephesians makes the biblical case for the benefits of developing volunteers God's way.

Old Testament: Example of Equipping

Perhaps in a bit of irony, the biblical vision of equipping is seen through the eyes of a concerned father-in-law whose daughter had married the minister of an enormous ministry. The daughter was none other than Zipporah, the daughter of a Midianite priest named Jethro and the wife of Moses. Zipporah had been visiting her father and, it can be surmised, had likely discussed the many things Moses was busy doing. Soon after, Jethro returned Zipporah and her sons to Moses's side. At the time, Moses was at the height of his ministry and was essentially the only visible leader in charge of the affairs of all the Israelite people.

Upon seeing Moses's crushing and unsustainable workload, Jethro became understandably concerned and lovingly confronted the prophet, encouraging him to distribute his work so as to avoid burnout (Exod. 18:17–24). This episode is not unlike what many church leaders experience today. Whether pastors, church staff, or volunteers, many struggle with the demands of ministry leadership. Rather than express surprise about today's reality of ministry burnout and the disappointed expectations of both ministry leaders and the people they serve, one need only hear the words of Jethro still echoing through time. He explicitly warned that without proper equipping, leaders would burn out (v. 18), and the people would be frustrated with them (v. 23). This is because one person, or even a few, cannot meet the needs of both congregants and the community at large. It requires mobilizing many leaders, each with different degrees of responsibility and authority (vv. 25–26).

New Testament: Benefits of Volunteer Development

The results of effective volunteer development are beautifully described by the apostle Paul in his vision for ministry given to the Ephesian church. In Ephesians 4:11–16, we see that a biblical approach to volunteer development results in (1) the skillful and meaningful use of leaders' equipping gifts, (2) edification of the body of Christ, (3) greater church unity, (4) a growing knowledge of Christ, (5) believers reaching their full potential of spiritual maturity, (6) increased biblical fidelity and doctrinal purity among members, and (7) the needs of people being met as believers learn to identify and exercise their spiritual gifts through acts of Christian service.

Paul's instruction about the biblical expectations of equipping and the practical benefits of volunteer development provide powerful motivation to ministry leaders. These principles must not be viewed as mere platitudes or suggestions but as biblical expectations that are tied to promises of divine blessing for doing God's work God's way.

Volunteer Mobilization Is an Aspect of Stewardship

The issue of mobilizing volunteers for ministry is rooted in the concept of divine stewardship, which centers on God as Creator. The doctrine of creation presents the God of the Bible as the self-existent and only true God. He created everything that exists: visible, invisible, material, immaterial, temporal, and everlasting (Col. 1:15–17). The divine power, knowledge, presence, and goodness necessary to create everything out of nothing establishes God as the greatest Being that could be imagined to exist. As Maker, God owns everything (Exod. 19:5). As a result, everything in the universe and everyone on earth owes allegiance to him.[1]

Humanity, made in God's image, was created to steward his resources (Gen. 1:28; 2:15). God commanded humans to subdue the earth and to rule over it as managers (Ps. 8:6). Indeed, everything in the world is now subject to human dominion. As the earth provides food, clothing, shelter, livelihood, and recreation for us, we are to exercise responsible care, cultivation, and control over it (Gen. 9:1–3). The New Testament similarly promotes stewardship, commanding us to manage our resources for the purposes of the Master (Matt. 25:14–30). We have been made stewards over everything God has specifically placed under our personal care.[2] Ministry leaders function as stewards of the church inasmuch as God has given each of them varying levels of authority in their local congregations.

Stewardship Is about Divine Ownership

When discussing the concept of Christian stewardship, Christians sometimes view the subject too narrowly and emphasize money nearly exclusively. While money is important to stewardship, it is not primary. Stewardship is about ownership. It is about God's creation and ownership of everything. Thus, it is important that we hold church leadership to the fundamental conviction that the church belongs to Christ—it is his body—and that leaders primarily steward it. Such stewardship assumes our management of and care for the church as both *organization* and *organism*.

Thinking about our stewardship of the church as an organization comes easy. Church leaders take great care in managing financial resources and distributing reports on budgets, income, expenses, salaries, and debt levels. Financial factors are sometimes even thought to indicate corporate church health. But biblical stewardship extends far beyond finances—it also involves the human resources entrusted to a congregation.

That is where the church must be understood as an organism. It is alive. The local church is composed of organic, living and breathing beings—people. Not only is it composed of people, but it also serves and ministers to people. And to do this well, the church must equip people to do the work of ministry (Eph. 4:11–13). This is done through volunteer engagement and development.

Stewardship Is about Honoring People

Churches do a good job counting offerings. This is an act of stewardship. Perhaps churches would benefit from giving the same type of attention to managing people as they do to managing pennies. Imagine being so focused on the stewardship of the organism known as the local church that you managed your volunteers with the same amount of care as you manage your money.

1. Cardoza, "Stewards of the Kingdom," 13–14.
2. Cardoza, "Stewards of the Kingdom," 14.

What if Christian educators carefully monitored volunteer engagement by logging volunteer hours served annually? Imagine calculating and reporting the financial equivalency of the valuable time invested in your ministry. Consider that, in a 2018 study, one hour of volunteer time was valued at $24.69,[3] with even higher rates for roles requiring skilled labor, such as accountants and heating/cooling professionals. Using this calculation, just one student ministries volunteer serving five hours per week over the course of a year is worth $6,419. Multiply that by the ten people serving in the ministry, and the real monetary value of that team's time exceeds $64,000 annually.

Many ministries do not enjoy monetary budgets even approaching $60,000 per year. They often have significantly less and carefully steward every penny of the financial resources they do have. It is critical that church leaders be just as exemplary in stewarding the human resources God has given them as in stewarding their physical resources. If we find we are failing to honor people with the highest level of respect possible, that faulty mind-set must change.

Treating volunteer involvement as a stewardship issue encourages leaders to utilize others' time more purposefully and to invest more significantly in volunteer training. Church members having available time but limited financial resources might feel more valued and willing to serve. Those involved in ministry would realize that, in addition to having a biblical command to serve and having been given spiritual gifts to fulfill that command, church leaders also hold volunteers in high esteem. These are powerful motivators to increase one's service contributions.

3. "Value of Volunteer Time."

Volunteer Mobilization Is Integral to Following Christ

For Jesus, ministry involvement was central to discipleship. In Matthew 4, Jesus meets Peter and Andrew fishing on the shores of the Sea of Galilee. He says to them, "Come, follow me . . . and I will send you out to fish for people" (v. 19). A few chapters later, he teaches a larger group of disciples to "seek first his kingdom" rather than worry about other cares of life (Matt. 6:33). Later, Paul continues this theme by teaching that service comes out of life-changing faith. "For we are God's handiwork, created in Christ Jesus to do good works, which God prepared in advance for us to do" (Eph. 2:10). In each of these situations, the work of the kingdom is seen as primary and the mobilization of people is considered necessary.

With many church leaders feeling overwhelmed by the responsibilities of ministry and many church members not engaged in service, one wonders about the reasons for the disconnect. Perhaps some ministry leaders feel guilty about asking people to volunteer, given their busy lives with work, family, and other responsibilities. Instead, ministry leaders can, with confidence, invite God's people not to "volunteer" but to participate in his redemptive work, to provide the opportunity for life change in others, and to grow in likeness to Jesus, who "did not come to be served, but to serve, and to give his life as a ransom for many" (Mark 10:45). This is so much more than just volunteering!

Volunteer Mobilization Honors the Contribution of Each Person

In writing to the church in Corinth, Paul explained that the Holy Spirit provides for the needs of the church by giving individual members unique gifts for the benefit of the whole: "There are different kinds of gifts, but the same Spirit distributes them. There are different kinds of service, but the same Lord. There are different kinds of working, but in all of them and in everyone it is the same God at work. Now to each one the manifestation of the Spirit is given *for the common good*" (1 Cor. 12:4–7, emphasis added). Later, Paul emphasized that the contribution each person makes is indispensable and essential to the functioning of the whole (1 Cor. 12:15–25).

These teachings are critical to understanding volunteer mobilization. That task begins with the perspective that every follower of Christ plays a valuable role. Mobilizers must help disciples find service opportunities that suit their gifts, passions, and availability. This applies both to those with obvious gifts and abilities and to those whose contribution may be less obvious.

The Nature of Volunteerism

Aspects of Volunteerism

Volunteerism has two aspects. The most commonly understood aspect is *economic*, emphasizing that volunteer work is unpaid. This includes work that may be voluntary or required. In the case of some uncompensated academic internships or community service requirements, the fact that they are unpaid makes them "volunteer" even though the work may be compulsory. The second aspect is *volitional*. That is, unpaid work as an act of free will in which "volunteers feel they are engaging in a leisure activity, which they have had the option to accept or reject on their own terms."[4]

4. Stebbins, "Would You Volunteer?," 155.

R. Dale Safrit and Ryan Schmiesing suggest that true volunteer work is composed of four elements: (1) active involvement (2) that is uncoerced and (3) not motivated by financial gain and (4) that focuses on the common good.[5] A combination of altruistic intentions, motivations, and actions cause people to volunteer. Even though volunteer *ministry* is activated by some unique motivations and even divine commands, Christian educators should seek to understand the nature of volunteerism so that they can appreciate the sociological, psychological, and anthropological factors that impact people's willingness to serve.

Types of Volunteers

Building on the definition by Safrit and Schmiesing, researchers have identified various types of volunteers.[6] These types can be grouped according to common characteristics.

Reasons for Volunteering

Affiliation-oriented volunteers are drawn to a service opportunity primarily because they have an affinity with the cause or purpose of the ministry and/or relationships with others involved. For instance, affiliation-oriented volunteers might volunteer for a community garden project because of concern for the environment or because a friend is involved. Skill-oriented volunteers, on the other hand, are attracted to a volunteer experience because

5. Safrit and Schmiesing, "Volunteer Models and Management," 6.

6. Rehnborg and Moore, "Maximizing Volunteer Engagement," 103–10; Yallen and Wentworth, "Assessment, Planning, and Staffing Analysis," 131–32; Terry, Harder, and Pracht, "Options for Volunteer Involvement," D.7–D.11.

it allows them to offer some specialized expertise to the organization. For instance, a registered master gardener might assist with a community garden because of a desire to use specialized training and experience for a greater cause than might normally be found in a paid work environment.

Duration of Commitment

Short-term volunteers are those willing to participate in a service of short, limited duration. Examples include an accountant who assists with an annual audit, a high school student who edits a video for a children's ministry, or parents who run a youth group's annual beach trip. Other volunteers serve regularly, potentially for a long time. Examples include a third-grade Sunday school teacher, a bassist who plays weekly for Sunday services, and a leader of a yearlong adult Bible study.

Type of Volunteer Service

A direct service volunteer is one who works directly with the people being served by a ministry—the child in the midweek children's program, the teen in the after-school program, or the family at the homeless shelter. An indirect service volunteer provides more administrative support for a ministry—planning for an event, serving on a task force or committee, or setting up for a ministry function.

Special Location

A combination of volunteer and tourism, "voluntourism"[7] involves a person using vacation time to travel to a location some distance away from home to serve as a volunteer. Though also a marketing strategy within the

tourism industry, voluntourism in a Christian context is seen in the numerous short-term mission trips sponsored by churches, Christian schools, and other ministry organizations.

Virtual volunteers serve at a distance from a physical ministry location through the internet instead of through physical presence at a specific place and time. Such an arrangement allows those who have scheduling conflicts or disabilities or who live some distance from a ministry to work as volunteers. A virtual volunteer could accomplish administrative tasks such as designing a brochure or distributing weekly prayer requests, or they could engage in relational ministry activities such as mentoring a college student who lives away from home or tutoring a student enrolled in an English course sponsored by a ministry partner in a restricted-access country.

Student Volunteers

It is common today for high schools and colleges to require students to volunteer at a nonprofit organization and/or fulfill a field experience requirement. While this may lack the volitional aspect of volunteerism mentioned above, some students see the requirement as an opportunity to serve. A volunteer mobilizer should look for ways to create opportunities for service-minded student volunteers.

Strategically considering how to cultivate each category mentioned could provide Christian educators with a consistent flow of new ministry servants they might never have had if they had not considered the nature and types of volunteerism. In addition, by identifying the characteristics and needs of each volunteer type, a mobilizing leader can provide a more positive volunteer experience, strengthening the ministry and volunteer retention.

7. Connors, *Volunteer Management Handbook*, 132.

A Strategic Approach to Volunteer Mobilization

Church leaders need a clear, strategic approach to volunteer mobilization to ensure that they faithfully steward the human resources and spiritual gifts present within their churches, purposefully facilitate spiritual growth through service, and provide other leaders with tools for fulfilling this pivotal equipping role. The remainder of this chapter examines the key steps of volunteer mobilization: planning, recruiting, equipping, engagement, and recognition and appreciation.[8]

Planning

The first step in volunteer mobilization is planning. In this step, a volunteer manager identifies the essential tasks to be accomplished in order to fulfill the organization's mission, groups the tasks into appropriate roles, and then crafts volunteer job descriptions that outline the purpose, nature, and expectations of each position.

Ministry Task Analysis

As a leader considers the mission, strategy, and programming approach of the organization, they need to determine what needs to be accomplished in any given week, month, or year. Once the majority of tasks have been identified, they can begin to group related tasks into manageable roles for volunteers. They should consider limiting the number of hours per week that would be required of each volunteer, especially for entry-level positions. Doing so makes it easier to recruit new volunteers. For volunteers willing and

able to take on larger roles, positions can be combined and tasks can be rotated as appropriate. Structuring work in such a way that volunteers have greater flexibility is especially important.[9]

Ministry Position Descriptions

A well-crafted position description (service description,[10] volunteer expectations, position charter,[11] or terms of call statement[12]) serves as the foundation for recruitment, training, and retention of volunteers. It clarifies expectations for the organization and the volunteer. A volunteer position description typically includes position title; purpose/objective of the position; qualifications needed (skills, experiences, spiritual gifts, personal characteristics, etc.); time requirements (hours per week; days/times of service); duration of commitment; general expectations; job-specific responsibilities; reporting and supervision relationships; resources needed; and training provided.[13]

Recruiting

The second step in volunteer mobilization is recruitment. In this step, a mobilizer seeks to match potential volunteers to the various positions needed to fulfill the mission. While this is often the most daunting step, a number of principles can guide effective recruitment.

9. Safrit and Merrill, "Management Implications," n.p.

10. Anthony and Estep, *Management Essentials for Christian Ministries*, 178–79.

11. McKee and McKee, *New Breed*, 143.

12. Halverson, *Ready, Set, Teach!*, 15–17.

13. Brudney, "Preparing the Organization for Volunteers," 75, Yallen and Wentworth, "Assessment, Planning, and Staffing Analysis," 141; Anthony and Estep, "Management Essentials for Christian Ministries," 184–89; and McKee and McKee, *New Breed*, 143–47.

8. Connors, *Volunteer Management Handbook*, xxii, 18–19.

Prayerful Recruiting

God provides the workers needed for ministry. When Jesus saw the need for leaders to shepherd the people coming to him, he instructed his disciples to "ask the Lord of the harvest" for workers (Matt. 9:38). The Holy Spirit also distributes spiritual gifts to Christians for the benefit of the body (1 Cor. 12:7). The entire process of recruitment must be a work of God, grounded in prayer.

Invitational Recruiting

Recruiting is not a sales pitch or a guilt trip. With the freedom that comes with knowing this is God's work and that he provides the workers, volunteer mobilizers are able to approach the task of recruitment with a spirit of love and grace. They are simply inviting people into God's work, not theirs. The word *invitation* is therefore important. Though some might approach leaders to ask how they can get involved, most people need to be made aware of a ministry opportunity and invited to help. Sometimes that invitation is given broadly, through verbal and written announcements, but the most effective invitation is usually one that is personal.[14] One-on-one meetings are excellent ways to cast vision and challenge people to service. As a rule, the more detached the approach, the less effective it is.

Values-Supported Recruiting

The invitation, whether personal or organizational, is more likely to be well received in a church with a rich volunteer culture. This means creating a church-wide expectation

14. Safrit and Merrill, "Management Implications," n.p.

for service. For example, the church's spiritual growth strategy includes volunteer involvement; teaching and preaching regularly highlight the ways that ordinary people are involved in God's work; membership classes include teaching on spiritual gifts; a membership covenant includes a written agreement to volunteer for service;[15] and budgeting includes funding for training volunteers and their supervisors.

Team-Supported Recruiting

In a small church or organization, a leader may have a large enough network of relationships to recruit enough people for a ministry. As the ministry grows, however, the relational connections of the leader may not keep up with demand. In such cases, all team members can identify and invite others to serve. When each team member gets involved, the potential number of recruits multiplies exponentially. But such work still needs to be well coordinated. As team members get involved in recruitment, these efforts need to be organized administratively with the aid of support staff, deacons, ministers, and pastors.

Purposeful Recruiting

Too often in the past, churches approached recruitment with a goal of getting bodies into vacant positions. If all the positions in a given ministry were filled, then recruitment was successful. Along with this approach was a mentality that recruitment was an invitation based on guilt, pressure, or even coercion. In the short run, such a pragmatic strategy may have filled volunteer positions, but in the long run, it led to resentment, resistance,

15. Searcy and Henson, *Connect*, 88.

and problems with retention. Healthy recruitment mobilizes people for effective, fulfilling ministry and recognizes that God has called and equipped people for a particular type of service. Recruiters should help people discern where and how they can best serve by utilizing tools that facilitate identification of one's spiritual gifts.[16]

Selective Recruiting

Screening is necessary to assess whether someone has the spiritual maturity, knowledge, and character necessary for a particular ministry position. For instance, a gifted and engaging teacher with limited biblical knowledge or spiritual maturity may not be suited for many teaching opportunities. In such cases, recruiters have a protective function in volunteer mobilization. Though a prospective volunteer may express a sense of calling, giftedness, and passion for an area of ministry, a recruiter needs to protect those in the ministry. Mobilizers must screen workers for evidence of past misconduct or criminal activity during the application process, especially for those working with vulnerable populations (e.g., children, youth, the elderly, individuals with special needs). Screening includes checking personal references, conducting a criminal background check, and in-person interviews before offering volunteer positions.

Inclusive Recruiting

The screening process may prove that some applicants are unfit for ministry to certain populations. Yet God expects every believer to worshipfully present their body as a living sacrifice (Rom. 12:1). As redemptive communities, local churches must extend grace and mercy with accountability and find appropriate and meaningful ways for *all* members to serve. Though there may be seasons when a member is experiencing healing and therefore is not in visible ministry, there is nearly always something a struggling person can do in order to render service to God. Volunteer mobilizers, discreetly and responsibly, must find ways for all people to serve without placing others in danger of exploitation, abuse, or harm. The commitment to use all members in ministry, even those being redeemed from great brokenness, requires a delicate balance. Even so, it is biblical, possible, and necessary and often proves to be spiritually fruitful.

Progressive Recruiting

Rarely are new volunteers ready and willing to take on a major responsibility, particularly if they are new to the faith and/or to the church. Even those who are spiritually mature might be frightened away by a long-term commitment or a large ministry role. A helpful approach involves breaking ministry opportunities down into different levels, from small and limited to more ongoing and extensive ministry commitments. Nelson Searcy recommends developing a ministry ladder. Volunteers can begin with a limited role and increase their involvement over time.[17] He also emphasizes the need to create multiple entry points or on-ramps to help volunteers get involved in the process. Similarly, Jonathan McKee and Thomas McKee compare the recruiting process to a courting relationship, where there is a progression in asking for involvement and commitment rather than

---

16. Brennfleck and Brennfleck, *Live Your Calling*; Bugbee, *What You Do Best in the Body of Christ*.

17. Searcy and Henson, *Connect*, 106.

seeking the equivalent of a marriage proposal on the first meeting.[18]

The various aspects of recruitment help Christian educators think of recruitment as an ongoing process rather than a once-a-year task. Effective recruiters are always inviting, with flexibility and creativity, looking for the right people to meet the needs of the ministry.

Equipping

The third step in volunteer mobilization is equipping. This involves providing volunteers with information and skills for a productive, rewarding ministry experience. Here volunteers are oriented to the organization and then trained for ministry-specific tasks. While orientation and training overlap, there are differences: "Orientation includes a broad overview and introduction to the organization, its norms and culture, and other basic rules and regulations along with behavioral expectations. Training, on the other hand, provides methods for the volunteer to be successful in their specific position, tasks, or opportunities."[19]

Orientation

The orientation process welcomes volunteers and helps them to understand the organization, basic organizational functioning, and volunteer expectations. Orientation is also relational, as the volunteer is introduced to members of the team and becomes part of the ministry community. The orientation curriculum depends on the volunteer's responsibilities. Someone in an ongoing role will need

more detailed orientation, with ongoing access to key information. Those participating in a short-term opportunity need only an event-specific orientation. Topics commonly covered in an orientation include mission, vision, and values; organizational history, structure, and culture; profile of the population served by the organization; policies and procedures; volunteer expectations; facilities tour; introductions to staff and other ministry leaders; and calendar of key events.[20]

Training

The training process equips volunteers with skills and knowledge necessary to fulfill their specific ministry roles. The process begins as new volunteers become involved in the ministry and continues throughout their tenures of service. Training involves ongoing development and preparing volunteers for new responsibilities and commitment. David Eisner and his colleagues found that a lack of training is one of the top reasons people quit volunteering. However, only 25 percent of nonprofit organizations, including churches, regularly train their volunteers.[21]

Training curriculum is derived from position descriptions developed during planning. In that stage, roles and responsibilities were delineated, and essential knowledge and skills were identified. Some volunteers come to their roles with knowledge and skills from prior experience, education, and training. Others come with a willingness to serve but little knowledge or skill. The astute ministry leader will use position descriptions to assess the training needs of each volunteer. Addressing

18. McKee and McKee, *New Breed*, 25.
19. Hood, "Training Volunteers," 237.

20. H. Edwards, "Orientation," 229–31; Nagy, Berkowitz, and Wadud, "Developing Volunteer Orientation Programs."
21. Eisner et al., "New Volunteer Workforce," 34.

these training needs is essential for volunteer effectiveness and retention.

Approaches to Equipping Ministry Leaders

There are a variety of approaches for orienting and training volunteers for ministry: group seminars, a written handbook, webinars, and instructional videos. Training may be provided through on-the-job learning, group workshops, informational social media posts, media and magazine subscriptions, and mentoring. Team retreats foster more intensive training and team building. National and denominational ministry conferences often provide seminar options for volunteers with differing needs. Ultimately, approaches should reflect the ministry context, the assessed training needs of volunteers, and available resources.

Engagement

The fourth step in volunteer mobilization is engagement. Engagement involves ensuring that each volunteer has a satisfying and rewarding ministry experience. This is done by providing volunteers with shepherding and feedback while eliminating barriers that detract from the joy of service.

Pastoral Care and Shepherding

Each volunteer is a member of the body, and a ministry leader is responsible for shepherding and pastorally caring for each member. A ministry leader gets to know the joys and struggles of the volunteers and may speak truth into their lives, pray with them about personal needs, and guide them in the next steps on their spiritual journeys.

Mutual Feedback

The purpose of and primary motivation for volunteer service is the opportunity to positively impact the lives of others. Encouraging two-way feedback based on job descriptions can enhance the benefits of service for both the volunteer and the ministry. It is easy for mobilizers to avoid giving and receiving feedback for fear of alienating volunteers. Jeffrey Brudney challenges this fear: "A powerful motivation for volunteering is to achieve worthwhile and visible results; performance appraisal can guide volunteers toward improvement on this dimension. No citizen contributes his or her time to have her or his labor wasted in misdirected activity or to repeat easily remedied mistakes and misjudgments."[22]

Feedback is formative, helping both the volunteer and the ministry grow. The central vehicle for feedback is a one-on-one meeting between the volunteer and a ministry supervisor, centered on caring questions such as these:

- How is the position going for you so far?
- Are you doing what you thought you would be doing?
- What are you enjoying about volunteering?
- What do you find challenging, or what do you wish was different?[23]

This conversation encourages self-evaluation on the part of the volunteer, allowing the supervisor to encourage strengths and address weaknesses. The supervisor should request similar feedback through questions, for example,

22. Brudney, "Preparing the Organization for Volunteers," 77.
23. "Nonprofit Survival Guide."

What could I or the ministry be doing to help you be more effective in your ministry involvement? With this mutual feedback, a plan can be developed for more effective equipping.

Reimbursement for Ministry Expenses

Since volunteers donate time, it is tempting to think that such service comes without cost to the organization. However, there are many volunteer-related costs: event participation, training, supplies, and transportation. Volunteer youth leaders, for example, may incur costs by participating in retreats and activities, buying teaching resources, and paying for meals when meeting with a student. Leaders should seek to eliminate financial barriers to involvement by providing resources and reimbursing expenses associated with volunteer service. Not doing so may lead to volunteer attrition.

Recognition and Appreciation

The final steps in volunteer mobilization are recognition and appreciation. Taking the time to meaningfully recognize and genuinely thank volunteers for their service is essential to effective ministry. David Eisner and his colleagues suggest that one of the primary reasons volunteers leave an organization is lack of recognition. Sadly, only 35 percent of nonprofit organizations make this a regular part of their volunteer management practices.[24] Volunteers can and should be recognized both formally and informally.

Public Recognition

By publicly recognizing the work of volunteers, a leader communicates an organizational culture that values volunteer engagement. Such recognition might include asking volunteers to stand during worship services to be recognized, profiling longtime volunteers in a monthly newsletter, or hosting a volunteer appreciation luncheon. Along with including financial reports at the annual congregational meeting, a church could include a report of the number of volunteer hours served, possibly even listing all those who served in the various ministries over the past year. This can be a great encouragement to volunteers and congregational members as they reflect on what it means to share in the ministry of such an amazing church.

Personal Thanks

Ministry leaders should continually look for opportunities to affirm the work of volunteers and to give them thanks for their service in the course of day-to-day ministry. A ministry leader could make it a goal to write two or three thank-you cards per week, occasionally even adding a small gift card for a local coffee shop or church café. Even a quick text, social media message, or email can go a long way toward encouraging a volunteer.

Celebrating Accomplishments

One essential practice of effective leadership is to "encourage the heart" by celebrating the accomplishment of team goals.[25] For example, when the connections team contacts the one hundredth visitor for the month or the parking team efficiently gets all the cars in and out of the parking lot for the Easter services without incident, it is worth throwing a party, whether large or small, planned

24. Eisner et al., "New Volunteer Workforce," 34–35.

25. Kouzes and Posner, *Leadership Challenge*, 307.

or impromptu. Nelson Searcy suggests also celebrating individual accomplishments, such as when a volunteer serves for the first time, reaches a service milestone, or takes on a more advanced ministry commitment.[26]

Finishing Well

There will come a time for some volunteers to exit the ministry. Some will leave for personal reasons, while others will move on to a new area of ministry. Regardless of the reason, how a volunteer mobilizer handles the exit will affect future involvement, both for that volunteer and for others within the organization. Leaders should consider conducting a personal exit interview with each departing volunteer, at which the reasons for leaving can be assessed. If the volunteer had a positive experience within the ministry, leaders can ask them to suggest potential new volunteers, possibly even make the initial invitation, thus continuing the process of volunteer mobilization. Leaders should also be sure to recognize and thank the departing volunteer for their contribution.

Conclusion

Volunteers are essential to the life of every church and Christian ministry. Building on biblical principles and an understanding of volunteerism today, leaders can develop and implement a strategic process for volunteer mobilization that can facilitate significant growth in the church and for the kingdom of God worldwide.

---

26. Searcy and Henson, *Connect*, 159–63.

14

Digital Learning in Christian Education

JAMES T. FLYNN

Technology is human innovation in action—the generation of knowledge and processes to develop systems that solve problems, meet needs, and extend human capabilities.[1] It may take the form of hard objects such as tools or machines, or soft technology such as an alphabet, language, or computer software. *Educational* technology is any hard or soft technology applied to solve instructional problems or meet educational needs.

When new technology is introduced to a society, it has the potential to change society itself, often in unpredictable ways.[2] The alphabet allowed ideas to travel across time to impact future generations. Record those ideas in bound books rather than scrolls, and you create portable and accessible information that can be easily carried from place to place.

Create a machine to print those books cheaply enough for common people to have copies to read, and you create information-based social revolutions such as the Reformation and the Renaissance.[3]

Digital technology has created a modern-day Renaissance, which is still evolving. Before the advent of digital technology, words and music were physically printed to produce media. Digital technology has changed the way information is processed (as 0s and 1s) and stored. Create a machine that can quickly manipulate a series of 0s and 1s, and you have a computer. Create a device that can record and store a lot of 0s and 1s, and you have a hard drive. Write programs that can manipulate a

---

1. Manning and Johnson, *Technology Toolbelt for Teaching*, 4.
2. Miller, *Millennium Matrix*, 15–17.

3. Johannes Gutenberg is credited with the invention of mechanical movable print technology ca. 1450. Within five years, he had completed 180 copies of the Bible, and his now-famous Gutenberg Bible started a printing revolution that democratized access to information, paving the way to make the Scriptures and other published material available at an affordable price to ordinary people.

lot of 0s and 1s for the computer to read to produce a desired result, and you have software.[4] Link computers together through machines that manage and route the flow of 0s and 1s, and you have the internet. Changing the form of communication changes society and its institutions, including education.[5]

Distance Learning through Technological Development

Learning at a distance—a technology-dependent enterprise—began long before the advent of digital technology. Distance learning is more correctly called distributed education or learning, which is the delivery of educational resources, allowing instruction to occur independent of time and place.[6] Isaac Pitman pioneered the first period of distributed learning, offering a course via correspondence out of a private school in Bath, England, in 1840.[7] In 1873, the Society to Encourage Studies at Home was founded in the United States. Shortly thereafter, the Correspondence University was founded in 1883 in Ithaca, New York, "to supplement the work of other educational institutions by instructing persons who, from any cause, were unable to attend them."[8] In 1874, an entire degree could be earned via correspondence from Illinois Wesleyan University, followed by the University of Chicago in 1892.[9] By 1924, an estimated $70 million was received annually from tuition generated by 127 correspondence schools engaged in distributed learning.[10]

During World War II, the US Army began to use videotapes to train its employees, and shortly thereafter, video technology emerged for use in education.[11] This gave birth to a second period of distributed learning. As there was little interaction between audience and instructor, the term *distance education* came to describe this kind of education. The advent of computer technology in the 1960s ushered in a third period of distance learning. Computer-based instruction (CBI) and computer-aided instruction (CAI) were the first serious attempts to integrate digital information technology with educational theory by technologically facilitating interaction between student and teacher. At first, interaction was severely limited due to a lack of stability in hardware and software, but with the rapid advances in computer technology during the 1970s and 1980s, better computer operating systems, and the development of learning management software, distance education evolved dramatically. Advances in networked communication systems in the 1990s and the integration of multimedia with text, images, animation, video, and CD-ROMs increased the impact and reach of distance education.

---

4. Though there are many more nuances to digital communication, digital information can ultimately be reduced to a discrete series of 0s and 1s that are specifically arranged to represent specific pieces of information. When you press the letter *A* on your computer keyboard, it sends the code 01000001 to the computer as a piece of information, representing that letter. This is called binary code because it is composed of two numbers (0 and 1) corresponding to the ASCII (American Standard Code for Information Interchange) standard format for what series of 0s and 1s represents a particular letter or symbol.

5. Miller, *Millennium Matrix*, 15.

6. Silverman, Rudestam, and DeStefano, *Encyclopedia of Distributed Learning*, 129–33.

7. Snart, *Hybrid Learning*, 59.

8. Noffsinger, *Correspondence Schools*, 6.

9. Snart, *Hybrid Learning*, 59–60.

10. Snart, *Hybrid Learning*, 59–60 (quoting Noffsinger).

11. Shih and Hung, *Future Directions*, 2.

The convergence of multimedia, internet, and networking technologies created a Digital Revolution in teaching that defines a fourth distinct period in distance education.[12]

In this period of digitally mediated learning, face-to-face and online learning began to merge into new forms of hybrid learning, also called blended learning.[13] Face-to-face learning was complemented by online instruction to create a flexible learning environment that captured the best of both approaches, allowing students to self-select the delivery that best suited their learning style and needs.[14] The result is today's evolving online educational environment with versatile learning management system software, video-on-demand technologies, and streaming-resource capabilities. Use of digital technology presents an unparalleled opportunity for high-impact education and discipleship on a global scale, commensurate with the call of the Great Commission to "make disciples of all nations" (Matt. 28:19).

Making Sense of the Digital Revolution

The introduction of digital technology has greatly accelerated the rate of change in society. Clayton Christensen uses the term *disruptive innovation* to describe these kinds of changes in society.[15] We are now in a period of disruptive innovation in communication technology that is profoundly changing education. What forces are causing these changes? How can these forces be harnessed to create high-impact learning and discipleship?

Hardware and Processing Power

Computer hardware evolution is a key technology driving change. Back in 1965, Gordon Moore, cofounder of Intel, developed a formula to predict advances in computer processing power.[16] Moore's law predicts the doubling of computer processing power every two years, and that law has held true since 1965.[17] Increases in processing power are clearly evident, as computers, which used to fill entire rooms, are now handheld and wearable.[18]

Computer hardware innovation and miniaturization have profoundly impacted the way people communicate and learn. Increased processor speed and miniaturization have created a culture of convergence in communication in which smartphone and wearable technology are displacing entire categories of information-based technology with one device.[19] It should come as no surprise that education, an information-based enterprise, is also being profoundly affected. Mobile learning (m-learning) is being integrated for use both inside and outside the classroom.[20]

12. Shih and Hung, *Future Directions*, 3.
13. Snart, *Hybrid Learning*, xvi.
14. J. Anderson, Boyles, and Raines, "Future Impact of the Internet."
15. Christensen, *Innovator's Dilemma*.

16. Poeter, "Moore's Law Really Works after All," 10–13. This is an excellent article that explains Moore's law in layman's terms.
17. In 1965, there were approximately 2,300 transistors on a computer chip. As of 2011, there were approximately 2.6 billion transistors on a computer chip. In order to crowd that number of transistor circuits on a chip, incredibly small and detailed production capability is employed. In fact, the space between transistors on a chip is now so small that many scientists believe the physical limits of current chip technology will be reached in the near future if the density of transistors continues to increase and that a new kind of technology will be needed to produce more powerful processing chips beyond a currently predicted 15-billion-transistor theoretical limit.
18. Weiss, "Google Glass Now Available," 2.
19. The desktop and laptop computer, standard for decades, are being displaced by the tablet and the smartphone, which will be displaced by wearable technology.
20. Rogers, Houser, and Thornton, "Mobile Educational Technology," 1424.

Mobile technology will further evolve with increased connection speed, web-browsing capability, and processor speed, allowing for delivery of increasingly rich online learning content. M-learning is now being integrated into face-to-face classrooms as a connectivity tool, allowing for real-time surveys, responses, and quizzes through smartphone and wearable technology during face-to-face classes, resulting in increased participation, social interaction, and engagement.[21] The integration of m-learning presents a challenge to "digital immigrants" over age forty who are conditioned to tethered e-learning via desktop or laptop. "Digital natives" under thirty, for whom mobile and wearable technology are second nature, often embrace it without hesitation.[22] The m-learning revolution has begun and represents a moving target that Christian educators must plan for in curricular, pedagogical, and IT infrastructure design.

Software and Cognitive Computing

Advances in software are also driving the Digital Revolution. One of the most promising advances is the area of artificial intelligence. Artificial intelligence software allows a computer to simulate human thinking through a process commonly called cognitive computing.[23] IBM's Watson computer is just one example of cognitive computing technology that relies on artificial intelligence

software to simulate human thinking.[24] Watson is capable of answering questions posed in human language, offering financial advice, evaluating scientific hypotheses, and creating jokes and puns.[25] With artificial intelligence programs, computers are now able to generate new knowledge and make discoveries without the aid of human intervention. The idea of artificial intelligence in education, particularly Christian education, is off-putting for some. The idea of replacing a person with a machine seems to collide head on with Christian ideals of personal fellowship and communication. Yet as with all computer-assisted learning, artificial intelligence can function effectively *alongside* instructors to enhance efficiency and productivity. Common uses include grammatical editing of essays, evaluation of cogent structure and plagiarism checks, and accurate speech-to-text synthesis for evaluative feedback from instructors.

Networking

The effects of technology on culture and the way people perceive reality are nowhere more apparent than in the evolution of computer networking. Connecting computers together through cable wire, then fiber optic cable, and now wireless technology has created a "mobile-global" village.[26] In the 1960s, with the advent of television and satellite technology, news stories could be broadcast from remote parts of the world via video feed in real time. This advance made the world seem smaller but allowed communication in only one direction. Unlike television, the internet allows for interactive real-time text, audio,

21. Rogers, Houser, and Thornton, "Mobile Educational Technology," 1428.
22. Rogers, Houser, and Thornton, "Mobile Educational Technology," 1432.
23. Abate, "Stanford Bioengineers Create Circuit Board." In 2014, Stanford University began experimenting with a neural processing design that incorporated sixteen core chips, simulating one million neurons each, with over a billion neural synapse-like connections.

24. Hay, "New Technologies."
25. Hay, "New Technologies."
26. Snart, *Hybrid Learning*, 70.

and video communication to remote parts of the world at little cost. Many parts of the developing world are bypassing wired networks altogether and instead are opting to install high-speed wireless communication networks dedicated to smartphone connectivity. This kind of networking capability has created a mobile-global culture as people interact across geographical, political, and cultural borders.[27]

Whereas Moore's law predicts that computer processing power will double every eighteen to twenty-four months, Butter's law for fiber optic networks predicts that network data capacity will double every nine months with a corresponding 50 percent decrease in cost of transmission. Google is currently experimenting with ultrafast internet access services delivered by satellites and high-altitude balloons to expand low-cost internet access to developing nations that currently have little access.[28] This trend is affirmed by current work to create networks that are one thousand times more powerful than current mobile networks, able to download the equivalent of a high-definition movie in less than a second.[29]

Christian educators need to begin to integrate the use of digital web-based resources and books into curricular planning. Digital editions provide access to books previously too expensive to purchase or out of print. The use of ebooks illustrates how educational delivery must adapt to handheld or wearable technology. Advances in networking also open up opportunities for Christian educators to train and disciple the many emerging global leaders who are least served and least able to afford today's expensive models for education. However, higher education is one of the most change-resistant social institutions ever created.[30] Its constructs were perfectly suited for a time when students had little access to information or the world around them. Now, a recent Pew survey found that 75 percent of adults say college is too expensive to afford and 57 percent say higher education systems in the United States have failed to provide students with good value for their money.[31] These economic forces alone are likely to create a change-or-die environment for education generally, but for Christian education specifically, because of more limited financial resources. Those institutions that choose "click" over "brick" in their infrastructure plans are likely to have a significant advantage in the market, but planning for this direction must be accomplished far in advance.

Social Media and the Human Dimension

Increased network connection speeds, increased processing power, more substantial web-browsing capabilities, and advanced mobile technology have produced a revolution in social networking. Social networking will be a defining factor in twenty-first-century educational technology.[32] The advent and success of social networking endeavors such as Facebook, Twitter, Instagram, and Snapchat and niche communities such as LinkedIn illustrate a profound change in how community is defined and how it is integrated into everyday life. Nowhere is this more pronounced than in education.

Virtual tools and meeting environments make it possible to construct vibrant virtual

27. Snart, *Hybrid Learning*, 70.
28. "Project Loon."
29. Carroll, "Huawei Predicts First 5G Networks."

30. J. Anderson, Boyles, and Raines, "Future Impact of the Internet," 7 (quoting Cline).
31. J. Anderson, Boyles, and Raines, "Future Impact of the Internet," 3–4.
32. Snart, *Hybrid Learning*, 70.

learning communities as part of curricular design.[33] In order to adapt to student expectations for a robust social dimension in online learning, curricular design and pedagogy must take a more community-based approach to learning by creating shared goals, problems, and projects as well as shared resources, membership, and leadership. Collaborative approaches to group work with high levels of dialogue, interaction, and collaboration must become the norm for a generation conditioned by social networking and media. Whereas in the past, information and knowledge sharing was emphasized, now there must be an emphasis on knowledge construction and exchange through the use of communication technologies that take into account mobile learning capabilities.[34] Rather than following a paradigm in which knowledge flows from professor to student, the learning experience must involve a community of inquiry in which meaning is constructed in community through purposeful inquiry as individuals explore ideas and questions together.[35] These trends and changes resonate with the core values and beliefs of Christianity, because they capitalize on the idea of transformational community, a core value of Christian education.

Educational Technology and Digital Learning

Effective Christian education over the next several decades belongs to those who are skilled at spotting trends created by new technology,

understanding what drives those trends, and harnessing their power to create high-impact curriculum and delivery. While our focus is on educational technology, it is only a means to an end. If technology is properly understood and deployed, it should blend into the background and become invisible while increasing educational effectiveness. The important thing is not the technology but the trend, with its potential to positively impact teaching and ministry.

The Web as Technology

The internet itself is a powerful technology that can be redeemed for the propagation of the gospel and for high-impact education. When first introduced, the internet was a static technology. Webpages were first authored for viewing but little more.[36] The static internet that existed in the 1960s, 1970s, and a large part of the 1980s is often referred to as Web 1.0. Technological advances that allowed users to interact with the web produced an explosion of online interaction and knowledge content. This era of interactive internet technology is often referred to as Web 2.0. The technologies of Web 2.0 began to shape the idea of online virtual community, which has had a profound effect on education.[37]

The advent of virtual community made possible by Web 2.0 technology resulted in the idea of web-logs (blogs). Blogging drove online social interaction to new levels. In 1997, about one hundred blogs existed on an early blogging website called Xanga. By 2005, fifty million blogs existed. The more personal

33. D. Lewis and Allan, *Virtual Learning Communities*, 6.

34. D. Lewis and Allan, *Virtual Learning Communities*, 6.

35. Garrison and Vaughan, *Blended Learning in Higher Education*, 6, 13–16.

36. Garrison and Vaughan, *Blended Learning in Higher Education*, 5.

37. Garrison and Vaughan, *Blended Learning in Higher Education*, 5.

feeling of a blogging experience creates the kind of intimacy and relationship needed for transformational learning to take place. Some feel that the development of Web 2.0 technologies and the social interaction that has resulted will ultimately have more significant influence on society and culture than the printing press.[38]

New developments in web technology, known as Web 3.0, are being driven by increased internet traffic, the proliferation of high-speed networking, and hardware and its associated software that rely on the internet for their operation. As knowledge and cognitive content rapidly increase on the web, there is a shift toward a more semantic emphasis on the meaning of data and personalization.[39] An example of this shift is embodied in Second Life virtual community.[40] Second Life represents a technological shift toward finding personal meaning and toward a virtual social presence on the web that has profound implications for education in general and Christian education specifically. The propagation of the gospel has always been about connecting with other people, building relationships, and sharing the good news in community so that lives can be transformed. Because of Web 3.0 technology, digital *koinōnia* must increasingly be a

part of any endeavor in Christian education.[41] A shift in perception about what is "real" has already occurred for this generation. They value social interaction just as much as others before them but no longer define social interaction as purely face-to-face. Virtual interaction on the web, especially the kind of interaction that is now possible because of emerging Web 3.0 technologies, are just as real as face-to-face interaction was for past generations. The generation currently in preschool will be immersed in blended virtual and face-to-face social presence to the point that education that relies merely on face-to-face design will seem odd.

Learning Management Systems

In order to project social presence and educational content onto the web, one needs technology to host a web presence and build a learning community. That software is called a Learning Management System (LMS). One of the most versatile and popular LMS software packages currently available is Moodle.[42] Moodle is unique because it is open-source software, which means that users are encouraged to build their own software components

---

38. Garrison and Vaughan, *Blended Learning in Higher Education*, 5.

39. Garrison and Vaughan, *Blended Learning in Higher Education*, 7.

40. Second Life is an immersive 3-D virtual world parceled into virtual lands and places. The user chooses a 3-D representation called an avatar that allows them to walk or run through virtual places of their choice. The user can customize their avatar with clothing bought from online virtual malls that exist within Second Life. They can buy virtual houses and outfit them with furniture. They can go on vacations to virtualized real-world locations or purely imaginary places that don't exist in the real world.

41. The Greek term *koinōnia* is often translated "community" in the English Scriptures. The word is meant to frame the synergy that results from the interaction of two or more Christians when they connect in fellowship. Until the Digital Revolution, that connection was most often face-to-face. The advent of web technology, particularly Web 3.0 technology, introduced a new virtual dimension to *koinōnia* that is just as real to this generation as face-to-face interaction.

42. Ferriman, "20 Most Popular Learning Management Systems." As mentioned earlier in this chapter, rapid changes in technology can quickly modify what is available and the most effective LMS for your needs. This limited review of LMS software serves only as an example of the kinds that are available at the time this chapter is being written.

for the Moodle platform and then share them with other users in the Moodle community.[43] It is versatile enough to be used for higher education or local church discipleship needs. Blackboard is another example of an LMS, but unlike Moodle, it is not open source and can be pricey.[44] It is the LMS of choice for many schools and universities that can afford a more expensive and formal platform to mediate their distance and blended classes. Several other specialty LMS software packages are available, with varying capabilities and price. New LMS software, such as Edmodo, seems to have integrated significant aspects of social media into its design and look.[45]

Technological Tools for Learning

As technology continues to advance, an increasing number of functions will be web-based. Calendars that are web-based, such as Google Calendar and Microsoft Outlook, allow for time planning and scheduling in a collaborative manner. In Web 1.0 and 2.0, users could bookmark their favorite links on the web for convenient retrieval. Web 3.0 technology now allows for social bookmarking in which groups such as learning communities jointly mark common links to webpages, notes, images, and multimedia sources for common access and collaborative activities. Social bookmarking allows for aggregate sources from the web on the topic of focus to be easily integrated into curricular design.

Web 3.0 capabilities continue to move toward greater personalization and virtual community, opening up new opportunities in collaborative learning. This new social construct of community has radically altered how students learn. They are interactive learners rather than passive consumers of information and move between face-to-face and virtual relationship seamlessly. A blend of synchronous and asynchronous interaction in class pedagogy can greatly enhance social presence and create the kind of virtual community that is essential for effective learning.[46] As distance education progressed in the 1990s, discussion posts were often used as a tool to promote a modest forum for social interaction. Blogging technology has since displaced discussion posting as a richer means of interaction and can be effectively integrated into education either as part of an LMS or through one of the many stand-alone blogging platforms on the web.[47] The key is to provide multiple pathways for interactive discussion to enhance social presence in the learning process. Effective online pedagogy can involve the integration of other social networking platforms (Facebook, Twitter, etc.) in the educational process.

Wikis are another tool for collaboration and connection in online learning. A wiki is a virtual community of people who add, edit, and manage information on a particular subject.[48] As knowledge became more available

43. See https://moodle.org/.

44. See http://www.blackboard.com/.

45. See https://www.edmodo.com/.

46. Asynchronous interaction occurs when someone posts information at one time and others access that information and respond at a different time. Synchronous interaction occurs when individuals communicate in real time with one another, responding immediately to one another as would occur in face-to-face communication.

47. Examples of current blogging platforms available include WordPress and Blogger. Many LMSs also contain dedicated blogging features, behind a secure firewall to protect the communication.

48. Wikis came into prominence in the mid-2000s with the advent of Wikipedia, an online encyclopedia that was created, is edited, and is maintained exclusively by the online community: http://www.wikipedia.org/.

on the web, people began to view curation of knowledge and learning as a community effort. For local churches and higher education, wikis represent an ideal opportunity for students to collaborate in building a knowledge base on a particular subject related to their studies. An instructor can literally build different chapters or subject divisions that are focused on class subject matter into the wiki structure and ask students to populate those areas with a synthesis of what they have learned from reading, lecture, and discussion in class—in essence writing their own class book on the subject they are studying, chapter by chapter. Wikis, and any of the other technologies mentioned in this chapter, may be displaced by another kind of media; the important thing is the principle of learning in community and constructing a learning experience through social interaction.

Content Delivery

With the democratization of information on the web, knowledge is no longer possessed by a few people to be distributed to a class. More than likely, students can find the information somewhere online. Access to knowledge on the web has created a radical reconfiguration of what it means to teach a subject. Increasingly, technology is driving higher education to provide specialty skill sets, character formation, and the wisdom to apply knowledge successfully in the real world. Furthermore, the general availability of knowledge from web-based sources also has radical implications for how content is delivered and learning is assessed.

Ideally, content delivery designs should encompass a range of different learning styles and remove barriers of time and distance.

Lecture materials can be delivered online, in part or in whole, so that valuable time in the classroom can be used for discussion and application rather than lecture. Audio podcasts of recorded lecture information can now easily take the place of face-to-face lecture because of the advent of Really Simple Syndication (RSS) technology. RSS allows an audio or video recording to be made of learning content, which can then be uploaded to the web and accessed by the user. Large companies such as Google and Amazon may make major forays into the educational market soon.

Video uploads provide a multimedia dimension to the learning experience and can be easily produced via tablet or smartphone technology, then uploaded to a free hosting service such as YouTube or an LMS. As with audio lecture content, best practices suggest that audio or video recordings should be produced in segments no longer than fifteen to twenty minutes, preferably shorter. Other technology exists to produce PowerPoint presentations with streaming audio–PowerPoint technology produced by programs such as Adobe's Captivate software.[49] Software that captures screen content and allows one to build presentations from actual screenshots can be useful for instruction from web-based sources.[50]

As knowledge and content continue to migrate toward the web, an aggregation of web-based blogs, wikis, images, and multimedia on specialty subjects will be vital to the educational process and can be integrated into any online learning experience so that students can construct their own personal learning environment as best suits their individual needs.

49. See http://www.adobe.com/products/captivate .html.
50. See http://www.telestream.net/screenflow/over view.htm.

Students are being conditioned to go to the web for learning experiences, so aggregated learning sources from the web allow students to choose from a variety of supplemental sources to enhance their online learning experience. As an aggregator of key sources, the professor is modeling for students how to properly discern quality learning sources on the web, an increasingly important skill in light of the glut of low-quality information on the web today.

Assessment

As digital education continues to advance, the need to assess learning outcomes will only grow. In the past, cognitive results were emphasized in the educational process. Students were asked to memorize a set of facts and then reiterate them in written and oral examinations that demonstrated the students had learned what they had been told. Many times this manner of assessment is a better measure of how well a student can take a test than of how well they have mastered and can apply the knowledge in the real world. Technology is driving educational pedagogy and curriculum toward outcomes-based goals, which reinforce a set of knowledge, skill, and being formation (knowing, doing, and being) competencies. The aspect of being formation is critical to Christian education. Accordingly, assessment technology is already shifting toward new competency-based trends in education. Secular education acknowledges the importance of being formation by including a limited character formation aspect in its curriculum. Christian educators have the opportunity to nest that kind of character development in its proper biblical and ethical framework for a more holistic understanding of character as it relates to successful living. The fear of the Lord is the beginning of true knowledge properly grounded in the character of God himself (Prov. 1:7).

When specific outcomes are enumerated for a particular class, rubrics can become a useful tool to help students know how competency will be measured. Online rubric generation tools, such as Rubistar, can help educators construct easily understandable rubrics so that students understand how they are being assessed.[51] E-portfolio software allows students to take factual knowledge and apply it to their world through critical thought and reflection. Tools such as a personal learning portfolio create a more synthetic educational experience that often results in significant personal transformation far beyond what a cognitive or skill-based test would produce.[52] The trends toward competency- and outcomes-based education are important milestones in the development of educational process, because they emphasize the importance of holistic education involving both mind and spirit, which is at the heart of Christian education. With the advent of the Massive Open Online Class (MOOC), the first artificial intelligence assessment programs for written essay assessment emerged as a promising assessment tool.[53]

MOOC, Learning, and the Future

One example of disruptive innovation at work in education was the Massive Open Online Class (MOOC). MOOCs were case studies in disruptive innovation at work within a particular subsection of culture and its institutions. The first MOOC was offered in 2008 at the University of Prince Edward Island. The

51. See http://rubistar.4teachers.org/.
52. Donston-Miller, "7 Ways to Create E-Portfolios."
53. Balfour, "Assessing Writing in MOOCs."

class was open to twenty-five tuition-paying students, but others could enroll in the class online with no tuition cost. The online section had twenty-three hundred students and quickly eclipsed the importance of the face-to-face class. Salman Khan, a successful hedge fund manager, built on that idea when he began posting tutorials on YouTube to help relatives with mathematics. The collection of tutorials grew into the nonprofit Khan Academy and with the help of funding from the Bill Gates Foundation and Google now includes an extensive array of tens of thousands of video lectures on subjects including math, medicine, history, and economics that have been viewed at no cost by hundreds of millions of people.[54]

Sebastian Thrun, a Stanford research professor and Google fellow, along with his colleague Peter Norvig from Google, conducted the first full-fledged MOOC effort at Stanford in 2011. Thrun and Norvig, following the strategy of the first MOOC in 2008, opened an on-campus class with an enrollment of 200 students to anyone online at no cost. They could not have imagined how massive this open online class would become. The on-campus section of the class dwindled to 30 students, while the online section topped 160,000 students from 190 countries. The results spurred a proliferation of experiments with MOOCs, setting off an innovative tidal wave, and something of a panic in higher education, so that no one would be left behind. Thrun left Stanford and launched Udacity as a stand-alone MOOC, while Daphne Koller and Andrew Ng founded Coursera about the same time in late 2011. Coursera has since advanced a model that invites other universities to participate by building their own MOOC classes on the Coursera platform.[55]

There were significant problems with developing a viable economic model for MOOCs, given that educational access was free. MOOCs also had significant attrition rates, given the low degree of interaction because of the high numbers of students in classes. Some argue that MOOCs are a failed educational experiment, but the valuable lesson that can be learned from MOOCs has nothing to do with whether they survive or not. MOOCs embody some of the most important trends that will drive education in the future, including Christian education. MOOCs embody the democratization of knowledge due to advances in web and network technologies—a world in which knowledge is free. Their advent also emphasizes the trend toward global education that reaches those in most need who can least afford access to education. MOOCs radically reduced the cost of education and made it accessible at all times to all people in all places. They represent a growing trend toward more connectivist peer-to-peer learning architecture rather than classic education, which has a more professor-centered approach. MOOCs represent the opportunity for each learner to create their own learning environment through knowledge that is distributed across the web and an education that is highly self-directed. They leverage the power of social media and interaction to create social presence and are driving a push toward competency-based education that establishes certification based on measurable outcomes in the learning process. These facets embody the current trends in education, directly attributable to the introduction of new, innovative, and disruptive technology.

54. Ta'eed, "Will the Internet Replace Traditional Education?"

55. McKenna, "Big Idea That Can Revolutionize Higher Education."

Conclusion

Due to the rapid rate of technological change, it is more important than ever to understand the trends that are driving technology and their implications for education. The key is to remain flexible in pedagogical and curricular design so as to assimilate these trends for maximum impact and efficiency in Christian education. Christian education has always been a missional endeavor. We must have fluency in the technological language and tools of the coming generation as we prepare its emerging leaders. For centuries, we have expected nothing less than this on the mission field. So must it be for Christian education.

15

Executive Leadership

JANE CARR

When Jim Collins, author of *Good to Great*, asked Circuit City vice president Walter Bruckart to name the top five factors that moved the company from mediocrity to excellence during the company's heyday, Bruckart responded, "One would be people. Two would be people. Three would be people. Four would be people. And five would be people. A huge part of our transition can be attributed to our discipline in picking the right people."[1] An effective leader recognizes that one of their primary responsibilities is hiring well. An effective leader fills positions and promotes based on what a person can do, not based on personality or personal connections.

Matching a person to the right job, or a job to the right person, is one of the most complicated responsibilities any executive leader will face. Collins refers to this as "First Who"— get the right people on the bus. Once leaders have the right people in place, then they can figure out the best path to greatness.[2] This path to greatness involves preparing people to succeed, empowering people to lead, and helping people develop.

Hire the Best People

Most leaders prepare for an interview by glancing at a candidate's résumé as they walk down the hallway to meet the candidate. Throughout the entire interview, the leader is trying desperately to think of questions to ask and halfheartedly listening to responses. Since they are unprepared, they ask ineffective questions such as ones that every interviewer asks, or hypothetical questions that elicit hypothetical responses, or leading questions that virtually tell the candidate what they want to hear. In the first seven minutes of the interview, the leader makes a gut decision about whether

---

1. J. Collins, *Good to Great*, 55.

2. J. Collins, *Good to Great*, 47.

they like the person and then spends the remainder of the interview trying to confirm their intuition. At the end of the interview, the leader is left with no real information about the candidate or their ability to do the job, but they are ready to hire the person because they really liked them. Leaders need to prepare better to conduct interviews because taking greater care on the front end of hiring results in less turnover.

Hiring the best people involves identifying competencies and character traits, considering key responsibilities, reviewing résumés, scheduling interviews, and conducting a post-interview assessment.

Identify Competencies and Character Traits

If you are in a position to hire someone, the first step is knowing what you are looking for in a person. This does not mean simply having a job description, though that is an important part. It means taking time to ask the questions, What are the competencies and character traits that are critical to the success of this role? Are we looking for someone with excellent organizational skills, or someone who can conduct training and development, or someone who is highly relational? Are we looking for someone with great perseverance, or someone who is genuine and caring, or someone who is more direct, bold, and courageous? As you prepare to vet candidates, you need to create interview questions that are behavior based and will target the competencies and character traits you desire. When we ask hypothetical questions, we get hypothetical responses. Since the best predictor of future behavior is past behavior, asking behaviorally based questions is most effective (see table 15.1).

Table 15.1. Behavior-Based Interview Questions

Competency/Character Trait	Interview Question
Genuine care and concern	How do others know that you care about them?
Perseverance	Have you ever persevered through something even though doing so was difficult?
Direct, bold, and courageous	Have you ever disagreed with a supervisor or a peer colleague? How did you handle it?

Consider Key Responsibilities

Hiring the best people also involves considering the key responsibilities they will have. As you create interview questions, utilize the job description. Be sure to ask questions that will help you discover how a candidate will approach the most important aspects of their role. Such questions focus on the skills, knowledge, and experience needed to fulfill the responsibilities of the job. Let's consider, for example, three key responsibilities of a pastoral staff member: recruitment and selection of volunteers, leading change, and supervision of staff (see table 15.2).

Table 15.2. Responsibility-Based Interview Questions

Responsibility	Interview Question
Recruitment and selection of volunteers	How would you describe some of your best practices when it comes to recruiting and selecting volunteers?
Leading change	How did you introduce a change in your last ministry setting?
Supervision of staff	How would you describe what happened when you had a staff member who was underperforming in their role?

Notice that each question calls on the respondent to give an example of how they fulfilled a key responsibility. Each interview question is also open-ended. Any time you ask, "Tell us about a time when you had a staff member who was underperforming in their role. What did you do to fix it?" you are asking a leading question. In other words, you are leading the interviewee to answer in a way that shows them as the hero who rushed in, did something about the situation, and saved the day. In actuality, the interviewee might just tell you about their frustration with an underperforming employee, the impact it had on others, and how the person eventually found another job. In addition, since you are trying to evaluate whether the candidate has the skills, knowledge, and experience needed for the position, you should ask multiple questions in different ways for each area you are trying to evaluate. Doing so will prove helpful in the postinterview evaluation. Following are some prompts you can use to evaluate skills, knowledge, and experience.

- Give an example of an occasion when you used logic to solve a problem.
- Give an example of a goal you reached.
- Give an example of a goal you didn't meet.
- Describe a stressful situation at work.
- Tell me about a time you had to work under pressure.
- Talk about a challenging time in your life or ministry.
- Have you been in a situation in which you didn't have enough work to do?
- Talk about a time when you experienced failure.

- Describe a decision you made that was unpopular.
- Did you ever postpone making a decision? Why?
- Have you ever dealt with an organizational policy you didn't agree with?
- Have you gone above and beyond the call of duty? If so, how?
- When you worked on multiple projects, how did you prioritize them?
- How did you handle meeting a tight deadline?
- What do you do when your schedule is interrupted?
- Have you had to convince people to work on a project they weren't thrilled about? How did you do it?
- Give an example of how you have worked on a team.
- Describe a difficult situation with a coworker.
- What have you done when you have disagreed with a coworker?
- Share an example of how you were able to motivate employees or coworkers.
- What have you done when you have disagreed with your boss?

Review Résumés

Before conducting an interview, you should also review a candidate's résumé and look for gaps, missing information, and theological concerns based on past organizational ties. It is better to go deeper rather than wider by focusing on the last two or three positions they had rather than trying to examine their entire work history. As you look through a résumé, get curious. What do you want to know more about? Write down several questions to ask candidates based on their résumés.

Schedule Interviews

After you have prepared basic questions to ask all candidates based on competencies and characteristics desired for the position, questions related to the job description and the responsibilities of the position, and specific questions related to the candidates' résumés, schedule multiple interviews. An initial phone interview for fifteen to thirty minutes is a great start, especially if a face-to-face interview will require making significant travel arrangements for the candidate. Many organizations plan an entire weekend for one candidate when travel is involved. The weekend might include multiple interviews with various groups of people, social interactions, and opportunities to observe the person interacting with children, students, or congregation members.

At higher levels of leadership, a candidate might also be involved in theological interviews with key staff members and several elders of the church. Oftentimes candidates will respond in writing to a church's doctrinal statement or position statements (human sexuality, women in ministry, abortion, etc.) and then participate in an interview to clarify areas of potential concern.

Conduct a Post-Interview Assessment

A post-interview assessment is a key part of the process of vetting candidates.[3] After the interviews, based on candidates' answers and any other impressions received during the interviews, have everyone involved rate the candidates from 0 to 3 for each of the competencies/character traits and responsibilities

3. Andersen, *Growing Great Employees*, 51.

associated with the job: 0 = unacceptable, 1 = growth area, 2 = strength, 3 = key strength (see table 15.3). Leave blank any skills or competencies you weren't able to observe. Based on all you have seen and heard, give each candidate an overall rating.

Table 15.3. Post-Interview Assessment

Competency / Character Trait	Responsibility
Genuine care and concern _____	Recruitment and selection of volunteers _____
Perseverance _____	Leading change _____
Direct, bold, and courageous _____	Supervision of staff _____
Overall Rating _____	

Jim Collins says that good-to-great companies, when choosing the right people, place greater weight on character attributes than on specific educational background, practical skills, specialized knowledge, or work experience.[4] This doesn't mean that skills and knowledge aren't important, but such things can be taught. Dimensions such as character traits are ingrained and more difficult to change in a person.

A Sample Hiring Process

A sample hiring process for an associate staff member who will report to a pastor of high school students follows. In this case, both the supervisor (high school pastor) and the departmental leader (student ministries pastor) are involved in the process.

1. HR reviews and then routes résumés to the high school pastor and the student ministries pastor.

4. J. Collins, *Good to Great*, 51.

2. The high school pastor and the student ministries pastor review the résumés and indicate to HR which candidates to request applications from.

3. HR requests that approved applicants submit an application.

4. HR routes the applications to the high school pastor and the student ministries pastor.

5. The high school pastor and the student ministries pastor conduct prescreening phone calls with select candidates.

6. HR checks the references of the candidates to be interviewed.

7. The high school pastor and the student ministries pastor conduct interviews with the candidates.

   a. Candidates are encouraged to attend a service if they haven't already done so.

   b. Candidates are encouraged to attend a particular area of ministry as an observer.

   c. Candidates are asked to return for any additional interviews deemed necessary.

8. The high school pastor and the student ministries pastor give a final recommendation to HR.

9. HR conducts a background check on the recommended candidate (live scan, credit history, criminal history, DMV, etc.).

10. The executive or lead pastor conducts a final interview with the recommended candidate.

11. The candidate meets with the student ministry team.

12. HR sends an offer letter.

Prepare People to Succeed

In Christian organizations, leaders are infamous for hiring poorly and then throwing employees into the deep end to sink or swim. Erika Andersen says, "Getting an employee started right basically means providing the answers to the who, how, and what questions."[5] According to Gallup, only about 50 percent of employees know what is expected of them at work. Many people believe that simply giving someone a job description will do. However, knowing what is expected involves more than just a job description. It includes understanding how what one person is supposed to do fits in with what everyone else is supposed to do and how those expectations change when circumstances change.[6] Here are some questions every employee should be able to answer.

Question 1: Who do I need to know?
   • Who will I be interacting with, and what will we be doing together?
   • Who are the key people in the company, and what are their roles?
   • Who else will be important to my success, and why?

Question 2: How do things get done around here?
   • What systems or procedures do I need to understand and use?
   • What cultural expectations (unwritten rules) exist here?
   • What is definitely not okay to do here?

Question 3: What is expected of me?
   • How does my job description translate into day-to-day work?

5. Andersen, *Growing Great Employees*, 61.
6. Wagner and Harter, *12: The Elements of Great Managing*, 4.

- What short-term priorities are most critical?
- How will I communicate with my supervisor about expectations going forward?[7]

Most employees want to do a good job, and if they are set up for success, they will produce good results. Employees need more than information to succeed. They also need materials, resources, equipment, and adequate facilities. According to Gallup's research, only one-third of employees strongly agreed that they have the materials and the equipment they need to do their work well.[8] Executive leaders would do well to set employees up for success by providing them with not only the information they need to get started but also the material resources that will allow them to do their very best.

Empower People to Lead

According to Ken Blanchard, "Empowerment is the creation of an organizational climate that releases the knowledge, experience, and motivation that reside in people."[9] Simply put, empowerment is not giving power to people but rather releasing power that is already inside the people we lead. This is often easier said than done in churches today. Executive leaders are fearful of releasing power. Perhaps their role models were command-and-control, top-down, hierarchical-type leaders. Perhaps they are reluctant to relinquish control because they know they will still be held

accountable for outcomes. Perhaps their pride or need to be seen by others has created an internal obstacle for them and others.

As Blanchard points out, if leaders are going to move toward empowering others, they must adopt a new culture (see table 15.4).[10]

Table 15.4. Hierarchical Culture versus Empowerment Culture

Hierarchical Culture	Empowerment Culture
Planning	Visioning
Command and control	Partnering for performance
Manager monitoring	Self-monitoring
Individual responsiveness	Team responsibility
Pyramid structures	Cross-functional structures
Workflow processes	Projects
Managers	Coaches/team leaders
Employees	Team members
Participative management	Self-directed teams
Do as you are told	Own your job
Compliance	Good judgment

When leaders develop a culture of empowerment, they create opportunities for people to lead with greater pride and ownership. Such people make better decisions and are willing to take calculated risks. They do what is best, not just what is expected. They are more engaged on the job, which brings greater productivity and results.

Empowering others involves giving them information. We have all heard the saying that information is power. As Blanchard suggests, sharing information builds trust and promotes organizational learning.[11] In *The Leadership*

7. Andersen, *Growing Great Employees*, 61–64.

8. Wagner and Harter, *12: The Elements of Great Managing*, 24.

9. Blanchard, *Leading at a Higher Level*, 69.

10. Blanchard, *Leading at a Higher Level*, 72–73.

11. Blanchard, *Leading at a Higher Level*, 77.

Pipeline, the authors state, "Managers who issue orders, jealously guard information, and make unilateral decisions won't get the best performance from their people."[12] Managers who control people by controlling information will not get the best from people who expect to have access to information and be involved in the decision-making process.

Empowering others also involves giving them opportunities. One of the biggest leaps for executive leaders is moving from individual contributor to manager. As an individual contributor, they were responsible for everything. Therefore, the idea of releasing things to others can be overwhelming. In *HBR's 10 Must Reads for New Managers*, Carol Walker states in her article titled "Saving Your Rookie Managers from Themselves," "New managers should be encouraged to take small risks initially, playing to the strengths of their staff members. Early success will build the manager's confidence and willingness to take progressively larger risks in stretching each team member's capabilities. Reinforce to him that delegation does not mean abdication."[13] Ensuring that a sufficient number of meetings are set to outline the task, staying abreast of progress, and maintaining adequate accountability are essential.

There are several common signs that a manager is not empowering their team to lead. They view questions from their people as interruptions. They fix mistakes themselves rather than using them as an opportunity to teach others to do the work properly. They do not take credit for the successes of their people and distance themselves from their problems and failures.[14] Individual contributors are

used to spending their time doing rather than discussing. Yet managers need to engage in regular discussions with people. They need to monitor the completion of tasks and ask questions about what might be getting in the way. Management is an active not a passive process.

In the late 1960s, Ken Blanchard and Paul Hersey introduced four styles of leadership through what they would later call the situational leadership model.[15] The four styles of leadership are directing, coaching, supporting, and delegating—each style varying in the amount of direction provided, the amount of support provided, and the amount of leadership responsibility assumed by the employee. Directing behaviors include organizing, planning, teaching, focusing, and structuring, while supportive behaviors include affirming, involving, listening, and encouraging. The model is based on the premise that no single leadership style fits everyone. A leader must adapt their leadership style to the person they are leading depending on the experience of the person and their motivation to do a task. A leader might even use a different style with the same person depending on the task at hand.

The situational leadership model can help a leader determine the best way to empower those they lead. If a person has little to no experience or is insecure about taking on a new task, then the most empowering thing a leader can do is be more directing. If a person lacks experience but is highly motivated and enthusiastic about learning and jumping in and trying, then a coaching leader who gives direction but allows for more interaction in the process by asking questions, listening, giving feedback, and affirming will most likely empower the em-

---

12. Charan, Drotter, and Noel, *Leadership Pipeline*, 38.
13. Walker, "Saving Your Rookie Managers," 40.
14. Charan, Drotter, and Noel, *Leadership Pipeline*, 43.

15. Blanchard, *Leading at a Higher Level*, 89.

ployee. If a person has experience and is able to do a task on their own but lacks the motivation to do so, then a supporting leader who affirms, encourages, and provides accountability will make them feel empowered. Finally, if a person is highly experienced at a task and highly motivated to do the work independently of others, then a delegating leader will truly empower them to excel.[16]

Help People Develop

Gallup has discovered that four out of ten employees feel that neither their manager nor anyone else in the organization is looking out for their development. Despite the importance of development at any point in a person's career, the frequency with which managers invest in employee development declines with workers' age and tenure in an organization. More than half of employees age eighteen to twenty-four who are less than six months into a new job indicate that someone at work encourages their development. However, the percentage slips to just 25 percent (or one out of four) for workers over fifty-five years of age and to 20 percent (or one out of five) for workers with ten or more years at a particular company.[17]

Meeting regularly, one-on-one, with people gives leaders an opportunity to personally coach and develop them. "One-on-ones allow for focused time with a staff member to listen to them, debrief ministry events, consider upcoming needs, provide encouragement and correction, and troubleshoot challenges."[18]

These times are also beneficial for personal accountability, support, mentoring, and development. An important aspect of all these areas is feedback. In order to develop people, leaders must first be able to give feedback.

Give Feedback

Douglas Stone and Sheila Heen report that the feedback process strikes at the tension between two fundamental human needs: the need to learn and grow and the need to be accepted just the way we are.[19] James Kouzes and Barry Posner cite that a major reason people are not proactive in asking for feedback is that they are simply afraid of being exposed as not perfect, not knowing everything, not being as good of a leader as they should be, and not being up to the task.[20] A person's ability to receive feedback is also based on their mind-set.

Fixed and Growth Mind-Sets

Development requires feedback because it is essential for learning and growth. But a person's openness to feedback depends on their mind-set toward learning and growth. Benjamin Barber, an eminent sociologist, once said, "I don't divide the world into the weak and the strong, or the successes and the failures. . . . I divide the world into the learners and the non-learners."[21] Mind-sets are simply the beliefs we carry with us. Our beliefs can and do change over time. What we believe profoundly affects the ways in which we behave.

Someone with a fixed mind-set believes their qualities are set in stone. They have a certain amount of intelligence, and every

16. K. Lawson and Boersma, *Supervising and Supporting Ministry Staff*, 56.

17. Wagner and Harter, *12: The Elements of Great Managing*, 82.

18. K. Lawson and Boersma, *Supervising and Supporting Ministry Staff*, 55.

19. D. Stone and Heen, *Thanks for the Feedback*, 8.
20. Kouzes and Posner, *Learning Leadership*, 161.
21. Quoted in Dweck, *Mindset*, 17.

situation calls for them to confirm that intelligence. They must prove themselves, and every situation is about success or failure, looking smart or looking dumb, being accepted or being rejected, being a winner or being a loser. Someone with a fixed mind-set tries to repair their self-esteem after a failure by assigning blame or making excuses. They are always in danger of being measured by a failure.

Someone with a growth mind-set believes their basic qualities are things they can cultivate through effort. They believe everyone can change and grow and that every situation is an opportunity to challenge oneself and to learn something new. When people believe their basic qualities can be developed, then failures, though still disappointing, don't define them.[22]

The good news is that people can change their mind-set. Just by being aware of the mind-set and knowing their own tendencies, they can make different choices when faced with challenges (see table 15.5). When they catch themselves passing up a chance for learning, feeling labeled by a failure, or becoming discouraged when something requires a great deal of effort, they can choose to embrace a growth mind-set rather than a fixed mind-set. A growth mind-set also allows them to be more open to the feedback of others.

Managers with a fixed mind-set view others with a certain fixed ability. They praise ability and look down on the mistakes of others because they see mistakes as evidence of a lack of ability, they value the ability to consistently perform and provide feedback that is evaluative and critical, and they are concerned with the group being seen as good. Managers with a growth mind-set view others as resourceful and full of potential. They praise effort and

22. Dweck, *Mindset*, 245.

Table 15.5. Two Mind-Sets

Fixed Mind-Set	Growth Mind-Set
Intelligence Is Static	**Intelligence Can Be Developed**
Leads to a desire to look smart and therefore a tendency to . . .	Leads to a desire to learn and therefore a tendency to . . .
Challenges	
avoid challenges	embrace challenges
Obstacles	
give up easily	persist in the face of setbacks
Effort	
see effort as fruitless or worse	see effort as a path to mastery
Criticism	
ignore useful negative feedback	learn from criticism
Success of Others	
feel threatened by the success of others	find lessons and inspiration in the success of others
As a result, they may plateau early and achieve less than their full potential.	**As a result**, they reach even higher levels of achievement.

Adapted from Dweck, *Mindset*, 245.

persistence and embrace the mistakes of others by encouraging and helping people in order to get the most learning out of them, they value the ability to learn and perform and they provide feedback that promotes development, and they are concerned with the group getting better.

While managers with a growth mind-set believe it is important to hire talented people, they are extremely committed to their employees' development. They believe that people can change and grow, give more feedback and more developmental coaching than those with a fixed mind-set, and notice improvement in employees' performance.

For feedback to be beneficial, both leaders and those they lead must work to develop a growth mind-set.

Types of Feedback

There are two types of feedback that are beneficial: reinforcement feedback and improvement feedback. Reinforcement feedback says, "Hey, what you are doing is making a huge contribution here. Keep doing it." Ken Blanchard promotes setting aside at least two hours a week for cheering people on.[23] Reinforcement feedback is a wonderful tool for creating greater engagement.[24] Reinforcement feedback is appreciative, and appreciation is fundamentally about relationship and human connection. Appreciation says, "Thanks," but it also conveys, "I see you," "I know how hard you've been working," and "You matter to me."[25]

Yet people often hear managers say, "If I don't say anything, you're doing a good job." This is the idea that no news is good news. Others say, "I'm just not good at giving praise." According to Gallup's research, less than one out of three employees can strongly agree with the statement that in the last seven days they received recognition or praise for doing good work.[26] Employees who do not feel adequately recognized are more likely to say they will leave their company in the next year.

Improvement feedback says, "Hey, what you are doing is not working and it's having a negative impact. Something must change."

The timing of this type of feedback needs to be as immediate as possible. People have a difficult time accepting feedback that they do not understand. The more time that lapses between a behavior observed by a manager and the feedback given to the employee, the greater the likelihood that the feedback itself will be rejected. There are two simple guidelines for giving improvement feedback. First, ask for permission: something as simple as "Could I share something with you that might be helpful?" Second, be specific: focus on what you observed or heard, on what the individual did or said, and on the impact that this had on you, others, or the organization.[27]

John Zenger and Kathleen Stinnett encourage leaders to provide at least three times as much positive, reinforcement feedback as improvement feedback. They state that "this 3-to-1 ratio seems to be the secret to creating good feelings and improved results."[28]

How to Give Feedback

According to Erika Andersen, leaders often do one of five things when it comes to feedback: they give no feedback, they give delayed feedback, they give general feedback, they give softened feedback that lacks urgency, or they give feedback that is specific and timely (given as soon as possible) and includes why it is important to make changes in light of the feedback.[29] The last option is most useful.

Zenger and Stinnett created the fast-feedback test, six simple questions leaders can ask themselves before giving feedback.

23. Blanchard, *Leading at a Higher Level*, 158.
24. Zenger and Stinnett, *Extraordinary Coach*, 184.
25. D. Stone and Heen, *Thanks for the Feedback*, 31.
26. Wagner and Harter, *12: The Elements of Great Managing*, 52.

27. Zenger and Stinnett, *Extraordinary Coach*, 214–15.
28. Zenger and Stinnett, *Extraordinary Coach*, 185.
29. Andersen, *Growing Great Employees*, 149.

1. Will the information be useful to the recipient?

2. Do I have a trust-based relationship in place that will support the conversation?

3. Is the behavior change critical for the individual's success?

4. Will the feedback be new or surprising to hear? Will the data fall into a blind spot for the individual and perhaps be shocking to them?

5. Will the behavior change take significant time, effort, or support?

6. Am I personally invested in the behavior change?[30]

If, based on the answers to these questions, a leader decides to give feedback, they should ask permission to share the feedback and then be specific, focusing on what the individual did or said and its impact on the leader, others, or the results.[31]

Leaders tend to interpret behaviors and give feedback based on their interpretations rather than on the facts. Examples include "You are aloof" or "You aren't being a team player" or "You come across as arrogant." Andersen suggests a method she calls the camera check.[32] A leader should imagine watching the person in action like a camera recording the behavior that needs changing, then playing the tape in their head and noticing what they see and hear the person doing or not doing (see table 15.6).

Leaders also have to realize that for feedback to be helpful, people must understand it. Feedback often arrives packaged like generic

Table 15.6. Common Feedback versus Camera-Check Feedback

Common Feedback	Camera-Check Feedback
Aloof	Doesn't make eye contact with others in the room, looks at their phone often, and types on their computer rather than participating in the conversation
Arrogant	Doesn't speak to colleagues in the halls, rolls their eyes and shakes their head while others speak, and interrupts to disagree with others' ideas

items in the supermarket labeled "soup" or "cola." The feedback the leader gives seems clear—"You are aloof" or "You come across as arrogant"—but it actually contains little content and thus has little value. The more specific leaders are in their feedback, the more helpful it is to others.[33]

Leaders can help people develop through feedback. In every organization, explicit and implicit messages evolve about what is actually valued and what we say that we value. If we want learning and continuous improvement to be valued, it has to be embedded in what we talk about and celebrate. Do we take time to debrief and get feedback around our work, or do we save it all up for that once-a-year opportunity to let it all out in a performance review?

Ask Questions

Baseball coaches always tell players, "Keep your eye on the ball." In all sports that involve a ball, it is certainly important to watch the ball, but does telling someone to watch the ball actually cause them to do so? What if the coach instead asked questions to build awareness for

30. This list is from Zenger and Stinnett, *Extraordinary Coach*, 185.

31. Zenger and Stinnett, *Extraordinary Coach*, 217.

32. Andersen, *Growing Great Employees*, 152.

33. D. Stone and Heen, *Thanks for the Feedback*, 48.

the player—such as, "What do notice about this pitcher's routine?" or "Which way is the ball spinning as it comes toward you?" These questions would compel players to actually watch the ball. Players will have to focus and concentrate more on what is happening and how it is impacting their behavior. Their answers would be descriptive, so there would be no risk of self-criticism or self-defeat. The same approach can be used by leaders to help people discover for themselves, learn from an experience, and gain the skills they need to do something on their own.[34]

The most effective questions for raising awareness and helping people develop in their roles begin with words that help to quantify or gather facts, words such as *what*, *when*, and *who*. The word *why* is discouraged since it often implies criticism and evokes defensiveness, and *why* and *how*, if unqualified, both cause analytical thinking, which can be counterproductive. Analysis (thinking) and awareness (observation) are dissimilar mental modes that are virtually impossible to employ simultaneously to full effect. Why and how questions are better expressed as what questions: "What were the reasons . . ." or "What are the next steps . . ."[35]

How do leaders convert a discussion into a decision that employees will act on? A good manager can get an employee moving by asking simple questions such as these:

- What are you going to do?
- When are you going to do it?
- What obstacles might you meet along the way?
- Who needs to know about it?

34. Whitmore, *Coaching for Performance*, 44–45.
35. Whitmore, *Coaching for Performance*, 47.

- What support do you need along the way?
- On a scale of 1 to 10, rate the degree of certainty you have that you will carry this out. What prevents it from being a 10?

Telling someone how to do something or asking closed-ended questions saves people from having to think. This may appear more efficient for a leader who simply wants to move on to the next thing, but, ultimately, it does not help the employee develop. Asking open-ended questions encourages employees to think for themselves.

Conduct an After-Action Review

Too often leaders recognize people for getting a job done or for accomplishing a goal. John Zenger and Kathleen Stinnett state, "While it is important to acknowledge the attainment of the end result, if that is all we do, we miss the opportunity to truly reinforce the behaviors that made the individual successful."[36] In addition, people miss the learning that can be gleaned from their successes. An after-action review (AAR) is a structured review or debriefing process for analyzing what happened, why it happened, and how it could have been done better by the participants and those responsible for the project or event.[37] This process is useful for learning from both successes and

36. Zenger and Stinnett, *Extraordinary Coach*, 185.
37. After-action reviews in the formal sense were originally developed by the US Army. Formal AARs are used by all US military services and by many other non-US organizations. Their use has extended to business as a knowledge-management tool and a way to build a culture of accountability. An AAR occurs within a cycle of establishing the leader's intent, planning, preparation, action, and review.

failures. It is distinct from a debrief in that it begins with a clear comparison of intended versus actual results. It can also be a helpful tool for considering what was learned from both successes and failures. It focuses on participants' actions, and participants learn from the review. Recommendations for others are not produced. AARs in larger operations can be used to keep each level of an organization focused on its own performance within a particular event or project.

Here are some sample questions to use for an AAR.

1. *What was the intent?* What was the intended outcome? What was to be accomplished, and how was it to be accomplished?
2. *What happened, and why did it happen?* What were the results, and what contributed to them? What were the critical points or junctures along the way?
3. *What was learned?* What is known now that wasn't known before? What lessons learned will help you or someone else do better next time?

Form a Learning Plan

To develop and learn new behaviors we must have a plan that includes experimentation, practice, and feedback in safe settings and alongside supportive relationships. As we adopt new responses, patterns of behavior, and capabilities, we are essentially rewiring our brain.[38] A learning plan is simply a stated learning goal that you want to accomplish. It

could be something like, "I want to become a more empathetic leader" or "I want to become a leader who inspires and develops others." Having stated the learning goal, identify several milestones or noticeable markers that indicate that you are heading toward accomplishing the goal. For each milestone create several action steps that indicate what you will do to reach the milestone. For example:

Learning Goal: To become a more emotionally self-controlled leader.
Milestone 1: No longer be verbally and nonverbally reactionary in stressful situations.
Action Steps

1. Identify my triggers.
2. Ask myself, "Is it worth it?" when I want to interrupt or make a comment.
3. Practice patient listening, allow others to fully express everything before I speak.
4. Read a book or watch several TED Talks on listening.

Conclusion

At the executive level of leadership, people move from managing themselves to managing others. Perhaps the most difficult aspect of this transition is shifting from getting the work done by yourself to getting the work done through others. Executive leaders are in a significant position to hire the best people, prepare them to succeed, empower them to lead, and help them develop.

---

38. Zenger and Stinnett, *Extraordinary Coach*, 177.

PART 4

EDUCATIONAL MINISTRIES

I f Christian education is anything, it is ministry. When the average person thinks about Christian education, thoughts of children's ministry and youth ministry typically follow. This is understandable due to the tremendous impact age-group ministries have within the field. Even so, Christian education is much more comprehensive than the ministries that serve people in those few but important years of growth. It is concerned with ministry during all phases of life, because God has a plan for our *entire* lives—and that plan extends from prior to our conception throughout eternity (Eph. 3:1–14).

Understanding the Nature of Ministry

Christian education involves equipping people for disciple making and spiritual formation throughout life. For this reason, local churches and parachurch organizations invest their resources to meet the needs of all people at all ages. The Bible mentions the concept of ministry several times. Both the Old and the New Testament speak about it at length—and the

Word of God tells us both what ministry is and, often, how to do it.

The Bible describes all Christians as disciples, saints, priests, and ministers (Acts 11:26; Eph. 4:11–13; 1 Pet. 2:9–10).[1] Ministry is something all disciples should perform by serving as a priest, offering up "spiritual sacrifices acceptable to God" (1 Pet. 2:5). A priest is a divine representative who serves as a bridge builder between God and humanity. In the Old Testament, God assigned Moses's brother Aaron and his sons to be priests (Exod. 28:1). This was called the Aaronic priesthood. That priesthood existed from the time of the old covenant until Christ became our High Priest in the new covenant (Heb. 10:1–21). In the New Testament, Jesus abolished the Aaronic priesthood and replaced it with the priesthood of all believers. In this new-covenant-based priesthood, *all* believers are now priests. We serve under the Lord Jesus Christ, our High Priest (Heb. 4:14–16), and every Christian has the responsibility and the privilege to minister in his name (1 Pet. 2:9–10).

1. Cardoza, "Theology of Ministry," 25–26.

211

Why Professional Ministry Equipping Is Important

Clearly, God considers ministry a high priority. So should we. An important aspect of doing ministry is preparing for ministry—not just "doing" it. Being equipped to do ministry is a clear priority in Scripture (Eph. 4:11–13). Without proper equipping, ministry can be ineffective and even harmful. This is a direct challenge to those who reject the biblical command to be equipped, assuming that sincerity somehow eliminates ignorance. The truth is that we discover what ministry is by looking to the Word of God and by integrating other sources of truth God has given us.

As the author of Scripture, God has the prerogative to tell us what ministry is. For this reason, Christian leaders are responsible to construct a biblical understanding of doing God's work. In other words, Christian educators must develop a biblical theology of ministry. We do this by studying ministry and practicing it, sometimes called theory and praxis.

Theory has to do with studying what God's Word and educated and experienced ministry specialists have to say about each area of Christian ministry. This shapes our underlying assumptions, perceptions, beliefs, and strategies about ministry. Beyond theory is praxis.

Praxis isn't just practice. Praxis has to do with taking the learned theoretical knowledge and applying it to real life, practically. When we unite the theory that is within our heads and hearts with the praxis from our skilled hands, our ministries can make a powerful impact.

A Call to Be Equipped in Ministry

A lack of spiritual impact by many churches is undoubtedly related to confusion about the essence of biblical ministry. Those in ministry should be properly equipped in the areas in which they seek to serve. This part is designed to help you do just that. In it, you will learn from some of the most highly educated, skillfully trained, and practically effective ministers in the field of Christian education. Whether you are being equipped to serve in family ministry, children's ministry, youth ministry, emerging adult ministry, or adult ministry, specialized training can be found within this important section of the book. Read each chapter carefully. Think deeply about the depth and the breadth of each ministry area. Then work to assemble a strong biblical and theoretical basis for all phases of human life in order to be fully prepared to do the work of ministry for which God has called you. As you do, people will be impacted and your ministry will be blessed.

16

Family Ministry

HOLLY CATTERTON ALLEN

Family ministries in faith communities have proliferated in the United States during the past three or four decades. The particular form or model of family ministry employed depends on the perceived needs a church is seeking to address. Some churches want their family ministry to simply create opportunities to bring families back together, as they have realized that specialized children's and youth ministries have tended to separate families. Others have created family ministries specifically to provide support for hurting families who are experiencing marital discord, divorce, abuse, or loss. Still other congregations view family ministry as the chief vehicle to equip parents to be the primary spiritual nurturers of their children.

As churches have developed family ministries, Christian universities and seminaries have responded to the call to equip for this specialization. A survey among evangelical colleges and universities found that 80 percent require or recommend a family ministry course for an undergraduate degree in Christian education or Christian ministries; at the graduate level, 83 percent require or recommend a family ministry course for a Christian education/ministries master's degree.[1] This data indicates that family ministry is alive and well among evangelical programs that are preparing future ministers, spiritual formation leaders, and Christian educators.

Thousands of evangelical churches in the United States now offer family ministries.

1. In 2012, Kevin Lawson (Talbot School of Theology) in conjunction with the Society of Professors of Christian Education conducted research among Christian education/ministries professors who teach in evangelical colleges and universities that offer undergraduate and/or graduate degrees in Christian education (or Christian ministries). The survey focused on the types of Christian education/ministry degree specializations, majors, and courses the professors' colleges/universities offer. There were 174 respondents representing 166 Christian colleges/universities. K. Lawson and Wilhoit, "SPCE Report," 276–93.

Some employ full- or part-time family ministers; others combine positions—for example, hiring a youth and family minister or a children's and family minister. And others, especially larger churches, engage full- or part-time marriage and family therapists to work with families in distress.

This chapter describes the purposes and rationale for various forms of family ministry, offers basic biblical and theological underpinnings, outlines several general models that churches follow, and offers a gentle critique along the way.

Purposes and Rationale for Family Ministry

Family ministry has sometimes been offered *proactively* (e.g., promoting healthy communication) and sometimes *reactively* (responding to the perceived crisis of the family in North America). Indicators of family erosion include the rise of single-parent families, the prevalence of divorce, the incidence of juvenile delinquency, and the increase in the numbers of teens and emerging adults leaving the faith. Church leaders have created specialized family ministry approaches that both educate toward healthy relational and communication patterns in all families and offer robust help, concrete support, and encouraging hope for families in crisis.

Family Ministry to Promote Healthy Families and to Support Struggling Families

Family life education approaches have been among the most common means of formulating a family ministry that attempts to promote healthy families and address difficult issues families experience. Charles Sell's classic *Family Ministry*, first published in 1981 and revised in 1995, describes a two-pronged family life education approach to family ministry. First, Sell advocates a strong educational component that offers preparation and enrichment seminars/retreats/classes that promote healthy relationships and processes between spouses (marriage education) and between parents and children (parenting education). Second, he offers guidelines for both educational and therapeutic approaches for helping families struggling with serious marital discord, abusive relationships, codependency and addiction issues, and other troubling concerns. Sell then explores the idea of church as family, recommending whole-congregation (intergenerational) programming (e.g., camping, special events, education) as well as specific opportunities for nuclear family units to do things together. Sell acknowledges the diversity in family structures today, along with the unique needs of single adults, but not as thoroughly as more recent books on family ministry.

Don Hebbard's *Complete Handbook for Family Life Ministry in the Church* is another practical guide for family ministry that, like Sell's, advocates both educational and therapeutic approaches to family ministry. Hebbard defines family life ministry as "ministry of the church through preventive and therapeutic efforts designed to strengthen all forms of families in the church and the community."[2] Hebbard broadens some of Sell's concepts, using more holistic terminology and emphasizing outreach (serving those *outside* the faith community) as well as inreach (serving those *inside* the faith community). Hebbard underscores

2. Hebbard, *Complete Handbook*, 6.

the importance of addressing all forms of families, acknowledging the brokenness that is present in all families and the importance of the whole church as family (especially to single adults and seniors). He views family ministry as including both evangelism and edification.

Family Ministry to Bring Families Together

A less comprehensive approach to family ministry is taken by churches with a primary goal of counteracting the separating effect that children's and youth ministries have had on families. Mark DeVries's *Family-Based Youth Ministry*, first published in 1994, was a direct response to the generational segregation he witnessed (and participated in) as a youth minister for two decades. DeVries realized that perennially separating youth from their families did not serve teenagers or families well.

In the realm of children's ministry, Ben Freudenburg and Rick Lawrence's *Family-Friendly Church* and Ivy Beckwith's *Postmodern Ministry to Children in the 21st Century* echo DeVries's key point that regularly segregating parents and children does not bless families spiritually. These authors attempt to frame children's ministry within a larger theology of family, avoiding the compartmentalized approach of stand-alone children's ministries that nurture and minister to young children but segregate families in ways that are unnecessary and less helpful.

In response to these criticisms, some churches have added family-integrated components to their specialized youth and children's ministries. Others have added a stand-alone family ministry program to provide intentional family gatherings in spiritual settings: coordinating a Passover event for families,

sponsoring family retreats, or offering family Bible studies. In these ways, churches benefit families by providing both age-specific and whole-family ministry.

Family Ministry to Promote Parents as Spiritual Shepherds

Other faith communities have observed that the prevalence of children's and youth ministries has inadvertently led to another unintended consequence: parents abdicating their role as primary spiritual nurturers of their children because the church's specialized ministries have in some ways appropriated that role.

Timothy Paul Jones and Randy Stinson[3] describe the family-equipping model of family ministry in which "every practice at every level of ministry is reworked completely to champion the place of parents as primary disciple-makers in their children's lives."[4] In this model, children's and youth ministries are redeveloped to train parents and to involve them in the various programs or activities that take place. According to Jones and Stinson, "Every level of the congregation's life is consciously reworked to 'co-champion' the church's ministry *and* the parent's responsibility."[5]

Whatever iteration family ministry takes, church leaders are clearly concerned for the families in their churches and desire to help with the ordinary life tasks in families while also providing assistance when life falls down. Other influencers in the field of family ministry

3. Timothy Jones and Stinson, "Family Ministry Models," 155–80. See also Timothy Jones, *Perspectives on Family Ministry*.
4. Timothy Jones and Stinson, "Family Ministry Models," 175.
5. Timothy Jones and Stinson, "Family Ministry Models," 176.

are Diana Garland (former sociology professor at Baylor University),[6] Denise Kjesbo (professor and lead faculty of children's and family ministry at Bethel Seminary),[7] and Michael and Michelle Anthony (longtime academic and ministry leaders).[8]

Sticking Points in Discussions of Family Ministry

Any discussion of family ministry must inevitably address the question, What do we mean by family? Often the word *family* in family ministry refers primarily to families in the church who are raising children (emphasizing how to parent, discipline, and nurture children spiritually); it sometimes includes a focus on married couples (emphasizing how to communicate, manage conflict, etc. between spouses); and sometimes, though less commonly, the word *family* in family ministry means everyone in the family of God. The way a congregation defines family will inescapably influence how family ministry is accomplished in that setting.

Defining family today is a complex task. This discussion has been made more challenging due to movements seeking to redefine the nature and the composition of the family, sometimes in ways that compromise traditional biblical understandings. Diana Garland has worked to address this definitional task comprehensively. Her book on family ministry, *Family Ministry* (originally published in 1999 but substantially revised for the 2012 edition), takes a wide-ranging, nuanced look at families, their relationships,

the role of church and society in their healthy development, and the serious issues families face today. Garland says that the sociological study of families has taken two approaches to defining family: the first is *structural*—that is, describing "the ways persons are related to one another biologically and/or legally"—and the other is *functional*, meaning "based on the ways persons relate to one another, or function in one another's lives, in ways expected of family members."[9]

Churches (as well as Western society) have tended to utilize the structural definition of families—that is, people are family because of legal relationship (marriage or adoption) or biological relationship with one another (e.g., children, siblings). Structural definitions include extended family, blended families, and stepfamilies.[10] As churches developed family ministries in the past, they usually retained this structural understanding of families, focusing, as noted earlier, primarily on nuclear families but more recently acknowledging and addressing the unique needs of blended families and stepfamilies. However, churches are made up of many kinds of families and various household arrangements: grandparent/grandchildren families, single-parent families, and cohabiting couples with children. If a church is going to have a family ministry based on family structure, it should acknowledge the presence of these diverse households and intentionally minister with and to all these families.

One last sticking point in discussions of family ministry is that a focus on families excludes single adults of various stripes, childless married couples, couples who have adult children, and anyone not currently raising chil-

---

6. Garland, *Family Ministry.*
7. Kjesbo, "Five Models of Family Ministry."
8. Anthony and Anthony, *Theology for Family Ministries.*

9. Garland, *Family Ministry*, 53.
10. Garland, *Family Ministry*, 54.

dren. If family ministry *by definition* focuses on families with children, it unavoidably earns one of the criticisms of children's and youth ministries of the past—that is, it has a segregating effect on faith communities. In these instances, families with children will be the focus, and people of all ages who do not fit that definition will often feel sidelined.

Another way of conceiving family ministry is to explore Garland's functional definition of family. Garland says that *family* can be defined functionally as "the organization of relationships that endure over time and context, through which persons attempt to meet their needs for belonging and attachment and to share life purposes, help and resources."[11] If we consider faith communities to be the family of God, this functional definition could work very well.[12]

As this chapter unfolds, it will begin to explore family ministry in a broader sense, employing this more functional definition of family, in order to help us begin to think of family ministry in terms not only of how nuclear families can grow and become healthier but also of how the body of Christ, the family of God, can grow and become healthier. In this sense, family ministry can help us do the following:

- relate to one another—married persons, parents, singles, sisters, brothers, widows, old and young, male and female—in our homes as well as in our faith communities

- meet one another's needs for belonging and attachment so that none are family-less
- focus together on the shared tasks of building up the body (edification), reaching others who do not know Christ (evangelism), and caring for the marginalized, the oppressed, the powerless, and the hungry among us and also in our larger communities

Biblical and Theological Underpinnings for Family Ministry

Since family ministry has most commonly tended to focus on married couples and families with children, those who promote traditional family ministry ground their biblical foundations in Scripture's teaching regarding spouses and parenting. The creation of the male-female couple, their mutual role in ruling creation, and their relationship with God and with each other are described early in Genesis. The disconnects that ensued as a result of the fall are also described in Genesis and beyond. These original intentions and ultimate consequences, coupled with the teachings of Paul,[13] Peter,[14] and Jesus[15] in the New Testament, explain the mutual love, care, and respect that should characterize marriage and family relationships.

Family Structure in Scripture

With God's admonishment to Adam and Eve to populate the earth, the role of parenting came into being. Throughout the Old Testament, various stories of parents and children

---

11. Garland, *Family Ministry*, 56.
12. Garland does not use this functional definition in regard to faith communities; she offers it as an alternative to the structural definition of families as a way to encompass broader understandings of families that include households made up of those who are family to one another regardless of biological or legal connection.

13. For example, Eph. 5:22–32; Col. 3:18–22.
14. 1 Pet. 2:13–3:7.
15. For example, Matt. 19:1–11; Mark 10:2–12.

are depicted: Abraham's family (Sarah and Isaac, Hagar and Ishmael), Isaac's family (Rebekah, Jacob, and Esau), Jacob's family (Rachel, Leah, Bilhah, and Zilpah and their twelve sons and one daughter), and David's family (his wives and children). The New Testament offers glimpses of family life through Jesus's family, some of Jesus's parables (e.g., the prodigal son), people who came to Jesus and the apostles for healing, and other examples (e.g., Timothy's family).

Structurally, families in Scripture represent a broad spectrum:

- nuclear families (e.g., Adam, Eve, and their sons)
- extended, multigenerational families (e.g., Laban's family and many others)
- polygamous marriages (e.g., Jacob with Leah and Rachel)
- cross-cultural marriages (e.g., Ruth and Mahlon)
- marriages between believers and unbelievers (e.g., Eunice, a Jewess, and her Greek husband)
- single-parent families (e.g., the widow and her son in the story of Elijah)
- adult children and their parents/in-laws (e.g., Ruth and Naomi)
- adult siblings living with one another (e.g., Mary, Martha, and Lazarus)
- households that include those related by blood and marriage as well as slaves and servants
- arranged marriages (e.g., Isaac and Rebekah)
- adoptive families (e.g., Moses, Eli and Samuel)
- single persons (e.g., Jesus, Paul, the Ethiopian eunuch)

There were royal families, wealthy families, poor families, deeply flawed families (e.g., Solomon's harem and his many children), and even incestuous families. Among them, there does not seem to be a truly ideal or perfect family. Nevertheless, God accomplished his good purposes through them, working within and through imperfect families across thousands of years.[16]

Biblical Wisdom for Parenting Families

Besides offering descriptions of families and family life, the Bible also contains wisdom and guidelines for parenting. In the Old Testament, Deuteronomy 6:5–9 is the most foundational passage used to support the key role parents play in training their children spiritually, an admonition repeated for millennia in both Jewish and Christian families articulating God's design for faithful parenting.

Love the LORD your God with all your heart and with all your soul and with all your strength. These commandments that I give you today are to be on your hearts. Impress them on your children. Talk about them when you sit at home and when you walk along the road, when you lie down and when you get up. Tie them as symbols on your hands and bind them on your foreheads. Write them on the doorframes of your houses and on your gates.

In addition, Proverbs offers specific wisdom for parenting, such as, "Discipline your children, and they will give you peace; they will bring you the delights you desire" (29:17).

16. For this material, I am indebted to Denise Kjesbo's discussion of flawed families in her address "Five Models of Family Ministry."

The New Testament builds on these key ideas, though only a few passages specifically address parenting. Ephesians 5:22–32 and Colossians 3:18–22 emphasize relationships in families in light of relationship with God; thus, husbands are to love, wives are to respect, children are to obey, and fathers are to discipline without provoking. These passages address relationships between spouses and between parents and children, and they form the biblical foundation for educational approaches to family ministry as it is typically conceived. However, less than half of most congregations are made up of families in which children are present. As this chapter looks at broadening the scope of family ministry, we will explore the idea of the faith community as the family of God.

Theological Reflections on Family Ministry with Family Conceived as Family of God

Both Diana Garland and Rodney Clapp have robustly examined the concept of church as family. Garland states unequivocally, "The church is our new family, bound together not by the biology of blood and flesh but by faith in Jesus Christ. . . . The role of the church is to follow Christ by ensuring that no one in the family of faith is family-less—that everyone is adopted into family. . . . The adoptive family has become the ideal, the model, the witness that there are no limits to God's ability to create goodness, not even the limits of biology."[17] Clapp states this premise somewhat differently: "The church is God's most important institution on earth. The church is the social agent that most significantly shapes and forms the character of Christians. And the church is the primary vehicle of God's grace and salvation for a waiting, desperate world."[18]

Both Garland and Clapp build their theological case for seeing the church as the new family to some degree on Jesus's teaching about family. When Jesus is told that his mother and brothers are waiting to see him, he asks, "Who is my mother, and who are my brothers?" (Matt. 12:48). He then points to his disciples and says, "Here are my mother and my brothers. For whoever does the will of my Father in heaven is my brother and sister and mother" (vv. 49–50). He reiterates this key point in a later setting when a woman in the crowd calls out, "Blessed is the mother who gave you birth and nursed you." Jesus replies, "Blessed rather are those who hear the word of God and obey it" (Luke 11:27–28).

Garland and Clapp develop the idea that, for Christians, biological ties no longer primarily create family but rather following God. Jesus also tells the crowds that his kingdom will turn brother against brother, children against their parents, and parents against their children and that those who love their parents more than him are not worthy of him (Matt. 10:37). In these remarks, Jesus does not denigrate biological families. In fact, he upholds the importance and the obligations of marriage and families in a variety of ways: he affirms marriage (Matt. 19:6), blesses children (e.g., Mark 10:13–16), and condemns those who use vows to defraud their parents of needed funds (Mark 7:9–13). According to Clapp, Jesus doesn't deny or destroy the biological family; he does, however, decenter and relativize it.[19]

Other strong theological support for church as family comes from Paul's frequent use of

17. Garland, *Family Ministry*, 104, 107.

18. Clapp, *Families at the Crossroads*, 67–68.
19. Clapp, *Families at the Crossroads*, 78.

familial language when referring to followers of Christ. He speaks of Christians as brothers and sisters (e.g., 1 Thess. 1:4), referring to the image of baptism as a new birth into a new family (Gal. 3:26–29; see also John 3) and beautifully appropriating the language of adoption for those reborn as sons and daughters of God who call him by the intimate term *Abba* (Gal. 4). All of these images connote church as family. Seeing our faith community as our primary family, our "first family," is quite countercultural, since in America, we have tended to view the nuclear family as almost singularly sacred. In contrast, Clapp says, "Now for those who follow Jesus, the critical blood, the blood that significantly determines their identity and character, is not blood of the biological family. It is the blood of the Lamb."[20]

Joseph Hellerman meticulously depicts first-century family culture to help us understand the richness of Paul's analogy of church as family, especially believers as brothers and sisters in Christ.[21] Hellerman envisions an intentionally intergenerational church in which the older, wiser sisters and brothers know their younger siblings well and advise, guide, and accompany them on their journeys, while the younger siblings work with, care for, and join their older siblings on their journeys. This is a powerful, inviting image, reflective of Paul's admonitions in 1 Timothy 5:1–2 regarding cross-generational relationships in the early church.[22]

If we construe family ministry to embrace the broader concept of church as the family of God, then our theological and biblical discussion will expand as well. How should brothers and sisters in the faith community relate to one another—in their homes and elsewhere? Paul answers this partly with his "one another" passages: be kind to one another; love one another; honor one another; live in harmony with one another; instruct one another; wait for one another; serve one another; carry each other's burdens; encourage one another and build each other up; live in peace with each other; bear with one another in love; submit to one another.[23]

As children, new believers, and seasoned saints participate in a community in which we are kind to one another, love one another, bear one another's burdens, and encourage one another, we truly learn these concepts and experience them at a deep level. We begin to live those ways in our homes, in our workplaces, and in the world. All the while, we are being formed spiritually into the image of Christ.

Categorizing and Applying Family Ministry Approaches

Diverse forms of family ministry can coexist; a church need not choose a particular form and ignore the others. Table 16.1 shows the various ways to characterize and categorize current approaches to family ministry. The beginning of this chapter introduced aspects of several models of family ministry. A more detailed explanation of how the approaches overlap and intersect is needed to more fully understand the nuances of how churches approach ministry with families in mind.

---

20. Clapp, *Families at the Crossroads*, 78.

21. Hellerman, *When the Church Was a Family*.

22. This paragraph on Hellerman is adapted from Allen and Ross, *Intergenerational Christian Formation*, 34, 68.

23. See Mark 9:50; Rom. 12:10; 13:8; Gal. 5:13; 6:2; Eph. 4:2, 32; 5:21; Col. 3:13, 16; 1 Cor. 11:33; 1 Thess. 5:11.

Table 16.1. Basic Approaches/Models of Family Ministry Described by Those Who Have Written about Family Ministry

Type	Sell[a]	TenElshof[b]	Garland[c]	Jones and Stinson[d]	Kjesbo[e]
Age-Graded	Age-group ministry to various family members	Preparational family life ministry (also "Educational")		Family-based ministry (with an intergenerational component)	
Educational	Program model of family life education	Enrichment family life ministry (as well as preparational family life ministry, see above)	Family life education programs		Educational model
Family-Focused				Family-equipping	Family-friendly
Therapeutic		Remedial family life ministry	Counseling		Counseling-therapeutic
Intergenerational	Intergenerational	Equipping family life ministry	Congregational life as family ministry	Family-integrated models	Family of families
Families Serving			Equipping families for service		Family in service

a. Sell, "Family Life Education," 288–89.
b. TenElshof, "Ministry to Families in the Local Church," 185–99.
c. Garland, *Family Ministry*.
d. Jones and Stinson, "Family Ministry Models," 173–76.
e. Kjesbo, "Five Models of Family Ministry."

A common approach that began in the 1970s and 1980s is family life education. Charles Sell says there are two key components: (1) teaching people the knowledge and the skills necessary for successful family living and (2) training parents to nurture their children's faith.[24] Churches offer different types of family life education. Some use a program model, offering occasional classes or seminars on marriage, parenting, communication, and so on. Others fold family education into traditional Sunday school classes and other age- and stage-grouped ministries such as single adult ministry, youth ministry, and young adult ministry. Sell also

24. Sell, "Family Life Education," 289.

references the importance of intergenerational experiences in family life education approaches to family ministry.

In the 1992 version of *Introduction to Christian Education* (edited by Michael Anthony), Judy TenElshof's chapter on family ministry outlined the following typical approaches:

- preparational family life ministry: preparation for developmental stages (birth, childhood, adolescence, adulthood [young, middle, and late], and death)
- enrichment family life ministry: addressing life issues throughout the developmental stages (marriage, parenting, career)

- equipping family life ministry: learning to minister to one another across all lines (body life)
- remedial family life ministry: therapeutic, ministerial counseling; crisis intervention[25]

Diana Garland takes a more holistic stance rather than advocating specific approaches or models. She addresses family ministry from a blended sociological and biblical approach, saying that family ministry consists of any activity of a congregation that directly or indirectly does the following:

- develops family relationships in the congregational community by encouraging the adoption of Christians as family so that no Christian is family-less (Ps. 68:5–6; Matt. 12:24–50; John 19:26–27)
- increases the Christlikeness of the family relationships of Christians (1 John 4:16–21)
- equips and supports Christians who use their families as a channel of ministry to others within and outside the community of faith[26]

Timothy Paul Jones and Randy Stinson describe three contemporary approaches to family ministry.

- family-*based* ministry: children's, youth, and other age- or stage-based ministries remain functioning but commit to planning frequent events

and experiences that bring families and generations together
- family-*integrated* ministry: an intentional intergenerational approach, with an abrupt move away from age-segmented programming, in which generations worship together and parents bear the responsibility for their children's faith development (i.e., Sunday school, children's church, and youth ministry do not carry this responsibility)
- family-*equipping* ministry: age-organized ministries remain but are redeveloped to train and equip parents to be the primary spiritual nurturers of their children[27]

Denise Kjesbo has helpfully synthesized the above approaches, noting five current models of family ministry.

- educational model: training for the upcoming stages and seasons of life
- counseling/therapeutic model: helping families who are dealing with heavy difficulties; help to restore to wholeness
- family-friendly model: parents are seen as the primary and best faith nurturers of their children, with the church's role being to support and equip the parents for that calling; shift from church-centered, home-supported ministry to home-centered, church-supported ministry
- family of families model: people experience family as a part of the family of God, with the entire church being

25. TenElshof, "Ministry to Families in the Local Church," 185–99.
26. Garland, *Family Ministry*, 92–106.

27. Jones and Stinson, "Family Ministry Models," 173–77.

a village for the children; may have no age-graded instruction (an intentionally intergenerational approach)

- families in service model: the family is the launchpad for service and ministry in the community; not just about caring for families inside the church but about deploying the family, sending the family out to serve in ministry in the community; the church's purpose is to equip, to provide opportunity and support, and to connect families with one another as they serve in the community in the name of Jesus[28]

Family ministry can be accomplished, then, in a variety of ways. Rather than determining which individual method is best, ministry leaders might consider the diverse populations of their congregations and the various ministries already in place, then begin to design a ministry to meet congregational needs. They can begin by asking questions such as,

- Are we helping all the persons in our faith community to walk faithfully in their life journeys?
- Are some groups neglected?
- Does everyone belong in our family?
- Do we segregate more than we integrate?
- Are we helping parents in their tasks?
- Are we supporting our singles and our widows/widowers?
- Does our faith community feel like the family of God?
- Is our church family serving the weak, the powerless, and the marginalized and inviting them to the family table?

28. Kjesbo, "Five Models of Family Ministry."

These questions can help leaders identify a church's strengths, weaknesses, opportunities, and challenges in order to create a more effective family ministry.

Reframing the Discussion

In most articles and research that focus on family ministry, the nuclear family (even in its various forms explored above) is typically considered preeminent. The nuclear family is the *kairos* ("opportune" or "ideal") place where children are formed into Christ, where they construct a worldview, and where they find their identity.

Though I recognize that the inherent lifelong influence of the family of origin on children is undeniable, I believe that a more holistic biblical and theological understanding is that spiritual development, character, worldview, morality—all of our basic personal-social-relational-spiritual ways of being—are to be formed principally in faith communities.

Family of God as Primary Source of Identity

A shorthand way to describe this premise is that our primary identity should ultimately come not from our family of origin but from the body of Christ. The name on my birth certificate reads Holly Jeanean Catterton. I am a Catterton by birth; I am proud of my maiden name, and I love my family of origin. It has shaped me and continues to shape me in countless ways both identifiable and mysterious. To honor that important identity, I have taken as my professional name Holly Catterton Allen, thus honoring my family of origin. However, as important as my family of origin is to me, being a Catterton (and now also an

Allen) is secondary to the fact that I am of Christ. I am a Catterton, an Allen, but most importantly a Christian.

Some years ago, I knew a family that was disfellowshipped from the body of Christ with which they ministered. The husband had developed an emotional relationship with someone else, and when he confessed his sin, the other leaders of the church deemed him not fully repentant. The couple and their children were told to leave this fellowship, and their brothers and sisters in that community were cautioned not to speak with them. Though all the members of the family (including a teenager and two preadolescent children) were devastated, the wife especially was shattered. When later describing her experience, she was finally able to articulate the source of her desolation: "I was able to move past the sense of betrayal I felt with my husband's confession. It was, of course, a source of deep sorrow, but nothing prepared me for the intense loss I felt when my brothers and sisters deemed me unworthy to worship with them. I now realize that my deepest identity was not as a wife or even as a mother. It was as a child of God in a community of believers I viewed as my fellow pilgrims. To be cast out struck at my very core."

Indeed, our earthly family (our family of origin or nuclear family) does not ultimately define us. Our place with Christ in the faith community does. Just as King David's identity was inherently embedded in the fact that he was part of God's people and a Hebrew of the tribe of Judah, our identities should be embedded in the fact that we are believers in Christ. As such, we have been added by God to his church, and we are part of a faith community that gathers to worship, minister, bless, and care for one another and for others.

The Family of God as a Lifelong Spiritual Family

Clearly, nuclear families in churches are indispensable. I don't disagree that parents deeply and permanently impact their children's spiritual growth and development (children breathe in the very essence of their parents' spirituality as well as specific teaching they receive from them). I also agree that faith communities can help parents *realize* their profound and lasting spiritual impact on their children, and that churches can and should intentionally equip parents to teach and lead their children spiritually.

However, despite the powerful, God-given influence of parents, I believe that it is the faith community as a whole that needs to have more, not less influence on children and youth. In general, the local church is meant to play a larger spiritual-familial role in *everyone's* lives. The equipping task for the faith community continues throughout the life cycle: helping twentysomethings navigate the work world; encouraging newlyweds in their adjustments; supporting the divorced and widows/widowers on their difficult journeys; and assisting seniors as they cope with losses and changes.

In other words, the faith community's role is the same for all populations—helping members of a particular group live into and out of their primary identities as children of God in the family of God in their particular season in life. This undertaking can be accomplished through various versions of family ministry, including age- or stage-focused instruction. Recovery ministries can play a role; counseling is sometimes imperative; worshipping together is crucial, and *learning* together can be a surprisingly effective avenue for embracing our primary identity at Christ followers. *Cross-generational* mission trips, service projects, and small groups are among the best ways to train and encourage the whole family of God.

Conclusion

In my four decades participating in (and leading) various forms of ministry (children's church, small groups ministry, family ministry, women's studies, youth ministry, teaching ministry), nothing has captured my imagination more than the current intense interest among churches in becoming more intentionally *intergenerational* in their ministry outlook and practices; interest in all things intergenerational is sweeping the globe. This new (yet actually quite old) approach to being church encompasses the essence of what I am saying when I recommend that the word "family" in family ministry should refer to the whole family of God.

This international, cross-denominational move to become more intentionally intergenerational in all its iterations around the globe (e.g., Messy Church, whole-church, "All In") has embraced the concept that intergenerational experiences especially and uniquely nurture spiritual formation across all ages.[29]

In the family of God, when we view church as family, children and youth as well as singles, couples, and seniors—that is, *everyone*—will come to know people across the age and experience spectrum. As they do, they will develop a fuller-orbed, more complex understanding of dwelling in Christ throughout their entire life span. Parents need not (and cannot) provide this breadth of experience. They can teach, model, love, train. But it is the entire body of Christ, along with the Holy Spirit, that helps children, teens, emerging adults and all the rest conform to the *imago Dei*—the image of God.

Family ministry can and should attend to relationships and responsibilities of parents, children, and marriages. *Family ministry* can and should offer guidance and assistance for families in distress. But ultimately, a comprehensive *family ministry* can and should center on the body of Christ as the family of God.

29. Allen and Ross, *Intergenerational Christian Formation,* 24; Allen, *InterGenerate,* 17–18.

17

Ministry with Children

LEON M. BLANCHETTE JR.

The title of this chapter, "Ministry with Children," embodies the chapter's content and ministry philosophy. When people hear the phrase "ministry with children," some think of Bible stories with a nice moral lesson and games, crafts, and activities that serve as childcare in order to free up adults to have authentic worship and ministry experiences. The truth is very different from these common misperceptions.

Children's ministry is much more than Bible stories, programs, and activities. Children's ministry is about preparing an environment in which God can transform lives and children can encounter a living, intimate God who desires to have a life-changing relationship with them. Children's ministry is about walking *with* children and their families on a journey of faith in partnership with the church.

In order to achieve these results, one must have a solid biblical understanding of God's call to journey with children as well as a solid theological understanding that guides the ministry Godward. One must understand the uniqueness of God's creation of humanity and how children enter into a relationship with Christ. This chapter discusses these important topics.

A Biblical and Theological Call to Journey with Children

An underlying premise of this chapter is that the community of faith is on a lifelong journey with Christ. This language has a variety of implications. The Christian life is not about a decision made in a moment in time but rather a commitment of walking with Christ. This involves learning from moments that include both faithfulness and straying from the path and growing closer to Christ along the way. It is a journey lived out in God's present kingdom.

A second premise is that this journey is for the *entire* community of faith—and this includes children. As adults in the faith community faithfully walk with Christ, they bring along their children. Adults model how the Christian life is to be lived, and children watch with intense interest. These children learn how to join the journey and live in Christ's kingdom as they interact with others in the community of faith.

Created in the Imago Dei

In the opening verses of Genesis, God is found actively involved in the creation process, from the separating of light from darkness on day one to the creation of all living creatures that roam the ground on day six. God speaks into his creation, and everything obeys and becomes what he desires. Then in Genesis 2, God's approach changes noticeably. He moves from a God who speaks, to a God who is intimately involved in his creation—the creation of humanity. God is seen bending over Adam as he breathes life into his motionless body. This creature that has been created in the *imago Dei* (image of God) becomes a living being. As he opens his eyes, the first thing he likely sees is the face of his Creator. This divine creation of humanity becomes the catalyst for understanding that all are created in the image of God and, as a result, that all have value and worth.

When considering ministry with children, one must acknowledge that they, too, are created in the image of God and have inestimable value and worth. Recognition of this reality informs all that takes place in ministry with children. Children must not be looked down on because they are young and do not have the cognitive ability to understand things as an adult. They are valuable to God and the community of faith just as they are. Jesus's own words address this issue in each of the Synoptic Gospels (Matt. 18:1–5; Mark 9:33–37; Luke 9:46–48) when he is asked, "Who is the greatest in the kingdom of heaven?" He replies by bringing a child close to him and proclaiming that the greatest is the one who is like a child. In this brief moment in the biblical text, Jesus is acknowledging that the one who is viewed as the least by society is the greatest in God's kingdom.

Teaching for Spiritual Capacity

Children are capable of a real, intimate relationship with Christ in spite of an often pervasive belief that what occurs in ministry with children is for the purpose of preparing them for serious decisions that may occur in their future. By affirming that children are created in the image of God, the church recognizes that children do have a spiritual capacity for loving God and serving him, even at a very young age. The Shema ("hear" or "listen") in Deuteronomy 6:4–9 functions as a call to parents and the family of faith to pass this faith on to children.

> Hear, O Israel: The LORD our God, the LORD is one. Love the LORD your God with all your heart and with all your soul and with all your strength. These commandments that I give you today are to be on your hearts. Impress them on your children. Talk about them when you sit at home and when you walk along the road, when you lie down and when you get up. Tie them as symbols on your hands and bind them on your foreheads. Write them on the doorframes of your houses and on your gates.

As adults love God with all that is within them and live that faith out in their lives, they are to teach children how to walk with God at every opportunity. Christians are to travel this journey together as fellow pilgrims on a journey.[1] As members of the believing community live their daily lives, they are to instruct children. Whether adults realize it or not, they are constantly modeling behaviors and teaching their children by the way they live their lives.

Consider a young adult who does something and is startled when she realizes that her actions are identical to those of her mother: "I'm just like my mom!" She may not have been taught to mimic her mother through intentional or formal teaching, but nonetheless, she learned from her mother's example, which is the by-product of informal teaching. Faithful living in relationship with God is to be taught in the regular, informal moments of everyday life.

The Shema in Deuteronomy also directs adults to teach in an intentional way that is commonly called nonformal education. The "tying and binding" that the text describes is best understood as the intentional activities of life in which training occurs. This would be demonstrated by the family that has devotions together or the little girl who attends Sunday school and learns the stories of Scripture.

Finally, there is a formal approach to teaching. This usually occurs in an environment that includes curriculum, children sitting at a table, and a teacher communicating information to the children. The image of the typical school classroom is a good example of a formal approach to teaching.

Each of these three approaches to teaching is a valuable way of instructing children to grow in their faith, and ministries should help facilitate all three types of learning.

A closer examination of Moses's words to parents and the believing community reveals that growing in faith occurs as life is lived together, whether in formal or informal moments. The focus of the Shema is on training and modeling. The focus of this training and modeling is not acquisition of more information or knowledge of the Bible alone but life transformation. Christian educator Perry Downs stated it well when he said, "Some teachers confuse means with ends. They so focus on methods that they forget their objectives. Teaching the Bible is a method; changing lives is an objective. The reason we teach in the church is that lives may be changed."[2]

In other words, the purpose of teaching and learning God's Word is for life change, not solely for knowledge. If followers of Christ are not transformed and living what they have been taught, then one could say that the teacher did not teach and the student did not learn.[3] Teaching must lead to a changed life or education has not occurred. Deuteronomy 4:5–9 teaches that the decrees and laws of the Lord are to be taught for the purpose of obedience. Teaching is much more than communicating information; the purpose of teaching is to produce a life of loving obedience.

If this is the case, then why is teaching children for the purpose of life change often neglected? The neglect may come from a belief that a learner's cognitive or mental ability is closely and directly linked to their spiritual capacity. This view seems to originate

1. This language is taken from May et al., *Children Matter*, 16–19.

2. Downs, *Teaching for Spiritual Growth*, 33.

3. Blanchette, *Relationship between Ministry Praxis and Spiritual Development*. The words that mean "to teach" and "to learn" come from the same Hebrew root word, *lamad*. The implication is that if a student did not learn what was taught, the teacher did not really teach the information. There is an intimate connection between teaching, learning, and applying what is learned.

in the School Model[4] approach to education. In this approach, the focus of teaching is building knowledge rather than facilitating an encounter with Christ. Much of Christian education has relegated teaching to a focus on the acquisition of data, especially with children.

Teachers often judge their teaching effectiveness based on a child's ability to "spit back" the information that was transmitted to them during the lesson. This is often described as a *passive* understanding of the role of the child. Rather than the child being an *active* learner and the teacher being a shepherd or a colearner in the educational experience (an approach that honors both the teacher and the student), the child is merely a recipient of information.[5]

Teachers must recognize that the spiritual capacity of a child does not depend on their cognitive ability—and that is why we must teach for the purpose of life change. The results of a biblical understanding of the faith journey lead to a lesson that focuses on the truth of the text being taught in such a way that a child learns, believes, and implements the truth in their life so that they are forever changed.

The Role of Parents in Ministry with Children

Parents play a significant role in God's design for teaching children to walk with him. The Shema is not the only text that instructs parents to teach children the commandments of the Lord. The psalmist writes these words in Psalm 78:5–7:

> He decreed statutes for Jacob
>   and established the law in Israel,
> which he commanded our ancestors
>   to teach their children,
> so the next generation would know
>   them,
>   even the children yet to be born,
>   and they in turn would tell their
>   children.
> Then they would put their trust in
>   God
>   and would not forget his deeds
>   but would keep his commands.

These verses not only reinforce the command to teach children the statutes and laws of God but also explain the reason for doing so. The focus is on passing the faith from one generation to the next. Notice that the focus is not passing down the faith for the sole purpose of *knowing* the commandments of the Lord. The intention is to pass knowledge on so that the next generation will *keep* his commands. Another way of stating this is teaching the next generation both formally and informally, as life is being lived daily, so that they will learn and obey. Loving obedience to the commands of God must be the ultimate goal of passing down the faith.

What are the consequences of not passing down the faith to the next generation? The answer to that question can be found in 2 Kings 17:7–23. This text functions as a detailed explanation for Israel's exile during the days of Assyrian reign. The text clearly states that the people had turned to other gods and were committing all kinds of evil, which led to God removing them from his presence and

---

4. The School Model approach to ministry is described in May et al., *Children Matter*. The School Model is taken from the public school system of sitting children in chairs at desks and measuring successful learning by the cognitive ability to remember what was taught.

5. May, et al., *Children Matter*, 8–9.

giving them into the hands of their enemy (vv. 18–20). It is a harsh reminder of what happens when one generation neglects the command to teach the next generation in ways that transform.

Despite exceptions like this, the Old Testament highlights examples of nurturing faith in children. These include the value God places on families coming together for worship (Deut. 12:7–28; 16:9–15; 31:9–13). It was important that children be included in the rituals, customs, celebrations, and traditions of the Hebrew people, for through these worship experiences, instruction occurred. These were significant and intentional teaching moments. Encountering God together caused questions to be asked, allowing adults to tell the story of God's provision to their children (Deut. 6:20). Spiritually intimate times such as these became moments of passing on the faith as God had commanded.

The New Testament also provides instruction for parents regarding the training of children. In the Synoptic Gospels, including children in the activity of the community is reinforced by the words of Jesus (Matt. 19:14; Mark 10:14; Luke 18:16). In an attempt to protect Jesus, while unconsciously holding the belief that young children were of less value than others, the disciples rebuked parents for bringing their children to Jesus. Jesus's response is significant. He included them in the moment, gave them value, and identified them as the model for entrance into the kingdom of God: "Let the little children come to me, and do not hinder them, for the kingdom of God belongs to such as these. Truly I tell you, anyone who will not receive the kingdom of God like a little child will never enter it" (Mark 10:14–15; cf. Luke 18:16–17).

In another instance, Jesus was at the temple, and the priests and teachers of the law were outraged that the children were shouting, "Hosanna to the Son of David." In response, Jesus quoted Psalm 8:2: "From the lips of children and infants you, Lord, have called forth your praise" (Matt. 21:15–16). The value of the thoughts and words of children and their wisdom in recognizing Jesus as the Son of David are contrasted with the lack of wisdom demonstrated by the religious leaders who did not acknowledge Jesus as Messiah. It is an easy leap from hearing what Jesus said to the priests to recognizing that children need to be a part of the community not only for what they can learn from other members but also for what they can contribute to the community.

In his letter to the church in Ephesus, the apostle Paul wrote about relationships and the responsibility of specific parties in each type of relationship. Toward the end of the letter, Paul discusses the relationship of parents and children and, in particular, the relationship of fathers and children. "Children, obey your parents in the Lord, for this is right. 'Honor your father and mother'—which is the first commandment with a promise—'so that it may go well with you and that you may enjoy long life on the earth.' Fathers, do not exasperate your children; instead, bring them up in the training and instruction of the Lord" (Eph. 6:1–4).

In this text, Paul instructs children to obey and honor their parents. While Paul's instruction to children was commonplace in the culture at that time, the imperative command for fathers not to exasperate their children but to train and instruct them in the ways of the Lord was a novel idea. Fathers were often seen as harsh disciplinarians who were most concerned with a child's obedience and honor. Here Paul emphasizes the important role that parents—fathers in particular—have in training and instructing their children in the faith. The focus became obedience as a result of trustworthy teaching and caring instruction rather than obedience out of instructional harshness and moral duty.

The parents' role in the development of a child's spiritual life is essential. Because parents are the most influential people in a child's spiritual development, the question is not, Do parents have an impact on a child's development? but rather, Is this impact positive or negative? This God-given responsibility for parents to be a positive influence in the spiritual development of their children is given in the midst of the reassuring discovery that parents are not alone in this role. Members of the faith community are to come alongside to support and equip parents while also being intentional in their role to provide spiritual guidance to all children in the community. Just as the well-known African proverb states, "It takes a village to raise a child," it can also be said, "It takes a faith community to raise a faithful follower of Jesus."

The Role of the Faith Community in Ministry with Children

Throughout most of Old Testament religious history and in the history of the church, family members of all ages worshiped together. Even so, ministry specifically directed to children and their unique needs was lacking.

Some of this began to be addressed with the introduction of Sunday school by Robert Raikes in 1780.[6] This is when the church began

to focus more intentionally on teaching and spiritually nurturing children. The motivation for teaching children at this time was not a newly discovered recognition of their ability to have a personal relationship with Jesus but a realization that some children were failing to receive any type of education at all. While the motivation for Sunday school could be described as primarily pragmatic, the ministry was also biblically based.

Through Sunday school, children were taught subjects of all types but were also included in the gathering of the community of faith and taught Christian education content at an appropriate level for their learning. Since the beginning of Sunday school, recognition that ministry and teaching specifically tailored to children is important has continued to grow. During the century and a half after Sunday school was introduced, a number of ministries for young people thrived. Even so, there was no formal understanding of the unique differences between childhood and adolescence, so children's ministry as we know it had not yet come into being.

It wasn't until the mid-twentieth century that developmental theory began to mature and to influence Christian educators' perspective of education in the church. At that time, leaders in the church began to recognize that while children were present with their parents in worship, they were often forgotten or neglected and their learning was limited. Leaders wondered if there was a more productive way of educating children.

During this time, education and learning became the focus, much as they were in the public educational system, but spiritual development was often neglected. Education was

---

6. While Robert Raikes is credited with the creation of the Sunday school movement, there is evidence that others began educating children in the church prior to 1780. It appears that one of the differences between Raikes and the others is that he used the Bible to teach children to read, while others used sources such as the catechism. For more information, see Towns, *Robert Raikes*.

deemed effective if a child acquired the knowledge that was taught. Learning theory discovered that the best way to educate children was to address their unique developmental needs. Ministries designed specifically for children were developed. In many cases, children were removed from their parents while at church and placed in ministries designed specifically for their age.

Age-group ministry had already existed in the Sunday school classroom, and over time, children began to be removed from corporate worship to attend age-group worship. Children attended children's church, where they learned from puppets, sang fun songs, created crafts, had a snack, and played games. The church was convinced that children could learn more about God through these ministries than they could by sitting in church with their parents. Yet despite these changes, the focus became *learning about* God rather than *encountering* God in a personal way.

Despite this shortcoming, it would be a mistake to believe that age-group ministry was a poor decision and that children have been harmed by it. The problem is not age-group ministry. The problem occurs when age-group ministry leads to the segregation of parents and children. When children are removed from the faith community to be isolated with children their age, parents are removed as the primary spiritual caregivers of their children and are replaced by a silo-type ministry.[7] Time has proven that age-focused

ministry has its benefits, but it has also shown that removing children from their families and from the community of faith leads to serious negative consequences.

When families worship together, children learn more than just the cognitive knowledge that many often deem most valuable. As the family of Christ engages in life together, children learn the customs, traditions, and rituals of the church. And as Dietrich Bonhoeffer noted, "The physical presence of other Christians is a source of incomparable joy and strength to the believer."[8] Children observe as their parents put offering in the plate and then ask why this is done. Children watch as adults have encounters with God. Children learn the songs of the faith community. All of this occurs as the children sit and watch during a worship service, learning what it means to be a follower of Christ and a part of the faith community.

Safety and Security

I would like to conclude this section with a brief word about the importance of safety and security. This is a critical component when considering ministry for children from both a biblical and theological perspective. Children are invaluable, and it is essential that the church provide a safe and secure environment for children to experience God. All too often, local churches approach the topic of safety as an issue that other churches need to worry about. A common belief is that the evil that affects other churches could never occur in one's own church. Sadly, this is often the reason that abuse and other issues of safety

---

7. A silo-type ministry is a ministry in the local church that, for all practical purposes, is disconnected from the faith community. The ministry is officially a part of the church but is isolated in its own location and often functions on its own. Many in the faith community are not aware of what actually takes place in these silo ministries. Stuart Cummings-Bond refers to this approach of isolating students from the faith community as "the one-eared

Mickey Mouse." Cummings-Bond, "One-Eared Mickey Mouse," 76–78.

8. Bonhoeffer, *Life Together*, 19.

occur in local churches. All churches must adopt a safety and security policy that protects both children and those serving with children. There are many great resources available to assist churches in this endeavor. It should never be said that a church chose not to have a policy in place because they felt immune to the evils of the world.

How God Created Children

Volumes have been written on developmental theory as it pertains to cognitive, moral, social, and faith development. Developmentalists have contributed significant understanding of the way God has created children and their developmental process. While some of the specifics of these theories may be questioned and challenged, the theories continue to significantly influence an understanding of the developmental process of children. Rather than focusing on the specific theories of social scientists, we will summarize their thoughts and consider how a Christian understanding of the developmental process can impact the way we understand children in the faith community.

God created children in his image with a desire to explore their world, depend on others, relate to others, and love God. Yet even with these precious inclinations, children need a personal relationship with God. It has been said that the human heart was designed by the Creator with a God-shaped hole that every person seeks to fill and that can be filled only by God himself.[9] Most attempt to fill this

void with the trappings of this world but never find complete satisfaction. While children, like adults, may be consciously unaware of their explicit need for an intimate relationship with God, they too have a God-shaped vacuum that they desire to fill. As children explore their world and attempt to find safety and satisfaction, they turn to those around them for help in understanding their discoveries. Relationships with parents, other key adults, and other children become the instruments through which God brings about development and satisfaction of the heart. While no individual can fill the void found in the heart of a child, God chooses to use key relationships in the life of a child to lead them to the one who can fill the void.

Nursery-Age Characteristics

From his work in the field of cognitive development, Jean Piaget discovered that young children demonstrate intelligence through sensory input and motor activity.[10] These children learn as they experience their world through touching, tasting, seeing, hearing, and smelling. This explains why very young children put almost everything in their mouths. They also learn about the world as they grab, throw, hold, and hit. Children process this information by establishing cause-effect relationships

---

9. While Blaise Pascal is often given credit for the phrase "God-shaped vacuum," "God-shaped void," or "God-shaped hole," there appears to be no evidence that he used any of these phrases in his book *Pensées*, published in 1670. The 1958 publication of the same book contains the following quotation, which may be the source of this later adapted quotation: "What is it then that this desire and this inability proclaim to us, but that there was once in man a true happiness of which there now remain to him only the mark and empty trace, which he in vain tries to fill from all his surroundings, seeking from things absent the help he does not obtain in things present? But these are all inadequate, because the infinite abyss can only be filled by an infinite and immutable object, that is to say, only by God Himself" (113).

10. Bybee and Sund, *Piaget for Educators*, 48–50.

between actions and their consequences, through memory, and through other experiences. All the while, children of this age completely rely on adults for their security and well-being.

Application for ministry. Ministry in nurseries provides a unique opportunity to capitalize on the learning experiences of newborns and babies. Providing a clean, safe, secure environment for them to explore their world is essential. Very young children develop physically, socially, and spiritually as loving adults interact with them while they explore their world. This is a time to sing songs and tell stories of Jesus's love for them. Repetition of stories and prayers facilitates familiarity with human language, while children experience God's love through encounters with caring adults. For these reasons, time spent with nursery children should not be seen as babysitting but as significant ministry to and with the youngest worshipers of a congregation.

Preschool-Age Characteristics

Preschool is a significant time of discovery. Children at this age are still understandably egocentric, seeing life from only their own limited perspective. While they may seem to enjoy playing with one another, a close examination of their play reveals deeper insights. The speech of preschool children is often monologue in nature, resulting in less interactive relationships and causing them to have a difficult time joining in the make-believe play of other children. They also struggle to organize items in patterns and are often unable to focus on more than one item or thought at a time. Preschoolers love to watch and imitate others. They are strongly influenced by their senses, and that is why they are drawn to

images, stories, and symbols.[11] These are the ways preschoolers understand and interpret their world.

Application for ministry. Preschool children are experts at make-believe play and using their imaginations. They enjoy acting out Bible stories and putting themselves in the place of biblical characters. They also readily believe what they are told by others, making this time of life a wonderful opportunity to teach children the basic stories of the Bible. Their attitudes and thoughts about God and church are strongly influenced by those with authority at this stage of life, so it is important that parents recognize this influence and are intentional about their own spiritual lives.

Because preschool children love to watch and imitate others, the selection of leaders in ministry with these children is critical. Social learning theorist Albert Bandura discovered the educational power of watching and imitating. He stated that much of human behavior is the result of observing and imitating others.[12] Leaders in ministry with these children will have a significant impact on their development and love for Jesus, so choosing leaders who model authentic faith is essential. Children often encounter God and his love for them through the interaction and modeling of these key adult servants.

Elementary-Age Characteristics

The elementary-school age is a time of intense learning. Children find learning new information exciting. They often find great joy correcting an incorrect answer, especially if it is given by an adult. Children this age have

11. Downs, *Teaching for Spiritual Growth*, 115.
12. Bandura, *Social Learning Theory*, 22.

moved from the strong egocentricity found in the previous stage toward greater interaction with others. While they are still limited to concrete thinking, they have developed the ability to classify objects (classification), put items in logical order (seriation), and recognize that attributes of an object remain the same (conservation). Spiritually speaking, these children tend to understand the Christian faith in literal terms and enjoy learning about God and his love for them.

Application for ministry. The excitement elementary-age children exhibit for learning provides a wonderful opportunity for the community of faith to teach them the wonderful stories of the Bible and the truths imbedded in those stories. This is a time to move beyond the mere acquisition of information to help them understand truth. While learning is intense in this stage of life, these children are still limited to concrete thinking, which means that many of the abstract concepts of the Christian faith (love, hope, salvation, etc.) are often difficult for them to fully understand.

One practice that can help is expressing abstract thoughts using concrete examples. In essence, this is what Jesus did when he told parables. He explained a difficult spiritual truth by referring to common, easily understood concepts. He spoke about seeds, pearls, nets, vineyard workers, talents, sheep, and goats. Each of these examples was a common part of the culture of the day, and those who heard would have understood the role that each played in society.

Because these children desire to know God and to obey him, this is the age when many children accept Jesus as their personal Savior. It is important that the key adults in their lives provide opportunities for them to hear and respond to the gospel message without pressure or reward. Ideally, parents should walk through this experience with their children.

Preteen Characteristics

As children move into their preteen years, they begin to think in more abstract terms. They are now able to process more complex thoughts. As a result, preteens begin to ask questions about things they previously accepted as unchallenged truth. They begin the process of puberty and often have many questions they do not feel comfortable asking, especially at church. They begin to question beliefs they had in childhood and may even question the existence of God as a result of their intellectual development and the incongruity of life.

Application for ministry. For many adults, especially parents, the thought that their children might question the existence of God is frightening. While these fears are understandable, the questioning of God that is so natural at this age provides an exciting opportunity for parents and the church. If these children are given a safe environment in which they are encouraged to ask difficult questions, which are often not verbalized out of fear of adult responses, caring adults can help them apprehend solid answers.

What would it look like to provide a class for preteens that focused on the doctrines of the church, obviously at a basic level? What if the class was discussion-based rather than lecture-based and together the members, guided by the teacher, worked through these difficult concepts? What if the teacher played the role of devil's advocate when the students were beginning to get the "right" answer and challenged them to defend their answer? What would the results be? Is it possible that the students would move from having the faith of their parents and the faith community to owning their own faith? Later in life, when difficulties arise and their faith is challenged, parents may not be there to protect their children. With this approach, students can stand strong because they know why they believe what they believe. What a great opportunity for families and the church to help preteens own their personal faith.

Another example of an opportunity to assist and equip parents while helping and challenging preteens is a sex education class for preteens and parents. The methods used to conduct such a class may vary, but what should not vary is the church being an authoritative voice in a world that has corrupted what God created as beautiful. Preteens are at a stage in their development when important decisions about faithfulness regarding issues of sexuality are congruent with important decisions they are making about their faith.

In all these stages, parents, the church, and friends play a significant role. As children and adults interact together, adults model the Christian life and children show adults what childlike faith looks like. As a result, the faith community grows, and individuals mature spiritually. What a wonderful picture of God's design for the community of faith, the church.

Children and Conversion

Earlier in this chapter, we discussed the spiritual capacity of children. We focused on their ability to have an authentic relationship with Christ. The final section of this chapter discusses how that authentic relationship begins and how it grows with regard to salvation.

The Conversion Process

The conversion process for children is not unlike the conversion process for adults. Children must recognize their need for forgiveness of sin and that Jesus is the only way to salvation. One major difference in the conversion process for children is that they do not have the same cognitive ability as adults. Young children, in particular, do not have the cognitive ability to understand sin and its abstract implications for the salvation process. This leads people to question, Does this mean that young children are not capable of a relationship with Christ? Perhaps the issue at hand is a matter of language.

Instead of asking when a child became a Christian, perhaps a more biblical approach would be to ask when the child entered into a relationship with Christ. Jesus did not make a mistake when he brought little children to him and used them as an example of faith. When Jesus said, "Let the little children come to me," he was not telling people to get out of the way of the children in a mere physical sense (Matt. 19:14). He was saying children should be allowed to come to him spiritually. He was stating that even though these children were not able to fully understand all that was to be known about him, they were welcome to come into his presence, they were welcome to enter into a relationship with him. He clearly stated that adults were not to hinder this experience.

It is necessary for children to have an authentic conversion experience. It must not be limited to a mere cognitive understanding. On the path toward salvation, many children will encounter Jesus through a loving relationship with him long before they have a cognitive awareness of sin and their need for forgiveness. For those children who love Jesus at a young age, the decision to ask Jesus for forgiveness of sin when they become aware of the need is the next step in their spiritual development. This decision to ask for forgiveness is often not a difficult decision because they already love Jesus and want to obey him. The most significant moment in this process is when children recognize their need for salvation and eagerly pursue his forgiveness. God faithfully and sovereignly superintends this process as he draws children into a loving relationship with him and his people.

Second-Generation Christians and Beyond

The traditional salvation prayer that has been the standard in the church for generations may not actually be appropriate or necessary for some children raised in strong Christian families. While this statement may be shocking to some, once the tradition is evaluated and considered, many find relief in the realization that their own experience has validity and merit. These are children who have been raised to love Jesus from the earliest days of their lives. They may have even included Jesus in their play. For them, as long as they can remember, they have always loved Jesus. Gordon T. Smith calls children who grew up in strong Christian families and were in love with Jesus from a very early age "second-generation Christians."[13] He proposes that these children experience faith and their relationship with Jesus differently than those who are saved out of the evils of the world.

In days past, many in the church felt that faith was too complicated for the young, and the best the church could do was to release them into the world in hope that they would come back to what they were taught, accept Christ, and reject the sin of their youth. Horace Bushnell proposed that a new approach be considered, "the child is to grow up a Christian, and never know himself as being otherwise."[14] The goal of every Christian family and church should be that their children grow up knowing the love of Jesus. It is a duty and responsibility to nurture trust in Jesus from an early age.

Many are concerned that children do not just "fall" into Christianity. The concern stems from an incorrect belief that salvation is about cognitive ability and understanding alone. It is an error to believe that a child can have a relationship with Christ only when they fully understand that they are a sinner in need of forgiveness. For second-generation Christians, loving Jesus precedes knowledge of sin by many years. These children love Jesus and try to obey him, and then something interesting happens. They discover, often as young elementary-age children, that there is this thing called sin and that it needs to be forgiven. When an adult tells them that they need to pray to ask Jesus to forgive them of their sin, they respond with a desire to do so. Why wouldn't they? They already love Jesus, and if he asks them to seek forgiveness of sin, why would they do anything else?

Conclusion

Ministry with children is about the family and the church coming together to faithfully fulfill the mandate to train children in the way of the Lord so that they will be faithful followers of Christ. This process requires intentionality on the part of the family and the church.

---

13. G. Smith, *Beginning Well*, 208.

14. Bushnell, *Christian Nurture*, 4.

As the church provides age-group ministries, includes children in the faith community, and walks with them on this journey, children will observe, imitate, and discover what it means to love Jesus and follow him. As these children mature, they will begin to own the faith as their own and eventually will be the ones to pass the faith on to the next generation. But until that day arrives, they will develop and mature as productive members of the body of Christ.

18

Ministry with Youth

DAVID ODOM

Youth ministry is about inviting young people into a relationship with Jesus Christ and helping them grow toward spiritual maturity. It means coaching, guiding, leading, prodding, facilitating, and developing students to become more like Christ. Youth ministry leaders can expect triumphs and failures, tears and laughter, and heartbreak and joy. This chapter will help leaders develop a strategy and a practice for ministering to young people by identifying biblical and historical foundations for youth ministry, describing the unique characteristics of adolescent development and sociocultural influences, and reviewing current approaches to youth ministry.

The development of a vision and strategy for youth ministry does not take place in a vacuum. Figure 18.1 describes the cyclical nature of the process. Youth leaders begin with personal presuppositions. A person's presuppositions come from family background and personal experiences. A leader may have attended church and youth group, connected meaningfully with a small group, become a Christian at camp, felt called to ministry during high school—or had a negative church experience. Whether experiences were positive or negative, they shape a youth leader's presuppositions about ministry.

Youth leaders must realize that although personal experiences shape who they are, they also need a solid biblical understanding of God and ministry. This training can be formal and informal. One of the important things about this training is that leaders allow the Scriptures to override their presuppositions. Youth leaders often enter ministry with a zeal to see lost youth follow Christ. They love engaging teens in conversation and sharing the gospel. However, in a seminary class or through the counsel of a pastor, they are also challenged to provide opportunities for youth to be discipled in their faith. In this way, a leader allows the Bible

Figure 18.1
Developing a Youth Ministry Strategy and Practice

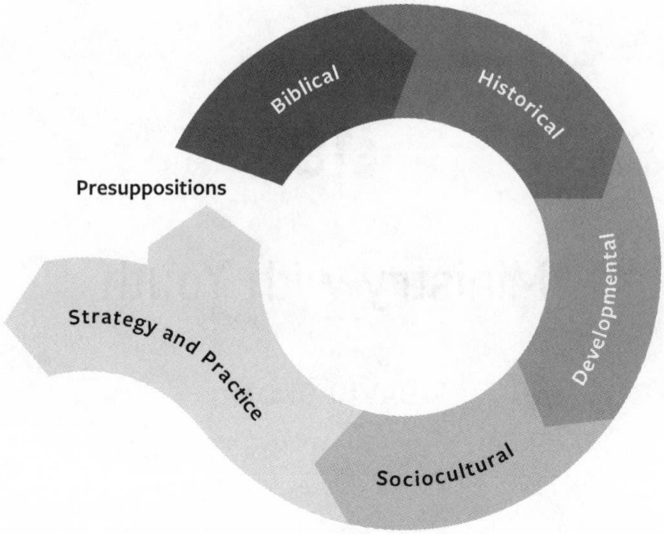

Adapted from Dunn, *Putting Youth Ministry in Perspective*, 30. The figure has been modified to emphasize the evaluative and cyclical nature of the process.

and theology to impact the strategy and the practice of youth ministry. Leaders must also learn about the history of youth ministry in the local context and the field of youth ministry in general. To avoid repeating the mistakes of the past, wise leaders spend time researching time-tested strategies, purposes, and decisions.

Then they must consider developmental issues related to adolescence and how they impact youth ministry. Again, this may come formally or informally. Adolescent development is a well-researched field with many valuable resources, both Christian and secular. Leaders study adolescence to understand how God designed humans as developmental beings. Pastors and congregations will depend on a youth leader's understanding of teenagers to help them minister to young people. The parents of teenagers may also look to youth leaders for guidance.

Leaders should also examine sociocultural influences. Here youth leaders focus on the social interactions of teenagers and the environment in which they live, allowing their observations to inform ministry strategy and practice.

Thus far a youth leader has allowed presuppositions, biblical understanding, historical context, adolescent development, and sociocultural influences to inform ministry strategy and practice. The last step is to allow ministry strategy and practice to inform thinking. After synthesizing all the information, a youth leader can develop a coherent ministry plan. The unseen component of the cycle is the Holy Spirit. Youth leaders must seek guidance from the Holy Spirit throughout the entire process.

The end of the process launches a new, evaluative beginning. Youth leaders must evaluate their strategy and their practice in light of everything that has come before. Wise youth leaders regularly take time to evaluate programs and strategy to determine the most effective way to reach students for Christ and help them grow toward spiritual maturity.

Biblical Foundations for Youth Ministry

In recent years, the nature and the value of youth ministry in the church have been attacked. Some say such ministry is unbiblical since it lacks a clear biblical mandate.[1] It is true that the Bible does not mention youth ministry. However, the Bible is silent about teenagers because adolescence was not a concept in that context.[2] While some suggest that Jesus was a youth minister because many of the disciples were probably in their late teen years, "it is anachronistic to call Jesus a youth minister" because adolescence is a modern phenomenon.[3] The absence of scriptural reference does not disqualify youth ministry from being legitimate and vital. A study of Scripture reveals seven characteristics that can be used to describe youth ministry: incarnational, shepherding, relational, communal, evangelistic, disciple making, and missional.

Youth Ministry as Incarnational

Jesus is God. He is both fully human and fully God. As the Second Person of the Trinity, Jesus left heaven to become a man on earth—this is the incarnation of Jesus Christ (Phil. 2:5–11). Jesus came to earth and became one of us. "In a very real sense, persons who work with youth (whether paid or volunteer) model the theological truth that we call incarnation."[4] As followers of Christ, youth workers must enter the world of teenagers. Jim Rayburn, the founder of Young Life, was one of the first to emphasize the incarnational nature of youth ministry. Youth leaders go where youth are and seek to come alongside them to present the gospel and nurture faith.

Youth Ministry as Shepherding

A pastor is the servant-leader of a local church. The Bible teaches that God gave the church pastors and teachers to equip believers to do the work of ministry (Eph. 4:11–12). A youth minister serves a shepherding role in the lives of students, volunteers, and parents. The apostle Peter describes the shepherding role of pastors as selfless, humble service to those in one's care (1 Pet. 5:1–4). Youth ministers preach, teach, pray, disciple, lead, and, most significantly, serve the congregation.

Youth Ministry as Relational

Rather than a program, a leader's priority should be to build godly relationships.[5] Jesus focused on relationships. When he called his disciples in Matthew 4:19, it was a relational invitation: "Follow me." In fact, one can practice true discipleship only in the context of a relationship. Youth leaders must intentionally invest in relationships with teenagers. God-centered relationships produce faithful and mature disciples.[6] To build relationships, youth leaders should intentionally initiate interaction with young people, going wherever they gather.

1. Baucham, *Family Driven Faith*, 179.
2. Keehn, "Youth Ministry from a Family Perspective," 226.
3. Crosby, "Responses to the Gospel Advancing View," 18.

4. A. Jackson, "Theology and Youth Ministry," 40.
5. Ogden, *Transforming Discipleship*, 121.
6. Kinnaman with Hawkins, *You Lost Me*, 206.

Youth Ministry as Communal

A community of believers is essential for spiritual growth. Youth leaders must help students see the value of being part of a Christ-centered community. The problem is that traditional youth ministry has not been congregation focused. It has been youth group focused. But fellowship within a youth group does not constitute fellowship with the entire body of Christ. Prevalent in youth ministry today is the conviction that leaders must help teenagers become rooted in a local congregation.[7] They must tear down the silos. Segregated youth ministry is over.

Here are a few things to remember about the church. Christ died for the church (Eph. 5:25). Christians develop community as they pray for and support one another (Acts 2:42–47; Gal. 6:2). The writer of Hebrews teaches that believers are to make the church a priority by not giving up meeting together (Heb. 10:25). Believers serve God by using their gifts in the church (Rom. 12:4–8). Youth, not just adults, should be a part of this community.

Youth need godly relationships with adults for their faith to mature. A congregation creates a sense of family. The spiritual family of the church provides security, stability, accountability, and a sense of belonging.[8] Community provides social settings for teenagers in which they can be transformed.[9] Youth leaders provide opportunities for community through small groups, fellowship activities, and service projects. When students make relational connections in a congregation, they are more likely to value the place of church in their lives as adults. Ultimately, it is not theological

conviction that leads to regular church attendance; it is relationships and community.[10]

Youth Ministry as Evangelistic

The greatest need of every teenager is to come to faith in Christ. Youth ministry has historically created opportunities for young people to hear and respond to the truth of the gospel. Here are a few reminders why it is important to share the gospel with teenagers. Evangelism is part of the Great Commission (Matt. 28:19–20). God desires for every person to repent and turn to him (John 3:17; 1 Tim. 2:3–4; 2 Pet. 3:9). Jesus died for everyone (1 Tim. 4:10; Heb. 2:9; 1 John 2:2). God will forgive any teenager who calls on him (Rom. 10:13). Youth leaders should faithfully share the gospel with students and invite them to respond.

Youth ministers must develop a strategy for clearly presenting the gospel to students that includes space for their questions and doubts.[11] A reasoned response, supported by a personal relationship of mutual trust, is key. Many of today's young people desire a sense of belonging before they believe. Relationships provide a safe environment for questions and doubts related to salvation.

An issue many youth leaders struggle with is the dichotomy between evangelism and discipleship. Mark Senter referred to this as a dynamic tension in youth ministry between attracting people and training them (see fig. 18.2).[12] In many churches, the same tension exists today. The tension is between an attraction-based youth ministry approach (evangelism) and one that focuses on training

7. C. Clark, *Adoptive Youth Ministry*, 17.
8. Packard, *Church Refugees*, 50.
9. Ketcham, "Faith Formation with Others," 101.

10. Packard, *Church Refugees*, 47.
11. Stier, "Gospel Advancing View of Youth Ministry," 13.
12. Senter, "Historical Framework for Doing Youth Ministry," 111.

Figure 18.2
The Dynamic Tension in Youth Ministry

Attract ◄──────────┼──────────► Train

(discipleship). However, a comprehensive model of youth ministry can include both evangelism and discipleship, along with worship, ministry, and fellowship.[13]

Youth Ministry as Disciple Making

The apostle Paul used developmental language to describe the process of spiritual growth (Eph. 4:13–16). He explained it as a natural progression from infancy to adulthood. According to Paul, maturing faith is strong enough to withstand "every wind of teaching" and "evil scheming." He also defined a person with maturing faith as one who understands their place in the body of Christ.

Youth leaders begin the disciple-making process by leading young people to a saving relationship with Jesus Christ. The next step is providing teenagers with the spiritual food necessary for growth. In the church, this means Bible study and discipleship.

"For an increasing number of teenagers today, the church is not just another place to receive biblical guidance and instruction; it is the only place to receive biblical guidance and instruction."[14] Biblical illiteracy is a growing problem in the church today.[15] Research shows that many young people lack a deep understanding of their faith.[16] Christian Smith, lead researcher for the National Study of Youth and Religion, found that most students were unable to articulate their faith. Instead, they expressed a belief system similar to but not quite orthodox Christianity.[17] Studying the Bible can help young people understand and articulate their faith. Bible study leads to spiritual wisdom and helps teenagers understand their identity in Christ.[18]

A mentor-and-mentee relationship provides a strong basis for discipleship. Learning from the example of others is a model used throughout Scripture. Older believers often mentored younger believers.[19] Youth leaders must intentionally seek out godly adults willing to mentor teenagers. Today's adolescents are often isolated from adults.[20] As a result, the advice or counsel they receive is limited.[21] They often do not have relationships with older and wiser believers.[22] Youth leaders must recruit disciple-making adults who demonstrate faithfulness, reliability, and dependability.[23]

Youth Ministry as Missional

The mission of the church is the mission of youth ministry. "Clearly, Jesus calls his disciples to be more than learners; he calls them to a radical commitment to himself and to the kingdom."[24] It is not enough to focus merely on evangelizing and discipling youth; youth leaders must create disciples who produce disciples. The goal is replication.[25]

---

13. Cannister, *Teenagers Matter*, 35.
14. Crosby, "Reformed View of Youth Ministry," 50.
15. C. Smith and Snell, *Souls in Transition*, 291.
16. Kinnaman with Hawkins, *You Lost Me*, 115.
17. C. Smith with Denton, *Soul Searching*, 162.
18. Kinnaman with Hawkins, *You Lost Me*, 210.
19. Keehn, "Youth Ministry from a Family Perspective," 230.
20. C. Smith et al., *Lost in Transition*, 241.
21. C. Smith et al., *Lost in Transition*, 234.
22. C. Smith et al., *Lost in Transition*, 235.
23. Ogden, *Transforming Discipleship*, 179.
24. Cannister, *Teenagers Matter*, 37.
25. Keehn, "Youth Ministry from a Family Perspective," 232.

Leaders should lead teenagers to share their faith with others as a natural result of their discipleship. Leaders can teach students the steps to become a Christian and how to share their testimony with others and can challenge them to engage their peers in gospel conversations.

The History of Youth Ministry

The church has ministered to young people throughout history. The first specific example in modern history of ministry to teenagers was Robert Raikes's Sunday school in 1780.[26] Raikes gathered children and youth and used the Bible for education. Although salvation and discipleship were not the focus of this early Sunday school, it set the stage for intentional youth ministry to come.

In his *When God Shows Up: A History of Protestant Youth Ministry in America*, Mark Senter notes four distinct cycles of youth ministry in America. The first cycle (1824–75) involved Christian societies such as the YMCA and Protestant juvenile temperance societies. The second cycle began as Francis Clark founded Christian Endeavor in 1881. Christian Endeavor was defined largely by a pledge that emphasized personal devotion through prayer and Bible reading.[27] Mainline denominations capitalized on the success of Christian Endeavor by forming groups called societies.[28]

The third cycle began with Evelyn McClusky's Miracle Book Club (1933) and employed youth fellowships. Jay Rayburn's Young Life and the Youth for Christ rallies began

in the 1940s. As before, church-based youth ministry adopted the methods of parachurch organizations. Youth groups played games, worshiped with praise bands, and featured an evangelistic message. In 1968, Wayne Rice and Mike Yaconelli founded Youth Specialties. A few years later, in 1974, Thom Schultz founded *Group* magazine. The seeker-driven youth services of Son City (later called Student Impact) began in the late 1970s.

According to Senter, a fourth cycle began in the 1990s.[29] Doug Fields wrote *Purpose Driven Youth Ministry* in 1992. Mark DeVries wrote *Family-Based Youth Ministry* in 1996 and began Youth Ministry Architects (now Ministry Architects) in 2002. The family-integrated movement or intergenerational youth ministry is the current theme of the fourth cycle of youth ministry. While many others have encouraged integration, two voices have significantly influenced current youth ministry trends: (1) Christian Smith and the National Study of Youth and Religion and (2) the Fuller Youth Institute research on Sticky Faith.

Adolescent Development

To effectively minister to young people, leaders must appreciate the transitional nature of adolescence. "Understanding youth experience is an essential prerequisite to gaining influence with them, and the disciple-making task at the heart of youth ministry is a task of influence."[30] Adolescence as a separate developmental stage is relatively new. Child labor laws and mandatory education in the early 1900s drove children out of the factories and into schools. In 1904, educational psycholo-

26. Senter, *When God Shows Up*, 56.

27. Senter, *When God Shows Up*, 57.

28. Senter, *When God Shows Up*, 57. See also Cannister, *Teenagers Matter*, 34.

29. Senter, *When God Shows Up*, 308.

30. Rahn, "Ministry to Youth," 221.

gist G. Stanley Hall wrote *Adolescence: Its Psychology and Its Relations to Physiology, Anthropology, Sociology, Sex, Crime, Religion, and Education*. He described adolescence as a time between childhood and adulthood characterized by "storm and stress."[31] Adolescence research has since become a crucial part of the study of human development. Physical and mental changes occur during adolescence that impact self-image and identity.

The transition from childhood to adolescence begins with the onset of puberty.[32] The average age for the onset of puberty is 11.5 years for girls and 13.5 years for boys.[33] Body weight and sociocultural and environmental influences are thought to impact the start of puberty.[34]

Physical characteristics of puberty
- growth spurt: the most rapid increases in growth since infancy
- sexual maturation: increased penis and testicle size in males and breast development and first menstruation in females
- hair growth: facial, chest, armpit, and pubic hair growth
- voice change: noticeable changes in voice among boys

Psychological characteristics of puberty
- body image: adolescents become more aware of their body changes and increasingly compare their bodies to others

- emotional changes: hormone changes are thought to be a contributing factor in the emotional responses of adolescence
- risky behavior: teenagers tend to engage in more risky behavior than children
- early and late maturity: early-maturing boys view themselves more positively and have better peer relations than late-maturing boys; early-maturing girls are more likely to date, engage in sexual experiences sooner, smoke, drink alcohol, and be depressed than their peers[35]

Developmental Stages

The formal study of the development of young people began with the work of Sigmund Freud. With a focus on sexuality, Freud divided the early childhood years into three stages. Jean Piaget studied Freud's theories and later developed his stages of cognitive development. Erik Erikson was a student of Freud's who felt that the latter's focus was too narrow. Erikson's work focused on a broader spectrum of development from childhood to adulthood.

The pioneering work of these psychologists set the stage for more in-depth research into adolescent development. In recent years, developmental theorists have increasingly referred to adolescence in terms of stages: early (sixth to eighth grade), middle (ninth to twelfth grade), and late (ages eighteen to twenty-nine).[36] For youth ministry, it is helpful to examine the work of developmental

31. Hall, *Adolescence*, xiii.
32. Santrock, *Adolescence*, 18.
33. Santrock, *Adolescence*, 54.
34. Santrock, *Adolescence*, 53.

35. Santrock, *Adolescence*, 59.
36. Santrock, *Adolescence*, 26; Arnett, *Emerging Adulthood*, 4; and C. Clark, *Hurt*, 34–37.

theorists as a whole. Three descriptors of adolescence are learning by doing, relationships matter most, and meaning making.[37]

Early Adolescence: Learning by Doing

Generally speaking, early adolescence is the period from sixth to eighth grade. Students at this stage, for the most part, remain concrete thinkers. They are on their way to abstract thought but learn best through experiences with the physical world. These young adolescents enjoy active and participatory learning. Faith experiences are also tied to concrete experiences. Youth may gauge faithfulness by referring to specific expressions of the spiritual disciplines such as prayer and Bible reading.

Middle Adolescence: Relationships Matter Most

Students in middle adolescence (ninth to twelfth grade) can certainly still enjoy experiential learning, but their focus moves to relationships with others. As teens mature, they develop an increased sense of self. Erikson described identity formation as the primary task for students at this stage.[38] These teens view life through relationships, and the social focus shifts from parents to peers.[39] Lev Vygotsky theorized that culture and social interaction guide cognitive development.[40] According to Piaget, peers also influence identity formation and the development of social skills.[41] Adolescents learn about companionship, intimacy, and supportive relationships through friendships.[42] Of course, peer influence can be both positive and negative. Adolescents are more likely than children to go along with peer pressure.

Piaget would say that students at this stage have developed formal operational thinking.[43] They are now able to utilize abstract thinking—the ability to see the relationship between reality and possibility. Abstract thinking impacts their perspectives on life and relationships. They can consider the thoughts and feelings of others in new ways. Dwelling on the possible thoughts and feelings of others can lead to the self-centeredness associated with many teens.

Young people at this stage are concerned with who is attending an event. Leaders can plan exciting activities in state-of-the-art facilities, but if a young person's friends will not be present, it is unlikely that individual will attend. Therefore, relationships and social interactions impact faith formation. Learning at this stage is reciprocal—there is give-and-take.[44] When students share what they believe, leaders and peers respond. Bible studies with opportunities for small group discussion are beneficial at this stage.

Late Adolescence: Meaning Making

Older adolescents continue to value relationships, but as teenagers reach the end of high school, priorities shift to the meaning and purpose of life. Formal operational thinking is at full capacity, and they are further along in the process of identity formation.[45] A healthy sense of self enables older adolescents to make

37. Patty, "Developmental Framework for Doing Youth Ministry," 74–83.

38. Erikson, *Identity*, 128.

39. Santrock, *Adolescence*, 29.

40. Vygotsky et al., *Mind in Society*, 57.

41. Piaget, *Moral Judgment of the Child*, 93.

42. Santrock, *Adolescence*, 301.

43. Santrock, *Adolescence*, 29.

44. Erwin, *Critical Approach to Youth Culture*, 108.

45. Santrock, *Adolescence*, 394; Snailum, "How Families Shape the Faith," 179.

meaningful decisions about education and careers.[46] Students at this stage have a higher capacity to articulate beliefs and convictions.[47]

As adolescents get older, they begin to face the realities of adulthood. Young people generally agree on three markers of adulthood: "accepting responsibility for oneself, making independent decisions, and becoming financially independent."[48] In recent years, many have observed a lengthening of adolescence, as more and more adolescents fail to reach these markers. Chap Clark notes, "The problem is that what has always been a tricky and often painful time of relational and identity experimentation now takes a person much longer."[49] Jeffery Arnett prefers to call this group not older adolescents but rather emerging adults. He describes five key features of emerging adulthood: identity exploration, instability, self-focused, feeling in between, and the age of possibilities.[50] This age is characterized by volatility, as emerging adults experience instability in love, work, and education. People at this stage respond to deeper, weightier conversations about faith. They are increasingly concerned about the future and their role in the world. Bible studies with opportunities for lively debate and expressions of doubt are beneficial to late adolescents.

Faith Development

Building on the work of Piaget, Erikson, and others, James Fowler wrote the *Stages of Faith*, which provides an interesting framework for youth leaders to consider when thinking about faith as developmental. The adolescent stage of Fowler's work is synthetic-conventional. Fowler believed that young adults synthesize the belief systems of others (parents, pastors, and peers) and form belief. The next stage is individuative-reflective. Fowler believed this stage was for older adolescents (emerging adults). At this stage, adolescents individualize their faith by adopting it as their own. This process happens through personal reflection. Duffy Robbins reminds youth leaders, "We are never working with a faithless teenager. They may not be conscious of their beliefs, or the implications of their beliefs, or even how those beliefs came to be. But we are not trying to start a fire from coals that do not exist."[51]

Sociocultural Influences

Cultural influences impact the theology of today's students. Walt Mueller defines culture as "what we believe, what we do, and how we live our lives from day to day."[52] The experience of teenagers varies within each cultural context.[53] "Culture is not evil, but neither is it neutral."[54]

Today's young people are growing up in a post-truth culture. *Post-truth* refers to "circumstances in which objective facts are less influential in shaping opinion than appeals to emotion and personal belief."[55] Some of the challenges youth ministry faces today are rising Bible skepticism, pervasive pornography, and confusion regarding human sexuality.[56]

46. Porfeli and Lee, "Career Development," 11.
47. Patty, "Developmental Framework for Doing Youth Ministry," 81.
48. Arnett, *Adolescence and Emerging Adulthood*, 14.
49. C. Clark, "Creating a Place for a New Generation," 97.
50. Arnett, *Emerging Adulthood*, 10.

51. Robbins, *This Way to Youth Ministry*, 408
52. Mueller, *Engaging the Soul of Youth Culture*, 109.
53. Kelly, "Theology of Youth," 5.
54. Mike Yaconelli, *Core Realities of Youth Ministry*, 4.
55. "Post-truth."
56. Barna Group, *State of Youth Ministry*, 84.

According to a recent Barna study, the worldview of today's adolescents is post-Christian.[57] The study defines post-Christian in terms of declining spiritual indicators such as church attendance, belief in God, prayer, and Bible reading. The research notes that the percentage of people with a biblical worldview declines with each generation: boomers, 10 percent; Gen X, 7 percent; millennials, 6 percent; Gen Z, 4 percent.[58] The Barna research highlights another interesting fact about adolescence today: a new name—Generation Z.

Over the last decade, discussions of young people centered on millennials. But now attention is shifting to Generation Z (born 1996–2010 or 1999–2015). There are about 1.8 billion Gen Zers worldwide—the largest youth population ever.[59] They make up 25.9 percent of the US population.[60]

So far research on this new generation has been primarily market and educational research. Here are a few of the findings.

- Fifty-seven percent use a smartphone four or more hours a day.[61]
- They daily interact with three to five screens (compared to one to two for millennials).[62]
- Fifty-seven percent use a screen (TV, computer, video game, phone) four or more hours a day.[63]
- They experience eight hours of total electronic exposure daily.[64]

- Ninety-four percent (of eighteen- to twenty-four-year-olds) watch YouTube.[65]
- Fifty-seven percent have met a new friend online.[66]
- They have a lower attention span (eight seconds, down from twelve seconds in 2000).[67]
- They communicate with images (photos, emojis, gifs, etc.).[68]
- They are concerned for the planet.[69]
- They want to create media, not just view it.[70]
- They prefer "snackable" content (think social-media-sized content).[71]
- They prefer face-to-face communication.[72]
- They are open minded.[73]
- They feel empowered to change institutions (including the church).[74]
- Seventy-eight percent believe in God, and forty-one percent attend weekly religious services.[75]
- They are twice as likely as adults to be atheist.[76]
- They are social activists who want to join a cause.[77]

57. Barna Group, *Gen Z*, 24.
58. Barna Group, *Gen Z*, 24.
59. S. Edwards, "10 Things You Didn't Know."
60. Sparks and Honey, "Meet Generation Z."
61. Barna Group, *Gen Z*, 16.
62. Sparks and Honey, "Meet Generation Z."
63. "Common Sense Census."
64. Turner, "Generation Z," 105.

65. Turner, "Generation Z," 105.
66. Lenhart, "Teens, Technology and Friendships."
67. Lenhart, "Teens, Technology and Friendships."
68. Lenhart, "Teens, Technology and Friendships."
69. Lenhart, "Teens, Technology and Friendships."
70. Lenhart, "Teens, Technology and Friendships."
71. Sparks and Honey, "Meet Generation Z."
72. Turner, "Generation Z," 105.
73. Seemiller and Grace, *Generation Z Goes to College*, 10.
74. Seemiller and Grace, *Generation Z Goes to College*, 44.
75. Seemiller and Grace, *Generation Z Goes to College*, 43.
76. Barna Group, *Gen Z*, 14.
77. Vallone, Smith, Kenney, et al., "Agents of Social Change," 418.

Generation Z has a pluralistic ideology and a superficial theology.[78] They have a hard time believing in a good God who would allow evil and pain in the world.[79] Christian Smith, the lead researcher for the National Study of Youth and Religion, discovered that the spiritual beliefs of most teenagers and young adults do not match the traditional Christian faith. Smith describes their belief as Moralistic Therapeutic Deism.[80] Kenda Creasy Dean explains that the problems in youth ministry are representative of problems in the church as a whole. "The religiosity of American teenagers must be read primarily as a reflection of their parents' religious devotion (or lack thereof) and, by extension, that of their congregations."[81] Consequently, most people ages eighteen to twenty-five do not have a relationship with Christ and are not prepared for a lifetime of faith.[82] The faith of most young adults is weak and anemic. David Kinnaman asserts that "the next generation is caught between two possible destinies—one moored by the power and depth of the Jesus-centered gospel and one anchored to a cheap, Americanized version of the historic faith that will snap at the slightest puff of wind."[83] As a result, 60 percent stray from their faith during the college years.[84]

Even if today's young people do not drop out of the church, they are more likely to have developed an immature faith. In fact, the faith of many adults in the church could be considered immature. Tom Bergler calls this immature faith the juvenilization of American Christianity. He defines it as "the process by which the religious beliefs, practices, and developmental characteristics of adolescents become accepted as appropriate for Christians of all ages."[85]

Is there hope? How can we help today's young people develop mature faith? The answer lies in a commitment from youth leaders to develop strategies to disciple teenagers.

Strategy and Practice

Youth ministers cannot continue to maintain past strategies and expect different results. Leaders must see themselves not as leaders of youth but as people who influence the entire family.[86] This will not be easy. In many churches, parents have grown accustomed to youth leaders taking the lead in the discipleship of teenagers.[87] Others are content for young people to have their own worship experiences separate from the congregation. Parents may feel it takes a "professional" to shape the spiritual formation of their teenagers. Responding to each of these realities requires youth leaders to expand their reach into new arenas of ministry.

The arenas of youth ministry are the domains in which leaders operate. For most of the history of youth ministry, youth leaders have worked solely with teenagers. Working solely with teenagers is what most people think of when considering youth ministry. After all, it is ministry to *youth*. In many cases, the reason someone chooses to work in youth ministry is that they love young people and want to spend time with students. Unfortunately, though, as youth leaders have spent

78. Elmore with McPeak, *Marching Off the Map*, Kindle location 1014.
79. Barna Group, *Gen Z*, 38.
80. C. Smith with Denton, *Soul Searching*, 162.
81. Dean, *Almost Christian*, 4.
82. Ross, *Accelerate*, 4.
83. Kinnaman with Hawkins, *You Lost Me*, 28.
84. Parr and Crites, *Why They Stay*, 121.

85. Bergler, *Juvenilization of American Christianity*, 2.
86. Keehn, "Youth Ministry from a Family Perspective," 235.
87. Hayes, *Shift*, 36.

most of their time with students, many teenagers have developed a weak faith and have not remained in the church.

A growing number of leaders are calling for an expanded view of youth ministry. Expanding youth ministry to more than just spending time with students is imperative. Most notably, the arena of focus in recent years has been parent/family ministry. After all, the single most important influence on the spiritual lives of adolescents is their parents.[88] Some youth ministers are planning their week around time with both students and parents. The result is a deeper and broader perspective on what it means to be in youth ministry.

In addition to the parent/family arena, many are calling for a third arena: the congregation.[89] This arena involves time spent developing ways to help teenagers fully engage in the overall life of the church. Youth want relationships with adults.[90] "Adults underestimate how much kids want to be with us. Kids are far more interested in talking to caring, trustworthy adults than we think they are."[91] Youth ministry no longer means constructing "a parallel church experience for youth that operates separately and independently of the work, worship, education, and service going on in the rest of the congregation."[92]

Conclusion

Key leaders in the movement for an expanded view of youth ministry include Chap Clark, Kara Powell, and Richard Ross. Chap Clark, in his book *Adoptive Youth Ministry*, challenges youth leaders to integrate youth into a congregation by having members spiritually "adopt" students. Kara Powell, executive director of the Fuller Youth Institute and coauthor of several Sticky Faith resources, advocates intergenerational relationships and partnerships with parents in youth ministry. Richard Ross has championed what he refers to as "ministry in thirds."[93] Ross envisions a youth ministry with a balanced emphasis on teenagers, parents, and the congregation.

Entertainment- and experience-driven approaches to youth ministry have not produced a lifelong faith in students. As youth leaders enter the world of teenagers (incarnational), love and care for them (shepherding), spend quality time with them (relational), help them develop relationships in the congregation (communal), share the faith with them (evangelistic), help them grow in Christlikeness (disciple making), and align them with Christ's kingdom (missional), they can develop strategies to reach today's adolescents for Christ.

88. C. Smith with Denton, *Soul Searching*, 56.
89. Ross, *Youth Ministry That Lasts a Lifetime*, 6.
90. Mark Yaconelli, *Contemplative Youth Ministry*, 24.
91. K. Powell, Shelley, and O'Brien, "Is the Era of Age Segregation Over?," 47.
92. Mercer, "Emerging Scholarship," 77.

93. Ross, *Youth Ministry That Lasts a Lifetime*, 6.

19

Emerging Adult Ministry

CHRIS KIESLING

f we consider the entire human life span and set the young adult years from ages eighteen to twenty-nine, we quickly get a sense of their crucial position. It is during these years that the consolidations of the childhood and adolescent years come together to form an initial structure for adult life.[1] For the first time, many young adults find themselves living away from home and making their own choices about beliefs, values, affiliations, time, fashion, entertainment, lifestyle, and spending. It is during these years that most young adults discern a vocation to pursue and clarify ideologies and commitments worthy of their fidelity. The twentysomething years are most commonly the decade when romantic partners are sought for establishing a sustainable long-term relationship or marriage. For many, college represents an attempt to find belonging in a community of shared vision and values.

1. Erikson, *Childhood and Society*.

All of these represent gateway decisions that shape, if not determine, outcomes for the rest of one's life. The ancient wisdom speaks resoundingly to this season of life: "Watch over your heart with all diligence, for from it flow the springs of life" (Prov. 4:23 NASB).

Social Changes in Early Adult Life

Structurally, sociologists have charted five key markers or events that, once attained, indicate a movement toward and into full adulthood: leaving home, finishing formal education, landing a job sufficient to support financial independence, getting married, and having children. The Research Network on Transitions to Adulthood and Public Policy reported that in 1960, two-thirds of all adults in America had attained all five of these marker events by the age of thirty. Today, less than one-third of males and less than half of females have

251

attained all five of these marker events by the same age.[2]

The social and cultural reasons seem driven by a few factors. In the past fifty years, more young adults have waited longer to get married. In 1950, women on average married at age twenty and men at age twenty-two. Fifty years later, women on average marry at age twenty-five and men at age twenty-seven.[3] In some areas of the United States the average age is even higher. This postponement of marriage is coupled with an extension of higher education. Young adults are pursuing more education in hopes of enhancing career opportunities and earning potential. A reliance on financial help from parents or governmental loans diminishes independence and delays readiness to start a family.[4]

Changes in the journey to adulthood are not solely structural. Following periods of societal upheaval, the Depression and World War II generations placed premium value on settling down, regarding the attainment of the marker events as achievements that signified a sense of stability. Today, as society has reorganized around the value of a particular kind of individualism, these same events may signify the end of independence, the diminishment of freedom and spontaneity, and the narrowing of possibilities.[5]

The Phenomenon of Emerging Adulthood

The significance of these changes has created a need to recognize emerging adulthood as a new stage in the life course, roughly involving the ages eighteen to twenty-nine.[6] Emerging adulthood constitutes an in-between stage, a stage when transient and tentative explorations in vocation and romance go through many revisions on the way toward something more serious and permanent. It is a stage that is necessarily self-focused, a moratorium before the enduring responsibilities of full adulthood are enjoined.[7]

Particularly troublesome for those invested in Christian education is the discovery that, according to most measures, emerging adults are "the least religious adults in America today."[8] On average, the young adult years are marked by significant declines in religious belief, behavior, and one's subjective experience of feeling close to God.[9] Some may argue that this is not surprising, since college students have often made an exodus from church only to come back when they marry and begin to have children. Research does give some credence to this point. Of concern, however, is that with delays in marriage and childbearing, this disaffiliation from the church may now be extending for more than a decade. Some have called it the driver's-license-to-marriage-license hiatus. The great concern is that if young people diminish or abandon their purposeful engagement with Christian formation for a decade or more, can we be assured that they will still return? If they do return, what will have been forming their social visions and convictions during those crucial hinge years? Furthermore, what is likely to be the outcome when emerging adults navigate identity, mar-

2. https://www.macfound.org/networks/research-network-on-transitions-to-adulthood/. Publications at this site document these trends.

3. Arnett, *Emerging Adulthood*, 4.

4. C. Smith and Snell, *Souls in Transition*, 5.

5. C. Smith and Snell, *Souls in Transition*, 5.

6. Arnett, *Emerging Adulthood*, 7–25.

7. Arnett, "Emerging Adulthood," 469.

8. C. Smith and Snell, *Souls in Transition*, 102.

9. For a full review of this research, see Setran and Kiesling, *Spiritual Formation in Emerging Adulthood*, 12–17.

riage, vocation, and worldview choices without theological resources from which to derive meaning for their adult lives?

Of equal concern for many is that those who do stay affiliated in some way with Christianity through their emerging adult years may be adopting a rather innocuous form of faith, a faith that Christian Smith labeled Moralistic Therapeutic Deism (MTD). MTD presents such a challenge because it dresses up in Christian garb, convincing the "believer" that they have ascertained the fullness of faith, undermining any need or compulsion for investing in further Christian education or engaging in ongoing practices of spiritual formation. MTD is made up of convictions that undergird a sort of divinely sanctioned pursuit of personal happiness coupled with a vague moralism made up of niceness and tolerance. Primary beliefs in this imposter religion include the following:

- A God exists who created and orders the world and watches over life on earth.
- God wants people to be good, nice, and fair to one another as taught by the Bible and most world religions.
- The central goal of life is to be happy and to feel good about oneself.
- God is not involved in life except when I need God to resolve a problem.
- Good people go to heaven when they die.[10]

Notice that these beliefs have several implications. First, they have little to do with placing oneself in the narrative of God's redemptive history—meaning that knowing or enacting the biblical story is at best supplemental. Second, MTD requires no real identification with the people of God. Involvement in the church or other forms of faith community is largely deemed irrelevant and unnecessary. Third, this approach to faith eliminates any cost of discipleship. The requirements and implications of Christian living are radically minimized. Fourth, MTD requires little wrestling to overcome vices or sin and provides no motivation to acquire virtue through sustained practices. Finally, Moralistic Therapeutic Deism lends great support to a narcissistic pursuit of the American dream.[11]

With these understandings, those facing the challenge of Christian education among emerging adults have to take into consideration several central questions: What is the matrix of forces at play that gives shape to the young adult spirit? What social visions are presented to twentysomethings from which they make choices about identity, vocation, sexuality, politics, lifestyle, morality, church, and civic engagement? What dreams are worthy enough to capture their allegiance and toward which they can pledge lifelong fidelity?

Biblical, Historical, and Contemporary Ministries to Young Adults

Ministry with young adults has many biblical and historical precedents. In particular, Christian educational endeavors have a long history. The apostle Paul, for example, engaged scholars on his missionary journeys (Acts 17:16–34) and at one juncture stayed in place to establish a school of Tyrannus (Acts 19:8–10). Early church fathers resided in Alexandria to sustain

10. C. Smith with Denton, *Soul Searching*, 124.

11. For a full treatment of these issues, see Setran and Kiesling, *Spiritual Formation in Emerging Adulthood*, 29–53.

research and writing. Medieval monks established monasteries, cathedral schools, and universities. In New England, colonial colleges
were founded for the express purpose of training Christian leaders for the country. The vast
majority of these appointed ordained clergy
as presidents and hired faculty on the basis
of their theological persuasion and Christian
character.[12]

After World War I, land grants in the
United States promoted universities as public
institutions separate from denominational
loyalties and governing boards. This changed
significantly the role of the college president
and in many ways established the context and
the challenges of emerging adult ministry in
the West today. Faith-based colleges hired
college chaplains, who became the spiritual
leaders of their campus communities. Black
colleges were founded, typically retaining a
relationship with the church and focusing on
service, much like the early colonial colleges.
Mainline denominations established campus
ministry foundations on state universities to
nurture their own and to protect against the
fierce secularity of modern culture.[13]

These educational "ministries beyond the
local church" were followed by the birth-
ing of parachurch groups—such as Campus
Crusade for Christ—usually with a zeal for
evangelism, discipleship, and training leaders.[14]
Today, 70 percent of high school graduates go
on to attend college. Furthermore, the university model of higher education has been ex-
ported and largely retained in its Western form
in most countries around the globe. Consequently, ministry to emerging adults typically

12. For more on this history, see Kiesling and Rosza,
"Campus Ministry," 184–85.
13. Shockley, *Campus Ministry*, 24–37.
14. Balmer, *Encyclopedia of Evangelicalism*, 106.

brings into view ministry that occurs on the
college campus.

Despite the prominence of ministry associated with higher education settings, significant emerging adult ministry is also being offered on military bases, in jails and prisons, to
those in recovery, to unwed mothers, to those
released from human trafficking, and so on.
Of particular import is the growing number
of international students who travel to other
countries for education. In many cases, dis-
location serves to create openness to the gospel. In other cases, transnationals now regard
themselves as "reverse evangelists," carrying
a robust form of Christian witness back to
increasingly secularized societies from which
the original missionaries to their countries
came. Internationally, contexts vary significantly in the way ministry to young adults occurs, but often similar factors (secularization,
church-state relations, denominational loyalties, mobilization of missionaries) pose the
most salient challenges to young adults.

Emerging Adult Challenges
to Involvement in Church

Personal, cultural, ecclesiastical, and theological factors may all contribute to the disengagement of emerging adults from the
church, from settings of Christian education,
and from the intentional pursuit of spiritual
formation. At the personal level, emerging
adults are constantly learning new life skills
(college and vocational discernment, managing finances, developing habits of study, doing
laundry, getting along with a roommate, preparing food, etc.) that can easily push faith
commitments to the periphery of life. The im-
mediacy of these decisions makes them feel

more urgent than attending to faith-building practices.

Entertainment options also present themselves in alluring ways (sporting events, video gaming, parties, concerts, movies), as most of them occur on weekends, competing with the times when most churches typically gather. Furthermore, if the type of entertainment one engages in is perceived as suspect to a particular faith community's ethos, it also presents a challenge to an emerging adult. In order to avoid discontinuity between lifestyle and faith, a young adult may decrease religious involvement, redefine Christian beliefs, or compartmentalize or privatize their faith.[15]

Increasingly, emerging adults spend inordinate amounts of time managing social networks via technology. Christian educators and others have raised concerns such as (1) whether this constant flow of sensory stimuli habituates the brain to browse and skim, inhibiting the capacity for focused depth and concentration;[16] (2) whether virtual dispersion becomes preferred over embodied and situated places of connection to God, people, and printed texts; and (3) whether always being virtually connected equates with an absence of solitude from which refreshment to live well in community is gained.[17] Personal transiency from moving also peaks during the emerging adult years, creating relational instability and problems finding a church home, staying involved with a like-minded group of friends, and maintaining contact with a mentor. Transitions disrupt spiritual rhythms and established patterns, and the eagerness to belong sometimes leads to less discriminating choices in associations.[18]

On a cultural level, the moratorium of the college experience often communicates to students that adult responsibilities of marriage, parenting, and career are near on the horizon. This causes some to utilize the decade of the twenties to maximize pleasure and minimize responsibility. While assuming they will settle down and enter full adulthood later, emerging adults may benignly neglect[19] the spiritual life. If they come to regard autonomy, choice, and personal freedom as unparalleled goods that exist for a limited time, they adopt a mentality that this is "my time," "I need to get this out of my system," or "I can sow my wild oats and then go home and pray for crop failure." College culture often supports the myth that one can amend the choices one makes now at a later time with little consequence.[20] Important in emerging adult ministry is helping twentysomethings see that (1) freedom can be enhanced by the stability of adulthood, (2) things are worked into one's life more than they are worked out of it,[21] and (3) eventually, "a man reaps what he sows" (Gal. 6:7).

Emerging adults may disengage from church at this stage of life for other reasons as well. Invested in the developmental task of differentiating from parents, emerging adults may feel they are failing at the tasks of becoming independent and taking responsibility for themselves if they subscribe to their parents' belief system or if they perceive involvement in organized religion as having someone else

---

15. Setran and Kiesling's *Spiritual Formation in Emerging Adulthood* provides a good elaboration on these sources of disengagement.

16. Carr, *Shallows*.

17. Setran and Kiesling, *Spiritual Formation in Emerging Adulthood*, 46–49.

18. Setran and Kiesling, *Spiritual Formation in Emerging Adulthood*, 20–21.

19. Jay, *Defining Decade*, xvii–xxxi.

20. C. Smith and Snell, *Souls in Transition*, 102.

21. Dewey, *Experience and Education*, 28.

tell them what to believe or how to behave. Hence, the core values that tend to be a part of the matrix of the journey to adulthood may seem out of sync with the perceived core values of most churches. Although there are no doubt variations among religious faith traditions and local congregations, the core values of many religious faith communities and the values often elevated in young adult culture may differ in the following ways.[22]

Religious Faith Communities
- Settled lives
- Otherworldly focus—eternity in heaven
- Family-oriented focus
- Commitment and investment
- Particularity and exclusivity—Jesus as "the way, the truth, and the life"
- Felt need for faith
- Abstinence, purity

Young Adult Culture
- Transition and disruption
- Focus on this world—my life now
- A breaking away from family
- Need to keep options open—commitment limits exploration
- Diversity and inclusivity—all perspectives accepted, no one judges another's beliefs/lifestyle
- Self-sufficiency
- Partying/sex, freedom, letting loose

The differences between these core values likely contribute to the negative perceptions that younger generations form about the church. Young adults have been cited as

holding the following opinions about the church: it fortresses away from and demonizes the world; its message is trivial and irrelevant to emerging adults; it comes across as anti-intellectual and antiscience; its teachings are sexually repressive; it is often judgmental and unsafe for those who don't fit well with majority culture.[23]

In response, some ministers who work with emerging adults are studying apologetics as a way of making the gospel more credible, yet the most convincing argument is quite often a life of grace, kindness, mercy, justice, and faithfulness. Additional challenges confront Christians at many universities, where making contacts in residence halls is being restricted and/or eligibility requirements to be recognized as a school-sponsored organization require full inclusion of any student regardless of whether this compromises a ministry's beliefs. As higher education is increasingly driven by market demand to focus on skills training for job performance rather than on character formation and the development of a meaningful philosophy of life, concerns of faith receive less investment of thought and reflection in the curriculum.

Theologically, the church must also recognize that even its most emblematic ministry approaches have inadvertently contributed to narcissism, individualism, and a diminished view of the church among young adult populations. Protestantism was birthed on the foundation of valuing the individual faith of a believer over church and tradition. Conventional evangelism strategies, which are eager to promote salvation by grace alone, have tended to offer a rather effortless prayer that portrays salvation as an exchange between a

---

22. Much of this material is derived from concepts presented in C. Smith and Snell, *Souls in Transition*.

23. Kinnaman with Hawkins, *You Lost Me*, 90–100.

believer and Jesus. With salvation perceived as easy to obtain and one's eternal status secured by repeating a prayer, young people do not see the profound need to reorder the affections of the heart to fear, love, and trust God above all things and to love one's neighbor as oneself.

Consequently, many emerging adults do not regard the church as essential or even necessary for a person to have a relationship with God. Many even call themselves spiritual but not religious as a way of disaffiliating from organized religion and doctrinal belief. Being spiritual, then, comes to mean something akin to customizing and personalizing beliefs and lifestyle. In the minds of many emerging adults, church is an accessory one can utilize as needed rather than an essential, identity-bestowing, life-sustaining community that shapes the desires and dispositions of the heart.

Tim Clydesdale has argued that faith in the emerging adult years may not be abandoned as much as it is stowed away, locked up, to be taken out at a later time.[24] This suggests a posturing that inner conviction can be held on to despite little practice to nurture or support it. Despite this perception, research has established that there tends to be a somewhat close correlation between a person's inward commitments and their outward commitments.[25]

It is difficult to sustain inward conviction without a plausibility structure and a company of fellow sojourners who are seeking to cultivate Christian virtue under the guidance of the Holy Spirit. Indeed, there are myriad ways that the college experience challenges emergent faith. In some cases, revered professors hold intellectual positions that challenge

faith. Sometimes temptations force a choice between allegiance to God and pleasure. At times, difficult experiences are encountered, and God does not seem to intervene in the way desired or within a preferred time frame. Faith can be challenged by insufficient money or when time or energy isn't available to support perceived important tasks. Mental health challenges may undermine one's personal progress. A young adult may endure a romantic breakup that sabotages their sense of self—and the list could go on and on.

In order to sustain faith in these times, young adults need to see it being lived by someone they trust and respect and by a community to which they belong.[26] When this is not prevalent in their lives or on a college campus, it is almost inevitable that their faith will wane, morph, or even disappear.

The church can also inadvertently frustrate the involvement of emerging adults if it does not see them as having contributions to make. Many churches provide staff and resources to support children and youth ministry but offer little support for young adults. Some students find their way into campus ministries or Christian colleges that focus energy on helping young adults discern vocation and spiritual gifts, share leadership for worship and discipleship, and cultivate a rich context for spiritual formation only to struggle finding an equivalent in a local congregation after graduation.

Responses to Emerging Adult Challenges

The North American church does not seem to be unaware of the dearth of young adults in its midst. In fact, finding itself in an era of

24. Clydesdale, "Abandoned, Pursued, or Safely Stowed?"

25. Setran and Kiesling, *Spiritual Formation in Emerging Adulthood*, 18–20.

26. Garber, *Fabric of Faithfulness*, 139–74.

anxiety, it has offered a plethora of strategies in response to the question, How do we get more young people to come to church? Proposals abound that focus on church growth strategies from the emergent church, the emotionally healthy church, the missional church, new monasticism, the ancient-future church, the family-friendly church, the intergenerational church, and so on.[27] Each of these proposals provides correctives to the downward trending of church vitality in the West. However, deeper theological and ministry questions must be answered.

- Why should emerging adults come to church?
- Why do we believe church is important for young adults?
- What does the church have to offer young adults?
- What do young adults bring to the church?

In the book of Acts, on the day of Pentecost, while 120 followers waited in a disposition of prayer, the Holy Spirit gave birth to the *koinōnia* (fellowship) (Acts 2–4), which some time later became the *ekklēsia* (the church) (Acts 5, 9, and following). The posture of waiting for the power and the guidance of the Holy Spirit is critical in the reclamation of ministry to emerging adults today. Historically, the great renewal movements of the church were birthed among young adults and were almost always the outcome of sustained, concerted prayer.[28] Rather than battling over which style of worship is best, what model of ministry surpasses others, or which leader has

the keenest vision, we need an outpouring of the Spirit, what Jason Vickers has called "a generous pneumatology," whereby the variety of gifts and graces being bestowed in fresh expressions of faithfulness today can be appreciated and contextualized.[29]

We must also note the relationship between the *koinōnia* and the *ekklēsia*, which may provide a helpful distinction for many campus ministry groups. Whereas the church (*ekklēsia*) is composed of the whole people of God, emerging adult ministries often function more as fellowships (*koinōnia*s) of homogeneously aged people. E. Stanley Jones suggests that the *koinōnia* may be related to the *ekklēsia* in much the same way that the soul is related to the body.[30] The body can become an empty shell if life is not poured into it by the soul, but the soul needs the support of the body, through which it finds its grounding. In the same way, innovative expressions of church often develop from the idealism, energy, exploration, and risk-taking of young people. Critical are the moments when visionaries determine whether old wineskins can contain the new wine that is fermenting. Yet fresh expressions also need the wisdom, historical perspectives, guidance, and traditions of established structures and mentors to guide and tether them. Both of these are captured in Peter's explanation at Pentecost: "I will pour out my Spirit on all people. Your sons and daughters will prophesy, your young men will see visions [hence the progressive movements in church renewal], your old men will dream dreams [typically more conservative]. Even on my servants, both men and women, I will pour out my Spirit [all ages and genders and societal statuses are included]" (Acts 2:17–18).

27. Vickers, *Minding the Good Ground*, 10–15.
28. For an excellent historical overview of such movements, see Sheppard, *God on Campus*.

29. Vickers, *Minding the Good Ground*, 59.
30. S. Jones, *Mastery*, 125–28.

Strategies for Ministry and Engagement with Emerging Adults

Important literature has contributed to our understanding of young adults. In 1986, Sharon Parks characterized young adulthood as "the critical years," signified by the experience of dissolution and recomposition of the meaning of self and world and its challenges to faith.[31] Christian Smith and Patricia Snell more recently titled their longitudinal study of young adults *Souls in Transition* (2009). In 2007, Robert Wuthnow coined the term *spiritual tinkerers*, portraying the faith lives of many young adults as a bricolage—the joining together of inconsistent, disparate components lived as a sort of constructed improvisation.[32] More recently, in 2012, Richard Dunn and Jana Sundene offered that the outcome of uncertainty and fluidity is that truth itself comes to feel uncertain and unstable. Today, just as textual images on digital screens can perpetually shift one's perception, so various perspectives can change the truth that a young adult knows. Truth to emerging adults easily becomes stylized like one's Facebook page.[33]

If emerging adulthood is a time of transition, fluidity, exploration, and instability, then it follows that the primary emotional matrix that most emerging adults carry with them on a daily basis is a mixture of exhilaration, optimism, fear, worry, and anxiety. With fewer scripted maps to chart when certain events are expected to occur in a young adult's life, like marriage and having children, an ambivalence occurs between loving

unprecedented freedoms and having to carry the culpability of personal responsibility. If life is "entirely mine to make," there are no alibis if I as an adult don't become something remarkable.

My counseling colleague, Steve Stratton, suggests that "anxiety is the new hermeneutic" useful to understanding emerging adults.[34] This has far-reaching implications for those who learned to present the gospel as an antidote to guilt. Certainly, the gospel offers forgiveness of sins and freedom from shame and guilt, but if the predominant felt need of emerging adults is relief from anxiety, what social and emotional intelligence do Christian educators need to adequately diagnose their students and respond accordingly?

To see how anxiety serves as a necessary hermeneutic for understanding the forays that many emerging adults undertake, consider the following experiences of many emerging adults.

- Cohabitation may differ in its various forms and rationales, but to some extent, it serves as a strategy to test-drive a relationship before entering marriage. The underlying, albeit misguided, rationale for cohabitation is that it is a way to avoid the pain of divorce likely witnessed in the parental generation.

- Matchmaking is increasingly occurring online, configured by algorithms designed to help a person find a compatible partner and reduce the risk of choosing poorly.

- Mentors, life coaches, therapists, social workers, and extended family members are consulted in an attempt to find

31. Parks, *Critical Years*, 10–27.

32. Wuthnow, *How Twenty- and Thirty-Somethings Are Shaping the Future*, 13–16.

33. R. Dunn and Sundene, *Shaping the Journey of Emerging Adults*, 29–36.

34. Stratton, "Today's Student Culture."

wisdom and guidance to navigate the tricky terrain of young adulthood.

- Parents seek educational routes that involve homeschooling and Christian colleges to ensure that emerging adults are grounded in a Christian worldview and avoid cultural secularization.
- Some young adults are attracted to ancient liturgical forms that anchor them to something beyond the here and now.
- Some in Christian subcultures adopt stricter moral codes to provide a sense of safety and belonging.

If these strategies are at least in part ways to manage the anxiety that accompanies the journey to adulthood, it follows that Christian educators might benefit by learning what concepts and remedies those who treat anxiety disorders employ. How do these concepts and remedies bear resemblance to practices in Christian education? Consider just a brief synopsis of phrases and methods that summarize best treatments for anxiety disorders, noting associations that can be made to the objective of Christian education.

- Therapy focuses on mindful awareness of behavior and the development of compassion that works toward purposive behavior.
- Therapy recognizes the value of accompaniment and that much can be gained in a relational context of high trust, deep listening, and a balance of support and challenge.
- Therapy asks a client to change how they think and consider the effects of their thoughts in the relationships they engage in.

- Therapy redirects attention and seeks to gradually move a client's actions toward their core values.
- Therapy balances a dialectic tension between becoming more accepting of oneself and looking for ways to change.

I hasten here to add that I am not attempting to psychologize Christian education. I am not advocating that we abandon theological or biblical concepts for the use of psychological constructs or that we attempt to do the work of therapy in the classroom. Rather, I am suggesting that we recognize that many of our existing practices have dynamics implicit in them that direct focus in ways that can reach emerging adults. Let me draw from the recent works of several colleagues to illustrate.

In 2010, David Setran, James Wilhoit, Donald Ratcliff, Daniel Haase, and Linda Rosema contributed an article to the *Christian Education Journal* that focused on soul projects. The opening paragraphs of the article referenced an oft-cited Higher Education Research Institute (HERI) study from 2006 that suggested that "spiritual growth is best facilitated when students are actively engaged in 'inner work' involving self-reflection and contemplation." Gleaning from other authors, the article went on to show that missing from the lives of many emerging adults is any "purposeful engagement with Christian formation."[35] A host of new life experiences—social media, entertainment options, and work and family stresses—create a distractedness that affords little opportunity for the transforming power of solitary encounters with God through deep

---

35. Setran et al., "Spiritual Formation Goes to College," 401–22.

reading and introspection that in turn allow one to bring their fullness to community.

Historically, Christian education has always insisted on connecting sound learning and vital piety, theory and practice, mind and body, knowing-being-doing. Cycles of enactment, reflection, prayer, and intentionality serve to reorganize life around convictions and virtue. Soul projects are effective because they involve transformative learning that is embodied, social, and purposeful.

Ministries should place a high priority on cultivating the spiritual lives of emerging adults. Following is a brief list of soul projects that offer salient ways of forming the inner convictions of young men and women in this season of life.

- Reflective exercises that engage classical discipleship books such as *The Pilgrim's Progress* to help one see parallels between the books' insights and one's own journey
- The encouragement of statements of personal intent that mark a commitment to embark on a strategy for positive change or engagement with others
- Kingdom projects that engage one in the gospel, including acts of mercy and justice
- Spiritual disciplines of *lectio divina*, Sabbath keeping, and holy leisure
- Experiments in fixed and prolonged times of prayer
- Journaling with discernment focused on themes such as gratitude and the wounded healer
- Awe-evoking exercises such as looking at Hubble telescope images of the birth of a star

- Composing and telling one's own story of Christian identity formation[36]

Discipleship Approaches for Emerging Adults

Others have called for similar shifts in the processes of small group discipleship and the role of the Christian educator. Richard Dunn and Jana Sundene posit that if young adults are to navigate the journey to adulthood well, investors who can pour their lives into the young must be available and accessible. Dunn and Sundene contrast the difference between an agenda of telling and the agenda of one who paces.

- Telling enters the relationship with an agenda—communicating what a person should be thinking, feeling, or doing. The agenda of pacing is to understand what a person is actually experiencing, thinking, or doing.
- Telling relies on the teaching and advice-giving abilities of the leader. Pacing requires the gifts of listening and caregiving.
- Telling relates the teacher's/adult's knowledge about God's will for a young person's life. Pacing relates the teacher's/adult's heart for hearing where God is at work in the life of a particular person.
- Telling aims at the initial goal of a student's assent to and application of godly advice. Pacing aims at a student's authenticity in relationship to God and the adult.

36. These are gleaned primarily from Setran et al., "Spiritual Formation Goes to College," 401–22, supplemented with additional ideas from my knowledge base.

- The delivery system for telling is controlled teaching times, ministry experiences, and discussions. The delivery system for pacing is the intentional, informal, interpersonal relationships that occur in the daily dynamics of life.

- Telling utilizes small groups to assist in application and accountability. Pacing uses small groups to build relationships that foster self-disclosure, affirmation, encouragement, and challenge.[37]

What these authors advocate is a form of spiritual guidance that avoids dictating. Wisdom emerges from opening conversation and exploration rather than closing conversation with predetermined answers. A spiritual guide engages in trilingual listening—tuning one ear to the student, one to themselves, and one to the Holy Spirit (physically impossible unless there is such a thing as an inner ear that can hear the soul of another).[38] This form of spiritual guidance/mentoring accompanies a student through personal and relational transitions, attending to how the student is posturing toward their past, present, and future. Sometimes young adults cling to their past, hanging on too long to adolescent identifications and shrinking back from taking on more adult responsibilities. Sometimes young adults become so immersed in the present that they ignore their personal history or overlook what God has already wrought. Many view young adulthood solely as preparation for the future and overlook opportunities for ministry and engagement in present circumstances.[39] The spiritual guide/mentor then becomes a "detective of divinity,"[40] helping the student grow in their awareness of how God may be active in all these places. Looking to the past solidifies God's trustworthiness and invites the student to become a steward of their own story. Looking at the present highlights patterns of meaning and encourages the development of finding one's voice and making contributions. Looking forward creates a faithful vision, naming giftedness and identifying infirmities to overcome.

Conclusion

There is little doubt that classical forms of Christian education involving lecture and formal classroom methods continue to have their place. Embedded in university and seminary settings and sanctioned by accreditation agencies, they serve important roles in sustaining quality of education, providing cross-fertilization of initiatives across institutions, and guiding the formation of students and institutions. Yet the missional imperative carried by many emerging adults and those who lead them is generating a vast array of informal training networks, field education experiences, and international partnerships. These have enabled emerging adults to "act justly and to love mercy and to walk humbly with [their] God" (Micah 6:8) in powerfully formative experiences, fostering entrepreneurial ways of engaging culture and cultivating innovation in the work of the kingdom.

---

37. R. Dunn and Sundene, *Shaping the Journey of Emerging Adults*, 18–19.

38. The term *trilingual listening* is found in K. Anderson and Reese, *Spiritual Mentoring*, 96–97.

39. For an elaboration on mentoring in relation to a student's posturing toward time, see Setran and Kiesling, *Spiritual Formation in Emerging Adulthood*, 212–30.

40. This term is credited to Barbara Brown Taylor by K. Anderson and Reese, *Spiritual Mentoring*, 26.

20

Adult Ministry

RANDALL L. STONE

merica has experienced radical upheaval since the turn of the twenty-
first century. Forces such as technology,
immigration, globalization, communication,
and change acceleration are reshaping economics, culture, and sociological norms and
constructs.[1] As the new millennium dawned,
Christian voices as diverse as futurist Leonard Sweet (*Soul Tsunami*, 1999) and researcher
George Barna (*Boiling Point*, 2001) forecasted
numerous trends likely to impact the Christian
community.

Many of these changes have been realized,
and that predicted future is now here. The
front line of change in the local church is primarily in adult ministry. This chapter provides
a biblical approach to adult ministry, introduces seven characteristics of contemporary
adults, recommends six strategies for creating
a comprehensive model of adult ministry in

the current context, and describes ministry in
a multigenerational congregation.

A Biblical Approach to Adult Ministry

The theological roots of adult ministry begin
in the garden of Eden, where God created
man and woman and dwelled with them. Interestingly, the biblical record does not start
with the creation of children and their need
to be nurtured to maturity. Rather, God created a fully formed male and female as representatives his image and commissioned them
to multiply humanity and care for and rule
over the rest of creation (Gen. 1:27–28; 2:15).
With God's creation and commissioning of
adult persons in mind, we may derive three
principles to guide our basic understanding
of adult ministry: (1) humans are designed
for intimate and dependent relationship with
God; (2) families, the first and central social

1. Singh, "10 Social and Tech Trends."

units of humanity, provide the primary relationships for socialization and regeneration; and (3) meaningful work is essential for purpose and significance.

Throughout the Old Testament, God's story continues to center primarily on adults. From the patriarchs to the prophets, adults are the primary human figures in the biblical record. Always interwoven into the stories of individuals are the three strands of divine relationship, family, and work. For example, after the Hebrew captivity in Egypt, God designed a new civil society, built on the commands and guidelines for life given to Moses. During this stage, the tabernacle became the central organizing feature. The people's relationship to God assumed a more group-oriented structure as the ritual requirements of the law took shape. Families camped around the tabernacle to symbolize a new order.

The unified kingdom era under Solomon brought prosperity and the construction of the temple (1 Chron. 28:9–11). The temple became the destination of worshipers from all across the promised land. Families remained important as the tribes and their heads were entrusted with the occupation, defense, and productivity of the land, which was meaningful work indeed. Later, when the synagogue was introduced into Hebrew communities, the teaching of adults played a major role in what became known as the Jewish school through the intertestamental period and beyond.

The coming of the Messiah introduced new paradigms into ministry. Jesus demonstrated attention and compassion for children, but adults remained the primary focus of his ministry. He called working men to follow him, encouraged outcast women to stand beside him, and challenged religious leaders to believe him. After his death and resurrection, Jesus revealed his Spirit and power to 120 adults who spearheaded the gospel mission in response to his Great Commission (Matt. 28:18–20).

The legacy of adult ministry continued as the church was launched. Bold men and women of God were disciple makers, missionaries, and evangelists who traveled to the far corners of the known world. They spread the message of reconciliation with God through Christ (2 Cor. 5:14–21), restoration of natural and spiritual families (Eph. 5–6), and mobilization to meaningful work, with the ultimate aim of building the kingdom of God (Eph. 2:10; 4:11–13).

Understanding Today's Adults

The task of adult ministry today continues along the three dimensions of relationship with God, family, and work. Thus, effective adult ministry should guide adults toward a relationship with God, strengthen families, and prepare adults for meaningful kingdom work for God's glory.

While the term *adult* once referred to anyone who had matured beyond childhood and adolescence, the popular gerund *adulting* connotes the range of responsibilities associated with adulthood. Contemporary adults, as a group, exhibit a paradoxical perspective. In many ways, adult life reflects universally accepted concepts and ideals. On the other hand, today's adult represents the most diverse and eclectic profile in human history.

Adults have experienced radical and fundamental shifts in human life due to the disruption caused by culture-shaping inventions and innovations. Though the effects of many of these changes were already being felt, their impact is being felt even more than before as the Digital Revolution continues to slingshot humanity into a new age. Following are some common characteristics of adults today and potential ministry implications.

Adults Today Are More Connected with and through Technology

Communication methods are expanding at exponential rates. Information is at our fingertips both literally and figuratively. Over three-fourths of adults report owning a smartphone.[2] Phones are now used partially or exclusively for navigation, banking, shopping, and monitoring personal health. Engagement with social media by adults increased from 11 to 69 percent in the span of a single decade.[3] In addition, at least one form of social media is used by a majority of every age group except those sixty-five and over.[4] Multiple platforms exist, but users tend to migrate toward preferred platforms by age group.[5] These trends certainly expedite connection possibilities while also creating challenges for communication between different generations.

Implications. Creating meaningful connections and building community among Christians and unreached adults are nonnegotiable goals. Since technology creates opportunities for and barriers to communication, new skills are needed for effective adult ministry.

Adults Today Are More Mobile

Large-scale human migration is a common phenomenon in today's world and even within the United States, where approximately 15 percent of the population moves, either across town or out of state, each year. Not surprisingly, younger adults (ages eighteen to thirty-four) move at a significantly higher rate than do other adults.[6] The US Census Bureau projects population shifts between regions in the country. The West and the South consistently exhibit growth, while populations in the Midwest and the Northeast have steadily declined.[7] Americans are on the move internationally as well. A record number of Americans are traveling outside the country,[8] with an increasing percentage of Americans holding passports.[9]

Travel and transition are now the norms for most adults. Life transitions and church participation transitions are linked. A Pew research study revealed that the primary reason people search for a new church is relocation.[10] Awareness and appreciation of congregational transience can provide the necessary motivation for outreach and ministry to adults in transition by local congregations.

Implications. Transitions hold potential for new ministry. International travel can remove the fear of both cross-cultural evangelism and international missions.

Adults Today Are More Racially and Ethnically Diverse

Increased immigration and higher birth rates among nonwhite Americans over the past two decades have reshaped the racial and ethnic composition of the adult population. In addition, the number of mixed-ethnic or

2. Rainie and Perrin, "FACTTANK."
3. A. Smith, "U.S. Smartphone Use in 2015."
4. "Social Media Fact Sheet."
5. Chaffey, "Global Social Media Research Summary 2017."

6. "What Percentage of Americans Really Move Each Year."
7. US and World Population Clock.
8. "Arrivals Report."
9. Bender, "Record Number of Americans Now Hold Passports."
10. "Choosing a New Church or House of Worship."

mixed-race individuals is growing, and identifying individual ethnic identity presents a new set of sensitivities and challenges.[11] Ethnicity and race are associated with much more than cultural familial and national heritage; they often reflect differences in language and culture as well as political or religious perspectives.

Implications. Programs and ministries must pursue racial and ethnic reconciliation in the body of Christ. On a practical level, those who plan programs and services should keep multiple languages and ethnic cultures in mind.

Adults Today Are Likely to Be Older Rather than Younger

The most recent projections show a static birth rate and a burgeoning number of older adults, primarily baby boomers (born 1946–64), in the US general population. The percentage of adults over the age of sixty-five is expected to continue rising,[12] eventually doubling within four decades.[13]

The aging of America can be attributed to two major factors. First, the life expectancy of adults is climbing. Second, the birth rate among native-born young adults remains stagnant. Immigrant birth rates are typically higher but do not statistically compensate.[14] This trend is not American or even North American exclusively. Rather, the direction is global and will impact almost every society.[15] "Growth of the world's older population will continue to outpace that of the younger population over the next 35 years."[16]

Implications. An aging population will dramatically impact health care, extend work life, and shift costs in government programs. Churches and adult ministries will have a window to respond creatively to the new demographics, including placing greater emphasis on median and late adult ministry.

Adults Today Are More Educated than Previous Generations

Educational achievement marked the last half century perhaps more than any other pursuit. Since the 1960s, Americans have sought greater educational opportunities. The fruit of that pursuit is the most educated populace in history. Since 1960, the number of adults with a high school diploma has risen from four out of ten to approximately nine out of ten. The percentage of college graduates grew from less than 10 percent to 33 percent in the same time period. Postgraduate studies reflect proportional growth rates.[17]

Implications. Adult church members expect their leaders to have an education. They also expect the use of contemporary learning approaches in teaching situations.

Adults Today Are More Detached from Organized Religion

A variety of studies show that adults are gradually rejecting Judeo-Christian traditions and institutions and embracing personal spirituality.[18] While most American adults still consider themselves Christians and the majority identify with Protestant denominations, that number is declining precipitously, and fewer

11. Patton, "Chapter 1: Estimates of Multiracial Adults."

12. Ortman, Velkoff, and Hogan, "Aging Nation."

13. "Fact Sheet: Aging in the United States."

14. Ortman, Velkoff, and Hogan, "Aging Nation."

15. He, Goodkind, and Kowal, "Aging World: 2015."

16. He, Goodkind, and Kowal, "Aging World: 2015."

17. Ryan and Bauman, "Educational Attainment in the United States: 2015."

18. Masci and Lipka, "Americans May Be Getting Less Religious."

are actually engaged in formal religious activity.[19] One out of five adults identifies with no specific religious identity, a disturbing trend compared to the 97 percent who identified with either Protestant or Catholic Christianity in the 1950s. Formal participation in religion may be on the decline, but spiritual acknowledgment is steady, as 89 percent report belief in some concept of a supreme being (God). Along with these trends, regular church attendance by adults is in decline.[20]

Implications. Christians have a new and growing mission field: adults who are disenfranchised, dechurched, and detached from local congregations.

Adults Today Are More Likely to Be Single

More than 45 percent of adults in America are single, being either never married, divorced, or widowed.[21] While advertisers have targeted the single population, churches have largely ignored or marginalized the singles within their midst.[22] Single adults are often the most unrecognized and underutilized segment of a congregation, though they have great potential for contribution to kingdom enterprises.

Implications. Leaders must intentionally identify, reach, and relate to single adults in the church and the community, then engage them in meaningful ways to join Christ's mission.

---

19. Newport, "Five Key Findings on Religion in the US."
20. Newport, "Five Key Findings on Religion in the US."
21. "Profile America Facts."
22. P. Dunn, "Researching and Profiling American Single Adults."

This examination of the dynamics of today's adults reveals that adulthood is being redefined by technological advancement, demographic shift, and evolving social and cultural norms. These changes, along with advances in health and medicine that have greatly extended life expectancy, call on churches to focus more intently on adult ministry strategies.

Strategies for Contemporary Adult Ministry

The practical, theological, and strategic importance of adults is undeniable; therefore, churches should prioritize ministry to this dynamic population segment. Strategic and intentional adult ministry contributes positively to all aspects of a congregation. Yet, the amount of attention and staffing dedicated to youth and children's ministry has resulted in the neglect of adult ministry—especially to single adults and men. Churches routinely hire youth or children's ministry staff members long before a Christian education generalist or trained adult ministry specialist. Such an approach is ecclesiastically and missionally shortsighted. Inattention to reaching, equipping, and ministering to adults will inevitably lead to weaker churches and a diminished Christian faith.

What might a vibrant and effective adult ministry look like? Here are six strategies for developing a ministry specifically for adults, with special attention given to local church contexts.

Strategy 1: Organize Adult Programming for Learning, Ministry, and Living

All ministries must have an organizational structure. Church ministries face the daunting task of effectively organizing adults in their congregation for Bible teaching, personal ministry, and congregational care. This typically results in church leaders creating various organizational communities or ministry programming groups to meet adult needs in three primary categories: learning, ministry, and daily Christian living.

The character of such groups should complement the pulpit priorities, worship style, and missional activities of a congregation. For example, churches that emphasize dynamic biblical messages from the pulpit may require small groups characterized by life application and congregational care. Thus, adult ministry must be both firm and flexible as staff and leadership priorities change.

Communities of Learning

Disciple making includes teaching Christ's commands (Matt. 28:20). This can and should take place in one-on-one settings, but it also occurs in communities of learning such as small groups and Sunday school classes. Important aspects of ministry leadership are planning and implementing these learning communities church-wide.

Adults may choose to attend learning communities for a variety of reasons: a specific topic of interest, teaching and learning styles, time or schedule, or common life stage (e.g., mothers of preschoolers or empty nesters). A more traditional age group structure is usually more manageable—especially for outreach purposes—but in today's culture, relationships and life roles may intersect or overlap several age groups.

Curriculum is a plan for teaching and learning that facilitates learning toward specific aims or outcomes. Therefore, curriculum considerations should to some degree inform ministry organization. Curriculum can be purchased as a complete set or selected piecemeal and customized. At other times, curriculum may need to be conceptualized and written in-house. Most ministries use a combination of these approaches for their curriculum needs.

Curriculum mapping is imperative for long-term spiritual development and leadership training. Curriculum mapping is the process of identifying all ministry teaching needs, then planning what will be taught, when, by whom, and how often. Proactive and professional curriculum mapping prepares and organizes ministry participants for the important task of teaching. When selected effectively, curriculum can attract nonattenders and provide a helpful path or framework for regular attendees. Of course, the Bible should be the centerpiece and foundation of all curriculum choices.

Malcolm Knowles initially embraced the term *andragogy* and introduced his basic assumptions for adult education in 1975. In subsequent years, he refined his ideas and assumptions into a six-point framework.

1. *The need to know*. Adults need to know why they need to learn something before undertaking to learn it.
2. *The learner's self-concept*. Adults have a concept of being responsible for their own decisions, for their own lives.
3. *The role of the learner's experience*. Adults come into an educational activity with both a greater volume and a different quality of experience than youths.
4. *Readiness to learn*. Adults are ready to learn the things they need to know and be able to do in order to

cope effectively with their real-life situations.

5. *Orientation to learning.* In contrast to children and youth, who have a subject-centered orientation to learning (at least in school), adults are life-centered (or task-centered or problem-centered) in their orientation to learning.

6. *Motivation.* Adults are responsive to some motivators (better jobs, promotions, higher salaries, and the like), but the most potent motivators are internal pressures (the desire for increased job satisfaction, self-esteem, quality of life, and the like).[23]

Knowles's androgogical principles are on full display in contemporary culture. Understanding adult learning patterns and motivations offers adult ministry leader directives for creating learning communities. People will go where they are drawn, not where they are assigned. Therefore, it is incumbent on ministry leaders to craft attractive and meaningful learning experiences.

Communities of Practice

Communities of practice (CoPs) are replacing communities of learning. Previous generations of adults gathered to learn in religious settings that often reflected public education models. The rise of alternative education models has prompted an examination of CoPs as a reliable organizational alternative to traditional learning communities. Etienne and Beverly Wenger-Treyner defined communities of practice as "groups of people who share a concern or a passion for something they do and learn how to do it better as they interact regularly."[24]

There are three required components of CoPs. First, a domain name must exist. A CoP has an identity defined by a domain of shared interest (e.g., radiologists, Star Trek fans, middle school history teachers, Seahawks football fans). A CoP is not just a network of people or a club of friends; membership implies a commitment to the domain. Second, community is cultivated. Necessary components are that members of a specific domain interact with one another, engage in shared activities, help one another, and share information with one another. They build relationships that enable them to learn from one another. Third, members must form a practice. Members develop a shared repertoire of resources through a variety of interactions over time. Communities cultivate their practice through a multiplicity of methods, including problem solving, requests for information, seeking the experiences of others, reusing assets, coordination and synergy, discussing developments, visiting other members, mapping knowledge, and identifying gaps.[25]

Adult ministries can capitalize on shared interests that bring people together by creating or partnering with communities of practice. Mature believers, especially baby boomers, often find church or community service organizations (food banks, pregnancy centers, ESL classes) a significant pathway to meaningful relationships, biblical knowledge, spiritual growth, and kingdom contribution.

23. Knowles, Holton, and Swanson, *Adult Learner*, 63–67.

24. Wenger-Treyner and Wenger-Treyner, "Introduction to Communities of Practice."

25. Wenger-Trayner and Wenger-Trayner, "Introduction to Communities of Practice."

Communities of Living

For the past century, church was often central to neighborhood life, and adult ministry was organized around church activities. Now, the focus has shifted significantly as life has become more compartmentalized. However, churches should not completely abandon attempts to connect people according to geographical location or neighborhood, as some adults still associate this way. Shared religious or spiritual values coupled with proximity can create an environment for continued spiritual growth and congregational care. From living in renewed urban condominiums to choosing senior adult living centers, adults of all ages are fighting compartmentalization by engaging in lifestyles that consolidate their normal activities of work, shopping, recreation, entertainment, and education. Worshipful religious activities should also be an important factor in choosing where to live. Ministry leaders should seek individuals who can attract and mobilize others to create life-sharing communities for the range of individuals they are seeking to serve.

Strategy 2: Apply Developmental and Life Span Theories to Ministry Practice

Established developmental and life span theories afford adult ministry leaders perspective while they implement pragmatic strategies for discipleship. From the wave of developmental theories introduced in the early and mid-1900s by Sigmund Freud, Erik Erikson, and Jean Piaget, new theories of adult development emerged. Robert Havighurst and Daniel Levinson associated age ranges with specific stages of adult development. However, life-stage patterns generally accepted in previous generations are now under greater scrutiny. Delayed

adolescence (or emerging adulthood) and repeated life tasks such as marriage and child rearing disrupt the traditional constructs.

Life Span Theories and Social Maturity

George Vaillant's life task sequence resembles Erikson's developmental stages but may be more applicable to adult ministry in postmodernity. Vaillant introduced the concept of social maturation in his 1989 book *Aging Well*.[26] The social maturation process is composed of six sequential adult life tasks necessary for full maturity.

1. *Identity*. Sustained separation from social, residential, economic, and ideological dependence upon family of origin.

2. *Intimacy*. The task of living with another person in an interpersonal, reciprocal, committed, and contented fashion. . . . This task involves expanding one's sense of self to include another person.

3. *Career consolidation*. Expanding one's personal identity to assume a social identity within the world of work. In this task, one finds a career, rather than a hobby or job, characterized by contentment, compensation, competence, and commitment.

4. *Generativity*. Demonstration of a clear capacity to unselfishly guide the next generation. This involves the unselfish will and capacity to give one's self away.

5. *Keeper of the meaning*. Focuses on the conservation and preservation of

26. Vaillant, *Aging Well*, 40–53.

the collective products of mankind—rather than on just the development of its children. This suggests a wider social interest in preserving tradition and meanings from the past.

6. *Integrity.* Peace and unity resulting from reconciliation of one's self and the world.[27]

Progressing through each of the tasks, according to Vaillant, involves cognitive awareness and personal volition. An individual is not passive in completing the tasks but an active participant in growing toward social maturity. A constructive response to developmental detours is imperative. Adults struggling with dystonic resolution to life stages require attention and support within the body of Christ.

Support Groups and Recovery Ministries

Maladaptation due to fatherlessness, addictions, abandonment, and abuse are growing concerns. Adults raised in broken or dysfunctional homes are more subject to developmental arrest or delay. Creating environments acceptable to adults desiring wholeness and seeking spiritual, emotional, and social growth is imperative. Partnerships between Bible teachers, care leaders, and ministry activators are a place to begin.

Divorce, grief, addictions, wounded pasts, abuse, and self-destructive behaviors have been linked to stalled spiritual growth.[28] Increasing numbers of churches offer support or recovery groups to help adults work through personal issues. Such programs promote emotional health and advance discipleship, which in turn promote spiritually healthy congregations. Successful support groups provide safe places where adults can share their stories and their lives in trusted circles facilitated by trained leaders.

Some churches may lack trained leaders or the church size to justify offering recovery and support ministries. A leadership vacuum can be handled in one of two ways: recruit a leader from another congregation to help launch a group, or partner with other ministries. Both of these options allow a congregation to address the life needs of adults.

Personal Faith Development

Spiritual development, as a unique dimension of overall development, is of utmost importance. Adult ministries must guide adults along their faith journeys. James Fowler extended the work of Levinson and Erikson when he introduced a theory of faith development in the early 1980s. The treatise has framed numerous studies and found favor in the social science community. Some evangelicals struggle with his conclusions because of their relationship to developmental theorists and a lack of focus on God or Jesus as the object of faith. However, adult ministry leaders would do well to consider the third, fourth, and fifth stages of Fowler's faith development theory: synthetic-conventional faith (adolescence), individuative-reflective faith (young adulthood), and conjunctive faith (midlife and beyond).[29]

According to Fowler, during adolescence, individuals possess a synthetic-conventional faith shaped primarily by the influence of authorities such as parents and significant religious figures.[30] As adults transition from adolescence to

---

27. These points are adapted from Vaillant, *Aging Well*, 40–53.

28. Hawkins and Parkinson, *Reveal*, 49.

29. Fowler, *Stages of Faith* (1981), 113.

30. Fowler, *Stages of Faith* (1981), 154.

stage 4, the individuative-reflective stage, they confront an internal dilemma juxtaposing a new self-identity with a new worldview.[31] Adults must take ownership of their faith during this stage. Stage 5 indicates a security of faith that allows mature adults to freely dialogue about and engage with truths and traditions beyond their own.[32] Stage 6, called universalizing faith, is the most controversial and demands consideration beyond the scope of this chapter. Many have observed the faith development of adults and believe Fowler's theory has merit, especially in regard to the young and middle-age adult stages. Further, sometimes the inability to know and understand biblical truth and faith concepts may be developmentally, rather than educationally, related.

Conscientious leaders discern the faith capacity of adults in their ministry by using assessment tools, meaningful dialogue, and storytelling. In addition to understanding the spiritual maturity level of adults, effective leaders guide the spiritual growth of participants by choosing appropriate curriculum, creating challenging learning environments, and initiating authentic small group experiences. Another way to facilitate social and spiritual growth is through mentoring. Fostering relationships between a mature adult and a growing adult reaps rewards. Mentoring experiences, even as short-term connections, have value for both parties.

Strategy 3: Develop a Multidimensional Communication Plan

In light of technology, language diversity, and learning modalities, ministry leaders often struggle with effective communication. Informing adults about ministry opportunities can be costly and time-consuming. Information overload and excessive data exposure overshadow mass communication efforts. Therefore, ministry leaders should emulate advertisers by narrowing and targeting their messages. Several factors require consideration: (1) generation, as adults in different generations have different preferences about how information is disseminated and received (e.g., paper versus digital); (2) language and literacy, as communication through words and images may exclude certain populations; and (3) scope, as mass distribution and personal methods must be employed for effective appeal. Whatever communication methods are chosen, they need to be timely, substantive, and relevant to the audience. Ministry leaders must become students of information distribution to design a clear and consistent system.

Strategy 4: Adapt to New Economic Realities

The earning power of adults continues to fluctuate. Annual incomes remained static until beginning to creep higher in the early 2010s. Social nets are swollen with many families unable to escape poverty. By 2017, personal debt climbed to more than 12.5 trillion dollars, of which 1.3 trillion was student debt.[33] Meanwhile, the national debt soars.[34] Extended life expectancy exerts pressure on older adults who will be working longer to preserve their lifestyles and prepare for their futures. The Centers for Disease Control and Prevention reports that among healthy adults, men who reach age sixty-five live almost 18 years longer on average. Women at the same age can an-

---

31. Fowler, *Stages of Faith* (1981), 182–83.
32. Fowler, *Stages of Faith* (1981), 186.

33. Vasel, "Household Debt."
34. US Debt Clock.

ticipate an additional 20.5 years.[35] The cost of living longer will cause many adults to reduce their standard of living. In the face of global competition, less disposable income, and escalating health care costs, adults are expected to struggle. This outlook paints a bleak picture for next-generation adults. Despite these challenges, aging adults can maintain a healthy, productive, and purposeful life.[36]

Leaders must emphasize cost-effective ministry opportunities, as failing to do so can exacerbate divisions between social classes or generations. Ministry does not have to be expensive. Rather than costly programs, ministry should promote genuine care for one another, intercessory prayer, shared learning, and worship experiences. The pending financial downturn may serve as a catalyst to move away from building-centric experiences and toward relational ministry.

One manifestation of economic distress is the rise in the number of adults living in blended or multigenerational households. Financial loss or limited income is driving more families together. At the same time, divorce, remarriage, and cohabitation rates continue to rise. Rather than see these transitions as obstacles for ministry, leaders should embrace them as opportunities to reach more adults under a single roof and minister to the family as a whole.

Strategy 5: Teach the Truth about Difficult Topics

Too often the church has been reluctant to speak about difficult issues, choosing to remain silent about topics that have moved into the mainstream. The headlines reveal conflict and confusion about some very important

matters. Gender confusion/identity, homosexuality, and transgenderism are at the point of the cultural spear. Social justice concerns such as racism, abortion, sanctity of life, religious liberty, sex trafficking, immigration, climate change, addiction, globalism, socialism, and citizenship also deserve truthful exploration. Who knows what issues will drive the news cycles and shape culture in the near future? The Bible speaks to real-life issues, and we need not shy away from addressing them. In his letter to the Corinthian church alone, Paul addressed false philosophies, church division, idol worship, greed, drunkenness, fraud, divorce, remarriage, spiritual abuse, incest, and sexual issues of various kinds. Adults must be prepared to engage their relational circles regarding tough subjects, not to argue but to relate and to proclaim biblical truth.

Perhaps one of the greatest needs today is a renewed emphasis on basic life skills. Because so many emerging adults were reared in fatherless or neglectful homes, the ability to succeed in or even manage the domains of everyday life is weak or absent. The Bible upholds the responsibility to care for one's own family as a qualification for spiritual leadership (1 Tim. 3:12; 5:8; Titus 1:7). Young adults are usually technology savvy yet need and desire instruction on parenting, money management, work ethics, or interpersonal skills. Older adults need assistance with technology, social media, and social justice concerns. Through personalized instruction and mentoring relationships, multiple generations can help one another.

Strategy 6: Prepare for Changes in Religious Orientation and Practice

The present and the future religious orientation revolves around three main themes:

35. "Older Persons' Health."
36. Irving, *Upside of Aging*.

biblical literacy, spirituality, and religious activities. Church leaders generally agree that as the church gets younger, biblical literacy diminishes. Churches are sensing the impact of two generations of adults raised in families and schools that devalued the knowledge of God and religious involvement. Biblical and doctrinal instruction must become part of the ministry plan; in fact, it must be at the center. As Paul reminded Timothy, "All Scripture is God-breathed and is useful for teaching, rebuking, correcting and training in righteousness, so that the servant of God may be thoroughly equipped for every good work" (2 Tim. 3:16–17). As noted earlier, while emerging adults demonstrate a lack of Bible knowledge, they do exhibit interest in greater spirituality, a characteristic that can be leveraged for evangelism and ministry engagement. Training adults to initiate spiritual conversations with the unchurched leads to certain growth.

Ministry in a Multigenerational Congregation

Thus far, the discussion has focused on ministering to adults, with respect for the various life stages they will encounter. In a local church, many generations typically worship and gather together. Cooperating generations can benefit one another. Yet as Gary McIntosh observed, "Most churches target one generation exclusively . . . while often ignoring the others."[37] The number of generations in churches has expanded from four to five, six, or even seven, depending on the way they are defined. Churches may have three or four generations of adults in a single congregation. Meeting the needs and expectations of all the generations simultaneously seems

37. McIntosh, *One Church, Four Generations*, 13.

overwhelming. Where does one start? Here are some suggestions for doing ministry with a multigenerational mind-set.

First, cultivate common causes or ministries in which multiple generations can serve. As members of the body find their place of service, we will see that unity, knowledge, and maturity will result (Eph. 4:11–15). Serving together brings individuals into deeper relationships with one another, causes natural mentoring scenarios to arise, and allows formal and informal teaching to occur.

Second, create shared experiences in corporate worship and beyond. As part of the Levitical law, God instructed the Israelites to observe seven key feasts and festivals (Lev. 23). Some of them were conducted at the tabernacle or temple, and others were celebrated in the home. All were to be observed as families. Children learned Jewish history, doctrine, character, and truth in a relational, multisensory experience. Adult ministry should similarly feature such intentional family times and congregational events for instruction and celebration.

Third, celebrate special days and events such as Grandparents' Day, Support Group Sunday, Serve Team Sunday, or Single Adult Day to engage and affirm adults within the congregation. Tie them to the adult ministry strategy and the church mission statement. Traditions and annual events are opportunities to transmit faith from generation to generation, recount the history of a congregation or denomination, reinforce the mission of the church, and affirm and honor leaders who made worthwhile contributions in the past.

Fourth, confront any fear that exists between generations by fostering conversations and dialogue. Connect adults from different generations in specialized Bible studies, communities of practice, and mentoring relationships. Help them communicate through stories and narratives by giving adults a chance to tell their faith stories to one another. Small groups, worship, special events, and service events can be catalysts for propelling spiritual growth and promoting ministry partnerships.

Conclusion

Too many churches leap at fads, miss the trends, and neglect the truth. Adult ministers must become astute observers and exegetes of culture in order to respond to trends appropriately. However, the Bible, which has given us fundamentals for adult ministry, should provide the foundation and the framework for ministry. Regardless of which practical approach is implemented, ministry leaders should seek to reconcile adults to God, help them establish and restore healthy familial relations, and participate in meaningful work for themselves and the kingdom of God.

PART 5

EDUCATIONAL SPECIALIZATIONS

As Christian education grows as a discipline, the breadth of its reach extends ever further. The first four parts of this book were devoted to many of the core concerns of traditional Christian education: foundations, theory, administration, and ministry. The final part focuses its attention on five areas of specialization that are of concern to effective educational ministry.

The Ever-Increasing Breadth of Christian Education

Around 1917, the first diplomas in religious or Christian education began to be offered, signaling the field as a formal discipline.[1] From its beginning, Christian education centered on the foundational areas and teaching. Ministry in the early years especially centered on young people, but it continued to expand to meet the

needs of all people, regardless of age. As the field expanded, the needs of growing churches increased, and academic programming became more complex. Christian education as a field responded by providing greater attention to various areas of administration. Then as the needs of people and Christian organizations in our ever-changing world continued to proliferate, ministry specializations under the banner of Christian education responded.

Christian education has been described as an academic professional degree. This distinction is based on the fact that it is an area of practical theology that responds to needs in the church, culture, and society by conducting research, building literature bases, and creating academic degree programs to meet those needs. For this reason, one can expect the borders of Christian education to continue to expand outward, while educators commit themselves to remaining faithful to the essence of their historical roots.

1. Briggs and Smith, "John Milburn Price."

Current Specializations

The final part of this book addresses five areas of specialization. Each represents an important area of emphasis in educational ministry. One such specialization is Christian spiritual formation (chap. 21). Spiritual formation is an ancient practice, centuries in the making. Even so, the evangelical study of Christian formation has continued to gain needed attention in the past few decades. Since the late 1970s, when modern evangelical literature on spiritual formation began to appear, formation has been a growing phenomenon.[2] As our world ushered in the digital age, it was accompanied by a palpable recognition of our need for grounding in the classic disciplines of the faith that lead to believers being formed in Christ (Gal. 4:19). Several Christian education programs have added spiritual formation to their curriculum, while other institutions have created entire degrees in the field. Because of its centrality to the process of nurturing people toward transformation and Christlike character, spiritual formation is included in this volume.

Other major developments in recent years have been the forces of digitalization, urbanization, and globalization. As nations' populations rapidly expanded, large percentages of the world's peoples moved into cities, especially along the world's coastal areas. What were formerly large monolithic areas of the world have become increasingly multicultural, resulting in greater distribution of the world's ethnic groups around the globe. These forces have been felt acutely in the United States, tre-

mendously impacting society and the church. These new realities require believers to develop greater understanding and savvy in ministering in diverse demographic settings, which is the theme of chapter 22.

As local churches have sought to meet the needs of our ever-changing world, greater specialization and attention has been needed. Because of the varied responsibilities of congregations at this time, parachurch ministries have flourished to help meet the needs. Parachurch organizations have increasingly targeted people and causes in need of sustained, specialized ministry. Because of the proliferation of these groups and their sometimes uneasy relationship with the church, greater attention to understanding parachurch organizations is needed. Chapter 23 addresses these issues and provides context and perspective regarding these helpful ministries and how they and local churches can cooperate for kingdom impact.

With the compounding cultural threats of both postmodernism and secularization, as well as the ministry opportunities they present for faithful disciples, quality Christian schooling has increasingly become a priority in our time. Christian education's long relationship with primary and secondary schooling is well established, and the current state of Christian schooling as a discipline is explored further in chapter 24.

One of the areas most important to those in educational ministry is Christian higher education. Every academic course, program, degree, and student in the field of Christian education is affected by what happens in academe. The final chapter provides an overview of formal education as it relates to Christian education in general and Christian higher education in particular. The issues discussed have

2. In 1978, Richard Foster's magnum opus, *Celebration of Discipline*, was published, and it was both a major milestone in the beginning of a modern evangelical movement and the primary work on which a literature base was built. See https://renovare.org/about/story.

a direct, immediate effect on every educational ministry professional, professor, and student. The hope is to offer a unified perspective on these issues to help those in Christian education find their way through the maze of the early to mid-twenty-first century so they can emerge as leading voices in both the church and the educational institutions serving it.

A Challenge to Become Conversant in These Specializations

Our time is one presenting enormous possibilities and pitfalls. In the past, Christian educators have responded with great vision and vitality to address cultural challenges. Whether in the early days of the Sunday school in Gloucester, England, through Christian youth societies that met the needs of broken young people during the Industrial Revolution, or through youth parachurch ministries that proactively reached disaffected youth of the 1960s and beyond, Christian education has always met society where it hurts.

The twenty-first century represents an epoch of unprecedented change. Christian institutions, congregations, parachurch organizations, and individual believers all feel the crush of human need and ministry possibilities. As we are surrounded by a cloud of faithful witnesses from the past, let us commit to meet these challenges together by being equipped in these important areas of specialization. Becoming conversant in these areas, combined with the training received in other core areas of Christian education, will help prepare us for effective kingdom impact for the glory of God.

21

Christian Spiritual Formation

MARK A. MADDIX

God created us as spiritual beings with the capacity, by God's grace, to experience and know God. Spirituality is a fundamental dimension of humanness, which suggests that we are distinctly spiritual beings who are capable of receiving a call from God. It is by God's grace that persons are transformed into the image and likeness of Christ. The process of becoming like Christ includes a journey of participation in the local church and an appropriation of a variety of practices that God uses to shape persons into Christlikeness.

This chapter begins by focusing on the relationship between spiritual formation and

Portions of this chapter were previously published in Mark A. Maddix, "Spiritual Formation and Christian Formation," in James Estep and Jonathan Kim, eds., *Christian Formation: Integrating Theology and Human Development*. Nashville: B&H Academic, 2010, and are used with permission.

Christian education. Then it traces the biblical and historical foundations of spiritual formation that provide the basis for a working definition of *spiritual formation*. Then it examines formational practices expressed through a means of grace, especially the reading of Scripture and the catechetical process that includes the church gathered around the Word and the Table.

Spiritual Formation and Christian Education

The field of Christian education has been greatly impacted by the emergence of Christian spiritual formation. Many congregations, universities, and seminaries have replaced the content and practices of Christian education with spiritual formation. This change has fueled a discussion about the relationship between the two disciplines. Some Christian educators view the similarities, while others argue they have distinct functions and purposes.[1]

Historically, the term *spiritual formation* originates from the Roman Catholic theology that represents a post–Vatican II notion of spirituality. Post–Vatican II spirituality includes a focus on liturgical piety by emphasizing the Eucharist and calling for holiness. Spiritual formation as a formal movement in Protestantism arose in part because of the inadequacy of Christian education to address the care and nurture of the soul. Spiritual formation, as an area of study, focuses on how a person's spiritual life is nurtured and formed.

Spiritual formation was also a reactive shift from a modernist view of Christianity, with its focus on rationalism and objectivism, to postmodernism, with its great emphasis on subjectivity and connectivity.[2] Because of this shift in focus, many Christian educators have moved to the more neutral term *Christian formation* to include both the transmissive and the formative aspects, thus providing a more encompassing term to describe the confluence of Christian education and spiritual formation. This chapter recognizes the overlap of the disciplines of Christian education and spiritual formation but argues that the content of spiritual formation and that of its processes are different from those of Christian education. The hope is that Christian educators will recognize the distinction and begin to incorporate the content and the processes of spiritual formation into their educational ministries.

1. Steibel, "Christian Education and Spiritual Formation," 340–55; cf. Bramer, "Christian Formation," 352–63; Pazmiño, "Christian Education Is More than Formation," 356–65.
2. Bramer, "Christian Formation," 356.

Biblical and Historical Foundations of Spiritual Formation

Spiritual formation is the primary task of the church. People are formed and shaped in the context of Christian community as they encounter the Triune God in worship, fellowship, discipleship, and service. Christians cannot be spiritually formed without participating in a faith community. It is through a community of faith that Christians gather around the Word and the Table, receiving healing and renewal, then go out into the world to fulfill God's redemptive mission. Since the very nature of God is missional, the nature of the church is missional. The mission of God for the church is established in Matthew 28:19–20, the Great Commission: "Go and make disciples of all nations . . ." When the church is being faithful to its mission, lives are formed and transformed into the image and likeness of Christ.

Since spiritual formation is the primary task of the church, we should look to the Bible for some images that explain the nature of the spiritual life. James Wilhoit summarizes these examples in three sets of images: nurture (agriculture, gardening, human growth, intimacy), journey (race, battle, struggle), and death and resurrection (dying with Christ, being born again).[3]

First, Wilhoit begins with the image of Christian life and nurture. The image of Jesus as the true vine (John 15) vividly communicates the truth that we need to stay spiritually connected to Christ.[4] As Wilhoit states, "We often misread this image as being just about 'me abiding in Jesus,' when the actual image and language has a strong community focus; when the branches are connected to the vine,

3. Wilhoit, *Spiritual Formation*, 19.
4. Wilhoit, *Spiritual Formation*, 19.

a marvelous crop of grapes is produced."[5] We live and have our being as we stay connected to the source, Jesus Christ.

Second, Wilhoit provides the image of Christian life as journey and struggle. Paul uses the imagery of training and discipline in the Christian life (1 Cor. 9:24–27). The race image is a call for the Corinthian believers to adopt the singular focus of a trained athlete in their pursuit of Christ.[6] The most popular example of this is Philippians 3:13–14, which depicts an athlete straining forward and pressing on toward the goal. The journey metaphor also incorporates the idea of struggle against spiritual forces (Eph. 6:12). Battle imagery reminds us that there is both struggle and risk, but they are necessary for growth and sanctification.

The third image Wilhoit offers is that of death and resurrection. Scripture is full of examples of the movement from death to life. Wilhoit states, "The death-rebirth pattern is an archetypal pattern present throughout the Bible. The pattern shows itself in the flood (Gen. 6–9) as God destroys the entire world . . . then brings forth life on the earth out of the barrenness of destruction."[7] Other examples include the death and resurrection of Christ; the new birth as recorded in John 3:1–8; and the symbolism of baptism, being buried in Christ's death and raised again in new life (Rom. 6:4). These three images of nurture, journey, and death and resurrection capture the essential aspects of spiritual formation.[8]

Dallas Willard argues that the primary image of spiritual formation is the life of Jesus Christ. He states, "Christian spiritual formation is focused entirely on Jesus. Its goal is an obedience or conformity to Christ that arises out of an inner transformation accomplished through purposeful interaction with the grace of God in Christ."[9] Willard builds his argument on Galatians 4:19, "until Christ is formed in you," and 2 Corinthians 3:6, "the spirit gives life" (NRSV).[10] Willard's primary thesis is that the biblical imagery of spiritual formation is most reflected in being a follower, a disciple, of Jesus Christ. For Willard, discipleship is central to spiritual formation and practice.

Apophatic and Kataphatic Spiritual Traditions

Some people have delineated different types of spiritual traditions according to their distinctive elements and characteristics. Barbara Bowe provides two types of spiritual traditions: the apophatic and the kataphatic.[11] Bowe states that the "apophatic spiritual traditions (from the Greek *apophasis*, which means 'denial, negation') affirm the absolute unknowability of God and reject all conceptual attempts to name, symbolize, or speak about God in concrete images."[12] Bowe finds the basis for such a spiritual path in the revelation of God to Moses on the holy mountain of Sinai/Horeb in Exodus 19 and 20.[13] There Yahweh spoke to Moses with the words "I am going to come to you in a dense cloud" (Exod. 19:9), and after Moses received the Ten Commandments we learn that "the people remained at a distance, while Moses approached the thick darkness where God was" (Exod.

---

5. Wilhoit, *Spiritual Formation*, 19–20.
6. Wilhoit, *Spiritual Formation*, 20.
7. Wilhoit, *Spiritual Formation*, 22.
8. Wilhoit, *Spiritual Formation*, 22.
9. Willard, *Renovation of the Heart*, 22.
10. Willard, *Renovation of the Heart*, 23.
11. Bowe, *Biblical Foundations of Spirituality*, 16–18.
12. Bowe, *Biblical Foundations of Spirituality*, 16.
13. Bowe, *Biblical Foundations of Spirituality*, 16–17.

20:21). Ways in which the church has focused on spirituality by leaving behind everything to follow God reflect Moses's example of the "way of negation."

The history of spirituality is also rich with examples of the kataphatic spiritual traditions (from the Greek *kataphasis*, which means "affirmation"). Bowe states, "These spiritual traditions affirm that God the Creator can be known, by way of analogy, through images, symbols, and concepts drawn from human experience in the created world." At the heart of these traditions is the conviction that God is fundamentally a revealing God who seeks to be made known to the world. This spiritual way also has deep biblical foundations, especially in the Wisdom literature of both testaments. In these texts, those who seek God are invited to discern the divine presence within all of creation.[14]

For Christian spirituality, God is made known through the revelation of his Son, Jesus Christ. Such texts as John 14:9, "Whoever has seen me has seen the Father" (NRSV), and John 1:18, "No one has ever seen God. It is God the only Son, who is close to the Father's heart, who has made him known" (NRSV), ground the conviction that God can be experienced and known in and through Jesus Christ. This kind of Christ-centered, kataphatic spirituality supports and undergirds Christian spirituality.[15]

Contemplative and Apostolic Spirituality

Another classic distinction in the history of spirituality is the difference between contemplative and apostolic dimensions of spirituality. The term *contemplative*—"that transforming and unitive movement, in love, toward the mystery of God"[16]—involves a person's desire or longing for God. Coupled with the realization that God lives in all created things, it implies the corresponding effort to make oneself present to and aware of the presence of God. Contemplative spirituality has often been linked with the mystical dimension of faith, which sees the inner harmony of all things and denies any dualistic notion of life that opposes spirit and matter, the divine and the human.[17] The contemplatives sought God in solitude and in communal settings (monastic tradition). They removed themselves from society in order to experience the presence of God. Examples include Meister Eckhardt (1260–1327), Julian of Norwich (1343–1415), Teresa of Avila (1515–82), and John of the Cross (1542–91). One of the best-known contemplatives is Thomas Merton (1915–68), who wrote extensively about spirituality. These people and others see the contemplative life as a way to be united with God and to recognize the unity of all life.

In contrast to the contemplative life of separation from the world, apostolic spirituality focuses on an active way of discipleship in which believers participate in and further God's saving mission.[18] At the heart of the apostolic tradition is living out the mission of Jesus Christ to go and fulfill the Great Commission (Matt. 28:19–20). Much of Christian spirituality focuses on discipleship as central to Christian faith and practice. Christian disciples are urged to take up their cross and follow Jesus daily. Dallas Willard argues that Christian discipleship is not an option. He states, "The disciple is one who, intent upon

14. Bowe, *Biblical Foundations of Spirituality*, 17–18.
15. Bowe, *Biblical Foundations of Spirituality*, 17.
16. Bowe, *Biblical Foundations of Spirituality*, 17.
17. Bowe, *Biblical Foundations of Spirituality*, 18.
18. Bowe, *Biblical Foundations of Spirituality*, 18.

becoming Christ-like and so dwelling in his 'faith and practice,' systematically and progressively rearranges his affairs to that end. . . . There is no other way."[19]

Both contemplative and apostolic spiritualities are ways of responding to God. They share a common core of reverencing the mysterious otherness of God and recognizing God's Spirit and presence at the heart of all of life. Both embrace God's design and purpose for the life of the world, both of which are manifest in the ministry of Jesus Christ.[20] Some faith traditions emphasize one over the other, but both are necessary for effective spiritual growth and formation.[21]

Toward a Definition of Spiritual Formation

The word *spirituality*, which is derived from the Latin word *spiritualitas*, is a suitable translation of the original Greek words *pneuma* and *pneumatikos*, which mean "spirit" and "spiritual." Paul, in 1 Corinthians 2:15, maintains that "those who are spiritual [*pneumatikos*] discern all things, and they are themselves subject to no one else's scrutiny" (NRSV). The spiritual person, the *pneumatikos*, is under the leadership of the Holy Spirit.[22] Therefore, Christian spirituality is that of those who are living by the presence and the power of God's Holy Spirit. Christian spirituality is a particular way of responding to the Spirit of God for progressive transformation into the likeness of Jesus Christ. It is the result of the cooperation of one's whole life with the power and presence of Christ's Spirit, alive and working within the whole person—body and soul, thoughts and feelings, emotions and passions, hopes and fears and dreams.

A definition of *spiritual formation* begins with a focus on being formed and transformed.[23] A human person is being transformed into the image and likeness of Christ. In Galatians 4:19, Paul wrote, "I am again in the pains of childbirth until Christ is formed in you." He used the word *morphoō* ("to form"), closely related to *metamorphoō* ("to transform")—and it refers to a change in the essential nature, not in mere outward form. Paul desired that the inward nature of the Galatian believers would become so like the nature of Christ that they would have real Christlike character and behavior.[24] Thus, according to Galatians 4:19, spiritual formation can be defined as "the whole person in relationship with God, within the community of believers, growing in Christlikeness, reflected in a spirit-directed, disciplined lifestyle, and demonstrated in redemptive action in our world."[25] Spiritual formation, then, is the outworking of the grace of God in the hearts and actions of human beings. Robert Mulholland says, "Spiritual formation is a process of *being conformed* to the image of Christ, a journey into becoming persons of compassion, persons who forgive, persons who care deeply for others and the world."[26] We cannot conform ourselves to the image of Christ; God is the one who conforms and transforms us by the power of the Spirit. Spiritual formation is the process of shaping one's spirit and giving it a definite character. It means the formation of one's spirit in conformity with the Spirit of

19. Willard, *Great Omission*, 7.
20. Bowe, *Biblical Foundations of Spirituality*, 18.
21. Bowe, *Biblical Foundations of Spirituality*, 19.
22. K. Collins, "What Is Spirituality?," 81.

23. Maddix, "Living the Life," 9–17.
24. Tracy et al., *Upward Call*, 9.
25. Tracy et al., *Upward Call*, 12.
26. Mulholland, *Invitation to a Journey*, 25.

Christar.[27] James Wilhoit defines *spiritual formation* as "the intentional communal process of growing in our relationship with God and becoming conformed to Christ through the power of the Holy Spirit."[28]

The second aspect of spiritual formation focuses on human participation and obedience to Jesus Christ. It is important to note that what we do does not transform us. Rather, through our participation in the means of grace that we receive from God, we are changed. Historically, the church has discovered that certain disciplines, devotional skills and practices, and acts of Christian service keep believers in the presence of Christ, where the Holy Spirit has an opportunity to continue transforming them.[29]

Third, spiritual formation takes place in the context of community. Much of Western Christianity views salvation and spiritual formation as individualistic. In ancient biblical times, with a collectivist form of social organization, the overriding significance of the community was taken for granted.[30] Today, however, the Western church is fragmented and individualistic, which makes spiritual formation more difficult. Christian faith is often practiced void of community. But the Christian life is best lived in community, where worship, fellowship, small groups, and service take place. In this context, spiritual formation happens that anticipates, proclaims, and celebrates the kingdom.[31]

Spiritual formation is also a lifelong process. Many who work and study in the field of spirituality and faith formation use the metaphor of a journey to describe the life of faith.[32] The phrase *journey of faith* connotes the process and the passages in our response to God's overture to us when we view our lives as wholes.[33] Janet Hagberg and Robert Guelich, in addition to James Fowler, have developed stages of faith as a way to look at the faith journey.[34] Just as a child grows through stages of physical development and growth, so believers grow spiritually.

The idea of spiritual formation as a continuous process runs counter to the instinct for instant gratification. The path to spiritual formation includes joy and success as well as struggle and disappointment.[35] Much of the history of Christianity focuses on struggle and suffering, based on the suffering of Christ, as necessary aspects of growth and maturity.[36] Robert Mulholland says that "life itself is a process of spiritual development. The only choice we have is whether that growth moves us toward wholeness in Christ."[37]

The Christian journey, therefore, is an intentional and continual commitment to a lifelong process of growth toward wholeness in Christ. It is the process of "we must grow up in every way into him who is the head, into Christ" (Eph. 4:15 NRSV), until we "come to . . . maturity, to the measure of the full stature of Christ" (Eph. 4:13 NRSV). It is for this purpose that God is present and active in every moment of our lives.[38]

27. Maddix, "Living the Life," 10–11.
28. Wilhoit, *Spiritual Formation*, 23.
29. Maddix, "Living the Life," 11–13.
30. S. Powell, *Theology of Christian Spirituality*, 36.
31. S. Powell, *Theology of Christian Spirituality*, 43.
32. Fowler, *Stages of Faith* (1995); and Hagberg and Guelich, *Critical Journey.*
33. Hagberg and Guelich, *Critical Journey*, 5.
34. Hagberg and Guelich, *Critical Journey*, 6.
35. For more on historical movements in spiritual formation, see James B. Smith and Graybeal, *Spiritual Formation Workbook.*
36. Maddix, "Living the Life," 13–14.
37. Mulholland, *Invitation to a Journey*, 24.
38. Mulholland, *Invitation to a Journey*, 24.

Fourth, spiritual formation includes the nurturing of self and relationship to others. We are created to be in relationship with God. This relationship is to be characterized by uniqueness, unity, and reciprocity. Similar to the interrelationships within the Triune God, we are to experience simultaneous communion with God that does not jeopardize our uniqueness.[39] In our union with the Triune God, our human particularity is not lost. God acts not as a dominating other but as one who allows us to become more fully who God created us to be.[40] Spiritual formation includes caring for ourselves and nurturing ourselves in light of the Triune God.[41]

Jack Balswick states, "Our understanding of God's intention for human development is for us to become particular beings in relationship with the divine and the human other. In mutually reciprocating relationships we encounter the other and ourselves most fully."[42] God's intention for spiritual development is for it to be intertwined with an understanding and care of self, a relationship with God, and a relationship with others. When we live in this reality, we become more fully human and bear the image of the Triune God.

Fifth, spiritual formation includes mission. Being transformed into the image of Christ is not only for ourselves but also for the sake of others. We are spiritually formed so that we can engage in God's mission in the world. As we participate with God in the restoration and renewal of human persons and all of creation, the kingdom of God is realized.[43] Through the practice of compassion, service, and caring for others, persons are shaped and formed into missional disciples.[44] Through the power of the Holy Spirit, spiritually formed persons are empowered to engage in kingdom work and to bring about the fullness of Jesus's prayer: "Your kingdom come, your will be done, on earth as it is in heaven" (Matt. 6:10).

A definition of *spiritual formation* includes a focus on the inner transformation of the human person into the likeness of Jesus Christ. This transformation takes place as humans participate in avenues of God's grace such as worship, prayer, Bible study, communion, and acts of service. This transformation takes place in community and is a lifelong process. Spiritual formation also takes place as humans care for the self, relate to God and others, and serve others. Therefore, a definition of *Christian spiritual formation* is as follows:

> a process of being transformed into Christlikeness, through communal practices and participation in the means of grace, while giving attention to the care of self, which is demonstrated in loving others and being actively engaged in God's redemptive mission in the world.

Spiritual Practices: Means of Grace

Spiritual growth takes place through a variety of Christian practices. Christians view practices as a way to participate in the process of becoming Christlike. John Wesley, the founder of Methodism, called these practices

39. Balswick, Reimer, and King, *Reciprocating Self*, 38.
40. Balswick, Reimer, and King, *Reciprocating Self*, 39.
41. Maddix, "Living the Life," 14–15.
42. Balswick, Reimer, and King, *Reciprocating Self*, 49.

43. Saucy, "*Regnum Spiriti*," 141–42.
44. Maddix and Akkerman, *Missional Discipleship*, 15–26.

the means of grace. The term *means of grace* was a particular term used in Protestant and Roman Catholic circles to describe the specific channels through which God conveys grace to his people.[45] These means in themselves do not save or sanctify, but they are channels by which the Holy Spirit works in extraordinary ways for Christians to respond to God's grace.

Wesley divided the means of grace into three divisions: the instituted means of grace, the prudential means of grace, and the general means of grace. The instituted means of grace are practices given directly by Jesus Christ. They are prayer, searching the Scriptures, participating in the Lord's Supper (Eucharist), fasting, and Christian conferencing (spiritual conversation). These means of grace, particularly in their corporate expressions, mirror the intended and ongoing sacramental life of the church. The prudential means of grace are practices that are wise and beneficial to do. They include obeying Christ, participating in small groups, taking part in special prayer meetings, visiting the sick, doing all the good we can to all the people we can, and reading from the devotional classics of the rich tradition of two thousand years of Christianity. The prudential means of grace were designed to meet a person at his or her point of need. Thus, they are adaptable to a person's particular historical situation or context. Wesley believed that a person should try to do all the good they can by caring for the needs of the poor and by loving one's neighbor. He also recognized the importance of attending public worship regularly. Thus, the means of grace have both individual and communal aspects necessary for spiritual formation and

discipleship. The general means of grace include watching, denying ourselves, taking up our cross daily, and exercising the presence of God.[46]

The means of grace are one way to talk about the role spiritual disciplines or practices play in the process of spiritual formation. Dallas Willard says, "The activities constituting the disciplines have no value in themselves. The aim or substance of spiritual life is not fasting, prayer, hymn singing, frugal living, and so forth. Rather, it is the effective and full enjoyment of active love of God and humankind in all the daily rounds of normal existence where we are placed."[47] He adds that spiritual disciplines do not make a person "spiritually superior" but create the conditions in which grace may flow more freely.

Richard Foster calls Christians to spiritual formation through participation in spiritual disciplines.[48] Foster and Willard argue that the primary means of spiritual formation is based on a disciplined life in the Spirit, which includes obedience to Christ and faithful engagement in spiritual practices.[49] While spiritual practices in themselves do not form or shape us, they do provide avenues by which we can practice a life of obedience to Christ. Many Christians struggle with developing intentional personal and communal practices. Others lose sight of the intent of spiritual disciplines by making them legalistic and strict requirements of the Christian faith. Robert Mulholland provides a helpful caution: "For those for whom disciplines becomes a rigid structure of life that al-

45. Wesley, *Works of John Wesley*, 1:381.

46. Blevins and Maddix, *Discovering Discipleship*, 72–75.

47. Willard, *Divine Conspiracy*, 137.

48. Foster, *Devotional Classics*; and Foster, *Celebration of Discipline* (1998).

49. Foster, *Celebration of Discipline* (1998), 74.

lows no room for divine serendipities or grace interruptions of the disciplines, they can lead to works righteousness."[50] Obviously, between the avoidance of disciplines and the imprisonment of disciplines is the holistic practice of balanced spiritual disciplines, which become a means of God's grace to shape us in the image of Christ.[51]

Historically, spiritual disciplines or practices have been divided into three areas: inward, outward, and corporate domains (see table 21.1). The inward domain focuses on the transformation and development of the inner aspects of the human person. Practices in this domain include prayer, Scripture reading, meditation, silence, fasting, and journaling. The outer domain focuses on the social and behavioral aspects of spiritual formation. These spiritual practices include blessed subtraction (taking away specific things in life), solitude, acts of mercy, physical exercise, rest/sabbatical, and tithing. The corporate domain helps people participate in practices of accountability through community and worship. Spiritual practices in this domain include public confession of sins, worship, celebration, and spiritual direction. When the disciplines of all three domains are being practiced, the person is being formed and shaped holistically.

In addition to these more traditional practices of spiritual formational, there is a renewed interest in resurrecting prayers, liturgies, and other practices from church history. Using Christian icons in worship, participating in a weekly Eucharist, practicing the labyrinth, experiencing the stations of the cross, and participating in the Ignatian *examen* are examples of Protestant interest in finding new avenues

Table 21.1. Domains of Spiritual Disciplines

Inward Domain	Outward Domain	Corporate Domain
This domain centers on the internal righteousness of a person.	This domain focuses on a person's call to discover the social implications of simplicity, submission, and service.	This domain helps people participate in practices of accountability through community.
Spiritual Practices prayer Scripture reading meditation silence fasting journaling	**Spiritual Practices** blessed subtraction solitude acts of mercy physical exercise rest/sabbatical tithing	**Spiritual Practices** public confession of sins worship (liturgy) celebration spiritual direction

of spiritual formation.[52] Another example is praying the sign of the cross or kneeling and genuflecting before participation in worship.[53] Also, many Christians are developing a "rule of life" as a commitment to intentional growth in all areas of their lives.[54] For many Protestants, these forms of prayers, practices, and aspects of worship are new. However, they are giving a new generation of Christians a renewed sense of connection to the catholicity of the church.

Scripture Reading

Christians believe that the Bible is authoritative for Christian faith and practice. In reading the Bible, Christians find guidance, inspiration, and knowledge as to how to live

50. Mulholland, *Invitation to a Journey*, 103.
51. Mulholland, *Invitation to a Journey*, 103.

52. For a discussion of the spiritual practices that many Protestants are reappropriating, see Tony Jones, *Sacred Way*; and DeSilva, *Sacramental Life*.
53. Tony Jones, *Sacred Way*, 175.
54. P. Jones, *Art of Spiritual Direction*, 79–81, 113–14.

out their faith. However, Christians have read the Bible primarily to master a body of information. The Bible is often read to instruct, teach, and give information. Robert Mulholland states, "We are more often seeking some tidbits of information that will enhance our understanding of the Christian faith without challenging or confronting the way we live in the world."[55]

One approach to reading the Bible for transformation is the ancient practice of *lectio divina*, meaning "sacred reading" of Scripture. Stemming from the Benedictines, a religious order founded by St. Benedict of Nursia in the sixth century, *lectio divina* is typically described as a series of prayer dynamics.[56] Together they move readers of Scripture, individually or communally, to a deep level of engagement with the text and with God's Spirit. Scripture is a powerful avenue by which the Holy Spirit works to transform believers into greater Christlikeness.

Word and Table

Historically, the gathering of Christians for worship has been marked by the proclamation of the Word and participation in the Lord's Table.[57] First, spiritual formation takes place through the proclamation of the Word. Preaching touched and transformed the lives of the early Christians. In similar ways, when Scripture is preached today, the hope is that lives are changed and transformed through the work of the Holy Spirit. The proclamation of Scripture emphasizes the spoken Word of God, which bears witness to the incarnate Word of Jesus Christ. Furthermore, through the proclamation of Scripture, the spoken Word becomes a fresh expression of the living and active Word of God, a means of grace.

Second, as worshipers gather around the Table, the Eucharist, they encounter the presence of Christ and receive healing and restoration. The Eucharist serves as a means of grace that transforms believers. Communion, as a "means of grace," matures those who are being drawn toward Christlikeness. As believers participate, their love for God and neighbor deepens. The Eucharist stokes the personal and the communal memory of Christ's suffering as well as the direct activity of the Holy Spirit, providing an immediate way of participating in the ongoing transforming grace of God.[58]

Conclusion

The primary role of Christian education is passing on the faith to the next generation. Such education should aim for transmission of truth that leads to life transformation. The continual task of Christian educators is to engage in the process of spiritual formation in order to help Christians grow in grace. Christian educators will need to find appropriate avenues to foster spiritual formation in the life of the church. They can promote practices such as the means of grace, including Word and Table, to help disciples experience the formative power of Scripture. As Christian educators increasingly emphasize the processes of spiritual formation in their ministries, persons will increasingly be formed into Christlikeness.

55. Mulholland, *Shaped by the Word*, 52.
56. Hardy, "Lectio Divina."
57. Blevins and Maddix, *Discovering Discipleship*, 188–89.

58. Blevins and Maddix, *Discovering Discipleship*, 189.

22

Ministering in Specialized Settings

CHERYL FAWCETT

Christian ministry isn't what it used to be. In the past, culture and society were not uniform, but at least they were consistent enough that generic ministry degrees offered in Christian colleges and seminaries met the needs of most. That has changed. Increasingly, Christian education and ministry degree programs are offering specializations intended to equip students more strategically for an increasingly diverse world. As we seek to be equipped for ministry in the twenty-first century, understanding the nature and the implications of cultural changes can help us become more strategic. That begs the question, What is going on in our world?

Global civilization, including in the United States, is experiencing an unparalleled period of flux. Ours is a world of complexity and contradictions that make Christian ministry increasingly challenging. While it is indisputable that paradigmatic changes have led to increasing diversity worldwide, it is also true that certain tucked-away places and cultures have remained, at least for now, much as they were in decades past. Even so, as the Digital Revolution continues to disrupt entire civilizations, a deep suspicion lurks that the changes we will endure have only just begun.

In various localities, one finds evidence of the confusing and conflicting forces representing both divergence and convergence. Some geographical areas, for example, are increasingly diverse in ethnicity, while other communities continue to be more segregated. In addition, enormous numbers of people are concentrated in cosmopolitan centers, while other regions are very sparsely populated. In other words, despite trends that point us to certain generalizations about society, there remain profound and pronounced differences that affect the work of ministry.

The practical implication of this reality is that Christian educators cannot expect to be effective by taking a monolithic approach to ministry training. To help people make an impact in today's world, education must expose students to many areas of competency that will ensure effectiveness in today's varied demographic settings. To put it plainly, Christian ministers cannot expect to be widely effective in today's ever-changing world without possessing a growing understanding of the many settings, environments, and forces at work around our planet.

Where the World Currently Finds Itself

As the digital age dawned, it provided unprecedented opportunities for the world's peoples. The past several decades of civilization's advancement have been a result of human progress fueled by divine blessing. Many changes have led to improvements in human existence throughout many parts of the world, but there are notable exceptions.

Because we live in a fallen world, the bright, shiny side of positive change has a dark underbelly that produces unintended negative consequences and social injustices. As believers, we continue to do our best to help people in their sometimes desperate plight in the world while recognizing that human life today is, overall, significantly better than ever before in history.

Industrialization has produced greater productivity. This has helped large swaths of the global population formerly living at the subsistence level to emerge from poverty. It has helped entire societies begin to move toward stability and sustainability.[1] In addition, nearly nine out of ten people in the world are now literate.[2] Regarding health and longevity, improvements in housing, sanitation, fertility, agriculture, and medicine have exponentially improved human life everywhere. Political freedom and human liberties have also revolutionized people's lives. Only two hundred years ago, less than 1 percent of the world's population lived in a democracy. Now over half of the world enjoys the blessings of some form of representative government.[3] Not surprisingly, many of these improvements have been aided by enhancements in education. Human learning has helped create much positive change, and, in turn, greater human learning is needed. Never have more people in the world been exposed to formal education, even though a notable gap still exists in some areas.

Despite these fabulous improvements, the condition of the human heart is as it has always been—in explicit need of the gospel and the transformative power of Jesus. This spiritual reality makes it clear that Christian ministers must work diligently to understand the world in all its diversity in order to minister effectively in the ever-changing twenty-first century. As they do, those in the field can play a strategic role in advancing the cause of Christ.

The Forces at Work in Our World

To be most effective, Christian educators must grasp the timeless truths of Scripture and the time-bound changes of civilization. Great attention has been given in this book to the importance of Scripture and the foundations of Christian education. It is also important to have a working knowledge of the anthropological and sociological forces creating change

1. Roser and Ortiz-Ospina, "Global Extreme Poverty."
2. Roser, "Proof That Life Is Getting Better."

3. Roser, "Proof That Life Is Getting Better."

in our world. By understanding these things, we will be better informed about the world in which we live and minister.

This raises the question, What is meant by these so-called anthropological and sociological changes? Anthropology and sociology, like psychology, concern themselves with human behavior. Whereas psychology is more focused on individual persons, anthropology and sociology are more concerned about humanity in general. Where anthropology and sociology differ, however, is in their emphasis. Anthropology focuses primarily on culture, while sociology centers its attention on society. In today's world, several forces related to culture and society have impacted people and, as a result, have affected ministry in the twenty-first century.

Digitalization

Though the Industrial Revolution began in the eighteenth century, some areas of the world remained outside the reach of its impact for quite some time. Even so, industrialization brought greater productivity and economic growth to many areas. It did this by enabling the mass production of goods through advances in machinery, automation, energy, and manufacturing. All of these resulted in a gradual rise in the world's standard of living and the slow movement of people out of extreme poverty over the following two centuries.

As industrialization matured, the world changed dramatically. People's lives improved and human existence began to flourish worldwide, though with exceptions. Large portions of civilization saw great advancements, which led to an increasing need for advances in knowledge to solve human problems and to improve our world. Throughout this time, a knowledge economy began to develop.

The need for greater learning launched the information age. As it did, advances in electronics and science produced greater forms of technology. This resulted in the development of digital methods of retrieving, storing, and calculating information. During this time, large mainframe computers began to be invented for business needs, followed by personal computers for individuals' needs. As computers became ubiquitous, the information age was born.

The information age marked the change from the world being driven by industry to it being driven by technology. Continued developments led to smartphones, the internet, and wireless internet or Wi-Fi. With these advances, society entered the Digital Revolution.

These changes are impacting enormous segments of our lives, including production, communication, education, and much more. Life as known by previous generations, the so-called digital immigrants, has changed at a fundamental level.[4] For those who grew up as digital natives—millennials, Generation Z, and Generation Alpha—the future remains unclear.[5] What is clear is that being conversant about the results of digitalization is a necessary part of being an informed minister in this age.

Urbanization

One of the fundamental impacts of industrialization and digitalization has been urbanization.[6] Urbanization, the migration of large

4. Prensky, "Digital Natives, Digital Immigrants, Part 1."
5. A. Williams, "Meet Alpha."
6. "Future World Population Growth."

numbers of people from rural areas into cities, is often the result of industrialization and the economic opportunities that stem from it.[7] Urbanization is expected to drive global urban growth to as many as five billion inhabitants living in the world's cities by the year 2030.[8] Similar to the first wave of urbanization in the eighteenth and nineteenth centuries, the current trend offers grand opportunities, but it is also creating massive challenges—particularly in the developing world, where the majority of these crises are being felt most.[9]

The rise of new megacities throughout our world sometimes produces alarming shortages of clean water, food, and energy-related products like gas and oil, along with the blight caused by overcrowding and environmental pollution. Urban sprawl has contributed positively to economic growth and a higher standard of living for many, but it has also had deleterious effects. The loss of agricultural lands being used for new housing construction and business expansion has resulted in population surges that are resulting in unsustainable overcrowding. These sometimes produce a lower standard of living overall due to human stress and higher crime rates, profound infrastructure problems, taxing effects on existing energy grids, and much more. The compounded effects of these issues represent significant human and environmental pain. Together, they create the need for planting more local churches and equipping greater numbers of believers who can offer the message of the gospel, practical ministry, and other solutions.

Historically, urbanization played a role in God's kingdom during the early church.

Though urban areas in those times were not as large as today's cities, they still influenced the surrounding culture, much as cities do today.[10] They were the centers of power and influence. Paul targeted cities, and as the gospel took hold in them, it naturally spread to the surrounding areas.[11] Later, the Reformation also began in European cities and then later spread to the countryside.

The cities of today have continued to grow, but the evangelical church has often been slow to respond to this movement. Statistically, the number of Christians and the sizes of churches in inner cities have continued to decrease.[12] This has led to a discussion about whether cities have a secularizing effect or whether cities will make urbanites more open to the gospel. Evidence has been found for both views. Either way, a major factor for evangelism and disciple making is the posture of the church toward the city.[13] Because of the long-term reality of urbanization, with nearly half of the global population living within cities,[14] urban training must become a much greater focus of ministry preparation in colleges and seminaries.

At the same time, eliminating targeted training for rural and suburban ministry is not the answer. Ironically, ongoing industrialization and economic development sometimes give way to counterurbanization and its closely related phenomenon, suburbanization.[15] Many people move away from cities into rural and suburban areas due to the unpleasant living conditions in cities, a desire

7. UNFPA, "State of World Population 2007," 6–13.
8. UNFPA, "State of World Population 2007," 1.
9. According to United Nations statistics, as many as 80 percent of urbanites will ultimately reside in these areas.

10. Conn and Ortiz, *Urban Ministry*, 34.
11. J. Watson, "Urban Churches."
12. Greenway, *Guidelines for Urban Church Planting*, 569–70.
13. R. White, *Journey to the Center of the City*, 43–50.
14. J. Watson, "Urban Churches."
15. Mitchell, "Counterurbanization," 117–28.

to live in less-threatening places as they age, and the recent development of industry in more rural and suburban areas.

Globalization

The forces of industrialization, digitalization, and urbanization helped bring about globalization and its effects. As with many loaded terms, defining *globalization* is challenging—especially in a postmodern world.[16] In essence, globalization is an ongoing process that has resulted in the worldwide mutual exchange of people, ideas, values, perspectives, and cultures. Globalization is both a cause of change in our world and the effect of change in our world. It sometimes involves the migration of people from one place to another but at the very least includes or is assumed to include the reciprocal sharing and integration of cultures and societies.

The concept of globalization is nothing new to Christianity, only the degree to which it is currently being seen in the world. The Christian gospel is an example of divine globalization. God anticipated and, indeed, even commanded the worldwide distribution of believers and Christian truth so that the gospel could infuse all places, peoples, cultures, and societies.[17] This has happened continually throughout history. Sometimes Christianity has strongly affected the world, whereas at times of spiritual weakness, the Christian church has become more *like* the world.

In the case of contemporary society, globalization is occurring more rapidly and obviously than ever before. These forces are changing the developing world and the developed world. Movement of people to and from the global South (including the so-called 10-40 Window in the world's Southern Hemisphere) has affected both those people groups and the societies to which they immigrated.

As globalization has occurred, American cities have been transformed into radically diverse immigrant communities. Most large urban areas are now places with vast expressions of cultural and ethnic variety.[18] No longer are inner cities simply generic melting pots of homogeneous races, if they ever were. Now numerous identifiable ethnic, multicultural, and even national identities are seen in cities everywhere.

With the large and growing percentages of Asian, African, and European people in American cities come unique ethnic identities and cultural expressions. Each group has a different value system, different traditions, different tastes, and differences in dress, food, etiquette, child raising, educational perspectives, and social mores. These realities are challenging in and of themselves, but when these differences are in conflict, they can stretch church leadership to the breaking point. Ironically, globalization is not occurring only in cities, though it often starts there. It is now an increasing reality in communities everywhere, including suburbia and rural areas.

The Impact on Christian Education Training

The result of these unstoppable realities is sustained and radical changes that affect civilization, culture, society, the community, and the church. To respond well, Christian leaders must understand the nature of these demographic realities in all their complexity

16. Al-Rodhan, "Definitions of Globalization."
17. Veronis, "Globalization."

18. Fuder, *Training Students for Urban Ministry*, 245.

and nuance. These demographic realities must influence Christian education curriculum, preparatory training, and programs, courses, and learning objectives. Christian educators must figure out a new ministry calculus that results in enhanced formal training that can be used to equip believers for effective ministry in the new world.

Christian education must take the effects of these global changes into consideration and adjust accordingly. Perhaps more than any other academic discipline, the field of Christian education may have the greatest advantage. It seems most poised to meet these challenges, and doing so could advance the impact of Christian education in the process. To do so, however, Christian educators must reject a monolithic approach to formal ministry training that sees degree programs and curriculum as largely static. Instead, Christian education training must adapt to the current cultural forces to equip people for rural, suburban, and urban ministry; church planting; ministry to churches of all types and sizes; and ministry to monocultural and multicultural churches. Following are observations, considerations, and questions to ask as starting points for developing ministry training targeted to our increasingly diverse world.

Rural Ministry

One of the factors influencing ministry in the twenty-first century is the fact that we live in an increasingly urbanized world, as was stated earlier. Because of this trend, researchers and missiologists have gravitated toward urban ministry. Though giving greater attention to urban areas and ministries is important, it must not be done to the exclusion of ministry in rural areas. In late 2016, nearly 20 percent of the American people lived in rural America, a figure that equates to sixty million people living in 97 percent of the land mass of the United States.[19] Yet because of the increasing attention given to urban ministry and its suburban counterpart, training and literature targeting rural ministry is increasingly hard to find.[20]

Some, like Drew University professor Leonard Sweet, are beginning to argue that ministry in rural churches has eluded our attention and that students should be more informed about these areas.[21] In our increasingly urban world, many people do not accurately understand rural areas and ministry, as life is different there than when most Americans lived in an agrarian society. As a result, perspectives on rural ministry sometimes suffer from overly broad and harmful stereotypes.[22]

Many people falsely believe that the only successful churches reside in thriving urban or affluent suburban areas. Some wrongly consider sparsely populated areas passé and not worth the investment.[23] This perspective persists even at some training institutions that should work to reverse such stereotypes.

Rural ministry sometimes conforms to the assumptions that many nonrural people have about it—for example, that it involves tiny congregations scattered across the bluegrass landscape—but more often than not, it doesn't. Large swaths of rural Americans suffer from dire poverty, underemployment, mental health issues, and a lack of healthy churches among large populations of completely unchurched

---

19. "New Census Data Show Differences."
20. Griggs, *Small Town Jesus*, 18.
21. This argument from Sweet is referenced in Roth, *God's Country*, i–ii.
22. Daman and Weschler, *Forgotten Church*, 23.
23. O'Dell, *Transforming Church in Rural America*, 15–18.

people. Despite this, some ministers show no interest in reaching this domestic mission field. In the words of rural ministry specialists Glenn Daman and Brian Weschler:

> Ask a Bible college or seminary student to pastor a rural church, and they will look at you like you were asking them to pastor a church on the moon, with no people, no potential for growth, surrounded by dust and empty lands. In one survey of students in a Bible college, only thirty-three percent did not consider the size of the community important for prospective ministry opportunities. . . . This raises serious concerns as to why so few are willing to serve small churches in rural areas.[24]

Rural ministry has been neglected in ecclesiastical dialogue, research, and ministry training. This is why it is important that good Christian education methods for rural ministry be taught. In some cases, small communities in prairie, tundra, desert, or mountainous terrain have only a few local churches, or maybe only one. This reality makes the ministry offered at such places incredibly important.

Suburban Ministry

Sometimes suburbia brings to mind a higher standard of living, away from the crime and grime of the urban core.[25] This is sometimes the case, but the suburbs are not what they used to be. In years past, and certainly in some places still today, suburbs were thought of as being the center of idyllic living. Due to their manicured lawns, paid gardeners, and

McMansion homes in gated communities, ministry there was considered safe, clean, comfortable, and sometimes relatively lucrative. Municipalities even opened their doors to churches, considering the "moral stability" they brought to be a selling point for suburban developers.[26]

To be sure, some of these factors remain true. Yet even with the pomp and circumstance of well-heeled living, human nature remains in desperate need of Christ.[27] In such suburbs, previous training offered in many schools remains relevant. Yet this pattern of suburban churches is reversing. Part of the change is due to the increasing industrialization of suburban areas, outside the city limits. In such cases, companies seek to escape less-incentivized tax rates and scoop up property in fringe suburban areas. The promise of new jobs draws people there, leading to more growth in the first- and second-ring suburbs that exist in major metropolitan areas.

Another sociological factor effecting change in suburbs is gentrification.[28] Gentrification is the phenomenon of developers and investors moving into depressed and run-down areas of the city, improving them, and increasing the lease amounts for business space, apartments, and condos. Gentrification often draws people of means back into the city while driving people without means out into the older suburbs.

For several years now, many people from upper-middle-class and upper-class society have been drawn back into the city.[29] An

24. Daman and Weschler, *Forgotten Church*, 26.

25. Conn, *American City and the Evangelical Church*, 56–58.

26. Buggeln, *Suburban Church*, 160–63.

27. DeKruyter with Schultze, *Suburban Church*, 22–37.

28. Fuder and Castellanos, *Heart for the Community*, 39–50.

29. Ziegenhals, *Urban Churches in Transition*, 163–64.

unforeseen consequence has been that an increasing number of good poor people and, in some cases, violent people and gang members have found their way into the suburbs. This has resulted in increased social ills in many previously peaceful neighborhoods and overwhelmed city services in unprepared agencies.

All these factors have created a new suburbia that can make Christian ministry more diverse and challenging. In the past, the suburbs of large cities had a monolithic quality, while many of today's first-ring suburbs have a split personality. One part of town may contain nice, safe neighborhoods of relative wealth, while another part of the same suburb might be a transitional area where streets show the gritty impact of crime and poverty. All these realities and their attendant factors impact church ministry in suburbs, creating challenges for Christian educators today.[30]

Urban Ministry

Urban ministry is a central aspect of God's economy. From the earliest days of the establishment of the first city, Enoch (Gen. 4:17), to the gathering of God's people in the new city of Jerusalem in heaven (Rev. 21:2), cities figure prominently in the unfolding of God's plan. As stated earlier, urban areas are disproportionately influential. In addition to the sheer size of urban centers, they wield even more impact than the sum of their parts. An indication of this importance might be seen in the attention given to them in the New Testament epistles. Note that it was not little-known rural areas that served as the focus of

apostolic church planting but rather the great megacities of ancient Rome, Corinth, Thessalonica, Ephesus.

Despite the biblical, historical, and societal importance of cities, a real and present danger is that some churches, denominations, and educational institutions do not properly emphasize cities.[31] This is because, historically, there has been a type of antiurban sentiment within evangelicalism.[32] In the two centuries since the dawn of the Industrial Revolution, the incredible impact of cities has always been coupled with some negative by-products.[33] As people flood into cities for good jobs and a better future, and as anonymous and rootless urbanites struggle with unstable value systems, human depravity expresses itself.[34] This has sometimes made cities less than appealing and the source of human pain and suffering. The struggles of urban ministry are so challenging that even seasoned urban leaders sometimes grow discouraged.[35]

Christian educators must provide relevant training to students heading to urban areas, including inner cities. They must become acquainted with the glory and the grime of our great cities, in all their diversity across the land, and work with seasoned and embedded ministry experts to identify the most effective equipping strategies available.

Church Planting

New church congregations are being planted at a significant rate, especially among non-

30. Fuder and Castellanos, *Heart for the Community*, 129–42.

31. Conn, "Christian Social Ministry."
32. R. White, *Journey to the Center of the City*, 43–50.
33. Conn and Ortiz, *Urban Ministry*, 161.
34. Senter, *Coming Revolution in Youth Ministry*, 86–90.
35. Boyer, *Urban Masses and Moral Order*, 136.

mainline denominations (81 percent).[36] A group of people is considered a church plant if it is a newly organized local gathering of followers of Jesus Christ that identifies itself as a church, meets regularly to engage in spiritual activity, and would broadly be defined as Protestant.[37]

Though the church-planting surge at the beginning of the twentieth-first century was new to some, starting new congregations has been in vogue since the apostolic age. The apostle Paul spoke to unbelieving Athenian philosophers at Mars Hill, declaring the gospel beside the statue to an unknown god (Acts 17:16–34). As he continued to preach Christ in other significant Greek city-states beholden to the Grecian cult religion, churches sprang up everywhere, including many mentioned in the New Testament: Pergamum, Thyatira, Sardis, Philadelphia, Laodicea, Colossae, Smyrna, Philippi, Thessalonica, and Corinth. Other apostles had similar experiences as they preached throughout cities steeped in the Roman cult religion. Though some periods of church history have emphasized church planting less than others, leaders in our time are making it a greater priority.

Some Christians are aware of the priority and the challenges of church planting, though others are not. Some have a favorable view of the practice, while others do not. Either way, this ongoing emphasis of the apostolic church works to stem the tide of increasingly unreached and unchurched populations. For this reason, it should be a priority in ministry training.[38]

Unfortunately, not all institutions see the vision, and not all academic programs offer degrees, or even courses, in this area. Courses are needed, however, because of the tremendous stressors and challenges faced by both church planters[39] and their spouses.[40] Because church planting is increasingly important in our culture, training for this task should be a priority for Christian colleges and seminaries.

Ministry to Churches of All Types and Sizes

Churches, like people, come in all shapes and sizes. Churches may consist of a dozen congregants meeting once a month in a rural setting or tens of thousands meeting in multiple locations at different times, or anything in between. Some churches have online campuses, while others are mobile. Some lease a building, while others own property and use a traditional building for worship gatherings.

There are theologically conservative, moderate, and liberal churches. For lack of better terms, there are complementarian and egalitarian churches. Some are Calvinistic, some are Arminian, and some are in between. There are churches with volunteer pastors, circuit-preacher pastors, single-staff teams, and multistaff teams. There are denominational, associational, nondenominational, and independent churches. Some are small,[41] while others are large or behemoth.[42] Some are newly formed, and some have been serving their communities for decades or centuries. Local churches are genuinely unique, and those who seek to serve local churches need

36. "Church Planters and the Cost of Starting a Church."

37. Stetzer and Bird, *State of Church Planting in the United States*, 2.

38. Stetzer and Im, *Planting Missional Churches*, 30–35.

39. "Church Planters and the Cost of Starting a Church."

40. Hoover, *Church Planting Wife*, 161–76.

41. Vaters, *Small Church Essentials*, 130.

42. Schaller, *Very Large Church*, 108–15.

good general ministry training as well as solid specialized equipping.

Whatever the size or type of church, God has a common, universal design for it that is consistent with his eternal purposes.[43] At the same time, church leaders need specialized training that helps them develop the competency and the versatility they need to take the congregations they serve to the next level, whatever that may be in a given church.[44] To provide this training, seminaries and Christian universities should seek out and hire ministers who have been both faithful and successful in ministry and who also have the academic credentials to teach in as many areas as possible. The days of hiring professors in Christian education roles based always and only on academic pedigree are coming to an end. Finding professors who have served in varied capacities is a necessity for ongoing institutional relevance.[45]

Ministry to Monocultural and Multicultural Churches

Contrary to commonly held belief, multicultural and multiethnic societies are not a new occurrence. The divine plan of God has always involved people of all races, nations, and tongues (Isa. 49:6). When God called Abraham, he promised to make Abraham and his seed a blessing to "all nations" (Gen. 22:17–18). Even God's covenantal relationship with the Israelites in the Old Testament did not preclude the possibility and the ultimate reality of gentile inclusion (Rom. 11:13–18). As a result, the people of God have been understood

throughout Scripture as having multicultural and multiethnic properties. When Jesus gave the Great Commission, he could not have made that truth clearer. His followers were, and are, to teach "all nations" (Matt. 28:19).[46]

Monocultural churches are made up of people who have a similar background and heritage. Multicultural congregations have attendees who are from diverse backgrounds. Both types exist, and there is no reason to believe that either will cease to exist, in spite of the tremendous impact of globalization in our world. Even so, one can expect more and more churches to become integrated as people become increasingly familiar with and open to reaching out to those not like them in the name of Christ.

Studies have been done comparing monocultural and multicultural churches.[47] It can safely be said that both have advantages and challenges. Biblical and practical arguments have also been made for the value of each.[48] Even so, a great many Scripture passages speak to the virtues and the blessings of knowing, serving, and worshiping with believers from other nations, cultures, or ethnic heritages.

Regarding monocultural churches, some have thought of these congregations as being examples of closet racism. Rather than assigning false motives to others, we should seek to understand what are sometimes good and reasonable explanations for the existence of monocultural churches, even in our multicultural society. For example, some congregations simply exist in geographical areas where little or no ethnic diversity exists. In areas where

43. Warren, *Purpose-Driven Church*, 75–84.

44. George and Bird, *How to Break Growth Barriers*, 97–115.

45. Babcox, "Ministers without Master's Degrees."

46. Cardoza, "Perceptions of Ministerial Effectiveness," 49.

47. Duncum et al., "Comparison of the Vitality," 2–4.

48. Warnock, "Why We Still Need (Some) Monocultural Churches."

diversity is found, there are still congregations that are exclusively white, black, Asian, and so on. I offer no judgment on this phenomenon, as there can be and are valid reasons for segregated worship. But I hope that persons are not actively excluded due to their ethnic or national heritage.

Multiculturalism often raises the issue of biblical justice. Biblical justice is based on the high ideals of Christian ethics and the timeless truth of God's jealousy for equity.[49] A commitment to what is good and just will take a variety of forms. Just as when dealing with the other cultural and societal factors affecting our world, Christian education students need to be equipped with a holistic and responsible hermeneutical approach to justice in our world as well as with the skills to conduct effective ministry with all people made in the image of God.[50]

Conclusion

Responding directly to ministry needs is the essence of Christian education. Because it is a primary field in practical theology, with the others being pastoral ministry–related areas such as preaching-homiletics and pastoral care, no other academic program is designed to meet the ministry and discipleship needs of people quite like Christian education. Its proximity to theology (historical, biblical, and systematic), the social sciences (anthropology, sociology, and psychology), and the applied area of leadership places it in the center of the cultural nexus.

If the new world is to be reached, especially across the human life span, Christian education has an important, even indispensable, role to play. Therefore, all areas of Christian education must respond accordingly. Those working in preschool and children's ministry, preteen and youth ministry, emerging and young adult ministry, median and senior adult ministry, administration and leadership, parachurch ministries, and Christian higher education should focus on responding to the unique challenges of ministry in the twenty-first century.

Though changes such as these always have both positive and negative effects, they present an unparalleled opportunity for ministry impact. The key is to identify the cultural codes that can be used in presenting the gospel and then to equip believers to penetrate those people groups and cultures with the life-transforming message of Christ.

49. Calhoun, *Life in the Image of God*, 225–26.
50. Neihof, "Social Justice or Biblical Justice?"

23

Parachurch Christian Formation

JIM DEKKER

Introduction

In a chapter on parachurch Christian formation, a reader might expect a detailed discussion of amazing curricula used by top parachurch organizations. Such an expectation would lead to the false notion that "If only I could do that curriculum, I would provide excellent discipleship for those I serve." We should know by now that this does not work for at least two reasons. First, recent history is replete with people failing at replicating other ministry paradigms. Second, there are innumerable models of parachurch Christian formation, and each may or may not work depending on a host of factors. In short, the above expectation could only be met with fatal assumptions and raving omissions.

The intention of this chapter is to challenge the reader to be discerning in recognizing an obvious and understated difficulty in the relationship between parachurch and church-based spiritual formation. This recognition will help those pursuing either church-based or parachurch vocations to discern the amazing resources each has for the other in providing powerful Christian formation for the people of God.

A Story

I was born into a Dutch immigrant family that has strong ties to the Christian Reformed Church (CRC). Out of sheer immigrant devotion, our family faithfully attended the CRC. The language of God, prayer, covenants, and baptism all wove their way into my upbringing, but I saw little meaning in them as a kid. In my teen years, I rebelled against this picture of Christianity. I loved to fish, so my mother convinced me to attend a summer camp that she said had good fishing. I heard "fish camp" and was sold. I quickly discovered that my mother's idea of fishing at InterVarsity's Ontario Pioneer Camp had little to do with the hook, line, and bait that I had in mind but rather was intended to guide me toward Jesus. During that summer, this parachurch organization presented Jesus to me, and I began a radical Christian formation process. I became unashamed of my relationship with Jesus as Lord. I discovered the Bible, prayer, worship, and fellowship in new and exciting ways. But this formation was very different from what I experienced at my Christian Reformed church. This was the beginning of my awareness that there was a divide between church and parachurch ministry.

For five years, the dominant force in my spiritual formation was InterSchool Christian Fellowship of Canada (ISCF).[1] They taught me the inductive Bible study method, and I became well rooted in Scripture. I was embraced by devoted and like-minded believers whose dynamic faith gave me a broad picture of what it means to be part of the people of God. Increasingly I began to live out my faith in the public square, and others were finding and growing in faith around me. My church experience plodded along as usual: go to church on Sunday, sing, sit, stand, give money, pray, go home, and repeat. All that seemed to have little relevance to the new world of faith I was experiencing in ISCF. Deep inside, I knew I was supposed to value the local church, but my contrasting Christian formation experiences led me to value the parachurch more than the church. I knew this was a problem, but I couldn't figure it out for years to come.

My undergraduate and seminary years pushed me into a greater awareness of the church and how it differed from parachurch ministries. I had friends who were strong advocates of parachurch ministries and others who were devout churchgoers. Both groups had their own logic about why their ministry preference was important and how the other was "okay" but not quite as good. We usually ended conversations by saying, "All of us are in the mission of the 'big C' Church, so let's get along." I was not quite satisfied with this but knew that parachurch organizations and churches are in "an uneasy marriage."[2]

Fast forward over forty years to a lunch appointment I had with a veteran church planter north of Grand Rapids, Michigan. As we talked about current cultural issues among young adults in small-town Michigan, I encouraged developing an awareness of what God may already be doing in the area through parachurch ministries. The church planter piped up and said, "I've worked with those leaders before. They say they want to serve the church. They say they will send their people to the local church, but they simply don't. I find those leaders don't really care about the local church." For many kingdom leaders, this uneasy marriage continues to be real! It has created unnecessary tensions, unhelpful debates, and false dichotomies over the role of each in the formation of God's people.

What follows addresses the tension by recognizing how the parachurch is different in definition, organization, expertise, and opportunity. Identifying these differences provides the reader with the axes of discernment so as to wisely take advantage of the powerful formative processes

---

1. InterSchool Christian Fellowship is the high-school version of the commonly known university-level InterVarsity Christian Fellowship in Canada.

2. See White, *Church and Parachurch: An Uneasy Marriage*. White's introduction describes a gathering of Christian leaders in which the divide is acutely articulated. I have experienced similar tensions in today's ministry gatherings.

of parachurch Christian formation for either parachurch or church-based ministry.

Defining Parachurch

Parachurches are Christian organizations designed to carry out very specific missions within culture. Defining parachurches by mission is nearly impossible, even if we create loose categories for them. Such a process fundamentally diminishes each of their missions. In short, we cannot justly categorize them into groups in order to determine general Christian formation patterns or insights.[3]

Defining parachurches as *Christian nonprofit organizations* may be helpful. But considering that churches are also Christian nonprofits, the sheer number of non-church Christian nonprofits makes it impossible to help our case for understanding their formation processes. In the United States, there are approximately one hundred thousand nonprofit organizations: hospitals, homeless shelters, at-risk help centers, Christian entrepreneur training centers, short-term missions agencies, Christian financial counseling centers, Christian health insurance agencies, and the list goes on. Many identify as being Christian in some form and each offers formation processes. Add to these over a thousand Christian educational institutions in the United States and they represent revenues of some $2 billion annually with assets exceeding $4 billion.[4] Based on nothing more than the sheer size of these statistics, parachurch groups represent a profound numerical and geographical breadth. Stop for a moment and fathom the degree to which these organizations create a footprint of what it means to be Christian in society.

While parachurches carry the name of Jesus to the broader society, by both term and definition, parachurches are not churches and therefore not local congregations. For this reason, parachurches can take the liberty of selecting certain causes they will champion and deselecting others. Said another way, parachurches have a self-limiting scope of ministry, one that local churches do not afford themselves. While parachurches focus their collective resources serving a specific Christian mission, churches embrace a more comprehensive responsibility that forces them to triage programs and resources in an effort to steward the broader mission.

Historically, parachurches begin when dedicated Christians see some distinct need in society and rally resources to create an organization to address that need. The YMCA, Moody Bible Institute, counseling centers, and more obviously, Youth for Christ, CRU (formerly Campus Crusade for Christ), and InterVarsity all have a similar tale. Revisiting each story one might observe that the local church was somehow unable or unqualified to meet that identified need. Although this may be a reality, it is important to recognize that the local church cannot always fulfill the vision of individual congregants nor can it release responsibility to its broader two-thousand-year-old mission.

Parachurch organizations support the work of the local church, but parachurches, with their specific mission in society, have separated themselves from the local church base.

---

3. I have researched parachurch youth at-risk ministries to discern their Christian formation processes. The scope of research had to be particularized to handle the amount of data available. It is impossible to do this across the breadth of parachurches.

4. Stiles, "Nine Marks of a Healthy Parachurch Ministry."

Christians have struggled to define *parachurch* in relationship with the church—especially theologically. Is a parachurch theologically still "the church"?

Without going into biblical or historical theology in detail, the church is generally understood as a local organization of believers voluntarily committed to God—in Christ by the Spirit—and one another, under the authority of God's Word, for the advancement of the gospel and God's kingdom. Local congregations recognize the offices of the church (pastors, elders, deacons, or some combination of these), practice the sacraments (baptism, communion), and fulfill the purposes of the church (evangelism and missions, fellowship, discipleship, worship, and prayer). This mission is broad and serves the general public in an ever-expanding way (Acts 1:8). If we were to simplify the theological definition of the church as "those gathered together in Christ" we might melt parachurch into church. Such a definition might help us avoid division, but it simply doesn't work. Unfortunately, this simple definition is not shared across churches and parachurches. Ask the president of any Christian university if they are the leader of the church, and they will tell you they are not and that their university could not replace the local church. We can go down the list of theological nuances within the doctrine of ecclesiology, but one quickly notices that regardless of nuance, the evidence is that churches and parachurches are theologically different entities.[5]

Etymologically, the term *parachurch* simply means an organization that comes alongside (Gk. *para*) the church. Some have used the term *para-local church* rather than *parachurch*,

but in this chapter both will refer to the same thing—ministry organizations that support the mission of the church.[6] If we take the etymological definition seriously we might find help understanding that parachurches exist to serve the church in its broader mission. They simply come alongside churches with specific targeted ministries that local churches cannot provide with the same level of quality or, in some cases, simply cannot provide at all.[7] A clever example of the unique roles parachurches fill has been given by Jared Wilson.[8] He describes how practically no church would be capable of meeting the need of Christian publishing. Christian publishing companies are a parachurch that offers powerful formative processes for people. The formative resources they produce are a tremendous blessing that bolsters church ministry. A local church or even a conglomeration of churches would find it more than difficult to specialize in mastering commercial printing, marketing, and distribution such that we see in today's Christian publishing houses. The parachurch publishing ministry is needed as a work beyond the local church's capacity. Therefore, publishers come alongside congregations to supplement the mission of the church. It is here where our definition of *para*-church helps in the uneasy marriage. Parachurches are partners in the mission of the church and seek to

5. Greer and Horst, *Mission Drift*, 171.

6. Saunders, "Place and Purpose of Parachurch Ministries." See also J. White, *Church and Parachurch*. This perspective underscores some parachurch leaders' conviction (see also Jerry White) that parachurch organizations are a part of the universal church but operate beside the local church; hence the coining of the *para-local church* term.

7. Mathison, "Historical and Theological Foundations."

8. Jared Wilson, "Defining Our Terms."

supplement or enhance the mission in ways that churches cannot.

Parachurch Organization

Recognizing that parachurch Christian formation will overlap with the mission of the church, we may begin to understand the differences in *organization* to better understand the strained relationship between the church's formation processes and the parachurch. Leadership autonomy and theological particularity shape the organizational strength of a parachurch's Christian formation process.

As a rule, parachurches are free from the control or authority of any local congregation. This is one thing that has been made abundantly clear by parachurch leaders since the late twentieth century.[9] Indeed, parachurch leaders have sometimes considered this issue the central or even sole defining feature of parachurch ministries. It is the essence of what separates them from local churches. Parachurches are not dependent ministries within a given local church but are independent entities. They operate with their own constitutions and bylaws, their own budgets, their own leadership hierarchies, and their own governing boards. Until more recently, there was significant historical agreement that parachurches do not have authority to ordain pastors or appoint deacons, present the sacraments, and perform other responsibilities that are within the purview of local churches.[10] Though a limited number of parachurches sporadically usurp some of these ecclesiastical responsibilities, many church leaders consider doing so unwise and inappropriate.

9. J. White, *Church and Parachurch*, 19.
10. Moore and Sagers, "Kingdom of God and the Church."

The parachurch's mission continues to be supported without the broad and diverse influence and agenda of the local church. This has been true of parachurches from their beginning, and it has remained true in the decades of their proliferation in the 1970s and 1980s. During that season, parachurches felt restrained by the theological debates and the church polity issues typical to churches and denominations. Churches had to determine their eschatology, their position on divorce and remarriage, alcohol use, and abortion, all the while doing youth ministry, children's ministry, adult Bible study groups, etc. Parachurch leaders wanted to empower their mission to address a specific need and not become caught up in the fray of broader contextual conversations.

I have worked with some who consider such a separation an abdication of accountability to the whole of theology. They see this as giving parachurches room to be theologically unaccountable. This notion is only powerful if one assumes the parachurch to be responsible for a whole theology. Parachurches by design do not begin with the responsibility to steward Christian theology in the way that the church does. They start within their mission. Parachurches are actually more accountable to their specific mission's theology. A church can form its theological commitment broadly and idealistically but functionally do any kind of ministry it deems important within that larger picture. The collection plate still circulates every Sunday, and when the question of what mission to support comes up, any given answer from within the broader mission can justify the giving: missionaries, youth group, short-term mission, building projects, and so on. A church's board can shift a ministry without theological conversation simply because their commitments are broad enough to embrace a wide range of ministries. A parachurch is forced to sustain its specific mission because its accountability is directly tied to the theology justifying its mission. The lines are quite clear.

This leads us nicely to the next point, which is that parachurch ministries are coalition movements that happen in the face of a particular need perceived in society.[11] A coalition gathers diverse people together who, despite other differences, are committed to a particular cause. Since there is a focus on the need observed, leaders generally concentrate on the theological convictions that facilitate their mission. Setting aside broader theological elements that concern a church, the parachurch's leadership commits to what might be called a "thinner theology" in order to facilitate the vision and mission of their organization. Such a focus on specific theology of their mission creates the possibility for a more coherent organizational culture that has particular language on relevant issues. This gives a sense that the parachurches provide coherent Christian formation processes. Arguing about various theological positions as held by various historical Christian traditions is simply not the activity of most parachurch organizations.[12]

In short, having a thinner theology around its mission gives parachurches the ability to unite diverse people under this mission and can give the impression to the broader society that they are more welcoming and coherent in their formation processes and are less

theologically exclusive. Despite such appearances, a parachurch is specifically missioned and is therefore exclusive to its mission. Such exclusivity to mission leads us to the next point.

Parachurches, with their focus on a specific need within society, can raise funds directed to those needs. Philanthropists typically give to causes aimed at particular outcomes that have proven measurements of success. A parachurch is more able to fulfill a philanthropic vision than a local church with varied ministries. A parachurch can report back to the philanthropist on how their money has met the stated need. And a parachurch has the freedom to design specific sustainability measures. This facilitates an ongoing relationship between the philanthropist and parachurch mission. Local churches simply do not function along these lines of resourcing and accountability in their organizational structure.[13]

The Parachurch's Expertise

Parachurches often work with remarkable efficiency as they unite people's collective efforts to fulfill their ministry purposes. The insistence that those involved focus solely on the parachurch's mission steers people away from peripheral issues. Such focus and efficiency to the mission sets the stage for high levels of expertise in the organization. The parachurch becomes proficient at naming the knowledge, interpersonal skills, and leadership qualities necessary to fulfill the mission. In light of such

11. Trueman, "How Parachurch Ministries Go Off the Rails."

12. Christian schools, universities, and seminaries are an exception here, but such differences are named as part of their mission and are therefore to be expected.

13. Admittedly, this may be changing with the dispersal of DeVos and Lilly grants intersecting churches with parachurch organizations. Again, these grants function with deliberate focus and often work through denominational colleges or seminaries (parachurches) as they serve churches.

focus, the hiring process becomes equally fine-tuned. InterVarsity is expected to hire people who are dedicated to the transformation of millennials on college campuses across the country and around the world. If you have a general MDiv and a church-based internship, you are not likely a strong candidate for a campus parachurch ministry. However, if you have spent time in a university campus ministry, recently graduated, or are in a graduate or doctorate program and have studied millennial faith formation, you have a better chance at being hired into campus-based ministry. This is only one example from my work with various campus ministries. Needless to say, parachurch organizations hire highly specialized people to meet their specifically articulated mission.

Similarly, parachurch leadership can expect professional development of their workers. This training is deliberately focused on its mission of making leaders more specialized in what they do. For example, InterVarsity leaders that I have worked with are highly trained in understanding millennials and their faith formation. Not only are these leaders reading about and researching millennials, they are also on the ground, engaging with millennials, and confirming and reformulating what they are learning about their faith formation. Such leaders are dedicated experts in understanding those they serve—such expertise cannot be resourced in the same way by the local church.

Parachurches also have an incredible capacity to develop amazing Christian formation initiatives for those they serve. With a focused hiring process and professional development of staff, the Christian formation process (curriculum) becomes incredibly refined. Most Christian education specialists realize that

passion and practice are easily at hand in a parachurch ministry. For example, an InterVarsity staffer might experiment with a particular small group process for studying Scripture. The staffer might dedicate three or four experiences to assess and then gather feedback from the people they serve. That person might then adjust the process and implement the new design within a month or two. That same staffer has access to other staffers who may be able to contribute input. Further conversations with likeminded associates leads to incredibly refined Christian formation processes for the demographic they serve. This cycle of curriculum refinement in a parachurch makes for incredibly powerful formative processes.

Opportunities

I have mentioned the uneasy marriage between parachurches and churches. The sticking point is in the differences each brings to faith formation. A parachurch provides a powerfully focused Christian formation process that churches can't provide for themselves without giving up too much of their broad mission. Somehow the marriage of the two organizations needs to be better-mediated for the impact of Christian formation to be mutually beneficial for the kingdom of God—but this takes wisdom.

Such wisdom is not found in letters on a page but lives in the stories of real people seeking practical application. I am not offering overly simplistic answers for a healthy marriage. It has to be lived out, in sacrifice and mutual respect between the characters in the ministry marriage, not by the therapist or the self-help book. As in most learning processes, stories are formative; therefore, this section concludes with three stories of good and bad situations. From these, I encourage readers to discern for themselves what kinds of opportunities parachurches bring to the mission of God wherever they will serve.

Max's Story

The first story begins near the north side of Chicago around 2010. A youth pastor acquaintance of mine named Max[14] asked me to help him process his frustration with ministry over a cup of coffee. He had an excellent experience with Young Life and was able to minister effectively to urban at-risk and immigrant young people living messy lives. A local neighborhood church of about three hundred was in need of a youth leader to disciple twenty church kids, and Max thought he could supplement his income in this position. During the interview process, he asked the church if they were supportive of outreach efforts in their ministry and they said they were; what church isn't these days?

Max transformed the whole ministry into the Young Life Safe Place model, the one he knew best, and the kids enjoyed the fun, safe spaces. In a short time, Max discovered a group of local unchurched kids that lived in the neighborhood. Having been expertly trained to meet their needs, and having shifted the ministry model to an outreach design, Max proceeded to create opportunities for the church and neighborhood kids to be together in order to build trust and share faith.

At first the church kids felt safe playing the games and eating snacks together, but then things began to go astray. The games became more competitive and the church kids became more isolated, but Max persisted because he

14. Names in these examples have been changed to protect identities.

had been through this before. He expected the well-trained church kids would take the opportunity to witness to the others. But the differences continued to emerge. The church kids began to feel uncomfortable, and the neighborhood kids felt judged. Max pushed harder and began training the church kids to share their faith through evangelistic relationships, but this didn't work. Max began to receive letters and complaints from parents: "You are paid by us to disciple our kids." "Do your job and serve our kids with Bible studies, not just fun and games."

It was at this point that Max came to me with his concerns. "Should I leave youth ministry because I can't handle the pressure? Do I give up on the church because it didn't believe in outreach after all? Why are Christian parents so protective of their kids?!" He was discouraged and the church was frustrated. There was a fundamental misunderstanding between the two. Max was highly skilled in Young Life's Safe Place model, and the church wanted a church-based discipleship model, but neither understood the difference until long after things had gone bad. One person needed a job and the church needed someone to minister to their kids, but their lack of clarity about expectations left them in an uneasy marriage. Eventually, Max left church-based ministry, returned to Young Life, and continued to resent the church for "rejecting good Christian outreach." The church simply hired someone else.

Emily's Story

This second brief story tells of a similar situation with different results. I was coaching Emily as she was considering a youth ministry position in a small urban church.

She too was involved part time in a para-church ministry serving junior high kids in the school system. The church eventually hired her as their youth director while she remained in her position with the parachurch.[15] This relationship worked because the church wanted a model of ministry that matched Emily's parachurch skills. It also helped that she could see that the church needed a different model than her parachurch context. It did get strange when 60 percent of the church kids were part of her parachurch ministry as well. Emily had to find a way to respect the distinctions between the two different ministries. Emily managed this gap, and the kids who were in both programs learned the expectations for each of the different ministries. The church funded Emily's church salary and also dedicated one collection each year to her parachurch ministry. She was in a very fortunate position, but the church members recognized her incredible skill developed in the parachurch and wanted this for their kids as well.

Lessons for Today

Finally, here is a collection of observations from my fifteen-plus years of teaching ministry in Christian higher education. First is that Christian college students live in a very particular culture within the university. Students dedicated to their faith are served with intense discipleship programs, either sponsored by the university's ministries or other parachurch organizations serving the campus. Students learn Scripture, worship, pray, hold each other accountable for areas of sin they are seeking to overcome, and

develop rhythms of faith formation that are unlike those in any church. Ministry happens throughout the day, often in intimate groups of three to eight people. Resident assistants, campus pastors, and faculty mentors all contribute to these young lives as they are preparing for life in the real world.

One might conclude from this that strong faith is being formed; however, my observation uncovered a discouraging trend. I discovered that many of even my ministry students didn't go to church. They simply had "church" in the dorms and everywhere else on campus. This disturbed me because I have a high view of traditional church and believe the parachurch (such as the Christian university and other ministries) should not take the place of the church. But in the minds of these students, the church is replaced by a personal faith formation process that they tailor for their own growth. As time went on and students graduated, I noticed two more things happening. Either they would not move into the church after graduation—since it did not conform to their university experience—or they would go to a new church plant that functioned much like the parachurch experience. This typically involved worship in small, intimate spaces (usually houses), where prayer, singing, and Bible studies were conducted and group accountability was expected. These were spaces where they felt safe to raise personal questions and have close friends engage them on possible directions for life.

Later, in my twelfth year of teaching ministry, I came to meet a church-planting consultant who worked with several denominations as they sought successful church plants. I raised this issue with him, asking if he saw a pattern of church plants that looked an awful lot like parachurch ministries. He concurred.

---

15. Bivocational ministry is becoming more attractive to churches.

Since then, I have been watching contemporary blogs and social media, keeping an eye on contemporary models of church plants to see if this continues to be confirmed—so far it remains so. Though I do not have space to unpack why this concerns me theologically and sociologically, this begs consideration of how to understand the uneasy marriage between excellent parachurch faith formation ministries and the faith formation responsibilities of the church.

In short, these three stories tell of the differences between church and parachurch, the organizational complexity, and the developed expertise expressed in the spaces between parachurch and church-based formation processes. It is undeniable that parachurch ministries are well equipped to do their special formative task, and since they are not the church, the local church must somehow understand its opportunity to partner with but also go beyond what parachurches bring to ministry. The church needs a discernment process that assesses the particular parachurch's specialization and asks the question, How does this fit within our vision and mission? A church has the incredible opportunity to intersect with multiple parachurch ministries at one time without betraying its mission. Congregations could tap into the expertise of a parachurch organization's formation processes, but a church must not simply adopt a parachurch model without first discerning the complexities that come with it.

The following section presents parachurch organizations by general categories. These categories are less important for accuracy than they are to frame possibilities for navigating relationships across parachurch and church-based faith formation processes.

Parachurch Ministry Categories

As stated earlier, parachurches tend to defy classification. Specialized ministries continue to proliferate, blurring the lines between one classification and another. The very entrepreneurial nature of parachurch founders show how diverse and particular ministries can get. In spite of this, within the evangelical tradition, Richard Leyda's seven-category classification provides a helpful guide. Leyda's categories are as follows:

- Missions
- Evangelism and discipleship
- Childhood and adolescent ministries
- Camping and recreation
- Schools and educational institutions
- Media and technology
- Special interest[16]

These categories hardly contain the host of "new" evangelical parachurch organizations, let alone the many mainline or fully independent Christian organizations that continue to grow. Having said this, these categories may provide a frame of reference for the reader to consider where and how they might engage opportunities for the church to partner with a parachurch resource. Specific examples are not given for all of these categories; rather, a few will be highlighted to illustrate the diversity and discernment needed to appreciate their formation processes.

Mission- and evangelism-focused parachurches tend to host evangelistic crusades and provide training for personal or mass evangelism. Evangelistic ministries provide live events, music, media, publications, and

16. Leyda, "Parachurch Ministries."

other gospel-sharing resources targeting various audiences. Examples of evangelistic organizations include the following: Billy Graham Evangelistic Association, Luis Palau Association, Open Air Campaigners, the Harvest Crusades, Dare2Share, Campus Renewal, Wycliffe Bible Translators, the Way of the Master, and Probe Ministries.

Discipleship-focused parachurch ministries exist to help people cultivate maturing relationships with God that result in personal transformation in Christ. Discipleship parachurches provide teaching and learning processes through very specific ideological perspectives and hold particular outcome expectations. Without distinct discernment, theological challenges will exist here. Some discipleship models can be quite behavioral, while others use ancient and contemplative traditions. Some follow a replication model where "successful" disciplers replicate themselves in other disciples. Some claim to disciple as Jesus did, but their hermeneutic of Jesus's life and teaching is selective. Some models have outcomes that are tied to twenty-first century American cultural values rather than a more biblical vision for the people of God. Some models have been adapted from a particular pastor's sermon series and are now published as a discipleship tool through a parachurch organization. Some models promote a strict interpretation of Scripture to combat negative forces they see in society. Some promote a particular ideology or church polity even though they are a parachurch.

Examples of discipleship parachurch ministries include the following: Navigators, Athletes in Action, Fellowship of Christian Athletes, InterVarsity, Renovaré, Bible Study Fellowship, AWANA, All About Following Jesus, Revolution Within, Grace to You,

Gospel Coalition, Sonlife, Alpha Ministries, Desiring God, Precept Ministries, Living Proof, Ligonier Ministries, In Touch Ministries, Academy for Spiritual Formation, Evangelical Spiritual Directors Association, and Titus 2 Mentoring.

Virtually anyone can create a discipling parachurch organization with an online presence. Though the breadth and depth of impact may be limited by a host of factors, real and actual ministry opportunities exist in that space. These can supplement the work done by congregations and provide an opportunity for focused ministries to target specialized groups and constituencies.

Educational Parachurch Ministries

Historically, Christianity has consistently made an impact on education, particularly from the earliest days of the American experiment.[17] It is general knowledge that essentially all the earliest higher educational institutions in the original thirteen colonies and, later, in the United States were religious—and specifically Christian—in origin.[18] These schools were built on the stated importance of acquiring biblical knowledge and moral excellence for the sake of society.

Today, large numbers and diverse types of Christian schools and educational parachurch groups exist. These include preschools, elementary and high schools, Bible colleges, liberal arts colleges and universities, seminaries, and divinity schools. Some of these are recognized by the Department of Education through their accreditation bodies. Others receive accreditation through independent associations.

17. Lucas, *American Higher Education*, 103–44.
18. Ringenberg, *Christian College*, 37–42, 58–66.

Examples of schools and educational parachurch ministries include typical Christian elementary and high schools with their specific associations (e.g., Association of Christian Schools International or Christian Schools International), and typical Bible schools or institutes (e.g., Moody Bible Institute or Christian liberal arts colleges). Seminaries at one time focused on training their students for church-based ministry, whereas divinity schools trained their students for parish ministry or general awareness of religious philosophy in society. These lines have blurred over the years, so churches need to become aware of how and under what paradigm their pastoral candidates are being trained.

Connected with these educational parachurches are organizations that provide professional development for their leaders. Organizations such as the Society of Professors in Christian Education, Association of Theological Schools, Evangelical Theological Society, and Society of Biblical Literature all challenge faculty in their professional development. There are even associations for school counselors and organizations that train student life personnel and resident directors. Each of these parachurch support organizations carries particular ideological leanings where leaders experience that particular formative processes.

Camping and Recreational Parachurch Ministries

One of the most familiar types of parachurch ministries is Christian camps and recreational conference and convention centers. Each camp or conference center has a particular mission, such as creating a space for people to retreat from their daily lives.

Some have a mission to foster discipleship or awareness of the gospel through exposure to God's majesty in creation. For the most part, these parachurches usually have a very clear curriculum that requires space and time that typical churches do not have. When "campers" experience a powerful formative process, oftentimes the person's experience is limited to the camp and has little application in regular life back home. Camp leaders have struggled to find ways to make their discipleship experience transferable to everyday living. Campers recognize the issue, although many continue to take advantage of the retreat experience year after year. But even so, discipleship becomes tied to a separated space (camp) from the rest of life and begs to be adapted to everyday living. Here is where a healthy marriage with the local church can provide the discipleship connection to regular life. Having said that, it takes very deliberate and strategic investment on behalf of the camp and the local church to make the healthy connections between camp discipleship and daily church discipleship. This is not easy since camp themes and processes are not simply accommodated in the church curriculum or vice versa.

Examples of camping and recreational parachurch ministries include the following: Lake Junaluska Conference and Retreat Center, Ridgecrest Conference Center, Word of Life, HoneyRock, Hume Lake Camps, Kanakuk Kamps, Pioneer Camp, Portage Lake Camp, Life Teen Camps, Yosemite Sierra, The Cove, Springhill Camps, Lake Ann and a host of others. These camps also have associations that provide resources for what they do, such as Christian Camp and Conference Association, Christian Retreats Network, and Christian Retreat Centers.

How Churches and Parachurches Can Work in Harmony

Parachurches and local church ministries are both wonderful expressions of God's kingdom in action. Parachurches are clearly not churches by their own definition and limited mission; however, they do contribute to and are evidence of the movement of God in the world today. Churches are distinctly broader and historically different institutions. Unlike parachurches, the church is an entity that God has established and sustained for over two thousand years, but this difference need not create unhealthy relationships with parachurch organizations. The past uneasy marriage is more of a commentary on our inability to get along than it is the fault of the church ignoring social needs or the parachurch going rogue. A healthy relationship between the two will require a lot of work, but first and foremost, churches and parachurch ministries need to share their spaces and appreciate the stories that bind us together in a common mission. I conclude with some suggestions for how churches and parachurches can help cultivate mutual respect and ministry effectiveness.

What Churches Can Do to Bless Parachurch Ministries

- Pray for, appreciate, and honor parachurch ministries and leaders for their powerful ministry impact[19]
- Call on parachurch ministries to supplement, and train local church leaders with their areas of specialization[20]

- Where appropriate, encourage equipped volunteers to provide service in parachurch ministries where their gifts can be especially useful
- Consider providing targeted funding for local parachurches that supplement the work of local churches
- Proactively foster healthy, respectful relationships with parachurch leaders by ministering to them through fellowship and equipping opportunities[21]

What Parachurches Can Do to Bless Local Churches

- Acknowledge the priority of local churches in the divine economy of advancing the kingdom of God and consciously commit to supplement their work where they need help[22]
- Pray for local churches and strictly avoid unredemptive criticism of them and their leaders[23]
- Encourage parachurch leaders and volunteers to value and participate in local churches, making them their primary place of participation in the body of Christ[24]
- Partner with church associations and denominations, including inviting church leaders to participate at various levels of the ministry, for when parachurches partner with local churches, their impact is increased[25]

21. Hammett, "How Church and Parachurch Should Relate," 201.
22. Menijoff, "Are Parachurch Ministries Evil?"
23. McKinney, "Church-Parachurch Conflict," 76–80.
24. Carson, "Praying for Parachurch Ministries."
25. Hammett, "How Church and Parachurch Should Relate," 201.

19. Carson, "Praying for Parachurch Ministries."
20. McKinney, "Church-Parachurch Conflict," 73–80.

24

Christian Schooling

KAREN LYNN ESTEP

C hristian schooling has existed almost since the birth of the church. As with the chosen people of God, Christian families and communities have endeavored to develop a unique form of education that is distinctly religious. This chapter looks at the biblical and historical backgrounds of Christian schooling, explores its various contemporary expressions, identifies philosophical commitments to Christian schooling, and looks at the various challenges and opportunities for Christian schools in the twenty-first century.

Biblical Backgrounds of Christian Schooling

The roots of Christian schooling are deep, reaching as far back as the preexilic Hebrews (2300–586 BC) and of course extending into the New Testament period (AD 30–100). The Old Testament, covering the Hebraic (pre-586

BC) and the early Jewish educational traditions (post-586 BC), demonstrates the adaptation of the community to its needs, from nomadic beginnings to urbanized cities with developed religious centers. Some adaptations required changes to the instructional methods used. For example, James Estep traces the adaptive development of Hebraic and Jewish education through eight periods of the Old Testament narrative, identifying the introduction of educational formats, the addition of new educational formats, and the removal of seemingly obsolete educational formats.[1] This includes the introduction of Wisdom literature, scribal schools, and instruction in the royal courts during the united and divided monarchies but the loss of these during the exile and possibly the postexilic period.

1. Estep, Anthony, and Allison, *Theology for Christian Education*, 63.

The primary lesson in biblical education was that there is only one God and that he is the God of all, not just the Hebrew nation.[2] Yet as with any aim, there were controversies concerning the methods and the purpose of religious education, which is similar to Christian schooling today. Other relevant educational principles and practices from biblical times include the following. First, life and religion were inseparable. Second, parents and the home were primarily responsible for religious education. Third, there was value in the variety of educational institutions, the development and use of several methods for teaching, and the diverse types of educators charged with the duty of religious education. Fourth, the purpose of education, despite any method, focused on knowing God and the preservation of the faith.[3] Fifth, religious education was at times evangelistic and missional, as God's chosen people were driven to look beyond themselves and their inclusive communities.[4]

Table 24.1 highlights the educational developments throughout the biblical period, both the Old Testament and the New Testament, many of which were precursors for current-day principles and practices of Christian schooling.[5]

Thus, emerging from the biblical foundations of early Christian education is the schooling tradition of which we are now a part. Based on this biblical heritage of Christian schooling, genuine institutionalized Christian

education began to occur in the late second century (i.e., the rise of Christian schools).

Historical Backgrounds of Christian Schooling

The Christian schooling tradition has its roots deep in the history of the ancient world. In fact, its roots extend into biblical times, with the rise of Judaism's synagogue and its schooling system. The school tradition of the Greeks and later the Romans would provide another influence on the formation of Christian schools. Based on the schooling traditions of Judaism, the Greeks, and the Romans, the Christian schooling tradition was formed in the late second century AD.

Schooling in the Early Church

Perhaps the earliest form of Christian schooling was the catechetical school, which was a formal model of Christian education designed to approach life through both faith and intellect, integrating the two into a unified view of life. Two early proponents of formal education in the early church were Clement of Alexandria (ca. AD 150–215) followed by his protégé Origen (AD 185–254).

Under the leadership of these men, Christian educators saw education as a missional effort, concerned with fusing secular and sacred knowledge by combining Greek philosophy with Christian theology into a unified worldview.[6] Thus, students were able to study secular literature and view it through the lens of their Christian faith, a practice recognized today as faith-learning integration and/or worldview studies. For example, Pantaenus

2. Meyer, "Education," 2:902.

3. Estep, "Among the Hebrews and Ancient Judaism," 2.2, 3.3.

4. Kim, "Early Church," 6.9.

5. Estep, C. E.: The Heritage of Christian Education; Pazmiño, Foundational Issues in Christian Education, 19–56; Meyer, "Education," 2:900–905; and Estep, "Biblical Foundations" 44–72.

6. Kim, "Early Church," 6.8.

Table 24.1. Educational Developments in Scripture

Biblical Period	Developments
Education in Early Israel	
Early Hebrew / Patriarchal Period	Religion and life were inseparable, and so education was very practical and faith based. Familial education was dominant, and both mother and father served as teachers. Often fathers trained sons in an occupation or trade, while mothers trained daughters to be future wives and mothers and to manage the household.
Time of Mosaic Legislation	Parents continued their educational role, as the Mosaic legislation identified the responsibility of parents to provide religious and moral instruction and training for their children (Deut. 6:7; 11:19). However, this instruction and training were provided not just by parents but also by others in the community such as priests and tribal leaders. One learning objective for some was the ability to read and write, and the books of the Law were the textbook and program of religious instruction.
United and Divided Monarchies	Religion first aided the unification of the tribes into a monarchy, then also in part led to the demise of that unified kingdom in 931 BC. However, education developed significantly during the monarchies. For example, King Josiah officially recognized the prophets who were practicing during his reign and required that their teachings be learned. These schools of the prophets were associations or brotherhoods established for mutual edification rather than education. However, religious training was likely included, though the Bible does not use the word *school*. To the body of teachers in ancient Israel were added wise men, sages, and scribes. The rise of Wisdom literature resulted (e.g., Proverbs was the oldest handbook of education outside the Torah). Professional teachers offered further instruction to those who could afford the time and the expense (Eccles. 9:17; 12:11).
Education in Later Israel	
Late Monarchy and Exilic/ Postexilic Periods	The prophets became the heralds of divine truth, calling the nation to personal and corporate repentance and piety. During the end of the monarchy, but also with the work of Ezra the Scribe in the postexilic period, collections of writings of poets, lawgivers, prophets, and sages entered the Old Testament canon, which was the most significant educational text at that time. Hence, the scribes became more influential in education as the preservers and interpreters of the biblical text. During the very last era of Old Testament education, the origins of the fundamental elements of Judaism emerged: the synagogue, sects (e.g., Pharisees and Sadducees), and the oral tradition among the scribal class. While these elements are common in the Judaism of the New Testament, they emerged only at the close of the Old Testament.
Education in New Testament Times	
Early New Testament Period	The New Testament records the character of Jewish education that was only emergent in the Old Testament. The home remained the principal educational institution, but the synagogue was added to it. In most synagogues, elementary and in some cases secondary schools began (e.g., Joshua ben Gamala, high priest from AD 63 to 65, ordered that teachers be appointed in every Jewish community). As one would expect, Jewish instruction and subject matter centered on the Old Testament, which by now was complete. In addition, the oral tradition of biblical interpretation provided by the sects was also part of the educational process.
Time of Jesus	Memorization was the exact reproduction by the pupil of the master's teaching. However, Jesus also engaged his disciples in theological reasoning and critical thinking when it came to the acceptance and application of tradition.
	Jesus adapted many of the teaching methods of the rabbis, gathering around him a group of chosen disciples (learners) whom he trained and taught more explicitly with a view to perpetuating his own influence and work through them. He and other rabbis used both parables and connected discourses; the rabbis demonstrated their teaching through their own manner of life, and their instruction included teaching others how to teach. However, Jesus diverged from his contemporaries by demonstrating his own authority and traveling with his disciples.
Early Church	Apostles were more than preachers and missionaries; they were the church's first teachers. As such, they appointed other instructors for the church. Pastors and elders both had permanent charge of individual churches. Before the close of the first century, the church's educational ministry was distinct from that of Judaism, was embedded in local congregations, and was led by laypeople.
	In the New Testament, all were taught, even the socially marginalized (e.g., women, gentiles, "sinners," slaves). Instruction was for anyone who responded to the gospel message. The focus of teaching was the gospel; the Old Testament interpreted in light of Christ's life, death, and resurrection; Christian confessions of faith (e.g., trustworthy sayings, the teachings of Jesus); and how to live, in response to God's love and saving work.
	Paul demonstrated an acquaintance with the Greco-Roman schooling tradition by his use of educational terms, but he redefined them in a Christian context and reassessed their worth for spiritual value rather than just physical or mental benefit.[a]

a. Estep, "Philosophers, Scribes, Rhetors . . . and Paul?"

(AD 179) used Greco-Roman philosophy, classic literature, and other academic disciplines to equip Christians of all ages and both genders to converse with educated nonbelievers and to share the gospel with them.[7]

However, this approach to Christian schooling was not universally welcomed and provoked its share of opponents. For example, Tertullian, a church leader in North Africa, was opposed to Christians studying in Greek schools and even studying anything not expressly Christian, feeling it endangered their faith. He advocated a separatist approach to the education of Christian children. However, most Christian educators promoted the more missional vision of the Alexandrian schools of Clement and Origen, and the Christian schooling tradition was born. Such early church authorities as Jerome, Ambrose, Chrysostom, and Augustine all promoted the missional and integrationist agenda of their predecessors. Paul Kienel notes, "For most early church Christians the choice was obvious. They would form their own schools. Nearly two thousand years later, Christian parents around the world are faced with the same dilemma—with one important difference. Paganism in non-Christian schools today is far less obvious than it was in Rome in AD 100."[8]

Schooling in the Medieval Church

Near the end of the early church era, several new initiatives in Christian schooling started, but they flourished during the medieval period. For example, cathedral schools started in the fifth century AD but reached their height in educational prominence in the tenth to twelfth

centuries AD. These schools, which instructed young boys who demonstrated an aptitude for the priesthood, became the prototype for the medieval university.

Parish schools, typically housed in church buildings, provided children with general education, usually through rote memorization, but offered little opportunity for higher learning. The first permanent institution of Christian education, one that persists today, was the monastic school. In these schools, a broader liberal arts curriculum was available to students. In fact, many of the subjects taught in the monastic school—the *trivium* and *quadrivium* or the seven humanities— are still in our curriculum today. Students studied music, math, science, philosophy, history, literature, and grammar. They also had access to libraries. However, not until the Reformation did education of the masses become the focus of Christian schooling's agenda.

Schooling in the Reformation

Protestantism's emphasis on the priesthood of all believers necessitated a literate population, one that could read and study the Bible. Hence, with the rise of Protestant theological reformation came a parallel educational reformation. Martin Luther (1483– 1546) was both a priest and a teacher. In 1524, he wrote "Letter to the Mayors and Aldermen of All Cities of Germany in Behalf of Christian Schools," advocating the spiritual, material, and political benefits of establishing tax-supported Christian schools in every major city in Germany. He further promoted his views through preaching and speaking, including a sermon titled "Duty of Sending Children to School" (1530).

7. K. Lawson, "Historical Foundations of Christian Education."

8. Kienel, *History of Christian School Education*, 1:4.

John Calvin (1509–64) also advocated the establishment of Christian schools for the advancement of the church through a literate and learned populace. The educational legacy of the Protestant Reformation is significant: the initiation of universal, compulsory public education; the integration of the sacred and the secular; the promotion of literacy; and the development of civic school systems as opposed to just individual schools.

Schooling in the Enlightenment

Following the educational ideals and endeavors of Protestantism, the Christian schooling tradition continued into the Age of Reason, the Enlightenment. The father of modern education, John Amos Comenius (1592–1670), maintained that education was for the purpose of shaping and nurturing the human soul, nurturing the faith of children. He advocated universal public education on both an elementary and a secondary level and a four-hour school day (with intermittent periods of independent study). Later, perhaps the most influential educator of the Enlightenment, John Locke (1632–1704), appeared on the scene. While Locke was regarded as a scholar, physician, scientist, and philosopher, he also turned his attention to educational matters. In his *Essay concerning Human Understanding* (1690), he presented the notion that children are a *tabula rasa* (a "blank slate"), just waiting to be written on. In 1697, he followed it up with *Some Thoughts concerning Education*, in which he outlined the curriculum, in terms of both content and instructional methods, that would produce the most desired results. Locke was not a Christian educator as such, but he influenced virtually every Christian educator in the eighteenth

and nineteenth centuries, including John Wesley, Alexander Campbell, and even Horace Bushnell.

The Pietistic tradition also arose during the Enlightenment, with its own version of the Christian schooling tradition. For example, Johann Pestalozzi provided the catalyst for a school that would later come to be known as the Children's Garden (or kindergarten). The Kingswood School, established by John Wesley, grew out of the Pietistic commitment not only to an intellectual education but also to spiritual formation and Christian service.[9] Unlike its modern-day expression, the Sunday school, first established by Robert Raikes in 1780, was indeed a school, scheduled on Sundays for the convenience of the impoverished child laborers in England who could attend school only on Sunday.

Across the Atlantic Ocean, in the early American colonies, the Christian schooling tradition took root in different forms. In the southern colonies, Christian schools, sponsored by the Society for the Propagation of the Gospel in Foreign Places, were relatively rare but could be found in most major cities. Parochial schools were established throughout the mid-Atlantic colonies, as were academies for career training. The Quakers, the Dutch Reformed Church, and the aforementioned Society for the Propagation of the Gospel in Foreign Places established elementary schools, some of which focused on the underprivileged.[10]

In the sectarian mid-Atlantic colonies, the Bible was frequently used as a textbook, as was Pastorius's *New Primer*, "a scriptural text."[11] However, perhaps the Puritans of

9. Estep, "Wesley's Educational Ideal," 55–72.
10. Gangel and Benson, *Christian Education*, 246.
11. Rippa, *Education in a Free Society*, 28–29.

New England, more than any others, characterize Christian schooling in early America. The Old Deluder Satan Act of 1647 required the establishment of a common school in every town of more than fifty families. In addition to the common school, several other institutions provided education, including religious instruction. One such school, the Dame school, even taught religion and literacy to girls.

The heritage of Christian schooling reveals several themes consistent with the contemporary Christian school: the integration of faith and knowledge into a consistent worldview, attention given to nurturing the spiritual lives of students, the theological and practical necessity of Christian education, and the necessity of qualified, trained teachers and administrators.

Various Expressions of Contemporary Christian Schooling

Christian schooling is not captured by any one form of Christian education but describes an umbrella that ranges from instruction in homes (e.g., homeschooling) to institutional varieties (e.g., Christian schools or even boarding schools). Some of these variations have arisen due to a number of factors, including the following:

- *Regulation.* Within the United States, many states provide oversight and regulation through yearly testing and reporting, though such oversight and regulation can vary by state.
- *Theory.* Within the Christian education community itself, various approaches

to and theories of education are adopted and used within schools.
- *Association and cooperation.* Several Christian schooling associations, such as the Association of Christian Schools International, provide resources and support in the form of curriculum resources, publications, teacher credentials, and accreditation to both individual homeschools and institutional Christian schools.

These various expressions of Christian schooling make up the vast landscape of Christian education in the twenty-first century.

Homeschooling

Nonformal teaching in the home has been around since the nomadic period of the patriarchs of the Old Testament. Today, this form of education goes by various names: homeschooling, home education, home-based learning, homeschool. While this format is common in Christian circles, it is not uniquely Christian. Many families use this format if they travel, have schedules that do not allow children to participate in traditional schooling, are in remote areas of the world, or are in areas without acceptable options. Some even use this method because they are opposed to government schools or their parental style dictates a preference for homeschooling.[12]

Various Approaches

Some Christian schools identify themselves by a particular teaching method or

12. Information about homeschooling in the United States can be accessed at http://www.homeschoolfacts.com/index.php.

model that they have adopted. However, some of these methods or models, though founded by a devoted Christian or adopted by Christians, are not unique to Christian schools. This is the case with Montessori schooling[13] and university model schools. Both models are used in secular and Christian schools.

The Montessori school[14] is one example of this; these schools can be Christian schools or nonsectarian. The method of teaching, which was developed by Maria Montessori, is not unique to Christian schooling, even though many Christian schools have adopted it, resulting in organizations such as Christian Montessori Fellowships.[15] Another model comes from the University-Model Schools International (UMSI).[16] This is presently an experimental model for Christian schooling based on the university model for education. Unique to this model is that the scheduling factor is more flexible.

Contemporary expressions of Christian schools are not limited to these examples. Rather, these examples demonstrate the unique approaches adopted by Christian schools. The diversity is as vast as that of traditional schooling.

Schooling Consortia and Co-ops

Parents interested in the traditional homeschool now have an opportunity to take part in homeschool consortia, Christian consortia, and homeschool co-ops, to name a few. Though not all homeschool groups identify as Christian, many do. These groups, which came about through networking, are support groups originally intended for educational and moral support. However, many of them have transformed "into grassroots lobbying bodies working for home-schooling legislation."[17]

Consortia are not-for-profit limited liability corporations with the goal of providing enrichment opportunities for homeschooled students. While joining a consortium requires no fee, a fee is assessed to students taking consortium courses. The curricula offered by consortia are designed for middle and high school students, and the opportunities include academic and social experiences. Both the Hudson Valley Consortium[18] and the Christian Educational Consortium[19] provide an online example of what a consortium is and can do for Christian families.

Homeschool co-ops are cooperatives built around homeschooling. Co-ops take on various formats and provide an assortment of offerings as determined by the people in them, so no two co-ops are alike. Parents work together to fill the areas often missed in homeschooling, such as life skills, academic resources, specialties, and social and group dynamics. Co-ops counter one of the major concerns and criticisms of homeschooling: a lack of social interaction with others. "Homeschooling has become more social. . . . Many homeschool families have found that they either aren't comfortable teaching all subjects, or they just like to supplement their teaching with outside activities. This is where you might find the homeschool

---

13. See http://www.montessori.org/.

14. Montessori schools stress independent, self-directed learning as their philosophy of education.

15. See http://www.christianmontessorifellowship.com/.

16. See http://umsi.org.

17. Bates, "Lobbying for the Lord," 3.

18. See http://albanykid.com/2011/04/27/home-school-consortium/.

19. See http://www.christianconsortium.org.

co-op to be an addition to your homeschool curriculum."[20]

Christian Schools

Rooted in the schooling tradition of the early church and dating back to the Alexandrian schools of Clement and Origen, Christian schools come in a variety of forms as defined by their form of governance, such as described in articles of incorporation. In general, they are either church-run or board-run varieties, though even these are varied (e.g., denominationally affiliated or community associations decide who can serve on the board). Christian schools can be privately owned, can take on some nontraditional formats such as boarding schools for missionary and military families, and can even provide online formats. The defining difference is their faith-based component, which has been added to the curriculum to distinguish it as a Christian school as opposed to a nonsectarian or public school.

Paul Kienel calls this the "age of Christian schools associations"[21] and lists twenty regional, national, and international evangelical Protestant Christian school associations. However, in addition to the Protestant associations, there are over seven thousand parochial schools within the United States.[22] Other associations that support Christian schooling include the Association of Christian Schools International (ACSI) (http://www.acsiglobal.org/about-acsi), the American Association of Christian Schools (AACS) (http://www.aacs.org/), the Ontario Alliance of Christian

Schools (OACS) (http://www.oacs.org/), the Association of Classical Christian Schools (ACCS) (http://www.accsedu.org/), and Christian Schools International (CSI) (http://www.csionline.org/home). These associations provide academic and curriculum resources, professional development, academic support, student activities, pre-K through twelfth grade school accreditation, and teacher credentials.

Protestant and Parochial Schools

Schools that started in response to a perceived threat to faith or tradition are typically identified as either Protestant or parochial. This is true historically of Protestant and Catholic schools as well as later emerging denominational and movement schools. "As early as 1840 Catholic leaders were expressing concern over the Protestant nature of public schooling and strongly encouraging Catholic parents to educate their children in parochial schools. Today, alienation from public schools and support for their religious alternatives are more likely to come from conservative Protestants than from Catholics, especially conservative Protestants with Pentecostal or charismatic identities."[23]

Protestant and parochial distinctions are yet another way to identify Christian schools. Protestant schools are similar to parochial schools, with parents sending their children for the benefit of both religious and academic goals. The term *parochial school* is a uniquely American term used to describe a school attached to a Catholic church parish. Like Protestant versions, these schools teach the same curriculum as found in public schools or even nonsectarian private schools but add courses

---

20. "Home School Families and Home School Co-ops."

21. Kienel, *History of Christian School Education*, 2:10–11.

22. See http://www.parochial.com/.

23. Uecker, "Catholic Schooling," 353. Uecker references both Hunt, Ristau, and Grant, "Catholic Schools," and Sikkink, "Social Sources of Alienation."

on church doctrines, dogma, and include faith-based interpretations of other subjects. Their intention is to provide a God-centered environment and alternative to secularized public schools as well as Protestantism.[24] The National Association of Parochial Schools provides an online directory of these schools (http://www.ncea.org/) and offers grants and scholarship assistance to those attending a parochial school.

Various denominational agencies have licensed or accredited Protestant and parochial schools alike. These agencies are unique to their denominational heritage. Examples include the National Lutheran Schools Accreditation (NLSA)[25] and the Nazarene Educators Worldwide, which is an international association.[26] The National Catholic Educational Association (NCEA) is the largest professional association in the world, serving students in pre-K through twelfth grade.[27] These associations serve schools by providing connections and resources and defining their mission.

In general, the contemporary expressions of Christian schooling are not limited by historical or denominational traditions, method of teaching, or home and traditional school models. What they have in common is the philosophical commitment to Christian education based on biblical teachings and understandings of Christian communities. While rooted in the history of Christian schooling, contemporary schools are not limited by the past but blend these historical commitments with the contemporary needs of students, churches, and culture.

Philosophical Commitments to Christian Schooling

Christian schools include doctrinal studies and intellectual reasoning in an effort to develop within each student a commitment to a biblical worldview. Kenneth Gangel reminds us of this, writing, "Christian educators share the awesome responsibility of helping young people develop the kind of worldview that leads to holy and responsible life choices."[28]

The integration of academics and Christian teaching has its roots in the traditions of the early church fathers and continues today in Christian schooling. However, integration is more than an academic ideal or an intellectual practice. Christian schools are committed to guiding students into an understanding of their relationship to God and preparing students to respond to God's calling to faithfulness. In fact, Richard Edlin describes Christian schooling as nurture and responsive discipleship.[29] Does Christian schooling contribute to the faith development of students? A recent study "based on longitudinal data, [indicated] that Protestant schools, but not Catholic schools, help to promote higher levels of religiosity that last at least until young adulthood."[30] Christian schooling's distinctive educational agenda arises from a comprehensive commitment to the integration of a Christian worldview into every dimension of life.[31] This integrative purpose of education has not changed in the twenty-first century.

It is relatively easy to speak of the integration of faith into life and academic pursuits,

24. "Parochial Schools."
25. See http://www.luthed.org/.
26. See http://www.naznew.net/.
27. See http://www.ncea.org/.

28. Gangel, "Biblical Foundations of Education," 55.
29. Edlin, "Core Beliefs and Values," 69.
30. Uecker, "Catholic Schooling," 366.
31. Edlin, "Core Beliefs and Values," 69–79.

but it is more difficult to describe or even make a viable model for doing so. This is perhaps one of the most challenging philosophical matters for contemporary Christian schooling (i.e., having an articulated commitment to an ill-defined or nebulous concept). However, Kenneth Badley has developed a matrix for faith-learning integration, one that speaks to the all-inclusive nature of the task and provides a means of describing it effectively.[32] In short, his theory maps the terrain of the essential philosophical distinctive of Christian schooling.

He describes faith-learning integration as existing along two axes with four points of orientation. The axes are (1) *faith* as the life of faith and/or body of doctrine and (2) *learning* as the process of learning and/or body of knowledge. On one end of the first axis is faith as life (e.g., the actual practice of genuinely living one's faith and the practices of Christian discipleship). On the opposite end of this axis is faith as doctrine (e.g., the content of faith, its stated beliefs and convictions and theological heritage). This axis is crucial to Christian schooling because it affirms the commitment to faith both academically and personally. The other two points of orientation are on the learning axis. On one end is learning as a process (e.g., the hermeneutics of Bible study, the scientific method, and rules of logic for argumentation). On the other end is learning as our existing knowledge (e.g., a field of study such as science, geography, history, literature, and mathematics). These four points create a matrix with which to describe faith-learning integration as a combination of some or all of the four quadrants.

Given Badley's paradigm, the distinctive philosophical commitments that are expressed in the mission of Christian schooling can be summarized in four statements: (1) Christian schooling is committed to the *spiritual formation* of students; (2) Christian schooling is committed to the integrity and preservation of *Christian beliefs*; (3) Christian schooling is committed to equipping the student's mind for *lifelong study*; and (4) Christian schooling is committed to giving students a *broad introduction* to every field of human learning. These form a matrix in which students' minds and spirits are nurtured toward Christian maturity.

Challenges and Opportunities for Christian Schools

The long-term effect of Christian schooling is in question. There are challenges and thus opportunities for Christian schools in the twenty-first century, five of which are discussed below.

First, developing the trade is important as we determine which schools and models do the best job at Christian education and, in particular, at promoting higher levels of religiosity into adulthood after graduation. As Christian schools seek to prepare students for college and to compete in the global marketplace, there is a concern for how academic excellence takes precedence over religious and faith teachings.[33]

Second, we live in a pluralistic society that not only is global but also has fast-moving flows of migration. This migration affects perspectives and theological thinking on a

32. Badley, "Faith/Learning Integration Movement," 28.

33. Justins, "Christian Schooling and Educational Excellence," 62–63.

grand scale not seen in previous centuries. "The irruption of migration," as Gioacchino Campese calls it, is the study of the growing theological thinking about human mobility, not unlike that of the nomadic precursors to Christianity found in our Hebraic history. "The impact of the irruption of these 'people on the move' on the contemporary scene has finally gotten the attention of Christian theology, as is evident by the growing number of publications and conferences organized on this subject."[34] Thus, it is also a concern for the future of Christian education.

Third, as we grow accustomed to the term *academic excellence*, we must determine what it means for Christian schooling. Do we water down the religious teachings of the faith intentionally or unintentionally? What should our goals be? What is the mission and purpose behind these goals?

Fourth, to ensure Christian freedoms, lifestyles, and moral expectations, more Christians will have to figure out their place on the political platforms of government. This is even true internationally. What should we lobby for or against? In the United States, this includes but is not limited to the issues surrounding school choice.

However, the school choice platform is likely the main issue facing Christian education in this nation. School choice continues to grow with additional state legislative support and new initiatives, with the hope of exploring political and moral legitimacy of religious education in light of the need for instruction for autonomy and instruction for civic education. These are the challenges faced by democratic society when opening up education, in particular faith traditions, to the demands of citizenship.[35]

For example, during the twentieth century, conservative Christianity began to have a presence in the political arena as Christians began to lobby for rights concerning many educational issues. Many special interest groups were formed from this somewhat successful movement, which is now known as the New Christian Right. However, this group does not represent all Christian schools or homeschools, though it has had a large following into the twenty-first century. It is clear that a continuing agenda for this century is maneuvering within the political sphere on behalf of Christians who use a form of homeschooling or Christian schooling in an effort to protect their convictions and lifestyles in an increasingly pluralistic and postmodern culture. The issues have moved beyond mobilizing resources for the purposes of education to mobilizing politically to preserve the faith, ethics, and ideology of Christians.[36]

School choice is an umbrella for many types of initiatives that will be further explored in the United States in the twenty-first century. Already there are varieties of program options, including tax-credit scholarships, vouchers, the Education Savings Act, and the Individual Income Tax Credits for Children with Disabilities Program.[37] The two most prominent are tax-credit programs and

34. Campese, "Irruption of Migrants," 3.

35. Rink, "Commitment, Character, and Citizenship," 128.

36. Bates, "Lobbying for the Lord," 14.

37. "School Choice Programs across the Nation." Statistical and other information on school choice can be found through the American Federation for Children (http://www.federationforchildren.org/), the Friedman Foundation for Educational Choice (http://www.edchoice.org/School-Choice/School-Choice-Programs.aspx), and the Alliance for School Choice (http://www.allianceforschoolchoice.org/yearbook).

vouchers. It should be noted that while the Christian school movement is supportive of these initiatives, they are not solely limited to or used for Christian schooling.[38] Currently, "thirteen states and the District of Columbia provide state-funded school vouchers to qualifying students."[39] While each state approaches school vouchers differently, the states address many of the same questions while developing their voucher programs. As these issues are considered and sifted through the legislative process, the strength and prominence of Christian schooling in the United States will be impacted. Christian schools must have the right to exist as guaranteed by the Bill of Rights, and adequate funding through vouchers and other means are necessary for Christian schools' long-term viability.

Conclusion

Christian schooling is a tradition rooted in Scripture and the heritage of Christian education in the church. Its unique contribution is its comprehensive integration of faith and learning in the lives of students in a way that most congregations or other educational endeavors cannot provide. It prepares students for a life of faith, success in higher education, and service in the church.

38. "Scholarship Tax Credits."
39. "School Voucher Laws."

25

Christian Higher Education

JOHN DAVID TRENTHAM

Christian higher education is not eternal and thus not an ultimate end in itself. It is, however, a means to an ultimate end. That end is the expansion and the enrichment of God's kingdom. To the extent that Christian higher education establishes itself and operates with the proper ultimate end in mind, it will represent an indispensable quality and element of God's church in the world, for the accomplishment of the Great Commission (Matt. 28:18–20). To the extent that Christian higher education exists under the authority of Christ, unto the mission of Christ, and according to the eternal promise of Christ, it will faithfully testify to the hope of Christ. And this testimony will necessarily yield increases for the gospel and human flourishing. Christian higher education thus strives to be a uniquely redemptive provision of salt and light—in the world, for the world, according to the purposeful wisdom of God (1 Cor. 1:24).

Within the scope of these convictions, we now introduce Christian higher education in its confessional Protestant expression through three contextual lenses: (1) conceptual context, (2) virtuous context, and (3) future context. The conceptual context will confirm its essence. The virtuous context will consider its priorities. And the future context will anticipate its direction and hope.

Through all of this, the aim is to set Christian higher education in its proper place and function as a unique gift to the church of God by which people may understand and know him as "the LORD who practices steadfast love, justice, and righteousness in the earth" (Jer. 9:24 ESV). May Christian higher education thus be a place for those who pray with St. Anselm, "I do not try, Lord, to attain Your lofty heights, because my understanding is in no way equal to it. But I do desire to understand your truth a little, that truth that my heart believes and loves."[1]

Christian Higher Education in Conceptual Context

An introduction to Christian higher education calls for a definition. The Council of Christian Colleges and Universities (CCCU) offers an answer with three commitments to the question, What is Christian higher education? These commitments may be summarized as (1) integration of biblical truth throughout every facet of an institution, (2) moral and spiritual formation of students unto wisdom, and (3) equipping students as redemptive influences in society.[2] While helpful, these three commitments may still leave one wondering how to conceptualize Christian higher education in its essence. To do this requires some unpacking.

First, we must clarify: What makes Christian higher education *Christian*? This engages the ontological dimension of Christian higher education. While this is not the only question, it is the most central and consequential one because it engages the matter of the "truth that our hearts believe and love" in Anselm's prayer. Qualifying the enterprise of higher education as Christian assigns a bedrock ontological identifier regarding the source of innermost *being*. On an individual level, to be a Christian is to confess Jesus as Lord in repentance and faith. Likewise, to be Christian in higher education is to maintain and abide in a Christian confessional identity. That Christian confessional identity necessarily entails a commitment to the biblical gospel and redemptive human flourishing.

The authenticity of the confessional identity of any Christian higher educational institution will be revealed in its approach to learning. All learning in the context of Christian higher education must be pursued from the foundation of scriptural and theological centrality and primacy. Scripture and theology articulate the basis of the Christian worldview, and the Christian worldview provides the unique normative perspective that makes authentically Christian education possible and sustainable. Nicholas Wolterstorff sums it up this way:

> Scripture is the fundamental source for one's speaking with a Christian voice and acting out of Christian conviction. And theology is disciplined reflection, in the light of Scripture, on God and God's relation to the world and humanity. Without such disciplined reflection one cannot build a community capable of speaking with a Christian voice and acting out of Christian conviction within the structure, solidarities, and practices of our common humanity. In particular, without knowledge of Scripture and theology one cannot build an academic community that speaks with a Christian voice and acts out of Christian conviction.[3]

Our second clarification in pursuit of a definition is this: What makes Christian higher education *educational*? This question directs us to consider the phenomenological dimension of higher education—that is, what should Christian higher education *do*, and how should it do it? In response, we must consider the priority of purposeful *mission*. Without an established core conviction, an institution is bereft of identity. Without a solid mission, an institution is bereft of a purposeful motive

1. Anselm, *Anselm of Canterbury*, 87.
2. "What Is Christian Higher Education?"

3. Wolterstorff, *Educating for Shalom*, 287.

to pursue its vision and calling. The most essential mission of Christian higher education is holistic learning within a biblical worldview framework.[4] Education is about learning, and learning is about growth and maturity. If students do not learn, education is not accomplished, regardless of whatever else may be achieved. And in Christian higher education, if students do not learn in the context of a thoroughgoing biblical worldview, education is stunted. The educational priority of higher education is thus to foster holistic growth and redemptive maturity in students, as a strategic investment in their influence, service, and stewardship in any number of future roles they inhabit along the trajectory of their lives.

Our final clarification in order to arrive at a proposed definition is as follows: What makes Christian higher education *higher*? Here we must consider the sociological dimension of Christian higher education. The unique outcomes of post-secondary education in the Christian context are pursued and realized in community and culture. College and graduate students, in order to officially matriculate into a degree program, must be formally accepted into a community in which organized learning takes place according to a particular set of parameters and systems which are established and maintained by an institution.

Throughout this chapter, the term *institution* will be used repeatedly to refer to colleges and graduate schools in Christian higher education. The reason for this is because "institution" characterizes schools as much more than just a product of formal classroom activities. In the most general sense, an institution is a *culture*, whether microcosmic (e.g., a married couple) or macrocosmic (e.g., the human race). Cultures are living, creative communities that are driven by a sense of virtue and responsibility to "make something of the world."[5] More specifically with regard to organizational entities, James Davison Hunter proposes that institutions comprise the most primary generative force in shaping the larger culture, because they represent the essential interface between symbolic ideas and the organization of human activity. Thus he asserts, "Culture is as much infrastructure as it is ideas. It takes shape in concrete institutional form."[6] It is thus ethically incumbent upon any institution, as a culture, to seek health, virtue, and human flourishing on the basis of the unique attributes of that institution.[7]

The institutional uniqueness of a Christian college or graduate school is chiefly manifested in the *curriculum*, which entails what is taught, what is not taught, and what is enculturated.[8] Stated in a different way, the institutional priority of any Christian institution of higher education is to engage and equip responsible adult learners in an

---

4. *Worldview* is a term with many definitions, some of which are inadequate due to a purely or overly cognitive-intellectual emphasis. The notion of worldview in view here is articulated by James Sire: "A worldview is a commitment, a fundamental orientation of the heart, that can be expressed as a story or in a set of presuppositions . . . which we hold . . . about the basic constitution of reality, and that provides the foundation on which we live and move and have our being." *Naming the Elephant*, 141.

5. See Crouch, *Culture Making*.

6. J. Hunter, *To Change the World*, 34.

7. J. Hunter says, "Institutions such as the market, the state, education, the media of mass communications, scientific and technological research, and the family in its socializing capacities are not organizationally neutral but have their own logic, place, and history that interact with the ideas and ideals for which they are carriers." *To Change the World*, 35.

8. The explicit, null, and hidden curricula. These are addressed later in this chapter.

organized, covenantal learning community with advanced competence and according to a prescriptive and developmentally-oriented curriculum.

Concentricity

Christian higher education is thus a product of three elements: ontological (confessional), phenomenological (missional), and sociological (institutional). Three crucial insights stem from this. First, these three elements are irreducible, which is to say that while Christian higher education may involve more than these, it cannot be composed of less. Second, these three elements are ordered: a school's Christian confession is the core of its identity, confessional priorities direct missional priorities, and missional priorities direct institutional priorities. Finally, though ordered, these elements are necessarily interactive and reciprocal. One element cannot be considered to the exclusion of another and all three must be healthy in order for a school to thrive in faithfulness and sustainability. We may thus conceptualize Christian higher education as a concentricity composed of elements that are distinct while mutually interactive and interdependent (see fig. 25.1).

A Proposed Definition

At this point, we may propose a comprehensive definition based on the three interactive elements just described:

Christian higher education is (1) a collective body of institutions that respectively exist and proceed on the basis of a Christian confessional identity, (2) for the purpose of promoting and facilitating student learning and formation according to a Christian worldview framework, (3) by the means

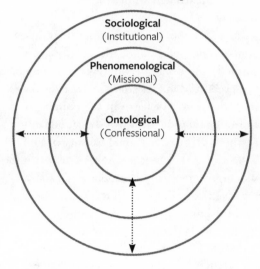

Figure 25.1
Christian Higher Education as a Concentricity

culture of one or more prescriptive post-secondary degree-based curricula.

One may note that the CCCU's three commitments correspond directly to this proposed definition and the comprising elements of Christian higher education (see table 25.1).

Table 25.1. Christian Higher Education and CCCU Commitments

Definition	Corresponding CCCU Commitment
A collective body of institutions that respectively exist and proceed on the basis of a Christian confessional identity	Integration of biblical truth throughout every facet of an institution
For the purpose of promoting and facilitating student learning and formation according to a Christian worldview framework	Moral and spiritual formation of students unto wisdom
By the means and culture of one or more prescriptive post-secondary degree-based curricula	Equipping students as redemptive influences in society

Having answered the conceptual or definitional context, we should now turn to consider some essential virtues. For the enterprise of Christian higher education, the goal cannot be merely to clarify an identity or to exist. The goal must be to thrive and flourish in society for the sake of the kingdom of God.

Christian Higher Education in Virtuous Context

What truly constitutes a Christian college in the current cultural milieu? In other words, what should an authentically Christian institution of higher education look like to the watching world? One helpful picture may be Robert Benne's notion of a "full-blooded" Christian college or university, in which "the Christian heritage is publicly relevant to the central endeavors of the college."[9] In order to achieve this, according to Benne, institutions must engender intentionally Christian priorities on three levels: (1) vision, a full account of reality based on the Christian narrative as revealed in Scripture and handed down through history; (2) ethos, a Christian way of life; and (3) persons, a community of believers who articulate the vision and embody the ethos.[10] We should note that these three levels correspond to the definition proposed above, entailing Christian higher education is irreducibly composed of confessional, missional, and institutional elements.

We may add two inverse corollaries to this triad of priorities. First, to the extent that authentic Christian community is engendered and facilitated, the Christian vision and ethos of an institution will be retained (or perhaps regained). Or inversely, to the extent that authentic Christian community is not engendered and facilitated, an institution's Christian vision and ethos will be relegated or lost. The beginning and end of virtue in Christian higher education is thus predicated on faithful stewardship in these three areas.

This section proposes a collection of virtues for Christian higher education stemming directly from the foregoing conceptual context and definition. To be clear, these virtues are intended to be categorically comprehensive (confessional, missional, and institutional) but not specifically exhaustive.

Confessional Virtues

Christian higher education is *Christian* by virtue of its confession. It must therefore be undertaken in the world and for the world but without capitulating to the ultimacy of the world. Christian learning and scholarship should be pursued and conducted publicly in society—that is, not in a sequestered enclave devoid of societal access. After all, if Christian learning communities are dichotomous or separated from the world, then Christian education and scholarship have no voice to be heard in the world. We must have access to society if we hope to impact society. This, according to Wolterstorff, is the crux of the Kuyperian vision for Christian higher education—namely, that "we are to speak and act within the structure of our common humanity but with a distinct Christian voice."[11]

In the World

When we call Christian higher education *Christian*, we clearly say something about

9. Benne, *Quality with Soul*, 6.
10. Benne, *Quality with Soul*, 6–18.

11. Wolterstorff, *Educating for Shalom*, 286.

what it is and what it is not—namely, secular. That isn't precisely accurate, however. The term *secular* may simply be defined as "in or relating to the world." Thus, to assert that Christian higher education is not secular is actually to say that it is not "in the world." But it is impossible to engage the Great Commission without being in the world. It is impossible to love one's neighbor without being in the world. We must remember the words of Jesus in his high priestly prayer: "As you sent me into the world, I have sent them into the world" (John 17:18). Christian higher education, in whatever institutional form, simply must be committed to being in the world and to being salt and light for the world (Matt. 5:13–14). But, of course, Christian believers and institutions must not be of the world (John 17:16). The critical observation here is that when Christian higher education is defined in contradistinction to "secular" higher education, it must not be assumed as sectarian and unengaged with the "real world." To say that Christian higher education is not secular is thus, more precisely, to say that it is not merely secular, ultimately secular, or secularist.

Christian versus Secularist Learning

The fundamental difference between confessionally Christian learning and secularist learning is a matter of one's motivation and appetite for obtaining and maintaining knowledge. A Christian will pursue learning according to the nature and purpose of all knowledge, which is to know God and to serve him accordingly (Jer. 9:24; Phil. 3:10). The secular appetite for learning may be categorized under three frameworks. First, the agnostic learner pursues knowledge for knowledge's sake, or according to mere curi-

osity.[12] The *pragmatic* or instrumental learner pursues knowledge for the sake of progress, or according to mere utility. The materialist learner pursues knowledge for the sake of promotion, or according to mere aspiration. Now, it should be acknowledged that each of these secular frameworks, from a biblical worldview perspective, identifies quite acceptable and commendable by-products or effects of learning. As primary motivations for learning, however, they are sub-biblical. There is thus a vital distinction between learning for self and learning for God, or between the pursuit of idolatry and the pursuit of sanctification with regard to the motivating impulse for learning, career preparation, and scholarship.

We may call this the "John 3:30 principle"[13] of Christian learning: learning will be motivated and directed either toward anthropocentric ends or toward Christocentric ends. Although they will never be fully Christlike in a Genesis 3 world, Christian learners will move toward Christlikeness as they are indwelled by the Holy Spirit and pursue sanctification with its eternal perspective. Conversely, secular learners, while possessing any number of righteous and God-honoring virtues, will move toward the pursuit and gratification of personal significance and achievement with its temporal perspective.

So now, the crucial diagnostic question for institutions of Christian higher education on a confessional level is this: What framework for learning is endorsed, embedded, and practiced

12. Regarding "curiosity," see Griffiths, "From Curiosity to Studiousness." Griffiths says, "The curious value learning for its own sake, alone, which is the precise Augustinian definition of idolatry: they exchange use for enjoyment," 108.

13. "He must increase, but I must decrease" (ESV).

in the curriculum of the school? In view of the secular frameworks, we may suggest that various types of Christian schools should be careful to avoid particular tendencies. Liberal arts colleges should take special care to avoid stoking vain curiosity. Bible colleges should take special care to avoid stoking utilitarianism. Seminaries and Christian graduate universities should take care to avoid stoking mere aspirationalism, as they are typically centers of elite scholarship, terminal degree offerings, influential publication, and prominent public platforms.

Missional Virtues

Christian higher education is educational by virtue of its mission. The thrust of that mission is, simply and profoundly, learning within a biblical worldview framework. That being the case, missional virtues in Christian higher education must begin from that point. A prioritized listing of virtues or "excellencies" may be articulated in this way:

- Excellence in learning is the primary telos of the mission.
- Excellent teaching (classroom and otherwise) is the means by which the mission is accomplished.
- Excellent students are the engine of the curriculum.
- Excellent faculty are the fuel of the curriculum.
- Excellent administrative leadership is essential to the navigational trajectory of the curriculum.
- Excellent scholarship and institutional support are the means by which faculty thrive and grow.

Learning as Pilgrimage

Learning is inherently human, purposeful, and worshipful. It is "a gift of God to humanity that we are to receive and practice with gratitude."[14] If education is fundamentally concerned with promoting learning, and if education must therefore personally engage and impact the learner, then higher education must be oriented around the developmental realities and possibilities in the lives of students. Learning in Christian higher education should therefore promote a pilgrimage mentality of Christian sanctification over and against a track-running mentality.

The educational aim of Christian higher education may thus be stated as the sustainable promotion of redemptive flourishing in the lives of students through learning. This pursuit of patterned learning and formation must necessarily invoke the ethic of Christian pilgrimage. Applied to the Christian life, the difference between pilgrimage and track running is the difference between an eternal and a momentary perspective. We Christians, after all, are "people who spend our lives going someplace, going to God, and whose path for getting there is the way, Jesus Christ."[15]

Here are a few ways that either perspective may be reflected in the lives of Christian college and graduate students:

- The pilgrim student is willing to engage in reflective consideration of a concept or issue, while the track-runner student seeks only immediate answers.
- The pilgrim is willing to engage a problem with an attitude of strategic

14. Wolterstorff, *Educating for Shalom*, 285.
15. E. Peterson, *Long Obedience in the Same Direction*, 17.

evaluation and compassion, while the track-runner seeks only ready-made, formulaic solutions.

- The pilgrim yearns for sustainable wisdom, while the track-runner yearns only for the accumulation of facts.
- The pilgrim pursues community, while the track-runner pursues only competition.
- The pilgrim values unity in diversity, while the track-runner values only unity in affinity.

Teaching as Sacred

Teaching in Christian higher education is a sacred trust. Excellent teachers will focus their prayer and energy primarily on engaging students to facilitate holistic learning unto biblical maturity. There are many modes of effective teaching as well as many modes that engender common pitfalls. Most importantly, however, we must affirm that the central virtue of teaching in Christian higher education is a desire for students in their learning to be progressively transformed into the image of Christ. In order for teachers to accomplish this, their teaching must be imbued with the Great Commandment (Matt. 22:37–39). They must "love the Lord" by teaching out of godly conviction and with a posture that reflects the fear of the Lord (Prov. 1:7). They must "love their neighbor" by knowing their students, challenging their students, motivating their students, and shepherding their students.

Institutional Virtues

Christian higher education is *higher* by virtue of its institutional community and culture. Institutions, as institutions, can and should be redemptive. Just as the institutions of marriage, the family, and the church are redemptive because of their institutional uniqueness and mission, so Christian higher educational institutions must seek to leverage their creative power for the sake of the kingdom. "Institutions are the only way that the gift of power can be fully expressed," Andy Crouch reminds us, "because institutions are essential for flourishing."[16]

In order for an institution of Christian higher education to sustain its confession and its mission faithfully, it must embrace and embed a transformational ethos throughout its entire structure—administratively, organizationally, culturally, academically, and pedagogically. A transformational ethos is evident in a Christian college and/or graduate school when every element of the institution is tailored to serve and influence the participants in that institution so that they establish patterns of progressive growth and maturity unto Christlikeness.

A Culture of Diversity

Christian community necessarily entails unity in diversity. Just as the culture of any local church will flourish most at the point of maximum unification across lines of worldly distinction such as race, ethnicity, class, generation, geography, and economy, so it is with confessional Christian higher education. More emphatically, if Christian higher education, as a vital extension of God's church, fails to present to the world a mosaic portrait of diverse people gathered and growing together, it will give the world a stunted picture of the hope of the gospel. That hope is the reality of eternity in heaven, with the entire family of God joined

16. Crouch, *Playing God*, 169.

together as every nation, tribe, people, and language (Rev. 7:9). Christian higher education simply must commit to embedding and celebrating godly diversity at every level: confessional, missional, and institutional.

With this imperative, it should be recognized that a wide door for redemptive flourishing is being opened to institutions of Christian higher education in this particular regard, given dramatic and rapid demographic shifts in the younger population of the United States.[17] The question is simply how the fields of diversity will be harvested and stewarded and whether confessional Christian institutions will find ways to share in that harvest and stewardship with the same level of intentionality as that of secular institutions. This begins, according to Justo González, with a humble recognition on the part of the evangelical church and Christian institutions of higher education within the United States: "We must acknowledge the cultural captivity of much of our institutional and ecclesiastical life, which prevents us from recruiting and making way for the growing minorities that will soon be the majority of the church."[18]

A Culture of Teaching and Learning

An unavoidable cultural question for any institution of Christian higher education, stemming directly from its mission, is whether it exists as an institution primarily for the purpose of (1) articulating, defending, and advancing the Christian worldview, (2) forming

students unto biblical maturity through excellent pedagogy and formative practices, or (3) a mutual combination of both of these aims. The culture created by the first purpose will be teacher/scholar-centric, while the culture created by the second purpose will be teaching/student-centric. A prime institutional virtue is to guard against making 1 and 2 mutually exclusive and to aim purposefully to realize 3.

According to David Smith and James K. A. Smith, much more intentionality and energy have been devoted to 1 rather than to 2. Scholarly endeavors have tended to trump pedagogical endeavors in garnering institutional support and energy in recent confessional higher education contexts.[19] Given the great struggle for confessional orthodoxy in Protestant-evangelical higher education in the last century, such an overcorrection or neglect of institutional balance may be understandable. Still, we must assert that institutions of Christian higher education are ethically bound and required to prioritize both teaching/scholarship and learning/formation. This necessarily follows from the biblical ethic of the Christian life, which is predicated on one's profession of faith necessarily coupled with one's love for God and neighbor as revealed in one's character and good works.

Curriculum as Culture Making

The uniqueness of an institution of Christian higher education is the curriculum, which entails every aspect of the institution that promotes and facilitates learning. As stated at the outset, authentically Christian learning is possible only within the framework of a Christian worldview, which is established

---

17. For example, according to the 2010 census results, the birthrate among African Americans, Asian Americans, and Hispanic Americans far outpaced the birthrate of European Americans. See González's brief treatment related to this in *History of Theological Education*, 133–39.

18. González, *History of Theological Education*, 139.

19. D. Smith and J. Smith, "Practices, Faith, and Pedagogy," 2–3.

on the basis of scriptural and theological primacy. Scripture is the fundamental source in which the Christian higher education curriculum must be rooted, and theology is the fundamental means of reflection according to which all learning must take place. This highlights the foremost curricular virtue with regard to Christian higher education: theological education must not be separated from Christian education. Justo González puts it well: "Theological studies are not the specialty of the ordained ministry, like medical studies are the specialty of physicians, but rather the way in which the church and all its members, both jointly and individually, express our love for God, as the commandment says, with all our minds."[20]

Orthodox scriptural and theological presuppositions must be in place to predicate all endeavors of learning, formation, and scholarship in the curriculum. At that point, Christians are not only at liberty to engage all fields of academic study but also responsible for engaging all disciplines. Further, Christians are uniquely free and responsible to faithfully interact with all knowledge and ideas for the purpose of being sharpened and enriched. It must be understood that neither knowledge nor insight is the exclusive possession of believers—even though redemptive, Christ-oriented knowledge and insight are possible only on the basis of the fear of the Lord (Prov. 1:7; 1 Cor. 1:18). In the Reformed tradition, recognition of the universal human capability for insight is predicated on "common grace."[21] And on the basis of common grace, Christians may seek and mine truth from a variety of disciplines and sources, even when those

sources may seem unlikely. John Calvin articulates this well:

> Whenever we come upon these matters in secular writers, let that admirable light of truth shining in them teach us that the mind of man, though fallen and perverted from its wholeness, is nevertheless clothed and ornamented with God's excellent gifts. If we regard the Spirit of God as the sole fountain of truth, we shall neither reject the truth itself, nor despise it wherever it shall appear, unless we wish to dishonor the Spirit of God. . . . Those men whom Scripture (1 Cor. 2:14) calls "natural men" were, indeed, sharp and penetrating in their investigation of inferior things. Let us, accordingly, learn by their example how many gifts the Lord left to human nature even after it was despoiled of its true good.[22]

Formally speaking, the curriculum of an institution of Christian higher education is actually a threefold unit of subcurricula—explicit, hidden, and null. The explicit curriculum is the content of what is explicitly taught in the classroom. The hidden curriculum is the content of what is learned through an institution's community and cultural ethos (i.e., what is caught rather than taught). The null curriculum is the content of what is learned through what is not taught. This includes "both the intellectual processes that are promoted or neglected, and the subject areas that are present or absent."[23] While much could be said with regard to the essential virtues of all three areas, the overriding virtue is that a curriculum will be effective only to the extent that the null and the hidden curricula receive due attention and care alongside the explicit

---

20. González, *History of Theological Education*, 118.

21. See Mouw, *He Shines in All That's Fair*.

22. Calvin, *Institutes*, 2.2.15.

23. Shaw, *Transforming Theological Education*, 79.

curriculum. This follows from the reality that a hidden curriculum and a null curriculum exist whether or not they are intended. And if they are not, the curriculum tends to reflect what Perry Shaw refers to as the "Schooling Paradigm," in which mere cognitive mastery is equivalent to learning and maturity, mere grade advancement is equivalent to education and formation, and mere degree completion is equivalent to competence and wisdom.[24]

A Culture of Redemptive Awareness

In the end, confessional Christian higher education is about influencing and promoting the Christian formation and maturity of students. Consider this critical question: How, and to what level of faithful effectiveness, do differing types of institutions shape and mold students? On an evaluative level for institutions, one should ask, "What inherent strengths and weaknesses regarding student formation and maturity are embedded in the framework of our school?" On an evaluative level for students, one should ask, "What unique opportunities for personal development and formative community does my school provide?" and "In what ways do I need to intentionally seek to mature in my faith and learning outside the context of my school community?" These questions constitute a posture of what may be called redemptive awareness—the commitment to honestly assess one's immediate context, identify the strengths and liabilities inherent in that context, and pursue redemptive maturity within and outside that context.

Every confessional institution of higher education will have redemptive cultural characteristics on which students should seek to

24. Shaw, *Transforming Theological Education*, 82.

capitalize, and every institution will have limiting or blind-spot cultural characteristics that students should seek to transcend. Furthermore, it should be understood that blind spots or limitations do not necessarily indicate institutional failure on an ethical level, though sometimes that may be the case. In the same way, it should be recognized that an inherent strength can become a liability if it is emphasized to the neglect of a different vital feature of learning, community, or some other component.

Redemptive awareness is thus an essential virtue for all Christian members of a Christian higher educational institution. Redemptively aware students, faculty, and administration will understand the features of their school's culture and will intentionally consider how they can pursue growth in Christlikeness by leveraging inherent strengths, transcending potential liabilities, and constructively engaging areas of weakness or shortcoming with a gospel-motivated sense of community and humility.

Christian Higher Education in Future Context

Christian higher education will persist, by God's grace. But the extent to which Christian higher education will be conducted responsibly and faithfully in the decades to come, and by whom, remains to be seen. That will be determined by a number of factors, some predictable, some unpredictable. As we look to the future, we may do so with these questions in view:

- How will God preserve confessional Christian higher education if orthodox confessionalism is culturally and/

or governmentally deemed inappropriate or noncredible as a foundation for institutional identity and mission?

- How will Christian institutions of higher education pursue excellence in pedagogy and scholarship compared to secular institutions?

- How will Christian higher education respond to, adapt to, and engage redemptively with rapidly shifting demographic trends in the United States?

- How will Christian higher education intentionally champion racial reconciliation and redemptive diversity as a fundamental point of emphasis related to confessional, missional, and institutional priorities?

- Will the bifurcation of theological centrality and expertise between seminaries and Christian colleges and universities persist, or will new modes of scholarly and collegial partnership continue to emerge and grow?

- To what extent will institutions of Christian higher education pursue innovative strategies to achieve holistic learning and formation in web-based or web-enhanced contexts?

As we conclude, we may do well to consider this classroom reflection question often proposed to college students: If you died today, what would be said of you at your funeral, and what do you wish would be said?[25] Your answer likely hinges on the conviction and depth of your personal character. You will consider what testimonial accounts would witness to

25. See DeYoung, "Pedagogical Rhythms." DeYoung describes how she uses a version of this question in the classroom to foster the practice of reflecting.

that and what prominent features of your persona and life would be invoked. Of course, the ultimate thrust of the question is, What is a life well lived? Biblically speaking, a Christian life well lived involves three elements: a biblical confession of the truth of salvation in Christ, through faith; a missional conviction that drives one to pursue discipleship by establishing and growing in Christlike virtue; and a practical, sustainable faithfulness of daily living that manifests in godly wisdom and testifies to the truth of the gospel by enriching others' lives. Now you may ask, "But what does this have to do with Christian higher education?" Everything.

Here is why: in order for higher education to be Christian, it must facilitate and cultivate an ecosystem in which students are engaged and compelled to mature according to this irreducible trifecta of a Christian life well lived. Truth without virtue is legalism or nominalism. Convictional virtue without truth is relativism or individualism. Truth and/or virtue without wisdom is superficial and represents a stunted, empty, hollow, or disjointed faith. Likewise, institutions of Christian higher education that emphasize truth separate from virtue may produce legalists or relativists. Institutions that do not embed practices tailored to engender practical, sustainable faithfulness will produce students with impressive credentials and without wisdom. May it not be so, for the future of Christ's church.

Conclusion

The triad of a life well lived is analogous to the threefold concentricity of Christian higher education presented at the beginning of this chapter. We may thus now assert that *if Christian institutions of higher education intend to facilitate lives well lived, churches well led, and societies well enriched, they must be institutions well stewarded.* If the mark of thoroughgoing Christian higher education is a commitment to a healthy confession, mission, and institution, then the success of any school is a function of its effectiveness in influencing students in each of these areas, simultaneously. In other words, a believer doesn't graduate from confession to virtue to wisdom; one grows according to the coordination of those elements. Confession, virtue, and wisdom are an interdependent set of attributes that compose redemptive development. Thus, "solid food is for the mature, who have their powers of discernment trained by constant practice"

(Heb. 5:14 ESV). And if the success of any institution depends on influencing students unto biblical maturity and wisdom, then this will be reflected in the chief concerns and energies of the institution's leadership, including faculty, administration, trustees, and student service professionals.

There is an inherent and solemn ethic at the heart of Christian higher education. It is this: institutions conduct themselves ethically and responsibly insofar as they cultivate education that equips students to produce well-lived lives in the economy of God's eternal kingdom. To the extent that this is realized in the coming years, Christian higher education will persist as both salt and light.

BIBLIOGRAPHY

Abate, Tom. "Stanford Bioengineers Create Circuit Board Modeled on the Human Brain." Stanford News Service, April 28, 2014. http://news.stanford.edu/pr/2014/pr-neurogrid-boahen-engineering-042814.html.

"The ADDIE Model." Instructional Design Expert.com. 2009. http://www.instructionaldesignexpert.com/addie.html#.Uy9CDM-n-BY.

"Administer." *Online Etymology Dictionary*. 2019. https://www.etymonline.com/word/administer.

Alexander, Patricia A. *Psychology in Learning and Instruction*. Upper Saddle River, NJ: Pearson Education, 2006.

Allen, Holly Catterton, ed. *InterGenerate: Transforming Churches through Intergenerational Ministry*. Abilene, TX: Abilene Christian University Press, 2018.

Allen, Holly Catterton, and Christine Lawson Ross. *Intergenerational Christian Formation: Bringing the Whole Church Together in Ministry, Community, and Worship*. Downers Grove, IL: InterVarsity, 2012.

Al-Rodhan, Nayef. "Definitions of Globalization: A Comprehensive Overview and a Proposed Definition." Program on the Geopolitical Implications of Globalization and Transnational Security, Geneva Centre for Security Policy, Geneva, Switzerland. June 19, 2006. http://citeseerx.ist.psu.edu/viewdoc/download?doi=10.1.1.472.4772&rep=rep1&type=pdf.

Andersen, Erika. *Growing Great Employees*. London: Penguin, 2006.

Anderson, Dave. "When 'Good' Isn't Enough: How to Overcome the 6 Temptations of Successful Organizations." *Arrivals*, January/February 2004, 39–41.

Anderson, Janna, Jan Boyles, and Lee Raines. "The Future Impact of the Internet on Higher Education." Pew Research Center. http://www.pewinternet.org/files/old-media/Files/Reports/2012/PIP_Future_of_Higher_Ed.pdf.

Anderson, Keith R., and Randy D. Reese. *Spiritual Mentoring: A Guide for Seeking and Giving Direction*. Downers Grove, IL: InterVarsity, 1999.

Anderson, Lorin W., and David R. Krathwohl, eds. *A Taxonomy for Learning, Teaching and Assessing: A Revision of Bloom's Taxonomy*. New York: Longman, 1992.

Angelo, Thomas A., and K. Patricia Cross. *Classroom Assessment Techniques: A Handbook for College Teachers.* San Francisco: Jossey-Bass, 1993.

Anselm. *Anselm of Canterbury: The Major Works.* Edited by Brian Davies and G. R. Evans. New York: Oxford University Press, 1998.

Anthony, Michael, ed. *Foundations of Ministry: An Introduction to Christian Education for a New Generation.* Grand Rapids: Baker Academic, 1992.

Anthony, Michael, and Michelle Anthony, eds. *A Theology for Family Ministries.* Nashville: B&H Academic, 2011.

Anthony, Michael J., and James R. Estep Jr., eds. *Management Essentials for Christian Ministries.* Nashville: Broadman & Holman, 2005.

"Are the Four Profitable Areas in 2 Tim 3:16 Covering Doctrine and Practice?" StackExchange. https://hermeneutics.stackexchange.com/questions/662/are-the-four-profitable-areas-in-2-tim-316-covering-doctrine-and-practice.

Arnett, Jeffery Jensen. *Adolescence and Emerging Adulthood: A Cultural Approach.* 5th ed. New York: Pearson, 2013.

———. "Emerging Adulthood: A Theory of Development from the Late Teens through the Twenties." *American Psychologist* 55 (May 2000): 469–80.

———. *Emerging Adulthood: The Winding Road from the Late Teens through the Twenties.* New York: Oxford University Press, 2004.

Arnett, Jeffrey Jensen, and Jennifer Tanner, eds. *Emerging Adults in America: Coming of Age in the Twenty-First Century.* Washington, DC: American Psychological Association, 2005.

"Arrivals Report." National Travel and Tourism Office. http://travel.trade.gov/view/m-2017-I-001/index.asp.

Augustine. "On the Catechising of the Uninstructed." Translated by S. D. F. Salmond. In vol. 3 of *The Nicene and Post-Nicene Fathers, Series* 1. Edited by Philip Schaff. Buffalo:

Christian Literature Publishing, 1887. Revised and edited for New Advent by Kevin Knight. http://www.newadvent.org/fathers/1303.htm.

Babcox, Emilie. "Ministers without Master's Degrees." *In Trust,* Spring 2014. http://www.intrust.org/Magazine/Issues/Spring-2014/Ministers-without-masters-degrees.

Badley, Kenneth. "The Faith/Learning Integration Movement in Christian Higher Education: Slogan or Substance?" *Journal of Research on Christian Education* 3, no. 1 (1994): 13–33.

Bain, Ken. *What the Best College Teachers Do.* Cambridge: Harvard University Press, 2011.

Balfour, Stephen. "Assessing Writing in MOOCs: Automated Essay Scoring and Calibrated Peer Review™." *Research & Practice in Assessment* 8 (Summer 2013). http://www.rpajournal.com/dev/wp-content/uploads/2013/05/SF4.pdf.

Balmer, Randal. *The Encyclopedia of Evangelicalism.* Louisville: Westminster John Knox, 2002.

Balswick, Jack O., Kevin S. Reimer, and Pamela Ebstyne King. *The Reciprocating Self: Human Development in Theological Perspective.* Downers Grove, IL: InterVarsity, 2005.

Bandura, Albert. *Social Foundations of Thought and Action: A Social Cognitive Theory.* Englewood Cliffs, NJ: Prentice-Hall, 1986.

———. *Social Learning Theory.* Upper Saddle River, NJ: Prentice-Hall, 1977.

Barna, George, and Mark Hatch. *Boiling Point.* Ventura, CA: Regal, 2001.

Barna Group. *Gen Z: The Culture, Beliefs, and Motivations Shaping the Next Generation.* Ventura, CA: Barna, 2018.

———. *The State of Youth Ministry: How Churches Reach Today's Teens—and What Parents Think about It.* Ventura, CA: Barna, 2016.

Bates, Vernon L. "Lobbying for the Lord: The New Christian Right Home-Schooling Movement and Grassroots Lobbying." *Review of Religious Research* 33, no. 1 (September 1991): 3–17.

Baucham, Voddie, Jr. *Family Driven Faith: Doing What It Takes to Raise Sons and Daughters Who Walk with God.* Wheaton: Crossway, 2007.

Beckwith, Ivy. *Postmodern Ministry to Children in the 21st Century.* Grand Rapids: Zondervan/Youth Specialties, 2004.

Bender, Andrew, "Record Number of Americans Now Hold Passports." Forbes.com. January 20, 2012. https://www.forbes.com/sites/andrew bender/2012/01/30/record-number-of-americans -now-hold-passports/#24c96f392f97.

Benne, Robert. *Quality with Soul: How Six Premier Colleges and Universities Keep Faith with Their Religious Traditions.* Grand Rapids: Eerdmans, 2001.

Bennis, Warren, and B. Nannis. *Leaders: Strategies for Taking Charge.* New York: Harper-Collins, 1985.

Benson, Warren S. "Parachurch Vocations in Christian Education." In *Introduction to Biblical Christian Education*, edited by Werner C. Graendorf, 348–67. Chicago: Moody, 1981.

Bergler, Thomas. *The Juvenilization of American Christianity.* Grand Rapids: Eerdmans, 2012.

Best, Ernest. "Ephesians." In *International Critical Commentary*, edited by J. Emerton, C. Cranfeld, and G. Stanton, 391. New York: T&T Clark International, 1998.

Bird, Michael B. *Evangelical Theology: A Biblical and Systematic Introduction.* Grand Rapids: Zondervan, 2013.

Black, Wesley. "Formal Education." In *Evangelical Dictionary of Christian Education*, edited by M. J. Anthony, W. S. Benson, D. Eldridge, and J. Gorman, 298–99. Grand Rapids: Baker Academic, 2001.

———. "Informal Education." In *Evangelical Dictionary of Christian Education*, edited by M. J. Anthony, W. S. Benson, D. Eldridge,

and J. Gorman, 362–63. Grand Rapids: Baker Academic, 2001.

Blanchard, Ken. *Leading at a Higher Level.* Upper Saddle River, NJ: Prentice-Hall, 2007.

Blanchette, Leon Marcel, Jr. *The Relationship between Ministry Praxis and Spiritual Development Milestones in the Lives of Children.* 2008. ProQuest Dissertations & Theses Global. 304461550. https://digitalcommons .olivet.edu/ched_facp/1.

Blevins, Dean G., and Mark A. Maddix. *Discovering Discipleship: Dynamics of Christian Education.* Kansas City, MO: Beacon Hill, 2010.

Bloom, Benjamin S., ed. *Taxonomy of Educational Objectives: The Classification of Educational Goals; Handbook I, Cognitive Domain.* New York: David McKay, 1956.

Boje, D. "The Isles Leadership: The Voyage of the Behaviorists." *The Leadership Box* (2000). Northern Michigan State University. http:// business.nmsu.edu/~dboje/teaching/338 /behaviors.htm#katz_michigan.

Bonhoeffer, Dietrich. *Life Together: A Discussion of Christian Fellowship.* San Francisco: Harper & Row, 1954.

———. *A Testament to Freedom: The Essential Writings of Dietrich Bonhoeffer.* Edited by Geffrey B. Kelly and F. Burton Nelson. San Francisco: HarperSanFrancisco, 1995.

Bowe, Barbara E. *Biblical Foundations of Spirituality: Touching a Finger to the Flame.* Lanham, MD: Rowman & Littlefield, 2003.

Boyer, Paul. *Urban Masses and Moral Order in America, 1820–1920.* Cambridge: Harvard University Press, 1978.

Boylan, Anne M. *Sunday School: The Formation of an American Institution, 1790–1880.* New Haven: Yale University Press, 1988.

Bramer, Paul. "Christian Formation: Tweaking the Paradigm." *Christian Education Journal* 4, no. 2 (2007): 352–63.

Brennfleck, Kevin, and Kay Marie Brennfleck. *Live Your Calling: A Practical Guide to Finding and Fulfilling Your Mission in Life*. San Francisco: Jossey-Bass, 2005.

Briggs, Philip H., and William Smith. "John Milburn Price." Christian Educators of the 20th Century. http://www.talbot.edu/ce20 /educators/protestant/john_price/.

Brown, Peter R. "Ambrose." *Encyclopedia Britannica Online*. http://www.britannica.com /EBchecked/topic/19014/Saint-Ambrose#toc 259.

Brudney, Jeffrey L. "Preparing the Organization for Volunteers." In *The Volunteer Management Handbook: Leadership Strategies for Success*, edited by Tracy Daniel Connors, 55–80. Hoboken, NJ: John Wiley & Sons, 2012.

Bugbee, Bruce. *What You Do Best in the Body of Christ: Discover Your Spiritual Gifts, Personal Style, and God-Given Passion*. Grand Rapids: Zondervan, 2005.

Buggeln, Gretchen. *The Suburban Church: Modernism and Community in Postwar America*. Minneapolis: University of Minnesota Press, 2015.

Bultmann, Rudolf. "Γινώσκω." In vol. 1 of *Theological Dictionary of the New Testament*, edited by G. Kittel, translated by G. W. Bromiley, 689–719. Grand Rapids: Eerdmans, 1964.

Bushnell, Horace. *Christian Nurture*. Grand Rapids: Baker, 1979.

Bybee, Rodger W., and Robert B. Sund. *Piaget for Educators*. 2nd ed. Prospect Heights, IL: Waveland, 1990.

Calhoun, Ronald C. Life in the Image of God: The Sermon on the Mount as a Hillside Holiness Message. Bloomington, IN: WestBow, 2013.

Calvin, John. *The Institutes of Christian Religion*. In *Library of Christian Classics*, edited by J. T. McNeill, translated by Ford Lewis Battles. Philadelphia: Westminster, 1977.

———. "The Way in Which We Receive the Grace of Christ." Book 3 of *Calvin: Institutes of Christian Religion*, edited by J. T. McNeill, translated by Ford Lewis Battles. Philadelphia: Westminster, 1960.

Campese, Gioacchino. "The Irruption of Migrants: Theology of Migration in the 21st Century." *Theological Studies* 73, no. 1 (March 2012): 3–32.

Cannister, Mark. *Teenagers Matter: Making Student Ministry a Priority in the Church*. Grand Rapids: Baker Academic, 2013.

Cardoza, Freddy. "Perceptions of Ministerial Effectiveness by Leaders of Urban Churches in the Southern Baptist Convention." PhD diss., Southern Baptist Theological Seminary, 2005.

———. "Stewards of the Kingdom." *Deacon Magazine*, Winter 2015–16, 13–14.

———. "A Theology of Ministry." *Deacon Magazine: Theology*, 2015, 25–26.

Carr, Nicholas. *The Shallows: What the Internet Is Doing to Our Brains*. New York: W. W. Norton, 2011.

Carroll, Michael. "Huawei Predicts First 5G Networks Will Go Live in 2020." FierceWirelessEurope. February 11, 2014. http://www .fiercewireless.com/europe/story/huawei-pre dicts-first-5g-networks-will-go-live-2020/201 4-02-11.

Carson, D. A. "Matthew." In *Matthew, Mark, Luke*. Expositor's Bible Commentary. Edited by Frank E. Gaebelein. Grand Rapids: Zondervan, 1984.

———. "Praying for Parachurch Ministries." *9Marks Journal*, March–April 2011. https:// www.9marks.org/article/praying-parachurch -ministries/.

Chaffey, Dave. "Global Social Media Research Summary 2017." Smart Insights. April 27, 2017. http://www.smartinsights.com/social -media-marketing/social-media-strategy/new -global-social-media-research/.

Charan, Ram, Stephen Drotter, and James Noel. *The Leadership Pipeline*. San Francisco: John Wiley & Sons, 2011.

Cherry, Kendra. "Understanding Accommodation in Psychology." VeryWell Mind. Updated November 5, 2018. http://psychology.about .com/od/glossaryfromatoz/g/Accommodation .htm.

Chick, Nancy. "Metacognition." Vanderbilt University Center for Teaching. http://cft.vander bilt.edu/guides-sub-pages/metacognition/.

Chittister, Joan. *The Sacred In-Between: Spiritual Wisdom for Life's Every Moment*. New London, CT: Twenty-Third Publications, 2013.

"Choosing a New Church or House of Worship." Pew Research Center. August 23, 2016. http://www.pewforum.org/2016/08/23/choos ing-a-new-church-or-house-of-worship/.

Christensen, Clayton M. *The Innovator's Dilemma: When New Technologies Cause Great Firms to Fail*. Boston: Harvard Business School Press, 1997.

"Church Planters and the Cost of Starting a Church." Barna. April 26, 2016. https://www .barna.com/research/church-planters-and-the -cost-of-starting-a-church/.

Clapp, Rodney. *Families at the Crossroads*. Downers Grove, IL: InterVarsity, 1993.

Clark, Chap, ed. *Adoptive Youth Ministry*. Grand Rapids: Baker Academic, 2016.

———. "Creating a Place for a New Generation: An Ecclesiological Perspective on Youth Ministry." *Christian Education Journal* 3, no. 2 (Fall 1999): 97.

———. *Hurt: Inside the World of Today's Teenagers*. Grand Rapids: Baker Academic, 2004.

Clark, Francis E. *World-Wide Endeavor: The Story of the Young People's Society of Christian Endeavor, from the Beginning and in All Lands*. Philadelphia, 1895.

Clark, Robert E., Lin Johnson, and Allyn K. Sloat, eds. *Christian Education: Foundations for the Future*. Chicago: Moody, 1991.

Clydesdale, Tim. "Abandoned, Pursued, or Safely Stowed?" Social Science Research Council. February 6, 2007. http:// www.ssrc.org.

Coleman, Robert E. *The Master Plan of Evangelism*. Old Tappan, NJ: Revell, 1964.

Coley, Kenneth S. "Active Learning Techniques in the Christian Education Classroom and in Ministry Contexts." *Christian Education Journal* 9, no. 2 (2012): 357–71.

———. *Teaching for Change: Eight Keys for Transformational Bible Study with Teens*. Nashville: Randall House, 2016.

Collins, Jim. *Good to Great*. New York: HarperCollins, 2001.

Collins, Kenneth. J. "What Is Spirituality? Historical and Methodological Considerations." *Wesleyan Theological Journal* 1 (1996): 76–94.

"The Common Sense Census: Media Use by Tweens and Teens." Common Sense Media. 2015. https://www.commonsensemedia.org/re search/the-common-sense-census-media-use -by-tweens-and-teens.

Conn, Harvie M. *The American City and the Evangelical Church: A Historical Overview*. Grand Rapids: Baker, 1994.

———. "Christian Social Ministry: What's the Problem?" *Urban Mission* 14, no. 1 (1996): 6–18.

Conn, Harvie M., and Manuel Ortiz. *Urban Ministry: The Kingdom, the City and the People of God*. Downers Grove, IL: InterVarsity, 2001.

Connors, Tracy Daniel, ed. *The Volunteer Management Handbook*. 2nd ed. Hoboken, NJ: Wiley & Sons, 2012.

Craig, William Lane. "Concluding Thoughts on the Two Tasks of the Christian Scholar." In *The Two Tasks of the Christian Scholar: Redeeming the Soul, Redeeming the Mind,* edited by William Lane Craig and Paul M. Gould, 177–90. Wheaton: Crossway, 2007.

Crosby, Brian. "The Reformed View of Youth Ministry." In *Youth Ministry in the 21st Century: Five Views of Youth Ministry*, edited by Chap Clark, 37–52. Grand Rapids: Baker Academic, 2015.

———. "Responses to the Gospel Advancing View." In *Youth Ministry in the 21st Century: Five Views of Youth Ministry*, edited by Chap Clark, 17–20. Grand Rapids: Baker Academic, 2015.

Cross, F. L. "Adoptianism." In *The Oxford Dictionary of the Christian Church*, edited by F. L. Cross and E. A. Livingstone, 19–20. New York: Oxford University Press, 2005.

———. "Nestorius." In *The Oxford Dictionary of the Christian Church*, edited by F. L. Cross and E. A. Livingstone, 1145–46. New York: Oxford University Press, 2005.

Crouch, Andy. *Culture Making: Recovering Our Creative Calling*. Downers Grove, IL: Inter-Varsity, 2013.

———. *Playing God: Redeeming the Gift of Power*. Downers Grove, IL: InterVarsity, 2013.

Cummings-Bond, Stuart. "The One-Eared Mickey Mouse." *Youthworker* 6 (Fall 1989): 76–78.

Daley, Brian. *The Hope of the Early Church: A Handbook of Patristic Eschatology*. Grand Rapids: Baker Academic, 1991.

Daman, Glenn, and Brian Weschler. *The Forgotten Church: Why Rural Ministry Matters for Every Church in America*. Chicago: Moody, 2018.

Dean, Kenda Creasy. *Almost Christian: What the Faith of Our Teenagers Is Telling the American Church*. New York: Oxford University Press, 2010.

DeKruyter, Arthur H., with Quentin J. Schultze. *The Suburban Church: Practical Advice for Authentic Ministry*. Louisville: Westminster John Knox, 2008.

DeSilva, David A. *The Sacramental Life: Spiritual Formation through the Book of Common Prayer*. Downers Grove, IL: InterVarsity, 2008.

DeVries, Mark. *Family-Based Youth Ministry*. Downers Grove, IL: InterVarsity, 1994.

———. *Sustainable Youth Ministry*. Downers Grove, IL: InterVarsity Press, 2008.

Dewey, John. *The Child and the Curriculum*. New York: Macmillan, 1902.

———. *Experience and Education*. New York: Collier, 1938.

———. "My Pedagogic Creed." *The School Journal* 54 (1897): 77–80.

DeYoung, Rebecca Konyndyk. *Glittering Vices: A New Look at the Seven Deadly Sins and Their Remedies*. Grand Rapids: Brazos, 2009.

———. "Pedagogical Rhythms: Practices and Reflections on Practice." In *Teaching and Christian Practices: Reshaping Faith and Learning*, edited by David I. Smith and James K. A. Smith, 24–42. Grand Rapids: Eerdmans, 2011.

Dillon, J. T. *Jesus as a Teacher: A Multidisciplinary Case Study*. Berkeley: University of California Press, 1995.

Dirkx, John M. "Engaging Emotions in Adult Learning: A Jungian Perspective on Emotion and Transformative Learning." In *Teaching for Change: Fostering Transformative Learning in the Classroom*, edited by Edward W. Taylor, 15–26. San Francisco: Jossey-Bass, 2006.

Dockery, David S. *Renewing Minds*. Nashville: B&H Academic, 2007.

Dodson, Jonathan K. *Gospel-Centered Discipleship*. Wheaton: Crossway, 2012.

Donahue, Bill. *Leading Life-Changing Small Groups*. Rev. ed. Grand Rapids: Zondervan, 2002.

Donston-Miller, Debra. "7 Ways to Create E-Portfolios." InformationWeek. July 9, 2013. http://www.informationweek.com/software /7-ways-to-create-e-portfolios/d/d-id/1110673?

Downs, Perry. *Teaching for Spiritual Growth: An Introduction to Christian Education.* Grand Rapids: Zondervan, 1994.

Dujarier, Michael. *A History of the Catechumenate: The First Six Centuries.* New York: William H. Sadlier, 1979.

Duncum, I., M. Pepper, N. Hancock, and R. Powell. "A Comparison of the Vitality of Monocultural and Multicultural Churches." NCLS Research *Occasional Paper* 24. Waterloo, New South Wales: 2014.

Dunn, Paul. "Researching and Profiling American Single Adults to Create a Ministry Launch Guide for American Churches." DMin project, New Orleans Baptist Theological Seminary, 2016.

Dunn, Richard R. "Putting Youth Ministry into Perspective." In *Reaching a Generation for Christ*, edited by Richard R. Dunn and Mark Senter, 25–44. Chicago: Moody, 1997.

Dunn, Richard R., and Jana Sundene. *Shaping the Journey of Emerging Adults: Life-Giving Rhythms for Spiritual Transformation.* Downers Grove, IL: InterVarsity, 2012.

Dweck, Carol S. *Mindset: The New Psychology of Success.* New York: Random House, 2006.

Eavey, Charles B. *History of Christian Education.* Chicago: Moody, 1964.

Edge, Findley B. *Teaching for Results.* Nashville: Broadman & Holman, 1995.

Edlin, Richard. "Core Beliefs and Values of a Christian Philosophy of Education." In *Foundations of Christian School Education*, edited by J. Braley, J. Layman, and R. White, 67–82. Colorado Springs: Purposeful Design, 2003.

Edwards, Harriett C. "Orientation: Welcoming New Volunteers to the Organization." In *The Volunteer Management Handbook: Leadership Strategies for Success*, edited by Tracy Daniel Connors, 227–36. Hoboken: John Wiley & Sons, 2012.

Edwards, Steven. "10 Things You Didn't Know about the World's Population." United Nations Population Fund. https://www.unfpa .org/news/10-things-you-didn%E2%80%99t -know-about-world%E2%80%99s-popula tion.

"Effective Use of Learning Objectives." *Teacher & Educational Development*, 2005. https:// www.slideshare.net/CristleAnnRivera/effective -use-of-learning-objectives.

Eggen, Paul, and Don Kauchak. *Educational Psychology: Classroom Connections.* 2nd ed. New York: Macmillan College, 1994.

———. *Educational Psychology: Windows on Classrooms.* 7th ed. Columbus, OH: Pearson Education, 2007.

Eisner, David, Robert T. Grimm Jr., Shannon Maynard, and Susannah Washburn. "The New Volunteer Workforce." *Stanford Social Innovation Review*, Winter 2009, 32–37.

Elliot, Stephen N., Thomas R. Kratochwill, Joan Littlefield Cook, and John F. Travers. *Educational Psychology: Effective Teaching, Effective Learning.* Boston: McGraw-Hill, 2000.

Elmore, Tim, with Andrew McPeak. *Marching off the Map: Inspire Students to Navigate a Brand New World.* Atlanta: Poet Gardener Publishing, 2017. Kindle.

Erickson, Millard J. *Christian Theology.* Grand Rapids: Baker, 1986.

Erikson, Erik. *Childhood and Society.* 2nd ed. New York: W. W. Norton, 1963.

———. *Identity: Youth in Crisis.* New York: W. W. Norton, 1968.

Erwin, Pamela. *A Critical Approach to Youth Culture: Its Influence and Implications for Ministry.* Grand Rapids: Zondervan, 2010.

Espinoza, Benjamin D., and Beverly Johnson-Miller. "Catechesis, Developmental Theory, and a Fresh Vision for Christian Education." *Christian Education Journal* 11, no. 1 (2014): 8–23.

Esqueda, Octavio J. "Biblical Worldview: The Christian Higher Education Foundation for

Learning." *Christian Higher Education* 13, no. 2 (2014): 91–100.

———. "God as Teacher." In *The Teaching Ministry of the Church*, edited by William R. Yount, 31–44. 2nd ed. Nashville: Broadman & Holman, 2008.

———. "The Holy Spirit as Teacher." In *The Teaching Ministry of the Church*, edited by William R. Yount, 74–87. 2nd ed. Nashville: Broadman & Holman, 2008.

———. "Sin and Christian Teaching." *Christian Education Journal* 8, no. 1 (2011): 164–76.

Estep, James R., Jr. "Among the Hebrews and Ancient Judaism." In *C. E.: The Heritage of Christian Education*, edited by James Riley Estep Jr. Joplin, MO: College Press, 2003.

———. "Biblical Principles for a Theology of Christian Education." In *A Theology for Christian Education*, by James R. Estep Jr., Michael J. Anthony, and Gregg R. Allison, 44–72. Nashville: Broadman & Holman, 2008.

———, ed. *C. E: The Heritage of Christian Education*. Joplin, MO: College Press, 2003.

———. "Conducting Performance Reviews." In *Management Essentials for Christian Ministries*, edited by Michael J. Anthony and James R. Estep Jr., 387–409. Nashville: Broadman & Holman, 2005.

———. "Leadership Strategies." In *Management Essentials for Christian Ministries*, edited by Michael J. Anthony and James R. Estep Jr., 349–64. Nashville: Broadman & Holman, 2005.

———. "Philosophers, Scribes, Rhetors . . . and Paul? The Educational Background of the New Testament." *Christian Education Journal* 2, no. 1 (2005): 30–47.

———. "A Theology of Administration." In *Management Essentials for Christian Ministries*, edited by Michael J. Anthony and James R. Estep Jr., 35–52. Nashville: Broadman & Holman, 2005.

———. "Toward a Theologically Informed Approach to Education." In *A Theology for Christian Education*, by James R. Estep Jr., Michael J. Anthony, and Gregg R. Allison, 264–95. Nashville: Broadman & Holman, 2008.

———. "Transforming Groups into Teams." In *Management Essentials for Christian Ministries*, edited by Michael J. Anthony and James R. Estep Jr., 333–48. Nashville: Broadman & Holman, 2005.

———. "Wesley's Educational Ideal at Kingswood and the Modern Christian School." *Journal of Christian Education and Information Technology* 14 (2008): 55–72.

Estep, James R., and Jonathan H. Kim, eds. *Christian Formation*. Nashville: B&H, 2010.

Estep, James R. Jr., Michael J. Anthony, and Gregg R. Allison. *A Theology for Christian Education*. Nashville: Broadman & Holman, 2008.

Etling, A. "What Is Nonformal Education?" *Journal of Agricultural Education* 34, no. 4 (1993): 72–77.

Etzel, Gabriel, Timothy Paul Jones, Chris Jackson, and John Cartwright. *Teaching the World: Foundations for Online Theological Education*. Nashville: B&H Academic, 2017.

"Fact Sheet: Aging in the United States." Population Reference Bureau. January 2016. http://www.prb.org/Publications/Media-Guides/2016/aging-unitedstates-fact-sheet.aspx.

Felder, Richard M. "Teaching Teachers to Teach: The Case for Mentoring." *Chemical Engineering Education* 27 (1993): 176–77.

Felder, Richard M., and Rebecca Brent. "Active Learning: An Introduction." *ASQ Higher Education Brief* 2, no. 4 (2009): 1–5.

Ferriman, Justin. "20 Most Popular Learning Management Systems." LearnDash. December 5, 2016. http://www.learndash.com/20-most-popular-learning-management-systems-infographic/.

Fink, Dee L. "A Self-Directed Guide to Designing Courses for Significant Learning." Fink Consulting. 2005. https://www.bu.edu/sph/files/2014/03/www.deefinkandassociates.com_GuidetoCourseDesignAug05.pdf.

Ford, Leighton. *Transformational Leadership.* Downers Grove, IL: InterVarsity, 1991.

Foster, Richard J. *Celebration of Discipline.* San Francisco: HarperCollins, 1978.

———. *Celebration of Discipline: The Path to Spiritual Growth.* 20th anniversary ed. San Francisco: Harper, 1998.

———, ed. *Devotional Classics: Selected Readings for Individuals and Groups.* San Francisco: HarperOne, 2005.

Fowler, James. *Stages of Faith.* New York: HarperCollins, 1981.

———. *Stages of Faith: The Psychology of Human Development and the Quest for Meaning.* San Francisco: HarperOne, 1995.

Frankena, W. K., ed. *Philosophy of Education.* New York: Macmillan, 1965.

Fraser, Craig J. "The Religious Instruction of the Laity in Late Medieval England with Particular Reference to the Sacrament of the Eucharist." DPhil diss., Oxford University, 1995.

Fraser, Robert E. *Marketplace Christianity: Discovering the Kingdom Purposes of the Marketplace.* Overland Park, KS: New Grid, 2004.

Freire, Paulo. *Pedagogy of the Oppressed.* New York: Continuum, 1970.

Freudenburg, Ben, with Rick Lawrence. *The Family-Friendly Church.* Loveland, CO: Group Publishing, 2009.

Fuder, John E. *Training Students for Urban Ministry: An Experiential Approach.* Eugene, OR: Wipf & Stock, 2001.

Fuder, John, and Noel Castellanos. *A Heart for the Community: New Models for Urban and Suburban Ministry.* Chicago: Moody, 2013.

"Future World Population Growth to Be Concentrated in Urban Areas of World." United Nations. March 21, 2002. http://www.un.org/esa/populationpublications/wup2001/WUP2001-pressrelease.pdf.

Gangel, Kenneth O. "Biblical Foundations of Education." In *Foundations of Christian School Education,* edited by J. Braley, J. Layman, and R. White, 55–65. Colorado Springs: Purposeful Design, 2003.

———. "What Christian Education Is." In *Christian Education: Foundations for the Future,* edited by Robert E. Clark, Lin Johnson, and Allyn K. Sloat, 13–29. Chicago: Moody, 1991.

Gangel, Kenneth O., and Warren S. Benson. *Christian Education: Its History and Philosophy.* Chicago: Moody, 1982.

Gangel, Kenneth O., and James Wilhoit. *The Christian Educator's Handbook on Family Life Education.* Grand Rapids: Baker, 1996.

Gannett, Lynn. "Teaching for Learning." In *Christian Education: Foundations for the Future,* edited by Robert E. Clark, Lin Johnson, and Allyn K. Sloat, 105–19. Chicago: Moody, 1991.

Garber, Steve. *The Fabric of Faithfulness: Weaving Together Belief and Behavior.* Downers Grove, IL: InterVarsity, 1996.

Gardner, Howard. *Multiple Intelligences: New Horizons.* New York: Basic Books, 2006.

Garland, Diana. *Family Ministry: A Comprehensive Guide.* Rev. ed. Downers Grove, IL: InterVarsity, 2012.

Garrison, D. R., and Norman D. Vaughan. *Blended Learning in Higher Education: Framework, Principles, and Guidelines.* San Francisco: Jossey-Bass, 2008.

George, Carl F., and Warren Bird. *How to Break Growth Barriers: Revise Your Role, Release Your People, and Capture Overlooked Opportunities for Your Church.* Updated ed. Grand Rapids: Baker Books, 2017.

González, Justo L. *The History of Theological Education.* Nashville: Abingdon, 2015.

Green, Ian. *The Christian's ABC: Catechisms and Catechizing in England, c. 1530–1740.* Oxford: Clarendon, 1996.

Greenway, Roger S., ed. *Guidelines for Urban Church Planting.* Grand Rapids: Baker, 1976.

Greer, Peter, and Chris Horst. *Mission Drift.* Bloomington, MN: Bethany, 2014.

Gregory, John Milton. *The Seven Laws of Teaching.* Lancaster, PA: Veritas Press, 2004.

Griffiths, Paul J. "From Curiosity to Studiousness: Catechizing the Appetite for Learning." In *Teaching and Christian Practices: Reshaping Faith and Learning,* edited by David I. Smith and James K. A. Smith, 102–22. Grand Rapids: Eerdmans, 2011.

Griggs, Donnie. *Small Town Jesus: Taking the Gospel Mission Seriously in Seemingly Unimportant Places.* Damascus, MD: Everyday Truth Publishers, 2016.

Groome, Thomas H. Foreword to *Christian Education as Evangelism,* edited by Norma Cook Everist, xi–xii. Minneapolis: Fortress, 2007.

Guillaume, Andrea M., Ruth Helen Yopp, and Hallie Kay Yopp. *50 Strategies for Active Teaching: Engaging K–12 Learners in the Classroom.* Upper Saddle River, NJ: Pearson Merrill Prentice-Hall, 2007.

Habermas, Ronald T., and Klaus Issler. *Teaching for Reconciliation.* Grand Rapids: Baker, 1992.

Hagberg, Janet O., and Robert A. Guelich. *The Critical Journey: Stages in the Life of Faith.* 2nd ed. Salem, WI: Sheffield, 2005.

Hall, G. Stanley. *Adolescence: Its Psychology and Its Relations to Physiology, Anthropology, Sociology, Sex, Crime, Religion, and Education.* New York: Appleton, 1904.

Halverson, Delia. *Ready, Set, Teach! Training and Supporting Volunteers in Christian Education.* Nashville: Abingdon, 2010.

Hammett, John. "How Church and Parachurch Should Relate: Arguments for a Servant-Partnership Model." *Missiology* 28, no. 2 (April 2001): 199–207.

Hardy, Doug. "Lectio Divina: A Practice for Reconnecting to God's Word." *Preacher's Magazine: A Preaching Resource in the Wesleyan Tradition* (2009): 38–41.

Harmless, William. *Augustine and the Catechumenate.* Collegeville, MN: Liturgical Press, 1995.

Hawkins, Greg L. *Move: What 1,000 Churches Reveal about Spiritual Growth.* Grand Rapids: Zondervan, 2011.

Hawkins, Greg L., and Cally Parkinson. *Reveal: Where Are You?* Chicago: Willowcreek Resources, 2007.

Hay, Maciamo. "The New Technologies That Will Change Human Civilization as We Know It." *H+ Magazine,* May 13, 2014. http://hplus magazine.com/2014/05/13/the-new-technolog ies-that-will-change-human-civilization-as-we -know-it/.

Hayes, Brian. *Shift: What It Takes to Finally Reach Families Today.* Loveland, CO: Group Publishing, 2009.

He, Wan, Daniel Goodkind, and Paul Kowal. "An Aging World: 2015." International Population Reports. US Census Bureau. March 2016. https://www.census.gov/content/dam/Census /library/publications/2016/demo/p95-16-1.pdf.

Hebbard, Don. *The Complete Handbook for Family Life Ministry in the Church.* Nashville: Thomas Nelson, 1995.

Hellerman, Joseph. *When the Church Was a Family: Recapturing Jesus' Vision for Authentic Christian Community.* Nashville: B&H, 2009.

Hendricks, Howard B. *Teaching to Change Lives.* Portland, OR: Multnomah, 1987.

Hippolytus. *On the Apostolic Tradition.* Translated by Alistair Stewart-Sykes. New York: St. Vladimir's Seminary Press, 2001.

"Home School Families and Home School Co-ops." Homeschool Central. http://homeschool central.com/articles/homeschool_coops.htm.

Hood, Mary Kay. "Training Volunteers." In *The Volunteer Management Handbook: Leadership Strategies for Success*, edited by Tracy Daniel Connors, 237–54. Hoboken, NJ: John Wiley & Sons, 2012.

Hoover, Christine. *The Church Planting Wife*. Chicago: Moody, 2013.

"How to Write Program Objectives/Outcomes." https://www.diabeteseducator.org/docs/default-source/education-and-career/ce-program-accreditation/howtowriteobjectivesoutcomes.pdf?sfvrsn=2%20.

Hull, Bill. *The Complete Book of Discipleship: On Being and Making Followers of Christ*. Colorado Springs: NavPress, 2006.

Hunt, T. C., K. M. Ristau, and M. A. Grant. "Catholic Schools." In *Religious Schools in the United States, K–12*, edited by Thomas C. Hunt and James C. Carper, 127–202. New York: Garland, 1993.

Hunter, James Davidson. *To Change the World:The Irony, Tragedy, and Possibility of Christianity on the Late Modern World*. New York: Oxford University Press, 2010.

Hunter, Madeline. *Enhancing Teaching*. New York: Pearson, 1994.

Hybels, Bill, and Mark Mittelberg. *Becoming a Contagious Christian*. Grand Rapids: Zondervan, 1994.

Irving, Paul H., ed. *The Upside of Aging*. Hoboken, NJ: John Wiley & Sons, 2014.

Issler, Klaus. *Wasting Time with God: A Christian Spirituality of Friendship with God*. Downers Grove, IL: InterVarsity, 2001.

Issler, Klaus, and Ronald Habermas. *How We Learn: A Christian Teacher's Guide to Educational Psychology*. Grand Rapids: Baker, 1994.

Jackson, Allen. "Theology and Youth Ministry: Then and Now." *Journal of Baptist Theology and Ministry* 13, no. 1 (Spring 2016): 34–47.

Jackson, Robyn Renee. *Never Work Harder than Your Students, and Other Principles of Great Teaching*. Alexandria, VA: ASCD, 2009.

Jay, Meg. *The Defining Decade: Why Your Twenties Matter and How to Make the Most of Them Now*. New York: Twelve, 2012.

Jensen, Robin. *Understanding Early Christian Art*. London: Routledge, 2000.

Johnson, L. Ted. *The Teaching Church*. Arlington Heights, IL: Harvest Publications, 1984.

Jones, E. Stanley. *Mastery: The Art of Mastering Life*. Nashville: Abingdon, 1991.

Jones, Paul W. *The Art of Spiritual Direction: Giving and Receiving Spiritual Guidance*. Nashville: Upper Room, 2002.

Jones, Timothy Paul, ed. *Perspectives on Family Ministry: Three Views*. Nashville: B&H, 2009.

Jones, Timothy Paul, and Randy Stinson. "Family Ministry Models." In *A Theology for Family Ministries*, edited by Michael Anthony and Michelle Anthony, 155–80. Nashville: B&H Academic, 2011.

Jones, Tony. *The Sacred Way: Spiritual Practices for Everyday Life*. Grand Rapids: Zondervan, 2005.

Jung, Joanne J. *Godly Conversation: Rediscovering the Puritan Practice of Conference*. Grand Rapids: Reformed Heritage Books, 2011.

Justins, Charles. "Christian Schooling and Educational Excellence: An Australian Perspective." *Journal of Education & Christian Belief* 13, no. 1 (Spring 2009): 49–64.

Keehn, David. "Youth Ministry from a Family Perspective." In *A Theology for Family Ministries*, edited by Michael Anthony and Michelle Anthony, 223–40. Nashville: B&H Academic, 2011.

Keller, Timothy. *Center Church: Doing Balanced, Gospel-Centered Ministry in Your City*. Grand Rapids: Zondervan, 2012.

Kelly, Paul. "A Theology of Youth." *Journal of Baptist Theology and Ministry* 13, no. 1 (Spring 2016): 3–19.

Ketcham, Sharon Galgay. "Faith Formation with Others." In *Teaching the Next Generations: A Comprehensive Guide for Teaching Christian Formation*, edited by Terry Linhart, 100–111. Grand Rapids: Baker Academic, 2016.

Khurana, Rakesh. *From Higher Aims to Hired Hands: The Social Transformation of American Business Schools and the Unfulfilled Promise of Management as a Profession.* Princeton: Princeton University Press, 2010.

Kienel, Paul A. *A History of Christian School Education.* Vols. 1–2. Colorado Springs: Purposeful Design, 2005.

Kiesling, Chris, and Victor Rosza. "Campus Ministry." In *Encyclopedia of Christian Education*, vol. 1, edited by George Kurian and Mark Lamport, 184–85. Lanham, MD: Rowman & Littlefield, 2015.

Kim, Jonathan. "The Early Church: Education of Heart and Mind." In *C. E.: The Heritage of Christian Education*, edited by James Riley Estep Jr. Joplin, MO: College Press, 2003.

Kinnaman, David, with Aly Hawkins. *You Lost Me: Why Young Christians Are Leaving Church . . . and Rethinking Faith.* Grand Rapids: Baker Books, 2011.

Kinnaman, David, and Gabe Lyons. *unChristian: What a New Generation Really Thinks about Christianity . . . and Why It Matters.* Grand Rapids: Baker Books, 2007.

Kjesbo, Denise. "Five Models of Family Ministry." Paper presented at Northwest Christian Education Conference, Overlake Christian Church, Redmond, WA, March 26–28, 2009.

Knight, G. *Philosophy and Education: An Introduction in Christian Perspective.* Berrien Springs, MI: Andrews University Press, 2006.

Knowles, Malcolm S. *The Modern Practice of Adult Education: From Pedagogy to Andragogy.* New York: Cambridge University Press, 1980.

Knowles, Malcolm S., Elwood F. Holton, and Richard Swanson. *The Adult Learner.* New York: Routledge, 2012.

Kolb, David A., and Ronald Fry. "Towards an Applied Theory of Experiential Learning." In *Theories of Group Practice*, edited by C. Cooper, 33–57. New York: John Wiley, 1975.

Kolb, David A., I. M. Rubin, and J. M. McIntyre. *Organizational Psychology: An Experiential Approach to Organizational Behavior.* 4th ed. Englewood Cliffs, NJ: Prentice-Hall, 1984.

Kouzes, James M., and Barry Z. Posner. *The Leadership Challenge.* 4th ed. San Francisco: Jossey-Bass, 2007.

———. *Learning Leaders.* San Francisco: Wiley, 2016.

Krathwohl, David R. *Taxonomy of Educational Objectives: The Classification of Educational Goals.* New York: Longman, 1984.

"Kubernēsis." Bible Tools. 2019. https://www.bibletools.org/index.cfm/fuseaction/Lexicon.show/ID/G2941/kubernesis.htm.

Lambert, Dan. *Teaching That Makes a Difference.* Grand Rapids: Zondervan, 2010.

Lanker, Jason. "Francis E. Clark: Founder of Christian Endeavor." *Christian Education Journal* 11, no. 2 (2014): 383–91.

Lawson, Kevin E. "Baptismal Theology and Practices and the Spiritual Nurture of Children, Part I: Early and Medieval Church." *Christian Education Journal* 8, no. 1 (2011): 135–39.

———. "Historical Foundations of Christian Education." In *Introducing Christian Education: Foundations for the Twenty-First Century*, edited by Michael J. Anthony, 17–25. Grand Rapids: Baker Academic, 2001.

———. "Learning the Faith in England in the Later Middle Ages: Contributions of the Franciscan Friars." *Religious Education* 107 (2012): 144–54.

———. "More than Silent Preaching: Didactic Use of Wall Painting in the Middle Ages." *Christian Education Journal* 11, no. 2 (2014): 327–30.

Lawson, Kevin E., and Mick Boersma. *Supervising and Supporting Ministry Staff*. Lanham, MD: Rowman & Littlefield, 2017.

Lawson, Kevin E., and James Wilhoit. "SPCE Report of the Core Curriculum Task Force: Expanded Executive Summary." *Christian Education Journal* 11, no. 2 (2014): 276–93.

Lawson, Michael S. "Biblical Foundations for a Philosophy of Teaching." In *The Christian Educator's Handbook on Teaching: A Comprehensive Resource on the Distinctiveness of True Christian Teaching*, edited by Kenneth O. Gangel and Howard G. Hendricks, 61–73. Grand Rapids: Baker, 1988.

———. *Grandpa Mike Talks about God*. Fearn, Tain, Scotland: Christian Focus Publications, 2007.

LeBar, Lois E. *Education That Is Christian*. Colorado Springs: Chariot Victor, 1995.

LeFrancois, Guy R. *Psychology for Teaching*. 8th ed. Belmont, CA: Wadsworth, 1994.

Lenhart, Amanda. "Teens, Technology and Friendships." Pew Research Center. August 6, 2015. http://www.pewinternet.org/2015/08/06/teens-technology-and-friendships/.

Lewis, Dina, and Barbara Allan. *Virtual Learning Communities: A Guide for Practitioners*. Berkshire, UK: Open University Press, 2005.

Lewis, Gordon R., and Bruce A. Demarest. *Integrative Theology*. 3 vols. Grand Rapids: Zondervan, 1996.

Leyda, Richard J. "Parachurch Ministries." In *Foundations of Ministry: An Introduction to Christian Education for a New Generation*, edited by Michael J. Anthony, 310–29. Grand Rapids: Baker Academic, 1992.

Lockerbie, D. Bruce. *A Passion for Learning: A History of Christian Thought on Education*. Colorado Springs: Purposeful Design, 2007.

Logan, F. Donald. *A History of the Church in the Middle Ages*. New York: Routledge, 2002.

Longenecker, Richard N. *Acts*. Expositor's Bible Commentary 9. Edited by Frank E. Gaebelein. Grand Rapids: Zondervan, 1981.

Louw, Johannes P., and Eugene A. Nida. *Greek-English Lexicon of the New Testament: Based on Semantic Domains*. New York: United Bible Societies, 1996.

Lucas, Christopher J. *American Higher Education: A History*. New York: Palgrave Macmillan, 2006.

MacCullough, Martha Elizabeth. *By Design: Developing a Philosophy of Education Informed by a Christian Worldview*. Langhorne, PA: Cairn University, 2013.

Maddix, Mark A. "Living the Life: Spiritual Formation Defined." In *Spiritual Formation: A Wesleyan Paradigm*, edited by Diane Leclerc and Mark A. Maddix, 9–17. Kansas City, MO: Beacon Hill, 2010.

———. "Spiritual Formation and Christian Formation." In *Christian Formation: Integrating Theology and Human Development*, edited by James R. Estep and Jonathan H. Kim, 237–72. Nashville: B&H Academic, 2010.

Maddix, Mark A., and Jay R. Akkerman, eds. *Missional Discipleship: Partners in God's Redemptive Mission*. Kansas City, MO: Beacon Hill, 2013.

Manning, Susan, and Kevin E. Johnson. *The Technology Toolbelt for Teaching*. San Francisco: Jossey-Bass, 2011.

Marthaler, Berard L. *The Catechism Yesterday and Today: The Evolution of a Genre*. Collegeville, MN: Liturgical Press, 1995.

Martin, Ralph P. *Worship in the Early Church*. Grand Rapids: Eerdmans, 1987.

Masci, David, and Michael Lipka. "Americans May Be Getting Less Religious, but Feelings of Spirituality Are on the Rise." Pew Research Center. http://www.pewresearch.org/fact-tank/2016/01/21/americans-spirituality/.

Mathison, Keith. "Historical and Theological Foundations." *TableTalk Magazine*, September 2014. https://tabletalkmagazine.com/article/2014/09/historical-and-theological-foundations/.

May, Scottie, Beth Posterski, Catherine Stonehouse, and Linda Cannell. *Children Matter: Celebrating Their Place in the Church, Family, and Community*. Grand Rapids: Eerdmans, 2005.

McGregor, Douglas M. "The Human Side of Enterprise." In *Adventure in Thought and Action, Proceedings of the Fifth Anniversary Convocation of the School of Industrial Management*. Cambridge: Massachusetts Institute of Technology, 1957.

McIntosh, Gary. *One Church, Four Generations: Understanding and Reaching All Ages in Your Church*. Grand Rapids: Baker Books, 2002.

McKee, Jonathan, and Thomas W. McKee. *The New Breed: Understanding and Equipping the 21st Century Volunteer*. Loveland, CO: Simply Youth Ministry, 2012.

McKenna, Laura. "The Big Idea That Can Revolutionize Higher Education: 'MOOC.'" *Atlantic*, May 11, 2012. http://www.theatlantic.com/business/archive/2012/05/the-big-idea-that-can-revolutionize-higher-education-mooc/256926/.

McKinney, Larry J. "The Church-Parachurch Conflict: A Proposed Solution." *Christian Education Journal* 10, no. 3 (Spring 1990): 73–80.

McMillan, Sally B. *To Raise Up the South: Sunday Schools in Black and White Churches, 1865–1915*. Baton Rouge: Louisiana State University Press, 2001.

McNeil, John D. *Contemporary Curriculum: In Thought and Action*. 7th ed. Hoboken, NJ: John Wiley & Sons, 2009.

Mears, Henrietta C. *431 Quotes from the Notes of Henrietta Mears*. Edited by E. L. Doan. Glendale, CA: Regal, 1970.

Melick, Rick, and Shera Melick. *Teaching That Transforms: Facilitating Life Change Through Adult Bible Teaching*. Nashville: B&H, 2010.

Menijoff, Aaron. "Are Parachurch Ministries Evil? Bad and Good Arguments for the Parachurch." *9Marks Journal* (March–April 2011). https://www.9marks.org/article/are-parachurch-ministries-evil-bad-and-good-arguments-parachurch/.

Mercer, Joyce Ann. "Emerging Scholarship on Youth and Religion: Resources for a New Generation of Youth Ministry." *Journal of Baptist Theology and Ministry* 13, no. 1 (Spring 2016): 77.

Meyer, H. H. "Education." In *The International Standard Bible Encyclopedia*, vol. 2, edited by James Orr. Grand Rapids: Eerdmans, 1957.

Mezirow, Jack. *Transformative Dimensions of Adult Learning*. San Francisco: Jossey-Bass, 1991.

Milavec, Aaron. *The Didache: Faith, Hope, and Life of the Earliest Christian Communities, 50–70 C.E.* New York: Paulist Press, 2003.

Miller, M. Rex. *The Millennium Matrix*. San Francisco: Jossey-Bass, 2004.

Mitchell, Clare J. A. "Counterurbanization and the Growth of Canada's Rural and Small Town Municipalities." *Canadian Journal of Regional Science* 31 (2008): 117–32.

Mocker, Donald W., and George E. Spear. "Lifelong Learning: Formal, Nonformal, Informal, and Self-Directed." ERIC Clearinghouse on Adult, Career, and Vocational Education. 1982. http://files.eric.ed.gov/fulltext/ED220723.pdf.

Moore, Russell D., and Robert E. Sagers. "The Kingdom of God and the Church: A Baptist Reassessment." *Southern Baptist Journal of Theology* 12, no. 1 (Spring 2008): 68–86.

Moreland, James P., and William Lane Craig. *Philosophical Foundations for a Christian Worldview*. Downers Grove, IL: InterVarsity, 2003.

Moreland, James P., and Klaus Issler. *In Search of a Confident Faith: Overcoming Barriers to Trusting in God*. Downers Grove, IL: InterVarsity, 2008.

Mounce, William D., gen. ed. *Mounce's Complete Expository Dictionary of Old and New Testament Words*. Grand Rapids: Zondervan, 2006.

Mouw, Richard J. *He Shines in All That's Fair: Culture and Common Grace*. Grand Rapids: Eerdmans, 2001.

Mueller, Walt. *Engaging the Soul of Youth Culture: Bridging Teen Worldviews and Christian Truth*. Downers Grove, IL: InterVarsity, 2006.

Mulholland, M. Robert Jr. *Invitation to a Journey: A Road Map for Spiritual Formation*. Downers Grove, IL: InterVarsity, 1993.

———. *Shaped by the Word: The Power of Scripture in Spiritual Formation*. Nashville: Upper Room, 2001.

Nagy, Jenette, Bill Berkowitz, and Eric Wadud. "Developing Volunteer Orientation Programs." Community ToolBox. https://ctb.ku .edu/en/table-of-contents/structure/volunteers /orientation-programs/main.

Naugle, David K. *Worldview: The History of a Concept*. Grand Rapids: Eerdmans, 2002.

Neihof, John. "Social Justice or Biblical Justice?" American Family Association. November 2, 2017. https://www.afa.net/the-stand/faith/201 7/11/social-justice-or-biblical-justice/.

"New Census Data Show Differences between Urban and Rural Populations (Release Number: CB16-210)." US Census Bureau. 2016. https://www.census.gov/newsroom/press-re leases/2016/cb16-210.html.

Newport, Frank. "Five Key Findings on Religion in the US." Gallup. December 23, 2016. http:// www.gallup.com/poll/200186/five-key-find ings-religion.aspx.

Newton, Gary C. *Heart-Deep Teaching: Engaging Students for Transformed Lives*. Nashville: B&H Academic, 2012.

———. "Nonformal Education." In *Evangelical Dictionary of Christian Education*, edited by M. J. Anthony, W. S. Benson, D. Eldridge, and J. Gorman, 505–6. Grand Rapids: Baker Academic, 2001.

Ninde, H. S., J. T. Bowne, and Uhl Erskine, eds. *A Hand-Book of the History, Organization, and Methods of Work of Young Men's Christian Associations*. New York: The International Committee of Young Men's Christian Associations, 1892.

Noddings, Nel. *Philosophy of Education*. Boulder, CO: Westview, 1998.

Noffsinger, John. *Correspondence Schools*. New York: Macmillan, 1926.

"Nonprofit Survival Guide: How to Manage Volunteers." Asia Catalyst. http://asiacatalyst .org/wp-content/uploads/2015/07/NPSG _EN.pdf.

O'Dell, Shannon. *Transforming Church in Rural America*. Green Forest, AR: New Leaf Press, 2010.

Odom, David. "Ministry Leadership with Emerging Adults." In *Together We Equip: Integrating Disciple and Ministry Leadership for Holistic Spiritual Formation*, edited by Jody Dean and Hal Stewart, 137–51. Bloomington, IN: WestBow, 2018.

Ogden, Greg. *Transforming Discipleship*. Downers Grove, IL: InterVarsity, 2003.

"Older Persons' Health." National Center for Health Statistics, Centers for Disease Control and Prevention. http://www.cdc.gov/nchs /fastats/older-american-health.htm.

Orme, Nicholas. *Medieval Children*. New Haven: Yale University Press, 2001.

Ormrod, Jeanne Ellis. *Educational Psychology: Developing Learners*. 5th ed. Columbus, OH: Pearson Education, 2006.

Ornstein, Allan C., and Francis P. Hunkins. *Curriculum: Foundations, Principles, and Issues*. 5th ed. Boston: Pearson, 2009.

Ortman, Jennifer M., Victoria A. Velkoff, and Howard Hogan. "An Aging Nation: The Older Population in the United States." United States Census Bureau. May 2014. https://www.census.gov/prod/2014pubs/p25-1140.pdf.

Osmer, Richard Robert. *The Teaching Ministry of Congregations.* Louisville: Westminster John Knox, 2005.

Ozmon, Howard A., and Samuel M. Craver. *Philosophical Foundations of Education.* 8th ed. Upper Saddle River, NJ: Prentice Hall, 2007.

Packard, Josh. *Church Refugees.* Loveland, CO: Group Publishing, 2015.

Packer, J. I. *Knowing God.* Downers Grove, IL: InterVarsity, 1974.

Parks, Sharon. *The Critical Years.* San Francisco: Harper & Row, 1986.

"Parochial Schools." *New World Encyclopedia.* Last modified January 15, 2019. http://www.newworldencyclopedia.org/entry/Parochial_school.

Parr, Steve, and Tom Crites. *Why They Stay: Helping Parents and Church Leaders Make Investments That Keep Children and Teens Connected to the Church for a Lifetime.* Bloomington, IN: WestBow, 2015.

Parrett, Gary A., and S. Steve Kang. *Teaching the Faith, Forming the Faithful.* Downers Grove, IL: IVP Academic, 2009.

Pascal, Blaise. *Pascal's Pensées.* New York: E. P. Dutton, 1958.

Patton, Eileen. "Chapter 1: Estimates of Multiracial Adults and Other Racial and Ethnic Groups across Various Question Formats." Pew Research Center. http://www.pewsocialtrends.org/2015/11/06/chapter-1-estimates-of-multiracial-adults-and-other-racial-and-ethnic-groups-across-various-question-formats/.

Patty, Steve. "A Developmental Framework for Doing Youth Ministry." In *Reaching a Generation for Christ,* edited by Richard R. Dunn and Mark Senter, 69–86. Chicago: Moody, 1997.

Pazmiño, Robert W. "Christian Education Is More than Formation." *Christian Education Journal* 7, no. 2 (2010): 356–65.

———. *Foundational Issues in Christian Education.* Grand Rapids: Baker Books, 2008.

———. *God Our Teacher: Theological Basics in Christian Education.* Grand Rapids: Baker Academic, 2001.

Pazmiño, Robert W., and Octavio J. Esqueda. *Anointed Teaching: Partnership with the Holy Spirit.* Salem, OR: Publicaciones Kerigma, 2019.

Petersen, Christine. "Bringing ADDIE to Life: Instructional Design at Its Best." *Journal of Educational Multimedia and Hypermedia* 12, no. 3 (2003): 227–41.

Peterson, Eugene. *A Long Obedience in the Same Direction: Discipleship in an Instant Society.* Downers Grove, IL: InterVarsity, 2000.

Peterson, Michael L. *Philosophy of Education: Issues and Options.* Downers Grove, IL: InterVarsity Press, 1986.

Phenix, Philip Henry. *Realms of Meaning.* New York: McGraw-Hill, 1964.

Piaget, Jean. *The Moral Judgment of the Child.* New York: Free Press, 1965.

Pippert, Rebecca Manley. *Out of the Salt Shaker and into the World: Evangelism as a Way of Life.* Downers Grove, IL: InterVarsity, 1995.

Plantinga, Cornelius, Jr. *Engaging God's World: A Christian Vision of Faith, Learning, and Living.* Grand Rapids: Eerdmans, 2002.

———. *Not the Way It's Supposed to Be: A Breviary of Sin.* Grand Rapids: Eerdmans, 1995.

Poeter, Damon. "Moore's Law Really Works after All: Study." *PC Magazine,* May 2013, 10–13.

Popham, W. James. "Formative Assessment: Seven Stepping-Stones to Success." *Principal Leadership* 9, no. 1 (2008): 16–20.

Porfeli, Erik F., and Bora Lee. "Career Development during Childhood and Adolescence."

New Directions for Youth Development 134 (Summer 2012): 11–22.

Posner, George J. *Analyzing the Curriculum.* 3rd ed. Boston: McGraw-Hill, 2004.

"Post-truth." *Oxford Living Dictionaries.* https://en.oxforddictionaries.com/definition/post-truth.

Powell, Kara, Marshall Shelley, and Brandon O'Brien. "Is the Era of Age Segregation Over? After 50 Years of Student Ministry, a Researcher Argues That the Future Will Require Bringing the Generations Together." *Leadership* 30, no. 3 (June 1, 2009): 43–47.

Powell, Samuel M. *A Theology of Christian Spirituality.* Nashville: Abingdon, 2005.

Prensky, Marc. "Digital Natives, Digital Immigrants, Part 1." *On the Horizon* 9, no. 5 (2001): 1–6. https://doi.org/10.1108/10748120110424816.

"Profile America Facts for Features: CB17-FF.16." Updated August 16, 2017. https://www.census.gov/content/dam/Census/newsroom/facts-for-features/2017/cb17-ff16.pdf.

"Project Loon." Project Loon homepage. http://www.google.com/loon/.

Rah, Soong-Chan. *The Next Evangelicalism: Freeing the Church from Western Captivity.* Downers Grove, IL: InterVarsity, 2009.

Rahn, Dave. "Ministry to Youth." In *Introduction to Christian Education: Foundations for the Twenty-First Century*, edited by Michael J. Anthony, 217–26. Grand Rapids: Baker Academic, 2001.

Rainer, Thom. "Dispelling the 80 Percent Myth of Declining Churches." Thom S. Rainer. July 28, 2017. http://thomrainer.com/2017/06/dispelling-80-percent-myth-declining-churches/.

———. *Unchurched Next Door.* Grand Rapids: Zondervan, 2008.

Rainie, Lee, and Andrew Perrin. "FACTTANK." Pew Research Center. June 28, 2017. http://www.pewresearch.org/fact-tank/2017/06/28/10-facts-about-smartphones.

Rehnborg, Sarah Jane, and Meg Moore. "Maximizing Volunteer Engagement." In *The Volunteer Management Handbook: Leadership Strategies for Success*, edited by Tracy Daniel Connors, 103–24. Hoboken, NJ: John Wiley & Sons, 2012.

Reisman, D. *The Lonely Crowd: A Study of the Changing American Character.* New Haven: Yale University Press, 1950.

Richards, Lawrence O. *Expository Dictionary of Bible Words.* Grand Rapids: Regency Reference Library, 1985.

Richards, Lawrence O., and Gary J. Bredfeldt. *Creative Bible Teaching.* Chicago: Moody, 1998.

Ringenberg, William C. *The Christian College: A History of Protestant Higher Education in America.* Grand Rapids: Baker Academic, 2006.

Rink, Rob. "Commitment, Character, and Citizenship: Religious Schooling in Liberal Democracy." *Journal of Education and Christian Belief* 17, no. 1 (2013): 128.

Rippa, S. Alexander. *Education in a Free Society.* New York: Longman, 1996.

Robbins, Duffy. *This Way to Youth Ministry: An Introduction to the Adventure.* Grand Rapids: Zondervan, 2004.

Robinson, Haddon W. *Biblical Preaching: The Development and Delivery of Expository Messages.* 3rd ed. Grand Rapids: Baker Academic, 2014.

Rogers, Patricia, Chris Houser, and Patricia Thornton. "Mobile Educational Technology." In *Encyclopedia of Distance Learning*, 2nd ed., edited by Patricia Rogers et al., 1424–31. Hershey, PA: Information Science Reference, 2009.

Rosebrough, Thomas R., and Ralph G. Leverett. *Transformational Teaching in the Information Age: Making Why and How We Teach*

Relevant to Students. Alexandria, VA: Association for Supervision & Curriculum Development, 2011. Kindle.

Roser, Max. "Proof That Life Is Getting Better for Humanity, in Five Charts." Vox Media. December 23, 2016. https://www.vox.com/the-big-idea/2016/12/23/14062168/history-global-conditions-charts-life-span-poverty.

Roser, Max, and Esteban Ortiz-Ospina. "Global Extreme Poverty." Our World in Data. Revised March 27, 2017. https://ourworldindata.org/extreme-poverty.

Ross, Richard. *Accelerate: Parenting Teenagers toward Adulthood.* Bloomington, IN: Cross Books, 2013.

———. *Youth Ministry That Lasts a Lifetime.* Fort Worth: Seminary Hill, 2017.

Roth, Brad. *God's Country: Faith, Hope, and the Future of the Rural Church.* Harrisonburg, VA: Herald, 2017.

Ryan, Camille L., and Kurt Bauman. "Educational Attainment in the United States: 2015." United States Census Bureau. March 2016. https://www.census.gov/content/dam/Census/library/publications/2016/demo/p20-578.pdf.

Sadker, Myra P., and David M. Sadker. *Teachers, Schools, and Society.* 4th ed. New York: McGraw-Hill, 1997.

Safrit, R. Dale, and Mary Merrill. "Management Implications of Contemporary Trends in Voluntarism in the United States and Canada." *Voluntary Action* 3, no. 1 (Winter 2000): n.p.

Safrit, R. Dale, and Ryan Schmiesing. "Volunteer Models and Management." In *The Volunteer Management Handbook: Leadership Strategies for Success,* edited by Tracy Daniel Connors, 3–30. Hoboken, NJ: John Wiley & Sons, 2012.

Santrock, John W. *Adolescence.* 16th ed. New York: McGraw-Hill, 2016.

Saucy, Mark. "*Regnum Spiriti*: The Kingdom of God and Spiritual Formation." *Journal of Spiritual Formation and Soul Care* 4, no. 2 (2011): 140–54.

Saunders, Jon. "The Place and Purpose of Parachurch Ministries: Serving the Local Church and Fulfilling the Great Commission at Her Side." The Gospel Coalition. August 31, 2015. https://www.thegospelcoalition.org/article/parachurch-ministry/.

Schaller, Lyle E. *The Very Large Church: New Rules for Leaders.* Nashville: Abingdon, 2000.

Schoenbach, Ruth, Cynthia Greenleaf, Christine Cziko, and Lori Hurwitz. *Reading for Understanding: A Guide to Improving Reading in Middle and High School Classrooms.* Jossey-Bass Education Series. San Francisco: Jossey-Bass, 1999.

"Scholarship Tax Credits." National Conference of State Legislatures. http://www.ncsl.org/research/education/school-choice-scholarship-tax-credits.aspx.

"School Choice Programs across the Nation." Center for Education Reform. http://www.edreform.com/in-the-states/know-your-choices/explore-choice-programs/.

"School Voucher Laws: State-by-State Comparison." National Conference of State Legislatures. http://www.ncsl.org/research/education/voucher-law-comparison.aspx.

Searcy, Nelson, and Jennifer Dykes Henson. *Connect: How to Double Your Number of Volunteers.* Grand Rapids: Baker Books, 2012.

Seemiller, Corey, and Meghan Grace. *Generation Z Goes to College.* San Francisco: John Wiley & Sons, 2016.

Sell, Charles. "Family Life Education." In *Evangelical Dictionary of Christian Education,* edited by M. J. Anthony, W. S. Benson, D. Eldridge, and J. Gorman, 288–89. Grand Rapids: Baker Books, 2001.

———. *Family Ministry.* Rev. ed. Grand Rapids: Zondervan, 1995.

Senter, Mark H., III. *The Coming Revolution in Youth Ministry: And Its Radical Impact on the Church.* Wheaton: Victor, 1992.

———. "A Historical Framework for Doing Youth Ministry." In *Reaching a Generation for Christ*, edited by Richard R. Dunn and Mark Senter, 69–86. Chicago: Moody, 1997.

———. *When God Shows Up: A History of Protestant Youth Ministry in America*. Grand Rapids: Baker Academic, 2010.

Setran, David, James Wilhoit, Donald Ratcliff, Daniel Hasse, and Linda Rosema. "Spiritual Formation Goes to College: Class-Related 'Soul Projects' in Christian Higher Education." *Christian Education Journal* 7, no. 2 (2010): 401–22.

Setran, David P., and Chris A. Kiesling. *Spiritual Formation in Emerging Adulthood: A Practical Theology for College and Young Adult Ministry*. Grand Rapids: Baker Academic, 2013.

Shaw, Perry. *Transforming Theological Education: A Practical Handbook for Integrative Learning*. Carlisle, UK: Langham Global, 2014.

Sheppard, Trent. *God on Campus: Sacred Causes and Global Effects*. Downers Grove, IL: InterVarsity, 2009.

Sherman, Amy. *Kingdom Calling: Vocational Stewardship for the Common Good*. Downers Grove, IL: InterVarsity, 2011.

Shih, Timothy K., and Jason C. Hung. *Future Directions in Distance Learning and Communications Technologies*. Hershey, PA: Information Science, 2007.

Shockley, Donald. *Campus Ministry: The Church beyond Itself*. Louisville: Westminster John Knox, 1989.

Sikkink, David. "The Social Sources of Alienation from Public Schools." *Social Forces* 78, no. 1 (1999): 51–86.

Silverman, Robert J., Kjell Erik Rudestam, and Anna DeStefano. *Encyclopedia of Distributed Learning*. Thousand Oaks, CA: Sage, 2004.

Simmons, T. F., and H. E. Nolloth, eds. *The Lay Folks' Catechism, or the English and Latin Versions of Archbishop Thoresby's Instruction for the People; Together with a Wycliffite Adaptation of the Same, and the Corresponding Canons of the Council of Lambeth*. New York: Scribner, 1901.

Simpson, B. J. "Learning Taxonomy—Simpson's Psychomotor Domain." http://iqac.uiu.ac.bd /UploadResourceFiles/20160719042515.pdf.

Singh, Sarwant. "The 10 Social and Tech Trends That Could Shape the Next Decade." Forbes .com. May 12, 2014. https://www.forbes.com /sites/sarwantsingh/2014/05/12/the-top-10- mega-trends-of-the-decade/#9647599a62c3.

Sire, James W. *Naming the Elephant: Worldview as Concept*. 2nd ed. Downers Grove: InterVarsity Press, 2015.

Skinner, B. F. *Beyond Freedom and Dignity*. New York: Bantam, 1971.

Slavin, Robert. *Educational Psychology: Theory and Practice*. 4th ed. Boston: Allyn and Bacon, 1994.

Smith, Aaron. "U.S. Smartphone Use in 2015." Pew Research Center. April 1, 2015. http:// www.pewinternet.org /2015/04/01/us-smart phone-use-in-2015.

Smith, Christian, Kari Christoffersen, Hilary Davidson, and Patricia Snell Herzog. *Lost in Transition: The Dark Side of Emerging Adulthood*. New York: Oxford University Press, 2011.

Smith, Christian, with Melinda Lundquist Denton. *Soul Searching: The Religious and Spiritual Lives of American Teenagers*. New York: Oxford University Press, 2005.

Smith, Christian, and Patricia Snell. *Souls in Transition: The Religious and Spiritual Lives of Emerging Adults*. New York: Oxford University Press, 2009.

Smith, David I., and James K. A. Smith. "Practices, Faith, and Pedagogy." In *Teaching and Christian Practices: Reshaping Faith and Learning*, edited by David I. Smith and James

K. A. Smith, 1–23. Grand Rapids: Eerdmans, 2011.

Smith, Gordon T. *Beginning Well: Christian Conversion and Authentic Transformation.* Downers Grove, IL: InterVarsity, 2001.

Smith, James Bryan, and Lynda Graybeal. *A Spiritual Formation Workbook: Small-Group Resources for Nurturing Christian Growth.* Englewood, CO: Renovaré, 1999.

Smith, James K. A. *Desiring the Kingdom: Worship, Worldview, and Cultural Formation.* Grand Rapids: Baker Academic, 2009.

Snailum, Brenda A. "How Families Shape the Faith of Younger Generations." In *Teaching the Next Generations: A Comprehensive Guide for Teaching Christian Formation*, edited by Terry Linhart, 176–86. Grand Rapids: Baker Academic, 2016.

Snart, Jason Allen. *Hybrid Learning: The Perils and Promises of Blending Online and Face-to-Face Instruction in Higher Education.* Santa Barbara, CA: Praeger, 2010.

Snowman, Jack, Rick McCown, and Robert F. Biehler. *Psychology Applied to Teaching.* 12th ed. Boston: Houghton Mifflin, 2009.

"Social Media Fact Sheet." Pew Research Center. February 5, 2018. http://www.pewinternet.org/fact-sheet/social-media/.

Sparks and Honey. "Meet Generation Z: Forget Everything You Learned about Millennials." LinkedIn SlideShare. June 17, 2014. https://www.slideshare.net/sparksandhoney/generation-z-final-june-17/2-2Meet_Generation_Z_Americans_born.

Sprinthall, Norman A., Richard C. Sprinthall, and Sharon N. Oja. *Educational Psychology: A Developmental Approach.* 6th ed. New York: McGraw-Hill, 1994.

"Stanford Bioengineers Create Circuit Board Modeled on the Human Brain." Stanford News. April 28, 2014. http://news.stanford.edu/pr/2014/pr-neurogrid-boahen-engineering-042814.html.

Stebbins, Robert A. "Would You Volunteer?" *Social Science and Public Policy* 46 (January 2009): 155–59.

Steibel, Sophia R. G. "Christian Education and Spiritual Formation: One and the Same?" *Christian Education Journal* 7, no. 2 (2010): 340–55.

Sternberg, Robert J., and Wendy M. Williams. *Educational Psychology.* Boston: Allyn and Bacon, 2002.

Stetzer, Edward, and Warren Bird. *The State of Church Planting in the United States: Research Overview and Qualitative Study of Primary Church Planting Entities.* Nashville: Lifeway Research, n.d.

Stetzer, Edward, and Daniel Im. *Planting Missional Churches.* 2nd ed. Nashville: B&H Academic, 2016.

Stewart, Edward C., and Milton J. Bennett. *American Cultural Patterns: A Cross-Cultural Perspective.* Boston: Intercultural Press, 1991.

Stier, Greg. "The Gospel Advancing View of Youth Ministry." In *Youth Ministry in the 21st Century: Five Views of Youth Ministry*, edited by Chap Clark, 3–16. Grand Rapids: Baker Academic, 2015.

Stiles, J. Mack. "Nine Marks of a Healthy Parachurch Ministry." *9Marks Journal* (March–April 2011). https://www.9marks.org/article/journalnine-marks-healthy-parachurch-ministry/.

Stone, Bryan. *Evangelism after Christendom: The Theology and Practice of Christian Witness.* Grand Rapids: Brazos, 2006.

Stone, Douglas, and Sheila Heen. *Thanks for the Feedback: The Science and Art of Receiving Feedback Well.* New York: Random House, 2014.

Stratton, Steve. "Today's Student Culture: Context for Change." Address presented to the faculty and staff of Union College, Barbourville, Kentucky, 2008.

Strong, J. *Enhanced Strong's Lexicon.* Bellingham, WA: Logos Bible Software, 2001.

Stronge, James H. *Qualities of Effective Teachers.* Alexandria, VA: ASCD, 2018.

Sweet, Leonard. *Soul Tsunami.* Grand Rapids: Zondervan, 1999.

Ta'eed, Collis. "Will the Internet Replace Traditional Education?" Insider. September 15, 2012. https://thenextweb.com/insider/2012/09/15/will-internet-replace-traditional-education/.

TenElshof, Judy. "Ministry to Families in the Local Church." In *Foundations of Ministry: An Introduction to Christian Education for a New Generation,* edited by Michael Anthony, 185–99. Grand Rapids: Baker Academic, 1992.

Terry, Bryan D., Amy M. Harder, and Dale W. Pracht. "Options for Volunteer Involvement." In *The Volunteer Management Handbook: Leadership Strategies for Success,* edited by Tracy Daniel Connors, Digital D Supplements. Hoboken: John Wiley & Sons, 2012. www.wiley.com/go/volhandbook.

Thiselton, Anthony C. *The Holy Spirit—In Biblical Teaching, through the Centuries, and Today.* Grand Rapids: Eerdmans, 2013.

Tolliver, Derise E., and Elizabeth J. Tisdell. "Engaging Spirituality in the Transformative Higher Education Classroom." In *Teaching for Change: Fostering Transformative Learning in the Classroom,* edited by Edward W. Taylor, 37–47. San Francisco: Jossey-Bass, 2006.

Tomlinson, Carol Ann. *How to Differentiate Instruction in Mixed-Ability Classrooms.* 2nd ed. Alexandria, VA: ASCD, 2001.

Towns, Elmer L. *Robert Raikes: A Comparison with Earlier Claims to Sunday School Origins.* Liberty University Digital Commons. 1971. http://digitalcommons.liberty.edu/towns_articles/22.

Tozer, A. W. *The Knowledge of the Holy: The Attributes of God: Their Meaning in the Christian Life.* Lincoln: Back to the Bible Broadcast, 1971.

Tracy, W. E., E. D. Freeborn, J. Metcalf-Tartaglia, and M. A. Weigelt. *The Upward Call: Spiritual Formation and Holy Living.* Kansas City, MO: Beacon Hill, 1993.

Tripp, Paul David. *Instruments in the Redeemer's Hands: People in Need of Change Helping People in Need of Change.* Phillipsburg, NJ: P&R, 2002.

Trotman, Dawson. *Born to Reproduce.* Colorado Springs: NavPress, 2008.

Trueman, Carl. "How Parachurch Ministries Go off the Rails." *9Marks Journal* (March–April 2011). https://www.9marks.org/article/journal/how-parachurch-ministries-go-rails/.

Turner, Anthony. "Generation Z: Technology and Social Interest." *Journal of Individual Psychology* 71, no. 2 (2015): 103–13.

Tyler, Ralph W. *Basic Principles of Curriculum and Instruction.* Chicago: University of Chicago Press, 2013.

Uecker, Jeremy E. "Catholic Schooling, Protestant Schooling, and Religious Commitment in Young Adulthood." *Journal for Scientific Study of Religion* 48, no. 2 (June 2009): 353–67.

UNFPA. "State of World Population 2007: Unleashing the Potential of Urban Growth." New York: UNFPA Publishing, 2007.

US and State Profiles. National Center for Charitable Statistics. http://nccs.urban.org/data-statistics/us-and-state-profiles.

US and World Population Clock. United States Census Bureau. https://www.census.gov/popclock/.

US Debt Clock. http://www.usdebtclock.org/.

Vaillant, George. *Aging Well: Surprising Guideposts to a Happier Life from the Landmark Harvard Study of Adult Development.* Boston: Little, Brown and Company, 2002.

Vallone, Donna, A. Smith, T. Kenney, and Robin Koval. "Agents of Social Change: A Model for Targeting and Engaging Generation Z across

Platforms." *Journal of Advertising Research* 56, no. 4 (2016): 414–25.

"Value of Volunteer Time." Independent Sector. https://www.independentsector.org/volunteer_time.

Van Brummelen, Harro W. *Steppingstones to Curriculum: A Biblical Path*. 2nd ed. Colorado Springs: Purposeful Design, 2002.

Vasel, Kathryn. "Household Debt Is Dangerously Close to 2008 Levels." CNN Money. February 16, 2017. http://money.cnn.com/2017/02/16/pf/americans-more-debt-in-2016/index.html.

Vaters, Karl. *Small Church Essentials: Field-Tested Principles for Leading a Healthy Congregation of under 250*. Chicago: Moody, 2018.

Veronis, Luke A. "Globalization." In *Dictionary of Mission Theology: Evangelical Foundations*, edited by John Corrie, 394–96. Downers Grove, IL: IVP Academic, 2007.

Vickers, Jason. *Minding the Good Ground: A Theology for Church Renewal*. Waco: Baylor University Press, 2015.

Vine, W. E. *An Expository Dictionary of New Testament Words*. 3 vols. Old Tappan, NJ: Revell, 1940.

"Volunteering in America." Corporation for National & Community Service. https://www.nationalservice.gov/serve/via.

Vos, Howard F. *Bible Study Commentary: Matthew*. Grand Rapids: Zondervan, 1979.

Vygotsky, Lev, Michael Cole, Vera John-Steiner, Sylvia Scribner, and Ellen Souberman, eds. *Mind in Society: The Development of Higher Psychological Processes*. Cambridge: Harvard University Press, 1978.

Wagner, Rodd, and James K. Harter. *12: The Elements of Great Managing*. New York: Gallup Press, 2006.

Walker, Carol A. "Saving Your Rookie Managers from Themselves." In *HBR's 10 Must Reads for New Managers*, edited by Harvard

Business Review, 35–48. Boston: Harvard Business Review Press, 2017.

Warnock, Chuck. "Why We Still Need (Some) Monocultural Churches." ChuckWarnock.com. November 4, 2013. https://chuckwarnockblog.wordpress.com/2013/11/04/why-we-still-need-some-monocultural-churches/.

Warren, Rick. *The Purpose-Driven Church: Growth without Compromising Your Message and Mission*. Grand Rapids: Zondervan, 1995.

Watson, David Lowes. *The Early Methodist Class Meeting*. Nashville: Discipleship Resources, 1985.

Watson, Jude Tiersma. "Urban Churches." In *Evangelical Dictionary of World Missions*, edited by A. Scott Moreau, Harold Netland, and Charles Van Engen, 990–91. Milton Keynes, UK: Paternoster, 2000.

Watson, Kevin M. *Pursuing Social Holiness: The Band Meeting in Wesley's Thought and Popular Methodist Practice*. New York: Oxford University Press, 2014.

Weiss, Todd R. "Google Glass Now Available for Sale to Anyone in U.S." *eWeek*, May 14, 2014, 2.

Wenger-Trayner, Etienne, and Beverly Wenger-Trayner. "Introduction to Communities of Practice: A Brief Overview of the Concepts and Its Uses." April 15, 2015. http://wenger-trayner.com/wp-content/uploads/2015/04/07-Brief-introduction-to-communities-of-practice.pdf.

Wengert, Timothy J. *Martin Luther's Catechisms: Forming the Faith*. Minneapolis: Fortress Press, 2009.

Wesley, John. *The Works of John Wesley*. Vols. 1–16. Edited by Albert Outler. Nashville: Abingdon, 1975–2003.

Weurlander, Maria, Magnus Söderberg, Max Scheja, Håkan Hult, and Annika Wernerson. "Exploring Formative Assessment as a Tool for Learning: Students' Experiences of Different Methods of Formative Assessment."

Assessment & Evaluation in Higher Education 37, no. 6 (2012): 747–60.

"What Is Christian Higher Education?" Council for Christian Colleges and Universities. https://www.cccu.org/about/#heading-what -is-christian-higher-4.

"What Percentage of Americans Really Move Each Year." Home Data. January 21, 2015. http://avrickdirect.com/homedata/?p=31.

White, Jerry. *The Church and Parachurch: An Uneasy Marriage*. Portland, OR: Multnomah, 1983.

White, Randy. *Journey to the Center of the City*. Downers Grove, IL: InterVarsity, 1996.

———. "Salvation." In *Evangelical Dictionary of Theology*, edited by W. Elwell, 1049. Grand Rapids: Baker Academic, 2001.

Whitmore, John. *Coaching for Performance*. Boston: Nicholas Brealey, 2007.

Wiggins, Grant P., and Jay McTighe. *Understanding by Design*. 2nd ed. Alexandria, VA: ASCD, 2005.

Wilhoit, James C. *Spiritual Formation as If the Church Mattered*. Grand Rapids: Baker-Books, 2008.

Wilkins, Michael J. *Discipleship in the Ancient World and Matthew's Gospel*. Grand Rapids: Baker, 1995.

———. *Following the Master: Discipleship in the Steps of Jesus*. Grand Rapids: Zondervan, 1992.

Willard, Dallas. *The Divine Conspiracy: Rediscovering Our Hidden Life with God*. New York: HarperCollins, 1997.

———. *The Great Omission: Reclaiming Jesus's Essential Teaching on Discipleship*. San Francisco: HarperCollins, 2006.

———. *Knowing Christ Today: Why We Can Trust Spiritual Knowledge*. New York: HarperOne, 2009.

———. *The Renovation of the Heart: Putting on the Character of Christ*. Colorado Springs: NavPress, 2002.

Williams, Alex. "Meet Alpha: The Next 'Next Generation.'" *New York Times*, September 19, 2015. https://www.nytimes.com/2015/09 /19/fashion/meet-alpha-the-next-next-gener ation.html.

Williams, Dennis. "Christian Education." In *Evangelical Dictionary of Christian Education*, edited by M. J. Anthony, W. S. Benson, D. Eldridge, and J. Gorman, 132–34. Grand Rapids: Baker Academic, 2001.

Williams, Donald T. *The Person and Work of the Holy Spirit*. Nashville: Broadman & Holman, 1994.

Williams, Peter. *Opening Up 2 Timothy*. Leominster, UK: Day One Publications, 2007.

Wilson, Elizabeth. *Fifty Years of Association Work among Young Women, 1866–1916*. New York: National Board of the Young Women's Christian Associations of the United States of America, 1916.

Wilson, Jared C. "Defining Our Terms." *Table-Talk Magazine*, September 2014. https://tablet alkmagazine.com/article/2014/09/defining -our-terms/.

Wilson, John. *Education in Religion and the Emotions*. London: Heinemann, 1971.

Wolterstorff, Nicholas. *Educating for Shalom: Essays on Christian Higher Education*. Grand Rapids: Eerdmans, 2004.

Woolfolk, Anita. *Educational Psychology*. 5th ed. Boston: Allyn and Bacon, 1993.

———. *Educational Psychology*. 8th ed. Boston: Allyn and Bacon, 2001.

———. *Educational Psychology*. 9th ed. Boston: Pearson Education, 2004.

Wuthnow, Robert. *How Twenty- and Thirty-Somethings Are Shaping the Future of American Religion*. Princeton: Princeton University Press, 2007.

Yaconelli, Mark. *Contemplative Youth Ministry: Practicing the Presence of Jesus*. Grand Rapids: Zondervan, 2006.

Yaconelli, Mike. *The Core Realities of Youth Ministry: Nine Biblical Principles That Mark Healthy Youth Ministries*. Grand Rapids: Zondervan, 2004.

Yallen, Cheryle N., and Barbara K. Wentworth. "Assessment, Planning, and Staffing Analysis." In *The Volunteer Management Handbook: Leadership Strategies for Success*, edited by Tracy Daniel Connors, 125–48. Hoboken, NJ: John Wiley & Sons, 2012.

Yount, William R. *Created to Learn: A Christian Teacher's Introduction to Educational Psychology*. 2nd ed. Nashville: B&H, 2010.

Zenger, John H., and Kathleen Stinnett. *The Extraordinary Coach*. New York: McGraw-Hill, 2010.

Ziegenhals, Walter E. *Urban Churches in Transition: Reflections on Selected Problems and Approaches to Churches and Communities in Racial Transition Based on the Chicago Experience*. Philadelphia: Pilgrim Press, 1978.

Zuck, Roy B. *Teaching as Jesus Taught*. Grand Rapids: Baker, 1995.

———. *Teaching with Spiritual Power*. Grand Rapids: Kregel, 1993.

Zylstra, Sarah E. "Pew: Evangelicals Stay Strong as Christianity Crumbles in America." *Christianity Today*, May 11, 2015. https://www.christianitytoday.com/news/2015/may/pew-evangelicals-stay-strong-us-religious-landscape-study.html.

SCRIPTURE INDEX

SUBJECT INDEX